Borland® C++

Version 3.0

Library Reference

BORLAND INTERNATIONAL, INC. 1800 GREEN HILLS ROAD
P.O. BOX 660001, SCOTTS VALLEY, CA 95067-0001

PRINTED IN THE USA.
R1 10 9 8 7 6 5 4 3 2

CONTENT

T A B L E S

INTRODUCTION

This manual contains definitions of all the Borland C++ library routines, common variables, and common defined types, along with example program code to illustrate how to use most of these routines, variables, and types.

If you are new to C or C++ programming, or if you are looking for information on the contents of the Borland C++ manuals, see the introduction in the *User's Guide*.

Here is a summary of the chapters in this manual:

Chapter 1: The main function discusses arguments to **main** (including wildcard arguments), provides some example programs, and gives some information on Pascal calling conventions and the value that **main** returns.

Chapter 2: The run-time library is an alphabetical reference of all Borland C++ library functions. Each entry gives syntax, portability information, an operative description, and return values for the function, together with a reference list of related functions and examples of how the functions are used.

Chapter 3: Global variables defines and discusses Borland C++'s global variables. You can use these to save yourself a great deal of programming time on commonly needed variables (such as dates, time, error messages, stack size, and so on).

Appendix A: Run-time library cross-reference contains an overview of the Borland C++ library routines and header files. The header files are listed; the library routines are grouped according to the tasks they commonly perform.

Class and member function documentation

Certain classes and class member functions are incorporated in Chapter 2. Here's a list of the classes and member functions and their page numbers.

The typefaces used in this manual are used as described in the User's Guide.

Name	Type	Page number
abs	member function	11
acos	member function	15
arg	member function	21
asin	member function	23
atan	member function	25
bcd	class	33
complex	class	86
conj	member function	87
cos	member function	90
cosh	member function	91
exp	member function	144
imag	member function	293
log	member function	340
log10	member function	341
norm	member function	373
pow	member function	396
polar	member function	394
real	member function	428
sin	member function	507
sinh	member function	508
sqrt	member function	518
tan	member function	554
tanh	member function	554

CHAPTER

1

The main function

Every C and C++ program must have a **main** function; where you place it is a matter of preference. Some programmers place **main** at the beginning of the file, others at the end. Regardless of its location, the following points about **main** always apply.

Arguments to main

Three parameters (arguments) are passed to **main** by the Borland C++ startup routine: *argc*, *argv*, and *env*.

- *argc*, an integer, is the number of command-line arguments passed to **main**.
- *argv* is an array of pointers to strings (**char** *[]).
  - Under 3.0 and higher versions of DOS, *argv*[0] is the full path name of the program being run.
  - Under versions of DOS before 3.0, *argv*[0] points to the null string ("").
  - *argv*[1] points to the first string typed on the DOS command line after the program name.
  - *argv*[2] points to the second string typed after the program name.
  - *argv*[*argc*-1] points to the last argument passed to **main**.
  - *argv*[*argc*] contains null.

- *env* is also an array of pointers to strings. Each element of *env*[] holds a string of the form `ENVVAR=value`.
  - ENVVAR is the name of an environment variable, such as PATH or 87.
  - *value* is the value to which ENVVAR is set, such as C:\DOS;C:\TOOLS; (for PATH) or YES (for 87).

If you declare any of these parameters, you *must* declare them exactly in the order given: *argc*, *argv*, *env*. For example, the following are all valid declarations of **main**'s arguments:

```
main()
main(int argc)                    /* legal but very unlikely */
main(int argc, char * argv[])
main(int argc, char * argv[], char * env[])]
```

The declaration `main(int argc)` is legal, but it's very unlikely that you would use *argc* in your program without also using the elements of *argv*.

The argument *env* is also available through the global variable *environ*. Refer to the *environ* entry in Chapter 3 and the **putenv** and **getenv** lookup entries in Chapter 2 for more information.

argc and *argv* are also available via the global variables *_argc* and *_argv*.

An example program

Here is an example that demonstrates a simple way of using these arguments passed to **main**.

```
/* Program ARGS.C */

#include <stdio.h>
#include <stdlib.h>

int main(int argc, char *argv[], char *env[])
{
   int i;

   printf("The value of argc is %d \n\n",argc);
   printf("These are the %d command-line arguments passed to"
          " main:\n\n",argc);

   for (i = 0; i < argc; i++)
      printf("   argv[%d]: %s\n", i, argv[i]);

   printf("\nThe environment string(s) on this system are:\n\n");

   for (i = 0; env[i] != NULL; i++)
```

```
        printf("   env[%d]: %s\n", i, env[i]);
    return 0;
}
```

Suppose you run ARGS.EXE at the DOS prompt with the following command line:

```
C:> args first_arg "arg with blanks" 3  4 "last but one" stop!
```

Note that you can pass arguments with embedded blanks by surrounding them with double quotes, as shown by `"argument with blanks"` and `"last but one"` in this example command line.

The output of ARGS.EXE (assuming that the environment variables are set as shown here) would then be like this:

```
The value of argc is 7

These are the 7 command-line arguments passed to main:

   argv[0]: C:\BORLANDC\ARGS.EXE
   argv[1]: first_arg
   argv[2]: arg with blanks
   argv[3]: 3
   argv[4]: 4
   argv[5]: last but one
   argv[6]: stop!

The environment string(s) on this system are:

   env[0]: COMSPEC=C:\COMMAND.COM
   env[1]: PROMPT=$p $g
   env[2]: PATH=C:\SPRINT;C:\DOS;C:\BORLANDC
```

The maximum combined length of the command-line arguments passed to **main** (including the space between adjacent arguments and the name of the program itself) is 128 characters; this is a DOS limit.

Wildcard arguments

Command-line arguments containing wildcard characters can be expanded to all the matching file names, much the same way DOS expands wildcards when used with commands like COPY. All you have to do to get wildcard expansion is to link your program with the WILDARGS.OBJ object file, which is included with Borland C++.

Once WILDARGS.OBJ is linked into your program code, you can send wildcard arguments of the type *.* to your **main** function. The argument will be expanded (in the *argv* array) to all files matching the wildcard mask. The maximum size of the *argv* array varies, depending on the amount of memory available in your heap.

If no matching files are found, the argument is passed unchanged. (That is, a string consisting of the wildcard mask is passed to **main**.)

Arguments enclosed in quotes ("...") are not expanded.

An example program

The following commands will compile the file ARGS.C and link it with the wildcard expansion module WILDARGS.OBJ, then run the resulting executable file ARGS.EXE:

```
BCC  ARGS  WILDARGS.OBJ
ARGS  C:\BORLANDC\INCLUDE\*.H  "*.C"
```

When you run ARGS.EXE, the first argument is expanded to the names of all the *.H files in your Borland C++ INCLUDE directory. Note that the expanded argument strings include the entire path. The argument *.C is not expanded as it is enclosed in quotes.

In the IDE, simply specify a project file (from the project menu) that contains the following lines:

```
ARGS
WILDARGS.OBJ
```

Then use the **R**un | **A**rguments option to set the command-line parameters.

If you prefer the wildcard expansion to be the default, modify your standard C?.LIB library files to have WILDARGS.OBJ linked automatically. In order to accomplish that, remove SETARGV from the libraries and add WILDARGS. The following commands invoke the Turbo librarian (TLIB) to modify all the standard library files (assuming the current directory contains the standard C and C++ libraries and WILDARGS.OBJ):

For more on TLIB, see the User's Guide.

```
tlib  cs  -setargv  +wildargs
tlib  cc  -setargv  +wildargs
tlib  cm  -setargv  +wildargs
tlib  cl  -setargv  +wildargs
tlib  ch  -setargv  +wildargs
```

Using –p (Pascal calling conventions)

If you compile your program using Pascal calling conventions (described in detail in Chapter 2, "Language structure," in the *Programmer's Guide*), you *must* remember to explicitly declare **main** as a C type. Do this with the **cdecl** keyword, like this:

```
cdecl  main(int argc, char * argv[], char * envp[])
```

The value main returns

The value returned by **main** is the status code of the program: an **int**. If, however, your program uses the routine **exit** (or **_exit**) to terminate, the value returned by **main** is the argument passed to the call to **exit** (or to **_exit**).

For example, if your program contains the call

```
exit(1)
```

the status is 1.

C H A P T E R

2

The run-time library

All programming examples in this chapter are in the online help system. This means you can easily copy them from help and paste them into your files.

This chapter contains a detailed description of each of the functions in the Borland C++ library. A few of the routines are grouped by "family" (the **exec...** and **spawn...** functions that create, load, and run programs, for example) because they perform similar or related tasks. Otherwise, we have included an individual entry for every routine. For instance, if you want to look up information about the **free** routine, you would look under **free**; there you would find a listing for **free** that

- summarizes what **free** does
- gives the syntax for calling **free**
- tells you which header file(s) contains the prototype for **free**
- gives a detailed description of how **free** is implemented and how it relates to the other memory-allocation routines
- lists other language compilers that include similar functions
- refers you to related Borland C++ functions
- if appropriate, gives an example of how the function is used, or refers you to a function entry where there is an example

The following sample library lookup entry explains how to find out such details about the Borland C++ library functions.

How to use function entries

Function Summary of what **function** does.

Syntax #include <header.h>

This part lists the header file(s) containing the prototype for **function** or definitions of constants, enumerated types, and so on used by **function**.

function(modifier *parameter*[,...]);

This gives you the declaration syntax for **function**; parameter names are *italicized*. The `[,...]` indicates that other parameters and their modifiers can follow.

DOS	UNIX	Windows	ANSI C	C++ only

The **function** portability is indicated by marks in the appropriate columns. Any additional restrictions are discussed in the **Remarks** section.

- `DOS` available for this system
- `UNIX` available under this system
- `Windows` compatible with Windows. **EasyWin** users should see Appendix C, "Using EasyWin," in the *User's Guide* for information about using certain non-Windows compatible functions (like **printf** and **scanf**) in programs that run under Windows.
- `ANSI C` defined by the ANSI C Standard
- `C++ only` requires C++; is not defined by the ANSI C Standard

If more than one function is discussed and their portability features are exactly identical, only one row is used. Otherwise, each function will be represented by a single row.

Remarks This section describes what **function** does, the parameters it takes, and any details you need to use **function** and the related routines listed.

Return value The value that **function** returns (if any) is given here. If **function** sets any global variables, their values are also listed.

See also Routines related to **function** that you might want to read about are listed here. If a routine name contains an *ellipsis* (**funcname...**, **...funcname**, **func...name**), it indicates that you should refer to a family of functions (for example, **exec...** refers to the entire family of **exe** functions: **execl**, **execle**, **execlp**, **execlpe**, **execv**, **execve**, **execvp**, and **execvpe**).

Example

```
/*Here you'll find a small sample program showing the use of function (and
possibly of related functions).*/
```

abort

Function Abnormally terminates a program.

Syntax #include <stdlib.h>
void abort(void);

DOS	UNIX	Windows	ANSI C	C++ only
■	■	■	■	

Remarks **abort** writes a termination message ("Abnormal program termination") on stderr, then aborts the program by a call to **_exit** with exit code 3.

Return value **abort** returns the exit code 3 to the parent process or to DOS.

See also **assert, atexit, exit, _exit, raise, signal, spawn...**

Example

```
#include <stdio.h>
#include <stdlib.h>

int main(void)
{
   printf("Calling abort()\n");
   abort();
   return 0; /* This is never reached */
}
```

abs

Function Returns the absolute value of an integer.

Syntax

Real version:
#include <math.h>
int abs(int *x*);

Complex version:
#include <complex.h>
double abs (complex *x*);

	DOS	UNIX	Windows	ANSI C	C++ only
Real **abs**	■	■	■	■	
Complex **abs**	■		■		■

Remarks **abs** returns the absolute value of the integer argument *x*. If **abs** is called when stdlib.h has been included, it's treated as a macro that expands to inline code.

If you want to use the **abs** function instead of the macro, include `#undef abs` in your program, after the `#include <stdlib.h>`.

Return value The real version of **abs** returns an integer in the range of 0 to 32,767, with the exception that an argument of –32,768 is returned as –32,768. The complex version of **abs** returns a **double**.

See also **cabs**, **complex**, **fabs**, **labs**

Example

```
#include <stdio.h>
#include <math.h>

int main(void)
{
   int number = -1234;
   printf("number: %d  absolute value: %d\n", number, abs(number));
   return 0;
}
```

absread

Function Reads absolute disk sectors.

Syntax #include <dos.h>
int absread(int *drive*, int *nsects*, long *lsect*, void **buffer*);

DOS	UNIX	Windows	ANSI C	C++ only
■				

Remarks **absread** reads specific disk sectors. It ignores the logical structure of a disk and pays no attention to files, FATs, or directories.

absread uses DOS interrupt 0x25 to read specific disk sectors.

drive = drive number to read (0 = A, 1 = B, etc.)
nsects = number of sectors to read
lsect = beginning logical sector number
buffer = memory address where the data is to be read

The number of sectors to read is limited to 64K or the size of the buffer, whichever is smaller.

Return value If it is successful, **absread** returns 0.

On error, the routine returns –1 and sets the global variable *errno* to the value returned by the system call in the AX register.

See also **abswrite**, **biosdisk**

Example

```
#include <stdio.h>
#include <stdlib.h>
#include <conio.h>
#include <dos.h>
#include <ctype.h>

#define SECSIZE 512

int main(void)
{
   unsigned char buf[SECSIZE];
   int i, j, sector, drive;
   char str[10];

   printf("Enter drive letter: ");
   gets(str);
   drive = toupper(str[0]) - 'A';

   printf("Enter sector number to read: ");
   gets(str);
   sector = atoi(str);
   if (absread(drive, 1, sector, &buf) != 0) {
       perror("Disk error");
       exit(1);
   }
   printf("\nDrive: %c   Sector: %d\n", 'A' + drive, sector);
   for (i = 0; i < SECSIZE; i += 16) {
      if ((i / 16) == 20) {
         printf("Press any key to continue...");
         getch();
         printf("\n");
      }
      printf("%03d: ", i);
      for (j = 0; j < 16; j++)
         printf("%02X ", buf[i+j]);
      printf("\t");
      for (j = 0; j < 16; j++)
         if (isprint(buf[i+j]))
            printf("%c", buf[i+j]);
         else printf(".");
      printf("\n");
   }
   return 0;
}
```

abswrite

Function Writes absolute disk sectors.

Syntax #include <dos.h>
int abswrite(int *drive*, int *nsects*, long *lsect*, void **buffer*);

DOS	UNIX	Windows	ANSI C	C++ only
■				

Remarks **abswrite** writes specific disk sectors. It ignores the logical structure of a disk and pays no attention to files, FATs, or directories.

➡ If used improperly, **abswrite** can overwrite files, directories, and FATs.

abswrite uses DOS interrupt 0x26 to write specific disk sectors.

drive = drive number to write to (0 = A, 1 = B, etc.)
nsects = number of sectors to write to
lsect = beginning logical sector number
buffer = memory address where the data is to be written

The number of sectors to write to is limited to 64K or the size of the buffer, whichever is smaller.

Return value If it is successful, **abswrite** returns 0.

On error, the routine returns –1 and sets the global variable *errno* to the value of the AX register returned by the system call.

See also **absread**, **biosdisk**

access

Function Determines accessibility of a file.

Syntax #include <io.h>
int access(const char **filename*, int *amode*);

DOS	UNIX	Windows	ANSI C	C++ only
■	■	■		

Remarks **access** checks the file named by *filename* to determine if it exists, and whether it can be read, written to, or executed.

The list of *amode* values is as follows:

06 Check for read and write permission
04 Check for read permission
02 Check for write permission
01 Execute (ignored)
00 Check for existence of file

Under DOS, all existing files have read access (*amode* equals 04), so 00 and 04 give the same result. In the same vein, *amode* values of 06 and 02 are equivalent because under DOS write access implies read access.

If *filename* refers to a directory, **access** simply determines whether the directory exists.

Return value If the requested access is allowed, **access** returns 0; otherwise, it returns a value of –1, and the global variable *errno* is set to one of the following:

ENOENT Path or file name not found
EACCES Permission denied

See also **chmod, fstat, stat**

Example

```
#include <stdio.h>
#include <io.h>

int file_exists(char *filename);

int main(void) {
   printf("Does NOTEXIST.FIL exist: %s\n",
      file_exists("NOTEXISTS.FIL") ? "YES" : "NO");
   return 0;
}

int file_exists(char *filename) {
   return (access(filename, 0) == 0);
}
```

Program output

```
Does NOTEXIST.FIL exist?  NO
```

acos, acosl

Function Calculates the arc cosine.

Syntax

Real versions:
#include <math.h>
double acos(double *x*);
long double acosl(long double *x*);

Complex version:
#include <complex.h>
complex acos(complex *x*);

	DOS	UNIX	Windows	ANSI C	C++ only
acosl	■		■		
Real **acos**	■	■	■	■	
Complex **acos**	■		■		■

Remarks **acos** returns the arc cosine of the input value. **acosl** is the long double version; it takes a long double argument and returns a long double result. Real arguments to **acos** and **acosl** must be in the range –1 to 1, or else **acos** and **acosl** return NAN and set the global variable *errno* to

EDOM   Domain error

The complex inverse cosine is defined by

acos(z) = $-i$ **log**($z + i$ **sqrt**($1 - z^2$))

Return value **acos** and **acosl** of a real argument between –1 and +1 returns a value in the range 0 to *pi*.

Error handling for these routines can be modified through the functions **matherr** and **_matherrl**.

See Also **asin, atan, atan2, complex, cos, matherr, sin, tan**

Example

```
#include <stdio.h>
#include <math.h>

int main(void)
{
   double result, x = 0.5;

   result = acos(x);
   printf("The arc cosine of %lf is %lf\n", x, result);
   return 0;
}
```

alloca

Function Allocates temporary stack space.

Syntax #include <malloc.h>
void *alloca(size_t *size*);

DOS	UNIX	Windows	ANSI C	C++ only
■	■	■		

Remarks **alloca** allocates size bytes on the stack; the allocated space is automatically freed up when the calling function exits.

Because **alloca** modifies the stack pointer, do not place calls to **alloca** in an expression that is an argument to a function.

If the calling function does not contain any references to local variables in the stack, the stack will not be restored correctly when the function exits, resulting in a program crash. To ensure that the stack is restored correctly, use the following code in the calling function:

```
char *p;
char dummy[1];

dummy[0] = 0;
...
p = alloca(nbytes);
```

Return value If enough stack space is available, **alloca** returns a pointer to the allocated stack area. Otherwise, it returns NULL.

See Also **malloc**

Example

```
#include <stdio.h>
#include <malloc.h>

void test(int a)
{
  char *newstack;
  int len = a;
  char dummy[1];

  dummy[0] = 0;           /* force good stack frame */
  printf("SP before calling alloca(0x%X) = 0x%X\n",len,_SP);
  newstack = (char *) alloca(len);
  printf("SP after calling alloca = 0x%X\n",_SP);
  if (newstack)
    printf("Alloca(0x%X) returned %p\n",len,newstack);
  else
    printf("Alloca(0x%X) failed\n",len);
}

void main()
{
  test(256);
  test(16384);
}
```

allocmem, _dos_allocmem

Function Allocates DOS memory segment.

Syntax #include <dos.h>
int allocmem(unsigned *size*, unsigned **segp*);
unsigned _dos_allocmem(unsigned *size*, unsigned **segp*);

DOS	UNIX	Windows	ANSI C	C++ only
■				

Remarks **allocmem** and **_dos_allocmem** use the DOS system call 0x48 to allocate a block of free memory and return the segment address of the allocated block.

size is the desired size in paragraphs (a paragraph is 16 bytes). *segp* is a pointer to a word that will be assigned the segment address of the newly allocated block.

For **allocmem**, if not enough room is available, no assignment is made to the word pointed to by *segp*.

For **_dos_allocmem**, if not enough room is available, the size of the largest available block will be stored in the word pointed to by *segp*.

All allocated blocks are paragraph-aligned.

allocmem and **_dos_allocmem** cannot coexist with **malloc**.

Return value **allocmem** returns –1 on success. In the event of error, **allocmem** returns a number indicating the size in paragraphs of the largest available block.

_dos_allocmem returns 0 on success. In the event of error, **_dos_allocmem** returns the DOS error code and sets the word pointed to by *segp* to the size in paragraphs of the largest available block.

An error return from **allocmem** or **_dos_allocmem** sets the global variable *_doserrno* and sets the global variable *errno* to

ENOMEM Not enough memory

See also **coreleft**, **freemem**, **malloc**, **setblock**

Example

```
#include <dos.h>
#include <stdio.h>

int main(void)
{
    unsigned int segp, maxb;
```

```
    unsigned int size = 64; /* (64*16) = 1024 bytes */
    int largest;

    /* Use _dos_allocmem, _dos_setblock, and _dos_freemem. */
    if (_dos_allocmem(size, &segp) == 0)
        printf("Allocated memory at segment: %x\n", segp);
    else {
        perror("Unable to allocate block.");
        printf("Maximum no. of paragraphs"
               " available is %u\n", segp);
        return 1;
    }
    if (_dos_setblock(size * 2, segp, &maxb) == 0)
        printf("Grew memory block at segment: %X\n", segp);
    else {
        perror("Unable to grow block.");
        printf("Maximum number of paragraphs"
               " available is %u\n", maxb);
    }
    _dos_freemem(segp);

    /* Use allocmem, setblock, and freemem. */
    if ((largest = allocmem(size, &segp)) == -1)
        printf("Allocated memory at segment: %x\n", segp);
    else {
        perror("Unable to allocate block.");
        printf("Maximum number of paragraphs"
               " available is %u\n", largest);
        return 1;
    }
    if ((largest = setblock(segp, size * 2)) == -1)
        printf("Grew memory block at segment: %X\n", segp);
    else {
        perror("Unable to grow block.");
        printf("Maximum number of paragraphs"
               " available is %u\n", largest);
    }
    freemem(segp);
    return 0;
}
```

arc

Function Draws an arc.

Syntax #include <graphics.h>
void far arc(int *x*, int *y*, int *stangle*, int *endangle*, int *radius*);

DOS	UNIX	Windows	ANSI C	C++ only
■				

Remarks **arc** draws a circular arc in the current drawing color centered at (*x,y*) with a radius given by *radius*. The **arc** travels from *stangle* to *endangle*. If *stangle* equals 0 and *endangle* equals 360, the call to **arc** draws a complete circle.

The angle for **arc** is reckoned counterclockwise, with 0 degrees at 3 o'clock, 90 degrees at 12 o'clock, and so on.

Note The *linestyle* parameter does not affect arcs, circles, ellipses, or pie slices. Only the *thickness* parameter is used.

If you're using a CGA in high resolution mode or a monochrome graphics adapter, the examples in this book that show how to use graphics functions may not produce the expected results. If your system runs on a CGA or monochrome adapter, pass the value 1 to those functions that alter the fill or drawing color (**setcolor**, **setfillstyle**, and **setlinestyle**, for example), instead of a symbolic color constant (defined in graphics.h).

Return value None.

See also **circle, ellipse, fillellipse, getarccoords, getaspectratio, graphresult, pieslice, sector**

Example

```
#include <graphics.h>
#include <stdlib.h>
#include <stdio.h>
#include <conio.h>

int main(void)
{
    /* request autodetection */
   int gdriver = DETECT, gmode, errorcode;
   int midx, midy;
   int stangle = 45, endangle = 135;
   int radius = 100;

   /* initialize graphics and local variables */
   initgraph(&gdriver, &gmode, "");

   /* read result of initialization */
   errorcode = graphresult();
   if (errorcode != grOk) {  /* an error occurred */
      printf("Graphics error: %s\n", grapherrormsg(errorcode));
      printf("Press any key to halt:");
      getch();
      exit(1);               /* terminate with an error code */
   }
```

```
   midx = getmaxx() / 2;
   midy = getmaxy() / 2;
   setcolor(getmaxcolor());

   /* draw arc */
   arc(midx, midy, stangle, endangle, radius);

   /* clean up */
   getch();
   closegraph();
   return 0;
}
```

arg

Function Gives the angle of a number in the complex plane.

Syntax #include <complex.h>
double arg(complex *x*);

DOS	UNIX	Windows	ANSI C	C++ only
■		■		■

Remarks **arg** gives the angle, in radians, of the number in the complex plane.

The positive real axis has angle 0, and the positive imaginary axis has angle *pi*/2. If the argument passed to **arg** is complex 0 (zero), **arg** returns 0.

Return value **arg**(*x*) returns **atan2**(**imag**(*x*), **real**(*x*)).

See also **complex**, **norm**, **polar**

Example

```
#include <complex.h>

int main(void)
{
   double x = 3.1, y = 4.2;
   complex z = complex(x,y);
   cout << "z = " << z << "\n";
   cout << "  has real part = " << real(z) << "\n";
   cout << "  and imaginary part = " << imag(z) << "\n";
   cout << "z has complex conjugate = " << conj(z) << "\n";

   double mag = sqrt(norm(z));
   double ang = arg(z);

   cout << "The polar form of z is:\n";
   cout << "   magnitude = " << mag << "\n";
   cout << "   angle (in radians) = " << ang << "\n";
```

```
   cout << "Reconstructing z from its polar form gives:\n";
   cout << "   z = " << polar(mag,ang) << "\n";
   return 0;
}
```

asctime

Function Converts date and time to ASCII.

Syntax #include <time.h>
char *asctime(const struct tm **tblock*);

DOS	UNIX	Windows	ANSI C	C++ only
■	■	■	■	

Remarks **asctime** converts a time stored as a structure in **tblock* to a 26-character string of the same form as the **ctime** string:

```
Sun Sep 16 01:03:52 1973\n\0
```

Return value **asctime** returns a pointer to the character string containing the date and time. This string is a static variable that is overwritten with each call to **asctime**.

See also **ctime, difftime, ftime, gmtime, localtime, mktime, strftime, stime, time, tzset**

Example

```
#include <stdio.h>
#include <string.h>
#include <time.h>

int main(void)
{
   struct tm t;
   char str[80];

   /* sample loading of tm structure */
   t.tm_sec    = 1;     /* Seconds */
   t.tm_min    = 30;    /* Minutes */
   t.tm_hour   = 9;     /* Hour */
   t.tm_mday   = 22;    /* Day of the Month  */
   t.tm_mon    = 11;    /* Month */
   t.tm_year   = 56;    /* Year - does not include century */
   t.tm_wday   = 4;     /* Day of the week  */
   t.tm_yday   = 0;     /* Does not show in asctime  */
   t.tm_isdst  = 0;     /* Is Daylight SavTime
                           Does not show in asctime  */

   /* converts structure to null terminated string */
```

```
   strcpy(str, asctime(&t));
   printf("%s\n", str);
   return 0;
}
```

asin, asinl

Function Calculates the arc sine.

Syntax

Real versions:
#include <math.h>
double asin(double *x*);
long double asinl(long double *x*);

Complex version:
#include <complex.h>
complex asin(complex *x*);

	DOS	UNIX	Windows	ANSI C	C++ only
asinl	■		■		
Real **asin**	■	■	■	■	
Complex **asin**	■		■		■

Remarks **asin** of a real argument returns the arc sine of the input value.

asinl is the long double version; it takes a long double argument and returns a long double result.

Real arguments to **asin** and **asinl** must be in the range –1 to 1, or else **asin** and **asinl** return NAN and sets the global variable *errno* to

EDOM Domain error

The complex inverse sine is defined by

$$\textbf{asin}(z) = -i * \textbf{log}(i * z + \textbf{sqrt}(1 - z^2))$$

Return value **asin** and **asinl** of a real argument return a value in the range *–pi*/2 to *pi*/2.

Error handling for these functions can be modified through the functions **matherr** and **_matherrl**.

See Also **acos, atan, atan2, complex, cos, matherr, sin, tan**

Example

```
#include <stdio.h>
#include <math.h>

int main(void)
{
   double result, x = 0.5;
   result = asin(x);
   printf("The arc sin of %lf is %lf\n", x, result);
```

```
   return(0);
}
```

assert

Function Tests a condition and possibly aborts.

Syntax #include <assert.h>
void assert(int *test*);

DOS	UNIX	Windows	ANSI C	C++ only
■	■	■	■	

Remarks **assert** is a macro that expands to an **if** statement; if *test* evaluates to zero, **assert** prints a message on *stderr* and aborts the program (by calling **abort**).

assert prints this message:

```
Assertion failed: test, file filename, line linenum
```

The *filename* and *linenum* listed in the message are the source file name and line number where the **assert** macro appears.

If you place the `#define NDEBUG` directive ("no debugging") in the source code before the **#include** <assert.h> directive, the effect is to comment out the **assert** statement.

Return value None.

See also **abort**

Example

```
#include <assert.h>
#include <stdio.h>
#include <stdlib.h>

struct ITEM {
   int key;
   int value;
};

/* add item to list, make sure list is not null */
void additem(struct ITEM *itemptr) {
   assert(itemptr != NULL);
   /* add item to list */
}

int main(void)
{
```

```
   additem(NULL);
   return 0;
}
```

Program output

```
Assertion failed: itemptr != NULL,
file C:\BC\ASSERT.C, line 12
```

atan, atanl

Function Calculates the arc tangent.

Syntax

Real versions:
#include <math.h>
double atan(double *x*);
long double atanl(long double *x*);

Complex version:
#include <complex.h>
complex atan(complex *x*)

	DOS	UNIX	Windows	ANSI C	C++ only
atanl	■		■		
Real ***atan***	■	■	■	■	
Complex ***atan***	■		■		■

Remarks **atan** calculates the arc tangent of the input value.

atanl is the long double version; it takes a long double argument and returns a long double result.

The complex inverse tangent is defined by

atan(*z*) = –0.5 *i* **log**((1 + *i z*)/(1 – *i z*))

Return value **atan** and **atanl** of a real argument return a value in the range –*pi*/2 to *pi*/2.

Error handling for these functions can be modified through the functions **matherr** and **_matherrl**.

See Also **acos, asin, atan2, complex, cos, matherr, sin, tan**

Example

```
#include <stdio.h>
#include <math.h>

int main(void)
{
   double result, x = 0.5;
   result = atan(x);
   printf("The arc tangent of %lf is %lf\n", x, result);
```

```
    return(0);
}
```

atan2, atan2l

Function Calculates the arc tangent of *y*/*x*.

Syntax #include <math.h>
double atan2(double *y*, double *x*);
long double atan2l(long double *y*, long double *x*);

	DOS	UNIX	Windows	ANSI C	C++ only
atan2	■	■	■	■	
atan2l	■		■		

Remarks **atan2** returns the arc tangent of *y*/*x*; it produces correct results even when the resulting angle is near *pi*/2 or –*pi*/2 (*x* near 0).

If both *x* and *y* are set to 0, the function sets the global variable *errno* to EDOM.

atan2l is the long double version; it takes long double arguments and returns a long double result.

Return value **atan2** and **atan2l** return a value in the range –*pi* to *pi*.

Error handling for these functions can be modified through the functions **matherr** and **_matherrl**.

See Also **acos, asin, atan, cos, matherr, sin, tan**

Example

```
#include <stdio.h>
#include <math.h>

int main(void)
{
   double result, x = 90.0, y = 15.0;
   result = atan2(y, x);
   printf("The arc tangent ratio of %lf is %lf\n", (y / x), result);
   return 0;
}
```

atexit

Function Registers termination function.

Syntax #include <stdlib.h>
int atexit(void (* *func*)(void));

DOS	UNIX	Windows	ANSI C	C++ only
■		■	■	

Remarks **atexit** registers the function pointed to by *func* as an exit function. Upon normal termination of the program, **exit** calls (**func*)() just before returning to the operating system.

Each call to **atexit** registers another exit function. Up to 32 functions can be registered. They are executed on a last-in, first-out basis (that is, the last function registered is the first to be executed).

Return value **atexit** returns 0 on success and nonzero on failure (no space left to register the function).

See also **abort, _exit, exit, spawn...**

Example

```
#include <stdio.h>
#include <stdlib.h>

void exit_fn1(void)
{
   printf("Exit function #1 called\n");
}

void exit_fn2(void)
{
   printf("Exit function #2 called\n");
}

int main(void)
{
   /* post exit function #1 */
   atexit(exit_fn1);

   /* post exit function #2 */
   atexit(exit_fn2);
   printf("Done in main\n");
   return 0;
}
```

atof, _atold

Function Converts a string to a floating-point number.

Syntax

#include <math.h>
double atof(const char *s);
long double _atold(const char *s);

	DOS	UNIX	Windows	ANSI C	C++ only
atof	■	■	■	■	
_atold	■		■		

Remarks

atof converts a string pointed to by *s* to double; this function recognizes the character representation of a floating-point number, made up of the following:

- an optional string of tabs and spaces.
- an optional sign.
- a string of digits and an optional decimal point (the digits can be on both sides of the decimal point).
- an optional *e* or *E* followed by an optional signed integer.

The characters must match this generic format:

[*whitespace*] [*sign*] [*ddd*] [.] [*ddd*] [e | E[*sign*]*ddd*]

atof also recognizes +INF and –INF for plus and minus infinity, and +NAN and –NAN for Not-a-Number.

In this function, the first unrecognized character ends the conversion.

_atold is the long double version; it converts the string pointed to by *s* to a long double.

strtod and **_strtold** are similar to **atof** and **_atold**; they provide better error detection, and hence are preferred in some applications.

Return value

atof and **_atold** return the converted value of the input string.

If there is an overflow, **atof** (or **_atold**) returns plus or minus HUGE_VAL (or _LHUGE_VAL), *errno* is set to ERANGE, and **matherr** (or **_matherrl**) is not called.

See Also

atoi, atol, ecvt, fcvt, gcvt, scanf, strtod

Example

```
#include <stdlib.h>
#include <stdio.h>

int main(void)
{
   float f;
   char *str = "12345.678";
```

```
    f = atof(str);
    printf("string = %s float = %5.3f\n", str, f);

    return 0;
}
```

atoi

Function Converts a string to an integer.

Syntax #include <stdlib.h>
int atoi(const char *s);

DOS	UNIX	Windows	ANSI C	C++ only
■	■	■	■	

Remarks **atoi** converts a string pointed to by *s* to **int**; **atoi** recognizes (in the following order)

- an optional string of tabs and spaces
- an optional sign
- a string of digits

The characters must match this generic format:

[*ws*] [*sn*] [*ddd*]

In this function, the first unrecognized character ends the conversion.

There are no provisions for overflow in **atoi** (results are undefined).

Return value **atoi** returns the converted value of the input string. If the string cannot be converted to a number of the corresponding type (int), the return value is 0.

See also **atof, atol, ecvt, fcvt, gcvt, scanf, strtod**

Example

```
#include <stdlib.h>
#include <stdio.h>

int main(void)
{
    int n;
    char *str = "12345";
    n = atoi(str);
    printf("string = %s integer = %d\n", str, n);
    return 0;
}
```

atol

Function Converts a string to a long.

Syntax #include <stdlib.h>
long atol(const char **s*);

DOS	UNIX	Windows	ANSI C	C++ only
■	■	■	■	

Remarks **atol** converts the string pointed to by *s* to **long**. **atol** recognizes (in the following order)

- an optional string of tabs and spaces
- an optional sign
- a string of digits

The characters must match this generic format:

[*ws*] [*sn*] [*ddd*]

In this function, the first unrecognized character ends the conversion.

There are no provisions for overflow in **atol** (results are undefined).

Return value **atol** returns the converted value of the input string. If the string cannot be converted to a number of the corresponding type (**long**), **atol** returns 0.

See also **atof, atoi, ecvt, fcvt, gcvt, scanf, strtod, strtol, strtoul**

Example

```
#include <stdlib.h>
#include <stdio.h>

int main(void)
{
   long l;
   char *lstr = "98765432";
   l = atol(lstr);
   printf("string = %s long = %ld\n", lstr, l);
   return 0;
}
```

bar

Function Draws a two-dimensional bar.

Syntax #include <graphics.h>
#include <conio.h>
void far bar(int *left*, int *top*, int *right*, int *bottom*);

DOS	UNIX	Windows	ANSI C	C++ only
■				

Remarks **bar** draws a filled-in, rectangular, two-dimensional bar. The bar is filled using the current fill pattern and fill color. **bar** does not outline the bar; to draw an outlined two-dimensional bar, use **bar3d** with *depth* equal to 0.

The upper left and lower right corners of the rectangle are given by (*left*, *top*) and (*right*, *bottom*), respectively. The coordinates refer to pixels.

Return value None.

See also **bar3d, rectangle, setcolor, setfillstyle, setlinestyle**

Example

```
#include <graphics.h>
#include <stdlib.h>
#include <stdio.h>
#include <conio.h>

int main(void)
{
   /* request autodetection */
   int gdriver = DETECT, gmode, errorcode;
   int midx, midy, i;

   /* initialize graphics and local variables */
   initgraph(&gdriver, &gmode, "");

   /* read result of initialization */
   errorcode = graphresult();
   if (errorcode != grOk) {   /* an error occurred */
      printf("Graphics error: %s\n", grapherrormsg(errorcode));
      printf("Press any key to halt:");
      getch();
      exit(1);               /* terminate with an error code */
   }

   midx = getmaxx() / 2;
   midy = getmaxy() / 2;

   /* loop through the fill patterns */
   for (i=SOLID_FILL; i<USER_FILL; i++) {
      /* set the fill style */
      setfillstyle(i, getmaxcolor());

      /* draw the bar */
      bar(midx-50, midy-50, midx+50, midy+50);
```

```
        getch();
    }
    /* clean up */
    closegraph();
    return 0;
}
```

bar3d

Function Draws a three-dimensional bar.

Syntax #include <graphics.h>
void far bar3d(int *left*, int *top*, int *right*, int *bottom*, int *depth*, int *topflag*);

DOS	UNIX	Windows	ANSI C	C++ only
■				

Remarks **bar3d** draws a three-dimensional rectangular bar, then fills it using the current fill pattern and fill color. The three-dimensional outline of the bar is drawn in the current line style and color. The bar's depth in pixels is given by *depth*. The *topflag* parameter governs whether a three-dimensional top is put on the bar. If *topflag* is nonzero, a top is put on; otherwise, no top is put on the bar (making it possible to stack several bars on top of one another).

The upper left and lower right corners of the rectangle are given by (*left*, *top*) and (*right*, *bottom*), respectively.

To calculate a typical depth for **bar3d**, take 25% of the width of the bar, like this:

```
bar3d(left,top,right,bottom, (right-left)/4,1);
```

Return value None.

See also **bar, rectangle, setcolor, setfillstyle, setlinestyle**

Example

```
#include <graphics.h>
#include <stdlib.h>
#include <stdio.h>
#include <conio.h>

int main(void)
{
   /* request autodetection */
   int gdriver = DETECT, gmode, errorcode;
   int midx, midy, i;
```

```
   /* initialize graphics and local variables */
   initgraph(&gdriver, &gmode, "");

   /* read result of initialization */
   errorcode = graphresult();
   if (errorcode != grOk) {   /* an error occurred */
      printf("Graphics error: %s\n", grapherrormsg(errorcode));
      printf("Press any key to halt:");
      getch();
      exit(1);               /* terminate with an error code */
   }

   midx = getmaxx() / 2;
   midy = getmaxy() / 2;

   /* loop through the fill patterns */
   for (i=EMPTY_FILL; i<USER_FILL; i++) {
      /* set the fill style */
      setfillstyle(i, getmaxcolor());

      /* draw the 3-d bar */
      bar3d(midx-50, midy-50, midx+50, midy+50, 10, 1);
      getch();
   }
   /* clean up */
   closegraph();
   return 0;
}
```

bcd

Function Converts a number to binary coded decimal (BCD).

Syntax #include <bcd.h>
bcd bcd(int *x*);
bcd bcd(double *x*);
bcd bcd(double *x*, int *decimals*);

DOS	UNIX	Windows	ANSI C	C++ only
■		■		■

Remarks All of the usual arithmetic operators have been overloaded to work with bcd numbers.

bcd numbers have about 17 decimal digits precision, and a range of about 1×10^{-125} to 1×10^{125}.

Use the function **real** to convert a bcd number back to a **float**, **double**, or **long double**.

The argument *decimals* is optional. You can use it to specify how many decimal digits after the decimal point are to be carried in the conversion.

The number is rounded according to the rules of banker's rounding, which means round to nearest whole number, with ties being rounded to an even digit.

Return value The bcd equivalent of the given number.

See also **real**

Example

```
#include <iostream.h>
#include <bcd.h>

int main(void)
{
   bcd a = bcd(x/3,2); // a third, rounded to nearest penny
   double x = 10000.0; // ten thousand dollars

   cout << "share of fortune = $" << a << "\n";
   return 0;
}
```

bdos

Function Accesses DOS system calls.

Syntax #include <dos.h>
int bdos(int *dosfun*, unsigned *dosdx*, unsigned *dosal*);

DOS	UNIX	Windows	ANSI C	C++ only
■		■		

Remarks **bdos** provides direct access to many of the DOS system calls. See your DOS reference manuals for details on each system call.

For system calls that require an integer argument, use **bdos**; if they require a pointer argument, use **bdosptr**. In the large data models (compact, large, and huge), it is important to use **bdosptr** instead of **bdos** for system calls that require a pointer as the call argument.

dosfun is defined in your DOS reference manuals.

dosdx is the value of register DX.

dosal is the value of register AL.

Return value The return value of **bdos** is the value of AX set by the system call.

See also **bdosptr, geninterrupt, int86, int86x, intdos, intdosx**

Example

```
#include <stdio.h>
#include <dos.h>

/* get current drive as 'A', 'B', ... */
char current_drive(void)
{
   char curdrive;

   /* get current disk as 0, 1, ... */
   curdrive = bdos(0x19, 0, 0);
   return('A' + curdrive);
}

int main(void)
{
   printf("The current drive is %c:\n", current_drive());
   return 0;
}
```

Program output

```
The current drive is C:
```

bdosptr

Function Accesses DOS system calls.

Syntax #include <dos.h>
int bdosptr(int *dosfun*, void **argument*, unsigned *dosal*);

DOS	UNIX	Windows	ANSI C	C++ only
■		■		

Remarks **bdosptr** provides direct access to many of the DOS system calls. See your DOS reference manuals for details of each system call.

For system calls that require an integer argument, use **bdos**; if they require a pointer argument, use **bdosptr**. In the large data models (compact, large, and huge), it is important to use **bdosptr** for system calls that require a pointer as the call argument. In the small data models, the *argument* parameter to **bdosptr** specifies DX; in the large data models, it gives the DS:DX values to be used by the system call.

dosfun is defined in your DOS reference manuals.

dosal is the value of register AL.

Return value The return value of **bdosptr** is the value of AX on success or –1 on failure. On failure, the global variables *errno* and *_doserrno* are set.

See also **bdos, geninterrupt, int86, int86x, intdos, intdosx**

Example

```
#include <stdio.h>
#include <dos.h>

/* get current drive as 'A', 'B', ... */
char current_drive(void)
{
   char curdrive;

   /* get current disk as 0, 1, ... */
   curdrive = bdos(0x19, 0, 0);
   return('A' + curdrive);
}

int main(void)
{
   printf("The current drive is %c:\n", current_drive());
   return 0;
}
```

bioscom

Function Performs serial I/O.

Syntax #include <bios.h>
int bioscom(int *cmd*, char *abyte*, int *port*);

DOS	UNIX	Windows	ANSI C	C++ only
■				

Remarks **bioscom** performs various RS-232 communications over the I/O port given in *port*.

A *port* value of 0 corresponds to COM1, 1 corresponds to COM2, and so forth.

The value of *cmd* can be one of the following:

0 Sets the communications parameters to the value in *abyte*.
1 Sends the character in *abyte* out over the communications line.
2 Receives a character from the communications line.

3 Returns the current status of the communications port.

abyte is a combination of the following bits (one value is selected from each of the groups):

0x02	7 data bits	0x00	110 baud
0x03	8 data bits	0x20	150 baud
		0x40	300 baud
0x00	1 stop bit	0x60	600 baud
0x04	2 stop bits	0x80	1200 baud
0x00	No parity	0xA0	2400 baud
0x08	Odd parity	0xC0	4800 baud
0x18	Even parity	0xE0	9600 baud

For example, a value of 0xEB (0xE0 | 0x08 | 0x00 | 0x03) for *abyte* sets the communications port to 9600 baud, odd parity, 1 stop bit, and 8 data bits. **bioscom** uses the BIOS 0x14 interrupt.

Return value

For all values of *cmd*, **bioscom** returns a 16-bit integer, of which the upper 8 bits are status bits and the lower 8 bits vary, depending on the value of *cmd*. The upper bits of the return value are defined as follows:

Bit 15	Time out
Bit 14	Transmit shift register empty
Bit 13	Transmit holding register empty
Bit 12	Break detect
Bit 11	Framing error
Bit 10	Parity error
Bit 9	Overrun error
Bit 8	Data ready

If the *abyte* value could not be sent, bit 15 is set to 1. Otherwise, the remaining upper and lower bits are appropriately set. For example, if a framing error has occurred, bit 11 is set to 1.

With a *cmd* value of 2, the byte read is in the lower bits of the return value if there is no error. If an error occurs, at least one of the upper bits is set to 1. If no upper bits are set to 1, the byte was received without error.

With a *cmd* value of 0 or 3, the return value has the upper bits set as defined, and the lower bits are defined as follows:

Bit 7	Received line signal detect
Bit 6	Ring indicator
Bit 5	Data set ready
Bit 4	Clear to send
Bit 3	Change in receive line signal detector
Bit 2	Trailing edge ring detector

Bit 1	Change in data set ready
Bit 0	Change in clear to send

Example

```
#include <bios.h>
#include <conio.h>

#define COM1       0
#define DATA_READY 0x100
#define TRUE       1
#define FALSE      0
#define SETTINGS (0x80 | 0x02 | 0x00 | 0x00)

int main(void)
{
   int in, out, status, DONE = FALSE;
   bioscom(0, SETTINGS, COM1);
   cprintf("... BIOSCOM [ESC] to exit ...\n");
   while (!DONE) {
      status = bioscom(3, 0, COM1);
      if (status & DATA_READY)
         if ((out = bioscom(2, 0, COM1) & 0x7F) != 0)
            putch(out);
         if (kbhit()) {
            if ((in = getch()) == '\x1B')
                    DONE = TRUE;
            bioscom(1, in, COM1);
         }
   }
   return 0;
}
```

_bios_disk

Function Issues BIOS disk drive services

Syntax #include <bios.h>
unsigned _bios_disk(unsigned *cmd*, struct diskinfo_t **dinfo*);

DOS	UNIX	Windows	ANSI C	C++ only
■				

Remarks **_bios_disk** uses interrupt 0x13 to issue disk operations directly to the BIOS. The *cmd* argument specifies the operation to perform, and *dinfo* points to a **diskinfo_t** structure that contains the remaining parameters required by the operation.

The **diskinfo_t** structure (defined in bios.h) has the following format:

```
struct diskinfo_t {
    unsigned drive, head, track, sector, nsectors;
    void far *buffer;
};
```

drive is a number that specifies which disk drive is to be used: 0 for the first floppy disk drive, 1 for the second floppy disk drive, 2 for the third, and so on. For hard disk drives, a *drive* value of 0x80 specifies the first drive, 0x81 specifies the second, 0x82 the third, and so forth.

For hard disks, the physical drive is specified, not the disk partition. If necessary, the application program must interpret the partition table information itself.

Depending on the value of *cmd*, the other parameters in the **diskinfo_t** structure may or may not be needed.

The possible values for *cmd* (defined in bios.h) are the following:

_DISK_RESET
: Resets disk system, forcing the drive controller to do a hard reset. All **diskinfo_t** parameters are ignored.

_DISK_STATUS
: Returns the status of the last disk operation. All **diskinfo_t** parameters are ignored.

_DISK_READ
: Reads one or more disk sectors into memory. The starting sector to read is given by *head*, *track*, and *sector*. The number of sectors is given by *nsectors*. The data is read, 512 bytes per sector, into *buffer*. If the operation is successful, the high byte of the return value will be 0 and the low byte will contain the number of sectors. If an error occurred, the high byte of the return value will have one of the following values:

0x01	Bad command.
0x02	Address mark not found.
0x03	Attempt to write to write-protected disk.
0x04	Sector not found.
0x05	Reset failed (hard disk).
0x06	Disk changed since last operation.
0x07	Drive parameter activity failed.
0x08	Direct memory access (DMA) overrun.
0x09	Attempt to perform DMA across 64K boundary.
0x0A	Bad sector detected.
0x0B	Bad track detected.
0x0C	Unsupported track.
0x10	Bad CRC/ECC on disk read.
0x11	CRC/ECC corrected data error.
0x20	Controller has failed.

0x40	Seek operation failed.
0x80	Attachment failed to respond.
0xAA	Drive not ready (hard disk only).
0xBB	Undefined error occurred (hard disk only).
0xCC	Write fault occurred.
0xE0	Status error.
0xFF	Sense operation failed.

0x11 is not an error because the data is correct. The value is returned to give the application an opportunity to decide for itself.

_DISK_WRITE
: Writes one or more disk sectors from memory. The starting sector to write is given by *head*, *track*, and *sector*. The number of sectors is given by *nsectors*. The data is written, 512 bytes per sector, from *buffer*. See _DISK_READ (above) for a description of the return value.

_DISK_VERIFY
: Verifies one or more sectors. The starting sector is given by *head*, *track*, and *sector*. The number of sectors is given by *nsectors*. See _DISK_READ (above) for a description of the return value.

_DISK_FORMAT
: Formats a track. The track is specified by *head* and *track*. *buffer* points to a table of sector headers to be written on the named *track*. See the *Technical Reference Manual* for the IBM PC for a description of this table and the format operation.

Return value **_bios_disk** returns the value of the AX register set by the INT 0x13 BIOS call.

See Also **absread, abswrite, biosdisk**

Example

```
#include <bios.h>
#include <stdio.h>

int main(void)
{
   struct diskinfo_t dinfo;
   int result;
   static char dbuf[512];

   dinfo.drive =  0;     /* drive number for A: */
   dinfo.head  =  0;     /* disk head number */
   dinfo.track =  0;     /* track number */
   dinfo.sector  =  1;  /* sector number */
   dinfo.nsectors =  1; /* sector count */
   dinfo.buffer = dbuf; /* data buffer */

   printf("Attempting to read from drive A:\n");
   result = _bios_disk(_DISK_READ, &dinfo);
```

```
    if ((result & 0xff00) == 0) {
       printf("Disk read from A: successful.\n");
       printf("First three bytes read are 0x%02x 0x%02x 0x%02x\n",
         dbuf[0] & 0xff, dbuf[1] & 0xff, dbuf[2] & 0xff);
    }
    else
       printf("Cannot read drive A, status = 0x%02x\n", result);
    return 0;
}
```

biosdisk

Function Issues BIOS disk drive services.

Syntax #include <bios.h>
int biosdisk(int *cmd*, int *drive*, int *head*, int *track*, int *sector*, int *nsects*, void **buffer*);

DOS	UNIX	Windows	ANSI C	C++ only
■				

Remarks **biosdisk** uses interrupt 0x13 to issue disk operations directly to the BIOS.

drive is a number that specifies which disk drive is to be used: 0 for the first floppy disk drive, 1 for the second floppy disk drive, 2 for the third, and so on. For hard disk drives, a *drive* value of 0x80 specifies the first drive, 0x81 specifies the second, 0x82 the third, and so forth.

For hard disks, the physical drive is specified, not the disk partition. If necessary, the application program must interpret the partition table information itself.

cmd indicates the operation to perform. Depending on the value of *cmd*, the other parameters may or may not be needed.

Here are the possible values for *cmd* for the IBM PC, XT, AT, or PS/2, or any compatible system:

0 Resets disk system, forcing the drive controller to do a hard reset. All other parameters are ignored.

1 Returns the status of the last disk operation. All other parameters are ignored.

2 Reads one or more disk sectors into memory. The starting sector to read is given by *head*, *track*, and *sector*. The number of sectors is given by *nsects*. The data is read, 512 bytes per sector, into *buffer*.

3 Writes one or more disk sectors from memory. The starting sector to write is given by *head*, *track*, and *sector*. The number of sectors is given by *nsects*. The data is written, 512 bytes per sector, from *buffer*.

4 Verifies one or more sectors. The starting sector is given by *head*, *track*, and *sector*. The number of sectors is given by *nsects*.

5 Formats a track. The track is specified by *head* and *track*. *buffer* points to a table of sector headers to be written on the named *track*. See the *Technical Reference Manual* for the IBM PC for a description of this table and the format operation.

The following *cmd* values are allowed only for the XT, AT, PS/2, and compatibles:

6 Formats a track and sets bad sector flags.

7 Formats the drive beginning at a specific track.

8 Returns the current drive parameters. The drive information is returned in *buffer* in the first 4 bytes.

9 Initializes drive-pair characteristics.

10 Does a long read, which reads 512 plus 4 extra bytes per sector.

11 Does a long write, which writes 512 plus 4 extra bytes per sector.

12 Does a disk seek.

13 Alternates disk reset.

14 Reads sector buffer.

15 Writes sector buffer.

16 Tests whether the named drive is ready.

17 Recalibrates the drive.

18 Controller RAM diagnostic.

19 Drive diagnostic.

20 Controller internal diagnostic.

➡ **biosdisk** operates below the level of files on raw sectors. *It can destroy file contents and directories on a hard disk.*

Return value **biosdisk** returns a status byte composed of the following bits:

0x00 Operation successful.
0x01 Bad command.

0x02	Address mark not found.
0x03	Attempt to write to write-protected disk.
0x04	Sector not found.
0x05	Reset failed (hard disk).
0x06	Disk changed since last operation.
0x07	Drive parameter activity failed.
0x08	Direct memory access (DMA) overrun.
0x09	Attempt to perform DMA across 64K boundary.
0x0A	Bad sector detected.
0x0B	Bad track detected.
0x0C	Unsupported track.
0x10	Bad CRC/ECC on disk read.
0x11	CRC/ECC corrected data error.
0x20	Controller has failed.
0x40	Seek operation failed.
0x80	Attachment failed to respond.
0xAA	Drive not ready (hard disk only).
0xBB	Undefined error occurred (hard disk only).
0xCC	Write fault occurred.
0xE0	Status error.
0xFF	Sense operation failed.

0x11 is not an error because the data is correct. The value is returned to give the application an opportunity to decide for itself.

See also **absread, abswrite**

Example

```
#include <bios.h>
#include <stdio.h>

int main(void)
{
   #define CMD    2    /* read sector command */
   #define DRIVE  0    /* drive number for A: */
   #define HEAD   0    /* disk head number */
   #define TRACK  1    /* track number */
   #define SECT   1    /* sector number */
   #define NSECT  1    /* sector count */

   int result;
   char buffer[512];
   printf("Attempting to read from drive A:\n");
   result = biosdisk(CMD, DRIVE, HEAD, TRACK, SECT, NSECT, buffer);
   if (result == 0)
      printf("Disk read from A: successful.\n");
   else
      printf("Attempt to read from drive A: failed.\n");
```

```
   return 0;
}
```

biosequip

Function Checks equipment.

Syntax #include <bios.h>
int biosequip(void);

DOS	UNIX	Windows	ANSI C	C++ only
■		■		

Remarks **biosequip** uses BIOS interrupt 0x11 to return an integer describing the equipment connected to the system.

Return value The return value is interpreted as a collection of bit-sized fields. The IBM PC values follow:

Bits 14-15 Number of parallel printers installed
00 = 0 printers
01 = 1 printer
10 = 2 printers
11 = 3 printers

Bit 13 Serial printer attached
Bit 12 Game I/O attached

DOS only sees two ports but can be pushed to see four; the IBM PS/2 can see up to eight.

Bits 9-11 Number of COM ports
000 = 0 ports
001 = 1 port
010 = 2 ports
011 = 3 ports
100 = 4 ports
101 = 5 ports
110 = 6 ports
111 = 7 ports

Bit 8 Direct memory access (DMA)
0 = Machine has DMA
1 = Machine does not have DMA; for example, PC Jr.

Bits 6-7 Number of disk drives
00 = 1 drive
01 = 2 drives

B

10 = 3 drives
11 = 4 drives, only if bit 0 is 1

Bit 4-5 Initial video mode
00 = Unused
01 = 40x25 BW with color card
10 = 80x25 BW with color card
11 = 80x25 BW with mono card

Bits 2-3 Motherboard RAM size
00 = 16K
01 = 32K
10 = 48K
11 = 64K

Bit 1 Floating-point coprocessor
Bit 0 Boot from disk

Example

```
#include <stdio.h>
#include <bios.h>

#define CO_PROCESSOR_MASK 0x0002

int main(void)
{
   int equip_check;

   /* get the current equipment configuration */
   equip_check = biosequip();

   /* check to see if there is a coprocessor installed */
   if (equip_check & CO_PROCESSOR_MASK)
      printf("There is a math coprocessor installed.\n");
   else
      printf("No math coprocessor installed.\n");
   return 0;
}
```

_bios_equiplist

Function Checks equipment.

Syntax #include <bios.h>
unsigned _bios_equiplist(void);

DOS	UNIX	Windows	ANSI C	C++ only
■		■		

Remarks **_bios_equiplist** uses BIOS interrupt 0x11 to return an integer describing the equipment connected to the system.

Return value The return value is interpreted as a collection of bit-sized fields. The IBM PC values follow:

Bits 14-15	Number of parallel printers installed 00 = 0 printers 01 = 1 printer 10 = 2 printers 11 = 3 printers
Bit 13	Serial printer attached
Bit 12	Game I/O attached
Bits 9-11	Number of COM ports 000 = 0 ports 001 = 1 port 010 = 2 ports 011 = 3 ports 100 = 4 ports 101 = 5 ports 110 = 6 ports 111 = 7 ports
Bit 8	Direct memory access (DMA) 0 = Machine has DMA 1 = Machine does not have DMA; for example, PC Jr.
Bits 6-7	Number of disk drives 00 = 1 drive 01 = 2 drives 10 = 3 drives 11 = 4 drives, only if bit 0 is 1
Bit 4-5	Initial video mode 00 = Unused 01 = 40x25 BW with color card 10 = 80x25 BW with color card 11 = 80x25 BW with mono card
Bits 2-3	Motherboard RAM size 00 = 16K 01 = 32K 10 = 48K 11 = 64K
Bit 1	Floating-point coprocessor
Bit 0	Boot from disk

DOS only sees two ports but can be pushed to see four; the IBM PS/2 can see up to eight.

Example

```
#include <stdio.h>
#include <bios.h>

#define CO_PROCESSOR_MASK 0x0002
```

```
int main(void)
{
   unsigned equip_check;

   /* Get the current equipment configuration. */
   equip_check = _bios_equiplist();

   /* Check to see if there is a coprocessor installed. */
   if (equip_check & CO_PROCESSOR_MASK)
      printf("There is a math coprocessor installed.\n");
   else
      printf("No math coprocessor installed.\n");
   return 0;
}
```

bioskey

Function Keyboard interface, using BIOS services directly.

Syntax #include <bios.h>
int bioskey(int *cmd*);

DOS	UNIX	Windows	ANSI C	C++ only
■				

Remarks **bioskey** performs various keyboard operations using BIOS interrupt 0x16. The parameter *cmd* determines the exact operation.

Return value The value returned by **bioskey** depends on the task it performs, determined by the value of *cmd*:

0 If the lower 8 bits are nonzero, **bioskey** returns the ASCII character for the next keystroke waiting in the queue or the next key pressed at the keyboard. If the lower 8 bits are zero, the upper 8 bits are the extended keyboard codes defined in the IBM PC *Technical Reference Manual*.

1 This tests whether a keystroke is available to be read. A return value of zero means no key is available. The return value is 0xFFFFF (-1) if *Ctrl-Brk* has been pressed. Otherwise, the value of the next keystroke is returned. The keystroke itself is kept to be returned by the next call to **bioskey** that has a *cmd* value of zero.

2 Requests the current shift key status. The value is obtained by ORing the following values together:

Bit 7	0x80	*Insert* on
Bit 6	0x40	*Caps* on
Bit 5	0x20	*Num Lock* on
Bit 4	0x10	*Scroll Lock* on
Bit 3	0x08	*Alt* pressed
Bit 2	0x04	*Ctrl* pressed
Bit 1	0x02	← *Shift* pressed
Bit 0	0x01	→ *Shift* pressed

Example

```
#include <stdio.h>
#include <bios.h>
#include <ctype.h>

#define RIGHT  0x01
#define LEFT   0x02
#define CTRL   0x04
#define ALT    0x08

int main(void)
{
   int key, modifiers;

   /* function 1 returns 0 until a key is pressed */
   while (bioskey(1) == 0);

   /* function 0 returns the key that is waiting */
   key = bioskey(0);

   /* use function 2 to determine if shift keys are used */
   modifiers = bioskey(2);
   if (modifiers) {
      printf("[");
      if (modifiers & RIGHT) printf("RIGHT");
      if (modifiers & LEFT)  printf("LEFT");
      if (modifiers & CTRL)  printf("CTRL");
      if (modifiers & ALT)   printf("ALT");
      printf("]");
   }
   /* print out the character read */
   if (isalnum(key & 0xFF))
      printf("'%c'\n", key);
   else
      printf("%#02x\n", key);
   return 0;
}
```

B

_bios_keybrd

Function Keyboard interface, using BIOS services directly.

Syntax #include <bios.h>
unsigned _bios_keybrd(unsigned *cmd*);

DOS	UNIX	Windows	ANSI C	C++ only
■				

Remarks **_bios_keybrd** performs various keyboard operations using BIOS interrupt 0x16. The parameter *cmd* determines the exact operation.

Return value The value returned by **_bios_keybrd** depends on the task it performs, determined by the value of *cmd* (defined in bios.h):

_KEYBRD_READ
: If the lower 8 bits are nonzero, **_bios_keybrd** returns the ASCII character for the next keystroke waiting in the queue or the next key pressed at the keyboard. If the lower 8 bits are zero, the upper 8 bits are the extended keyboard codes defined in the IBM PC *Technical Reference Manual*.

_NKEYBRD_READ
: Use this value instead of _KEYBRD_READY to read the keyboard codes for enhanced keyboards, which have additional cursor and function keys.

_KEYBRD_READY
: This tests whether a keystroke is available to be read. A return value of zero means no key is available. The return value is 0xFFFF (-1) if *Ctrl-Brk* has been pressed. Otherwise, the value of the next keystroke is returned, as described in _KEYBRD_READ (above). The keystroke itself is kept to be returned by the next call to **_bios_keybrd** that has a *cmd* value of _KEYBRD_READ or _NKEYBRD_READ.

_NKEYBRD_READY
: Use this value to check the status of enhanced keyboards, which have additional cursor and function keys.

_KEYBRD_SHIFTSTATUS
: Requests the current shift key status. The value will contain an OR of zero or more of the following values:

Bit 7	0x80	*Insert* on

Bit 6	0x40	*Caps* on
Bit 5	0x20	*Num Lock* on
Bit 4	0x10	*Scroll Lock* on
Bit 3	0x08	*Alt* pressed
Bit 2	0x04	*Ctrl* pressed
Bit 1	0x02	Left *Shift* pressed
Bit 0	0x01	Right *Shift* pressed

0x12 _NKEYBRD_SHIFTSTATUS

Use this value instead of _KEYBRD_SHIFTSTATUS to request the full 16-bit shift key status for enhanced keyboards. The return value will contain an OR of zero or more of the bits defined above in _KEYBRD_SHIFTSTATUS, and additionally, any of the following bits:

Bit 15	0x8000	*Sys Req* pressed
Bit 14	0x4000	*Caps Lock* pressed
Bit 13	0x2000	*Num Lock* pressed
Bit 12	0x1000	*Scroll Lock* pressed
Bit 11	0x0800	Right *Alt* pressed
Bit 10	0x0400	Right *Ctrl* pressed
Bit 9	0x0200	Left *Alt* pressed
Bit 8	0x0100	Left *Ctrl* pressed

Example

```
#include <stdio.h>
#include <bios.h>
#include <ctype.h>

#define RIGHT  0x01
#define LEFT   0x02
#define CTRL   0x04
#define ALT    0x08

int main(void)
{
   int key, modifiers;

   /* Wait until a key is pressed */
   while (_bios_keybrd(_KEYBRD_READY) == 0);

   /* Fetch the key that is waiting */
   key = _bios_keybrd(_KEYBRD_READ);

   /* Determine if shift keys are used */
   modifiers = _bios_keybrd(_KEYBRD_SHIFTSTATUS);
   if (modifiers){
      printf("[");
      if (modifiers & RIGHT) printf("RIGHT");
      if (modifiers & LEFT)  printf("LEFT");
      if (modifiers & CTRL)  printf("CTRL");
```

```
      if (modifiers & ALT)   printf("ALT");
      printf("]");
   }
   /* print out the character read */
   if (isalnum(key & 0xFF))
      printf("'%c'\n", key);
   else
      printf("%#02x\n", key);
   return 0;
}
```

biosmemory

Function Returns memory size.

Syntax #include <bios.h>
int biosmemory(void);

DOS	UNIX	Windows	ANSI C	C++ only
▪		▪		

Remarks **biosmemory** returns the size of RAM memory using BIOS interrupt 0x12. This does not include display adapter memory, extended memory, or expanded memory.

Return value **biosmemory** returns the size of RAM memory in 1K blocks.

Example

```
#include <stdio.h>
#include <bios.h>

int main(void)
{
   int memory_size;
   memory_size = biosmemory();   /* returns value up to 640K */
   printf("RAM size = %dK\n", memory_size);

   return 0;
}
```

_bios_memsize

Function Returns memory size.

Syntax #include <bios.h>
unsigned _bios_memsize(void);

DOS	UNIX	Windows	ANSI C	C++ only
■		■		

Remarks **_bios_memsize** returns the size of RAM memory using BIOS interrupt 0x12. This does not include display adapter memory, extended memory, or expanded memory.

Return value **_bios_memsize** returns the size of RAM memory in 1K blocks.

Example

```
#include <stdio.h>
#include <bios.h>

int main(void)
{
   unsigned memory_size;
   memory_size = _bios_memsize();    /* returns value up to 640K */
   printf("RAM size = %dK\n", memory_size);

   return 0;
}
```

biosprint

Function Printer I/O using BIOS services directly.

Syntax #include <bios.h>
int biosprint(int *cmd*, int *abyte*, int *port*);

DOS	UNIX	Windows	ANSI C	C++ only
■				

Remarks **biosprint** performs various printer functions on the printer identified by the parameter *port* using BIOS interrupt 0x17.

A *port* value of 0 corresponds to LPT1; a *port* value of 1 corresponds to LPT2; and so on.

The value of *cmd* can be one of the following:

- 0 Prints the character in *abyte*.
- 1 Initializes the printer port.
- 2 Reads the printer status.

The value of *abyte* can be 0 to 255.

Return value The value returned from any of these operations is the current printer status, which is obtained by ORing these bit values together:

B

Bit 0	0x01	Device time out
Bit 3	0x08	I/O error
Bit 4	0x10	Selected
Bit 5	0x20	Out of paper
Bit 6	0x40	Acknowledge
Bit 7	0x80	Not busy

Example

```
#include <stdio.h>
#include <conio.h>
#include <bios.h>

int main(void)
{
   #define STATUS  2    /* printer status command */
   #define PORTNUM 0    /* port number for LPT1 */

   int status, abyte=0;
   printf("Please turn off your printer. Press any key to continue\n");
   getch();
   status = biosprint(STATUS, abyte, PORTNUM);
   if (status & 0x01)
      printf("Device time out.\n");
   if (status & 0x08)
      printf("I/O error.\n");
   if (status & 0x10)
      printf("Selected.\n");
   if (status & 0x20)
      printf("Out of paper.\n");
   if (status & 0x40)
      printf("Acknowledge.\n");
   if (status & 0x80)
      printf("Not busy.\n");
   return 0;
}
```

_bios_printer

Function Printer I/O using BIOS services directly.

Syntax #include <bios.h>
unsigned _bios_printer(int *cmd*, int *port*, int *abyte*);

DOS	UNIX	Windows	ANSI C	C++ only
■				

Remarks **_bios_printer** performs various printer functions on the printer identified by the parameter *port* using BIOS interrupt 0x17.

A *port* value of 0 corresponds to LPT1; a *port* value of 1 corresponds to LPT2; and so on.

The value of *cmd* can be one of the following values (defined in bios.h):

_PRINTER_WRITE	Prints the character in *abyte*. The value of *abyte* can be 0 to 255.
_PRINTER_INIT	Initializes the printer port. The *abyte* argument is ignored.
_PRINTER_STATUS	Reads the printer status. The *abyte* argument is ignored.

Return value The value returned from any of these operations is the current printer status, which is obtained by ORing these bit values together:

Bit 0	0x01	Device time out
Bit 3	0x08	I/O error
Bit 4	0x10	Selected
Bit 5	0x20	Out of paper
Bit 6	0x40	Acknowledge
Bit 7	0x80	Not busy

Example

```
#include <stdio.h>
#include <conio.h>
#include <bios.h>

int main(void)
{
   unsigned status, abyte = 0;
   printf("Please turn off your printer. Press any key to continue\n");
   getch();
   status = _bios_printer(_PRINTER_STATUS, PORTNUM, abyte);
   if (status & 0x01)
      printf("Device time out.\n");
   if (status & 0x08)
      printf("I/O error.\n");
   if (status & 0x10)
      printf("Selected.\n");
   if (status & 0x20)
      printf("Out of paper.\n");
   if (status & 0x40)
      printf("Acknowledge.\n");
   if (status & 0x80)
      printf("Not busy.\n");
   return 0;
}
```

B

_bios_serialcom

Function Performs serial I/O.

Syntax #include <bios.h>
unsigned _bios_serialcom(int *cmd*, int *port*, char *abyte*);

DOS	UNIX	Windows	ANSI C	C++ only
■		■		

Remarks **_bios_serialcom** performs various RS-232 communications over the I/O port given in *port*.

A *port* value of 0 corresponds to COM1, 1 corresponds to COM2, and so forth.

The value of *cmd* can be one of the following values (defined in bios.h):

_COM_INIT	Sets the communications parameters to the value in *abyte*.
_COM_SEND	Sends the character in *abyte* out over the communications line.
_COM_RECEIVE	Receives a character from the communications line. The *abyte* argument is ignored.
_COM_STATUS	Returns the current status of the communications port. The *abyte* argument is ignored.

When *cmd* is _COM_INIT, *abyte* is a OR combination of the following bits:

Select only one of these:	
_COM_CHR7	7 data bits
_COM_CHR8	8 data bits
Select only one of these:	
_COM_STOP1	1 stop bit
_COM_STOP2	2 stop bits
Select only one of these:	
_COM_NOPARITY	No parity
_COM_ODDPARITY	Odd parity
_COM_EVENPARITY	Even parity
Select only one of these:	
_COM_110	110 baud

_COM_150	150 baud
_COM_300	300 baud
_COM_600	600 baud
_COM_1200	1200 baud
_COM_2400	2400 baud
_COM_4800	4800 baud
_COM_9600	9600 baud

For example, a value of (_COM_9600 | _COM_ODDPARITY | _COM_STOP1 | _COM_CHR8) for *abyte* sets the communications port to 9600 baud, odd parity, 1 stop bit, and 8 data bits. **_bios_serialcom** uses the BIOS 0x14 interrupt.

Return value

For all values of *cmd*, **_bios_serialcom** returns a 16-bit integer of which the upper 8 bits are status bits and the lower 8 bits vary, depending on the value of *cmd*. The upper bits of the return value are defined as follows:

Bit 15	Time out
Bit 14	Transmit shift register empty
Bit 13	Transmit holding register empty
Bit 12	Break detect
Bit 11	Framing error
Bit 10	Parity error
Bit 9	Overrun error
Bit 8	Data ready

If the *abyte* value could not be sent, bit 15 is set to 1. Otherwise, the remaining upper and lower bits are appropriately set. For example, if a framing error has occurred, bit 11 is set to 1.

With a *cmd* value of _COM_RECEIVE, the byte read is in the lower bits of the return value if there is no error. If an error occurs, at least one of the upper bits is set to 1. If no upper bits are set to 1, the byte was received without error.

With a *cmd* value of _COM_INIT or _COM_STATUS, the return value has the upper bits set as defined, and the lower bits are defined as follows:

Bit 7	Received line signal detect
Bit 6	Ring indicator
Bit 5	Data set ready
Bit 4	Clear to send
Bit 3	Change in receive line signal detector
Bit 2	Trailing edge ring detector
Bit 1	Change in data set ready
Bit 0	Change in clear to send

Example

```
#include <bios.h>
#include <conio.h>
```

B

```
#define COM1       0
#define DATA_READY 0x100
#define TRUE       1
#define FALSE      0
#define SETTINGS (_COM_1200 | _COM_CHR7 | _COM_STOP1 | _COM_NOPARITY)

int main(void)
{
   unsigned in, out, status;

   _bios_serialcom(_COM_INIT, COM1, SETTINGS);
   cprintf("... _BIOS_SERIALCOM [ESC] to exit ...\r\n");
   for (;;) {
      status = _bios_serialcom(_COM_STATUS, COM1, 0);
      if (status & DATA_READY)
         if ((out = _bios_serialcom(_COM_RECEIVE, COM1, 0) & 0x7F) != 0)
            putch(out);
      if (kbhit()) {
         if ((in = getch()) == '\x1B')
            break;
         _bios_serialcom(_COM_SEND, COM1, in);
      }
   }
   return 0;
}
```

biostime

Function Reads or sets the BIOS timer.

Syntax #include <bios.h>
long biostime(int *cmd*, long *newtime*);

DOS	UNIX	Windows	ANSI C	C++ only
■		■		

Remarks **biostime** either reads or sets the BIOS timer. This is a timer counting ticks since midnight at a rate of roughly 18.2 ticks per second. **biostime** uses BIOS interrupt 0x1A.

If *cmd* equals 0, **biostime** returns the current value of the timer.

If *cmd* equals 1, the timer is set to the **long** value in *newtime*.

Return value When **biostime** reads the BIOS timer (*cmd* = 0), it returns the timer's current value.

Example

```
#include <bios.h>
#include <time.h>
#include <conio.h>

int main(void)
{
   long bios_time;
   clrscr();
   cprintf("The number of clock ticks since midnight is:\r\n");
   cprintf("The number of seconds since midnight is:\r\n");
   cprintf("The number of minutes since midnight is:\r\n");
   cprintf("The number of hours since midnight is:\r\n");
   cprintf("\r\nPress any key to quit:");
   while(!kbhit()) {
      bios_time = biostime(0, 0L);
      gotoxy(50, 1);
      cprintf("%lu", bios_time);
      gotoxy(50, 2);
      cprintf("%.4f", bios_time / CLK_TCK);
      gotoxy(50, 3);
      cprintf("%.4f", bios_time / CLK_TCK / 60);
      gotoxy(50, 4);
      cprintf("%.4f", bios_time / CLK_TCK / 3600);
   }
   return 0;
}
```

_bios_timeofday

Function Reads or sets the BIOS timer.

Syntax #include <bios.h>
unsigned _bios_timeofday(int *cmd*, long **timep*);

DOS	UNIX	Windows	ANSI C	C++ only
▪		▪		

Remarks **_bios_timeofday** either reads or sets the BIOS timer. This is a timer counting ticks since midnight at a rate of roughly 18.2 ticks per second. **_bios_timeofday** uses BIOS interrupt 0x1A.

The *cmd* parameter can be either of the following values:

_TIME_GETCLOCK — The functions stores the current BIOS timer value into the location pointed to by *timep*. If the timer has not been read or written since midnight, the

B

	function returns 1. Otherwise, the function returns 0.
_TIME_SETCLOCK	The function sets the BIOS timer to the long value pointed to by *timep*. The function does not return a value.

Return value The **_bios_timeofday** returns the value in AX that was set by the BIOS timer call.

Example

```
#include <bios.h>
#include <time.h>
#include <conio.h>

int main(void)
{
   long bios_time;
   clrscr();
   cprintf("The number of clock ticks since midnight is:\r\n");
   cprintf("The number of seconds since midnight is:\r\n");
   cprintf("The number of minutes since midnight is:\r\n");
   cprintf("The number of hours since midnight is:\r\n");
   cprintf("\r\nPress any key to quit:");
   while(!kbhit()) {
      _bios_timeofday(_TIME_GETCLOCK, &bios_time);
      gotoxy(50, 1);
      cprintf("%lu", bios_time);
      gotoxy(50, 2);
      cprintf("%.4f", bios_time / CLK_TCK);
      gotoxy(50, 3);
      cprintf("%.4f", bios_time / CLK_TCK / 60);
      gotoxy(50, 4);
      cprintf("%.4f", bios_time / CLK_TCK / 3600);
   }
   return 0;
}
```

brk

Function Changes data-segment space allocation.

Syntax #include <alloc.h>
int brk(void **addr*);

DOS	UNIX	Windows	ANSI C	C++ only
■	■			

Remarks **brk** dynamically changes the amount of space allocated to the calling program's heap. The change is made by resetting the program's *break value*, which is the address of the first location beyond the end of the data segment. The amount of allocated space increases as the break value increases.

brk sets the break value to *addr* and changes the allocated space accordingly.

This function will fail without making any change in the allocated space if such a change would allocate more space than is allowable.

Return value Upon successful completion, **brk** returns a value of 0. On failure, this function returns a value of –1 and the global variable *errno* is set to

ENOMEM Not enough memory

See also **coreleft, sbrk**

Example

```
#include <stdio.h>
#include <alloc.h>

int main(void)
{
   char *ptr;

   printf("Changing allocation with brk()\n");
   ptr = (char *) malloc(1);
   printf("Before brk() call: %lu bytes free\n", coreleft());
   brk(ptr+1000);
   printf(" After brk() call: %lu bytes free\n", coreleft());
   return 0;
}
```

bsearch

Function Binary search of an array.

Syntax #include <stdlib.h>
void *bsearch(const void **key*, const void **base*, size_t *nelem*, size_t *width*,
int (**fcmp*)(const void *, const void *));

DOS	UNIX	Windows	ANSI C	C++ only
■	■	■	■	

Remarks **bsearch** searches a table (array) of *nelem* elements in memory, and returns the address of the first entry in the table that matches the search key. The array must be in order. If no match is found, **bsearch** returns 0. Note that because this is a binary search, the first matching entry is not necessarily the first entry in the table.

The type *size_t* is defined as an unsigned integer.

- *nelem* gives the number of elements in the table.
- *width* specifies the number of bytes in each table entry.

The comparison routine **fcmp* is called with two arguments: *elem1* and *elem2*. Each argument points to an item to be compared. The comparison function compares each of the pointed-to items (**elem1* and **elem2*), and returns an integer based on the results of the comparison.

For **bsearch**, the **fcmp* return value is

< 0 if **elem1* $<$ **elem2*
$==$ 0 if **elem1* $==$ **elem2*
> 0 if **elem1* $>$ **elem2*

Return value **bsearch** returns the address of the first entry in the table that matches the search key. If no match is found, **bsearch** returns 0.

See also **lfind, lsearch, qsort**

Example

```
#include <stdlib.h>
#include <stdio.h>

typedef int (*fptr)(const void*, const void*);

#define NELEMS(arr) (sizeof(arr) / sizeof(arr[0]))

int numarray[] = {123, 145, 512, 627, 800, 933};

int numeric (const int *p1, const int *p2)
{
   return(*p1 - *p2);
}

#pragma argsused
int lookup(int key)
{
   int  *itemptr;

   /* The cast of (int(*)(const void *,const void*)) is needed to avoid a type
      mismatch error at compile time */
   itemptr = (int *) bsearch (&key, numarray, NELEMS(numarray),
                              sizeof(int), (fptr)numeric);
   return (itemptr != NULL);
}

int main(void)
{
```

```
   if (lookup(512))
      printf("512 is in the table.\n");
   else
      printf("512 isn't in the table.\n");
   return 0;
}
```

cabs, cabsl

Function Calculates the absolute value of complex number.

Syntax #include <math.h>
double cabs(struct complex *z*);
long double cabsl(struct _complexl *z*);

	DOS	UNIX	Windows	ANSI C	C++ only
cabs	■	■	■	■	
cabsl	■		■		

Remarks **cabs** is a macro that calculates the absolute value of *z*, a complex number. *z* is a structure with type *complex*; the structure is defined in math.h as

```
struct complex {
   double x, y;
};
```

where *x* is the real part, and *y* is the imaginary part.

Calling **cabs** is equivalent to calling **sqrt** with the real and imaginary components of *z* as shown here:

```
sqrt(z.x * z.x + z.y * z.y)
```

cabsl is the long double version; it takes a a structure with type *_complexl* as an argument, and returns a long double result. The structure is defined in math.h as

```
struct _complexl {
   long double x, y;
};
```

If you are using C++, use the **complex** type defined in complex.h, and the function **abs**.

Return value **cabs** (or **cabsl**) returns the absolute value of *z*, a double. On overflow, **cabs** (or **cabsl**) returns HUGE_VAL (or _LHUGE_VAL) and sets the global variable *errno* to

ERANGE Result out of range

Error handling for these functions can be modified through the functions **matherr** and **_matherrl**.

See Also **abs, complex, fabs, labs, matherr**

Example

```
#include <stdio.h>
#include <math.h>

#ifdef __cplusplus
   #include <complex.h>
#endif

#ifdef __cplusplus /* if C++, use class complex */
void print_abs(void)
{
   complex z(1.0, 2.0);
   double  absval;

   absval = abs(z);
   printf("The absolute value of %.2lfi %.2lfj is %.2lf",
           real(z), imag(z), absval);
}
#else  /* Function below is for C (and not C++). */

void print_abs(void)
{
   struct complex z;
   double absval;

   z.x = 2.0;
   z.y = 1.0;
   absval = cabs(z);

   printf("The absolute value of %.2lfi %.2lfj is %.2lf",
           z.x, z.y, absval);
}
#endif

int main(void)
{
   print_abs();
   return 0;
}
```

calloc

Function Allocates main memory.

Syntax #include <stdlib.h>
void *calloc(size_t *nitems*, size_t *size*);

DOS	UNIX	Windows	ANSI C	C++ only
■	■	■	■	

Remarks **calloc** provides access to the C memory heap. The heap is available for dynamic allocation of variable-sized blocks of memory. Many data structures, such as trees and lists, naturally employ heap memory allocation.

All the space between the end of the data segment and the top of the program stack is available for use in the small data models (tiny, small, and medium), except for a small margin immediately before the top of the stack. This margin is intended to allow some room for the application to grow on the stack, plus a small amount needed by DOS.

In the large data models (compact, large, and huge), all space beyond the program stack to the end of physical memory is available for the heap.

calloc allocates a block of size *nitems* × *size*. The block is cleared to 0. If you want to allocate a block larger than 64K, you must use **farcalloc**.

Return value **calloc** returns a pointer to the newly allocated block. If not enough space exists for the new block or *nitems* or *size* is 0, **calloc** returns null.

See also **farcalloc, free, malloc, realloc**

Example

```
#include <stdio.h>
#include <alloc.h>
#include <string.h>

int main(void)
{
   char *str = NULL;

   /* allocate memory for string */
   str = (char *) calloc(10, sizeof(char));

   /* copy "Hello" into string */
   strcpy(str, "Hello");

   /* display string */
   printf("String is %s\n", str);

   /* free memory */
   free(str);
   return 0;
}
```

ceil, ceill

Function Rounds up.

Syntax #include <math.h>
double ceil(double *x*);
long double ceill(long double *x*);

	DOS	UNIX	Windows	ANSI C	C++ only
ceil	■	■	■	■	
ceill	■		■		

Remarks **ceil** finds the smallest integer not less than *x*.
ceill is the long double version; it takes a long double argument and returns a long double result.

Return value These functions return the integer found as a double (**ceil**) or a long double (**ceill**).

See Also **floor, fmod**

Example

```
#include <math.h>
#include <stdio.h>

int main(void)
{
   double down, up, number = 123.54;
   down = floor(number);
   up = ceil(number);
   printf("original number     %5.2lf\n", number);
   printf("number rounded down %5.2lf\n", down);
   printf("number rounded up   %5.2lf\n", up);
   return 0;
}
```

_c_exit

Function Perform _exit cleanup without terminating the program.

Syntax #include <process.h>
void _c_exit(void);

DOS	UNIX	Windows	ANSI C	C++ only
■		■		

Remarks **_c_exit** performs the same cleanup as **_exit**, except that it does not terminate the calling process. Interrupt vectors altered by the startup code are restored; no other cleanup is performed.

Return value None.

See Also **abort, atexit, _cexit, exec..., exit, _exit, _dos_keep, signal, spawn...**

Example

```
#include <process.h>
#include <io.h>
#include <fcntl.h>
#include <stdio.h>
#include <dos.h>

main()
{
    int fd;
    char c;

    if ((fd = open("_c_exit.c",O_RDONLY)) < 0) {
        printf("Unable to open _c_exit.c for reading\n");
        return 1;
    }
    if (read(fd,&c,1) != 1)
        printf("Unable to read from open file handle %d before _c_exit\n",fd);
    else
        printf("Successfully read from open file handle %d before _c_exit\n",fd);
    printf("Interrupt zero vector before _c_exit = %Fp\n",_dos_getvect(0));
    _c_exit();
    if (read(fd,&c,1) != 1)
        printf("Unable to read from open file handle %d after _c_exit\n",fd);
    else
        printf("Successfully read from open file handle %d after _c_exit\n",fd);
    printf("Interrupt zero vector after _c_exit = %Fp\n",_dos_getvect(0));
    return 0;
}
```

_cexit

Function Perform exit cleanup without terminating the program.

Syntax #include <process.h>
void _cexit(void);

DOS	UNIX	Windows	ANSI C	C++ only
■		■		

Remarks **_cexit** performs the same cleanup as **exit**, except that it does not close files or terminate the calling process. Buffered output (waiting to be output) is written, any registered "exit functions" (posted with **atexit**) are called, and interrupt vectors altered by the startup code are restored.

Return value None.

See Also **abort, atexit, _c_exit, exec..., exit, _exit, _dos_keep, signal, spawn...**

Example

```
#include <process.h>
#include <io.h>
#include <fcntl.h>
#include <stdio.h>
#include <dos.h>

main()
{
    int fd;
    char c;

    if ((fd = open("_cexit.c",O_RDONLY)) < 0) {
        printf("Unable to open _cexit.c for reading\n");
        return 1;
    }
    if (read(fd,&c,1) != 1)
        printf("Unable to read from open file handle %d before _cexit\n",fd);
    else
        printf("Successfully read from open file handle %d before _cexit\n",fd);
    printf("Interrupt zero vector before _cexit = %Fp\n",_dos_getvect(0));
    _cexit();
    if (read(fd,&c,1) != 1)
        printf("Unable to read from open file handle %d after _cexit\n",fd);
    else
        printf("Successfully read from open file handle %d after _cexit\n",fd);
    printf("Interrupt zero vector after _cexit = %Fp\n",_dos_getvect(0));
    return 0;
}
```

cgets

Function Reads a string from the console.

Syntax #include <conio.h>
char *cgets(char *str);

DOS	UNIX	Windows	ANSI C	C++ only
■				

Remarks **cgets** reads a string of characters from the console, storing the string (and the string length) in the location pointed to by *str*.

cgets reads characters until it encounters a carriage-return/linefeed (CR/LF) combination, or until the maximum allowable number of characters have been read. If **cgets** reads a carriage return/linefeed combination, it replaces the combination with a \0 (null terminator) before storing the string.

Before **cgets** is called, set *str*[0] to the maximum length of the string to be read. On return, *str*[1] is set to the number of characters actually read. The characters read start at *str*[2] and end with a null terminator. Thus, *str* must be at least *str*[0] plus 2 bytes long.

Return value On success, **cgets** returns a pointer to *str*[2].

See also **cputs, fgets, getch, getche, gets**

Example

```
#include <stdio.h>
#include <conio.h>

main()
{
   char buffer[83];
   char *p;

   /* there's space for 80 characters plus the NULL terminator */
   buffer[0] = 81;
   printf("Input some chars:");
   p = cgets(buffer);
   printf("\ncgets read %d characters: \"%s\"\n", buffer[1], p);
   printf("The returned pointer is %p, buffer[0] is at %p\n", p, &buffer);

   /* leave room for 5 characters plus the NULL terminator */
   buffer[0] = 6;
   printf("Input some chars:");
   p = cgets(buffer);
   printf("\ncgets read %d characters: \"%s\"\n", buffer[1], p);
   printf("The returned pointer is %p, buffer[0] is at %p\n", p, &buffer);
   return 0;
}
```

C

_chain_intr

Function Chains to another interrupt handler.

Syntax #include <dos.h>
void _chain_intr(void (interrupt far **newhandler*)());

DOS	UNIX	Windows	ANSI C	C++ only
■		■		

Remarks The **_chain_intr** functions passes control from the currently executing interrupt handler to the new interrupt handler whose address is *newhandler*. The current register set is NOT passed to the new handler. Instead, the new handler receives the registers that were stacked (and possibly modified in the stack) by the old handler. The new handler can simply return, as if it were the original handler. The old handler is not entered again.

The **_chain_intr** function may be called only by C interrupt functions. It is useful when writing a TSR that needs to insert itself in a chain of interrupt handlers (such as the keyboard interrupt).

Return value **_chain_intr** does not return a value.

See Also **_dos_getvect, _dos_setvect, _dos_keep**

Example

```
#include <dos.h>
#include <stdio.h>
#include <process.h>

#ifdef __cplusplus
    #define __CPPARGS ...
#else
    #define __CPPARGS
#endif

typedef void interrupt (*fptr)(__CPPARGS);

static void mesg(char *s)
{
  while (*s)
    bdos(2,*s++,0);
}

#pragma argsused
void interrupt handler2(unsigned bp, unsigned di)
{
```

```
  _enable();
  mesg("In handler 2.\r\n");
  if (di == 1)
    mesg("DI is 1\r\n");
  else
    mesg("DI is not 1\r\n");
  di++;
}

#pragma argsused
void interrupt handler1(unsigned bp, unsigned di)
{
  _enable();
  mesg("In handler 1.\r\n");
  if (di == 0)
    mesg("DI is 0\r\n");
  else
    mesg("DI is not 0\r\n");
  di++;
  mesg("Chaining to handler 2.\r\n");
  _chain_intr(handler2);
}

void main()
{
  _dos_setvect(128,(fptr) handler1);
  printf("About to generate interrupt 128\n");
  _DI = 0;
  geninterrupt(128);
  printf("DI was 0 before interrupt, is now 0x%x\n",_DI);
  exit(0);
}
```

chdir

Function Changes current directory.

Syntax #include <dir.h>
int chdir(const char **path*);

DOS	UNIX	Windows	ANSI C	C++ only
■	■	■		

Remarks **chdir** causes the directory specified by *path* to become the current working directory. *path* must specify an existing directory.

A drive can also be specified in the *path* argument, such as

C

```
chdir("a:\\BC")
```

but this changes only the current directory on that drive; it doesn't change the active drive.

Return value Upon successful completion, **chdir** returns a value of 0. Otherwise, it returns a value of –1, and the global variable *errno* is set to

ENOENT Path or file name not found

See also **getcurdir, getcwd, getdisk, mkdir, rmdir, setdisk, system**

Example

```
#include <stdio.h>
#include <stdlib.h>
#include <dir.h>

char old_dir[MAXDIR];
char new_dir[MAXDIR];

int main(void)
{
   if (getcurdir(0, old_dir)) {
      perror("getcurdir()");
      exit(1);
   }
   printf("Current directory is: \\%s\n", old_dir);
   if (chdir("\\")) {
      perror("chdir()");
      exit(1);
   }
   if (getcurdir(0, new_dir)) {
      perror("getcurdir()");
      exit(1);
   }
   printf("Current directory is now: \\%s\n", new_dir);
   printf("\nChanging back to orignal directory: \\%s\n", old_dir);
   if (chdir(old_dir)) {
      perror("chdir()");
      exit(1);
   }
   return 0;
}
```

_chdrive

Function Sets current disk drive.

Syntax #include <direct.h>
int _chdrive(int *drive*);

DOS	UNIX	Windows	ANSI C	C++ only
■		■		

Remarks **_chdrive** sets the current drive to the one associated with *drive*: 1 for A, 2 for B, 3 for C, and so on.

Return value **_chdrive** returns 0 if the current drive was changed successfully; otherwise, it returns –1.

See Also **_dos_setdrive, _getdrive**

Example

```
#include <stdio.h>
#include <direct.h>

int main(void)
{
   if (_chdrive(3) == 0)
      printf("Successfully changed to drive C:\n");
   else
      printf("Cannot change to drive C:\n");
   return 0;
}
```

_chmod

Function Gets or sets DOS file attributes.

Syntax #include <dos.h>
#include <io.h>
int _chmod(const char **path*, int *func* [, int *attrib*]);

DOS	UNIX	Windows	ANSI C	C++ only
■		■		

Remarks **_chmod** can either fetch or set the DOS file attributes. If *func* is 0, the function returns the current DOS attributes for the file. If *func* is 1, the attribute is set to *attrib*.

attrib can be one of the following symbolic constants (defined in dos.h):

FA_RDONLY	Read-only attribute
FA_HIDDEN	Hidden file
FA_SYSTEM	System file
FA_LABEL	Volume label
FA_DIREC	Directory
FA_ARCH	Archive

Return value Upon successful completion, **_chmod** returns the file attribute word; otherwise, it returns a value of –1.

In the event of an error, the global variable *errno* is set to one of the following:

ENOENT	Path or file name not found
EACCES	Permission denied

See also **chmod, _creat**

Example

```
#include <errno.h>
#include <stdio.h>
#include <dos.h>
#include <io.h>

int get_file_attrib(char *filename);
int main(void)

{
   char filename[128];
   int attrib;
   printf("Enter a file name:");
   scanf("%s", filename);
   attrib = get_file_attrib(filename);
   if (attrib == -1)
      switch(errno) {
         case ENOENT : printf("Path or file not found.\n");
                       break;
         case EACCES : printf("Permission denied.\n");
                       break;
         default:      printf("Error number: %d", errno);
                       break;
      }
   else {
         if (attrib & FA_RDONLY)
            printf("%s is read-only.\n", filename);

         if (attrib & FA_HIDDEN)
            printf("%s is hidden.\n", filename);

         if (attrib & FA_SYSTEM)
            printf("%s is a system file.\n", filename);

         if (attrib & FA_LABEL)
           printf("%s is a volume label.\n", filename);

         if (attrib & FA_DIREC)
            printf("%s is a directory.\n", filename);

         if (attrib & FA_ARCH)
            printf("%s is an archive file.\n", filename);
```



```
      }
   return 0;
}

/* returns the attributes of a DOS file */
int get_file_attrib(char *filename) {
   return(_chmod(filename, 0));
}
```

chmod

Function Changes file access mode.

Syntax #include <sys\stat.h>
int chmod(const char **path*, int *amode*);

DOS	UNIX	Windows	ANSI C	C++ only
■	■	■		

Remarks **chmod** sets the file-access permissions of the file given by *path* according to the mask given by *amode*. *path* points to a string; **path* is the first character of that string.

amode can contain one or both of the symbolic constants S_IWRITE and S_IREAD (defined in sys\stat.h).

Value of *amode*	Access permission
S_IWRITE	Permission to write
S_IREAD	Permission to read
S_IREAD | S_IWRITE	Permission to read and write

Return value Upon successfully changing the file access mode, **chmod** returns 0. Otherwise, **chmod** returns a value of –1.

In the event of an error, the global variable *errno* is set to one of the following:

ENOENT	Path or file name not found
EACCES	Permission denied

See also **access, _chmod, fstat, open, sopen, stat**

Example

```
#include <errno.h>
#include <stdio.h>
#include <io.h>
#include <process.h>
#include <sys\stat.h>
```

C

```
int main(void)
{
   char filename[64];
   struct stat stbuf;
   int amode;

   printf("Enter name of file: ");
   scanf("%s", filename);
   if (stat(filename, &stbuf) != 0) {
     perror("Unable to get file information");
     return(1);
   }
   if (stbuf.st_mode & S_IWRITE) {
     printf("Changing to read-only\n");
     amode = S_IREAD;
   }
   else {
     printf("Changing to read-write\n");
     amode = S_IREAD|S_IWRITE;
   }
   if (chmod(filename, amode) != 0) {
     perror("Unable to change file mode");
     return(1);
   }
   return(0);
}
```

chsize

Function Changes the file size.

Syntax #include <io.h>
int chsize(int *handle*, long *size*);

DOS	UNIX	Windows	ANSI C	C++ only
■		■		

Remarks **chsize** changes the size of the file associated with *handle*. It can truncate or extend the file, depending on the value of *size* compared to the file's original size.

The mode in which you open the file must allow writing.

If **chsize** extends the file, it will append null characters (\0). If it truncates the file, all data beyond the new end-of-file indicator is lost.

Return value On success, **chsize** returns 0. On failure, it returns –1 and the global variable *errno* is set to one of the following:

EACCESS	Permission denied
EBADF	Bad file number
ENOSPC	UNIX—not DOS

See also **close, _creat, creat, open**

Example

```
#include <string.h>
#include <fcntl.h>
#include <io.h>

int main(void)
{
   int handle;
   char buf[11] = "0123456789";

   /* create a text file containing 10 bytes */
   handle = open("DUMMY.FIL", O_CREAT);
   write(handle, buf, strlen(buf));

   /* truncate the file to 5 bytes in size */
   chsize(handle, 5);

   /* close the file */
   close(handle);
   return 0;
}
```

circle

Function Draws a circle of the given radius with its center at (*x*,*y*).

Syntax #include <graphics.h>
void far circle(int *x*, int *y*, int *radius*);

DOS	UNIX	Windows	ANSI C	C++ only
■				

Remarks **circle** draws a circle in the current drawing color with its center at (*x*,*y*) and the radius given by *radius*.

➡ The *linestyle* parameter does not affect arcs, circles, ellipses, or pie slices. Only the *thickness* parameter is used.

If your circles are not perfectly round, adjust the aspect ratio.

Return value None.

C

See also **arc, ellipse, fillellipse, getaspectratio, sector, setaspectratio**

Example

```
#include <graphics.h>
#include <stdlib.h>
#include <stdio.h>
#include <conio.h>

int main(void)
{
   /* request autodetection */
   int gdriver = DETECT, gmode, errorcode;
   int midx, midy, radius = 100;

   /* initialize graphics and local variables */
   initgraph(&gdriver, &gmode, "");

   /* read result of initialization */
   errorcode = graphresult();
   if (errorcode != grOk) {    /* an error occurred */
      printf("Graphics error: %s\n", grapherrormsg(errorcode));
      printf("Press any key to halt:");
      getch();
      exit(1);               /* terminate with an error code */
   }

   midx = getmaxx() / 2;
   midy = getmaxy() / 2;
   setcolor(getmaxcolor());

   /* draw the circle */
   circle(midx, midy, radius);
   /* clean up */
   getch();
   closegraph();
   return 0;
}
```

_clear87

Function Clears floating-point status word.

Syntax #include <float.h>
unsigned int _clear87 (void);

DOS	UNIX	Windows	ANSI C	C++ only
■		■		

Remarks **_clear87** clears the floating-point status word, which is a combination of the 80x87 status word and other conditions detected by the 80x87 exception handler.

Return value The bits in the value returned indicate the floating-point status before it was cleared. For information on the status word, refer to the constants defined in float.h.

See also **_control87**, **_fpreset**, **_status87**

Example

```
#include <stdio.h>
#include <float.h>

int main(void)
{
   float x;
   double y = 1.5e-100;
   printf("\nStatus 87 before error: %X\n", _status87());
   x = y; /* create underflow and precision loss */
   printf("Status 87 after  error: %X\n", _status87());
   _clear87();
   printf("Status 87 after  clear: %X\n", _status87());
   y = x;
   return 0;
}
```

cleardevice

Function Clears the graphics screen.

Syntax #include <graphics.h>
void far cleardevice(void);

DOS	UNIX	Windows	ANSI C	C++ only
■				

Remarks **cleardevice** erases (that is, fills with the current background color) the entire graphics screen and moves the CP (current position) to home (0,0).

Return value None.

See also **clearviewport**

Example

```
#include <graphics.h>
#include <stdlib.h>
#include <stdio.h>
#include <conio.h>
```

C

```
int main(void)
{
   /* request autodetection */
   int gdriver = DETECT, gmode, errorcode;
   int midx, midy;

   /* initialize graphics and local variables */
   initgraph(&gdriver, &gmode, "");

   /* read result of initialization */
   errorcode = graphresult();
   if (errorcode != grOk) {    /* an error occurred */
      printf("Graphics error: %s\n", grapherrormsg(errorcode));
      printf("Press any key to halt:");
      getch();
      exit(1);                 /* terminate with an error code */
   }

   midx = getmaxx() / 2;
   midy = getmaxy() / 2;
   setcolor(getmaxcolor());

   /* for centering screen messages */
   settextjustify(CENTER_TEXT, CENTER_TEXT);

   /* output a message to the screen */
   outtextxy(midx, midy, "Press any key to clear the screen:");

   getch();   /* wait for a key */
   cleardevice();   /* clear the screen */
   /* output another message */
   outtextxy(midx, midy, "Press any key to quit:");
   /* clean up */
   getch();
   closegraph();
   return 0;
}
```

clearerr

Function Resets error indication.

Syntax #include <stdio.h>
void clearerr(FILE **stream*);

DOS	UNIX	Windows	ANSI C	C++ only
■	■	■	■	

Remarks **clearerr** resets the named stream's error and end-of-file indicators to 0. Once the error indicator is set, stream operations continue to return error status until a call is made to **clearerr** or **rewind**.

The end-of-file indicator is reset with each input operation.

Return value None.

See also **eof, feof, ferror, perror, rewind**

Example

```
#include <stdio.h>

int main(void)
{
   FILE *fp;
   char ch;

   /* open a file for writing */
   fp = fopen("DUMMY.FIL", "w");

   /* force an error condition by attempting to read */
   ch = fgetc(fp);
   printf("%c\n",ch);

   if (ferror(fp)) {
      /* display an error message */
      printf("Error reading from DUMMY.FIL\n");

      /* reset the error and EOF indicators */
      clearerr(fp);
   }
   fclose(fp);
   return 0;
}
```

clearviewport

Function Clears the current viewport.

Syntax #include <graphics.h>
void far clearviewport(void);

DOS	UNIX	Windows	ANSI C	C++ only
■				

Remarks **clearviewport** erases the viewport and moves the CP (current position) to home (0,0), relative to the viewport.

Return value None.

See also **cleardevice, getviewsettings, setviewport**

Example

```
#include <graphics.h>
#include <stdlib.h>
#include <stdio.h>
#include <conio.h>

#define CLIP_ON 1   /* activates clipping in viewport */

int main(void)
{
   /* request autodetection */
   int gdriver = DETECT, gmode, errorcode, ht;

   /* initialize graphics and local variables */
   initgraph(&gdriver, &gmode, "");

   /* read result of initialization */
   errorcode = graphresult();
   if (errorcode != grOk) {   /* an error occurred */
      printf("Graphics error: %s\n", grapherrormsg(errorcode));
      printf("Press any key to halt:");
      getch();
      exit(1);               /* terminate with an error code */
   }

   setcolor(getmaxcolor());
   ht = textheight("W");

   /* message in default full-screen viewport */
   outtextxy(0, 0, "* <-- (0, 0) in default viewport");

   /* create a smaller viewport */
   setviewport(50, 50, getmaxx()-50, getmaxy()-50, CLIP_ON);

   /* display some messages */
   outtextxy(0, 0, "* <-- (0, 0) in smaller viewport");
   outtextxy(0, 2*ht, "Press any key to clear viewport:");

   getch();   /* wait for a key */
   clearviewport();   /* clear the viewport */
   /* output another message */
   outtextxy(0, 0, "Press any key to quit:");

   /* clean up */
   getch();
   closegraph();
   return 0;
}
```

clock

Function Determines processor time.

Syntax #include <time.h>
clock_t clock(void);

DOS	UNIX	Windows	ANSI C	C++ only
■		■	■	

Remarks **clock** can be used to determine the time interval between two events.

To determine the time in seconds, the value returned by **clock** should be divided by the value of the macro **CLK_TCK**.

Return value The **clock** function returns the processor time elapsed since the beginning of the program invocation. If the processor time is not available, or its value cannot be represented, the function returns the value –1.

See also **time**

Example

```
#include <time.h>
#include <stdio.h>
#include <dos.h>

int main(void)
{
   clock_t start, end;
   start = clock();
   delay(2000);
   end = clock();
   printf("The time was: %f\n", (end - start) / CLK_TCK);
   return 0;
}
```

_close, close

Function Closes a file.

Syntax #include <io.h>
int _close(int *handle*);
int close(int *handle*);

	DOS	UNIX	Windows	ANSI C	C++ only
_close	■		■		
close	■	■	■		

C

Remarks **_close** and **close** close the file associated with *handle*, a file handle obtained from a **_creat**, **creat**, **creatnew**, **creattemp**, **dup**, **dup2**, **_open**, or **open** call.

These functions do not write a *Ctrl-Z* character at the end of the file. If you want to terminate the file with a *Ctrl-Z*, you must explicitly output one.

Return value Upon successful completion, **_close** and **close** return 0. Otherwise, these functions return a value of –1.

_close and **close** fail if *handle* is not the handle of a valid, open file, and the global variable *errno* is set to

EBADF   Bad file number

See also **chsize**, **_close**, **creat**, **creatnew**, **dup**, **fclose**, **open**, **sopen**

Example

```
#include <string.h>
#include <fcntl.h>
#include <io.h>

int main(void)
{
   int handle;
   char buf[11] = "0123456789";

   /* create a file containing 10 bytes */
   handle = open("DUMMY.FIL", O_CREAT);
   write(handle, buf, strlen(buf));

   /* close the file */
   close(handle);
   return 0;
}
```

closedir

Function Closes a directory stream.

Syntax #include <dirent.h>
void closedir(DIR **dirp*);

DOS	UNIX	Windows	ANSI C	C++ only
■	■	■		

Remarks On UNIX platforms, **closedir** is available on POSIX-compliant systems.

The **closedir** function closes the directory stream *dirp*, which must have been opened by a previous call to **opendir**. After the stream is closed, *dirp* no longer points to a valid directory stream.

Return value If **closedir** is successful, it returns 0. Otherwise, **closedir** returns –1 and sets the global variable *errno* to

EBADF	The *dirp* argument does not point to a valid open directory stre

See Also **opendir**, **readdir**, **rewinddir**

Example See the example for **opendir**.

closegraph

Function Shuts down the graphics system.

Syntax #include <graphics.h>
void far closegraph(void);

DOS	UNIX	Windows	ANSI C	C++ only
■				

Remarks **closegraph** deallocates all memory allocated by the graphics system, then restores the screen to the mode it was in before you called **initgraph**. (The graphics system deallocates memory, such as the drivers, fonts, and an internal buffer, through a call to **_graphfreemem**.)

Return value None.

See also **initgraph**, **setgraphbufsize**

Example

```
#include <graphics.h>
#include <stdlib.h>
#include <stdio.h>
#include <conio.h>

int main(void)
{
   /* request autodetection */
   int gdriver = DETECT, gmode, errorcode, x, y;

   /* initialize graphics mode */
   initgraph(&gdriver, &gmode, "");

   /* read result of initialization */
   errorcode = graphresult();

   if (errorcode != grOk) {   /* an error occurred */
      printf("Graphics error: %s\n", grapherrormsg(errorcode));
```

C

```
      printf("Press any key to halt:");
      getch();
      exit(1);               /* terminate with an error code */
   }

   x = getmaxx() / 2;
   y = getmaxy() / 2;

   /* output a message */
   settextjustify(CENTER_TEXT, CENTER_TEXT);
   outtextxy(x, y, "Press a key to close the graphics system:");

   getch();   /* wait for a key */
   /* closes down the graphics system */
   closegraph();
   printf("We're now back in text mode.\n");
   printf("Press any key to halt:");
   getch();
   return 0;
}
```

clreol

Function Clears to end of line in text window.

Syntax #include <conio.h>
void clreol(void);

DOS	UNIX	Windows	ANSI C	C++ only
■				

Remarks **clreol** clears all characters from the cursor position to the end of the line within the current text window, without moving the cursor.

Return value None.

See also **clrscr, delline, window**

Example

```
#include <conio.h>

int main(void)
{
   clrscr();
   cprintf("The function CLREOL clears all characters from the\r\n");
   cprintf("cursor position to the end of the line within the\r\n");
   cprintf("current text window, without moving the cursor.\r\n");
   cprintf("Press any key to continue . . .");
   gotoxy(14, 4);
   getch();
```

```
   clreol();
   getch();
   return 0;
}
```

clrscr

Function Clears the text-mode window.

Syntax #include <conio.h>
void clrscr(void);

DOS	UNIX	Windows	ANSI C	C++ only
■				

Remarks **clrscr** clears the current text window and places the cursor in the upper left-hand corner (at position 1,1).

Return value None.

See also **clreol**, **delline**, **window**

Example

```
#include <conio.h>

int main(void)
{
   int i;

   clrscr();
   for (i = 0; i < 20; i++)
      cprintf("%d\r\n", i);
   cprintf("\r\nPress any key to clear screen");
   getch();
   clrscr();
   cprintf("The screen has been cleared!");
   getch();
   return 0;
}
```

complex

Function Creates complex numbers.

Syntax #include <complex.h>
complex complex(double *real*, double *imag*);

C

DOS	UNIX	Windows	ANSI C	C++ only
■		■		■

Remarks Creates a complex number out of the given real and imaginary parts. The imaginary part is taken to be 0 if *imag* is omitted.

complex is the constructor for the C++ class **complex**, which is defined in complex.h. Other applicable functions (listed under **See also** below) are also defined in complex.h. Some of these are overloaded versions of C library functions declared in math.h. C++ is required for the complex versions.

If you don't want to program in C++, but instead want to program in C, the only constructs available to you are **struct complex** and **cabs**, which give the absolute value of a complex number. Both of these are defined in math.h.

complex.h also overloads the operators **+**, **–**, *****, **/**, **+=**, **–=**, ***=**, **/=**, **=**, **==**, and **!=**. These operators give complex arithmetic in the usual sense. You can freely mix complex numbers in expressions with **int**s, **double**s, and other numeric types. The operators **<<** and **>>** are overloaded for stream input and output of complex numbers, as they are for other data types in iostream.h.

Return value The complex number with the given real and imaginary parts.

See also **abs**, **acos**, **arg**, **asin**, **atan**, **atan2**, **conj**, **cos**, **cosh**, **imag**, **log**, **log10**, **norm**, **polar**, **pow**, **real**, **sin**, **sinh**, **sqrt**, **tan**, **tanh**

Example

```
#include <iostream.h>
#include <complex.h>

int main(void)
{
   double x = 3.1, y = 4.2;
   complex z = complex(x,y);
   cout << "z = " << z << "\n";
   cout << "  has real part = " << real(z) << "\n";
   cout << "  and imaginary real part = " << imag(z) << "\n";
   cout << "z has complex conjugate = " << conj(z) << "\n";
   return 0;
}
```

conj

Function Returns the complex conjugate of a complex number.

Syntax #include <complex.h>
complex conj(complex *x*);

DOS	UNIX	Windows	ANSI C	C++ only
■		■		■

Remarks `conj(z)` is the same as `complex(real(z), -imag(z))`.

Return value The complex conjugate of the complex number.

See also **complex, imag, real**

Example

```
#include <iostream.h>
#include <complex.h>

int main(void)
{
   double x = 3.1, y = 4.2;
   complex z = complex(x,y);
   cout << "z = " << z << "\n";
   cout << "  has real part = " << real(z) << "\n";
   cout << "  and imaginary real part = " << imag(z) << "\n";
   cout << "z has complex conjugate = " << conj(z) << "\n";
   return 0;
}
```

_control87

Function Manipulates the floating-point control word.

Syntax #include <float.h>
unsigned int _control87(unsigned int *newcw*, unsigned int *mask*);

DOS	UNIX	Windows	ANSI C	C++ only
■				

Remarks **_control87** retrieves or changes the floating-point control word.

The floating-point control word is an **unsigned int** that, bit by bit, specifies certain modes in the floating-point package; namely, the precision, infinity, and rounding modes. Changing these modes allows you to mask or unmask floating-point exceptions.

_control87 matches the bits in *mask* to the bits in *newcw*. If a *mask* bit equals 1, the corresponding bit in *newcw* contains the new value for the

C

same bit in the floating-point control word, and **_control87** sets that bit in the control word to the new value.

Here's a simple illustration:

Original control word:	0100	0011	0110	0011
mask	1000	0001	0100	1111
newcw	1110	1001	0000	0101
Changing bits	1*xxx*	*xxx*1	*x*0*xx*	0101

If *mask* equals 0, **_control87** returns the floating-point control word without altering it.

_control87 does not change the Denormal bit because Borland C++ uses denormal exceptions.

Return value The bits in the value returned reflect the new floating-point control word. For a complete definition of the bits returned by **_control87**, see the header file float.h.

See also **_clear87**, **_fpreset**, **signal**, **_status87**

coreleft

Function Returns a measure of unused RAM memory.

Syntax *In the tiny, small, and medium models:*

```
#include <alloc.h>
unsigned coreleft(void);
```

In the compact, large, and huge models:

```
#include <alloc.h>
unsigned long coreleft(void);
```

DOS	UNIX	Windows	ANSI C	C++ only
■				

Remarks **coreleft** returns a measure of RAM memory not in use. It gives a different measurement value, depending on whether the memory model is of the small data group or the large data group.

Return value In the small data models, **coreleft** returns the amount of unused memory between the top of the heap and the stack. In the large data models, **coreleft** returns the amount of memory between the highest allocated block and the end of available memory.

See also **allocmem, brk, farcoreleft, malloc**

Example

```
#include <stdio.h>
#include <alloc.h>

int main(void)
{
   printf("The difference between the highest allocated block and\n");
   printf("the top of the heap is: %lu bytes\n", (unsigned long) coreleft());
   return 0;
}
```

cos, cosl

Function Calculates the cosine of a value.

Syntax

Real versions:
#include <math.h>
double cos(double *x*);
long double cosl(long double *x*);

Complex version:
#include <complex.h>
complex cos(complex *x*);

	DOS	UNIX	Windows	ANSI C	C++ only
cosl	■		■		
Real **cos**	■	■	■	■	
Complex **cos**	■		■		■

Remarks **cos** computes the cosine of the input value. The angle is specified in radians.

cosl is the long double version; it takes a long double argument and returns a long double result.

The complex cosine is defined by

cos(z) = (**exp**($i * z$) + **exp**($-i * z$))/2

Return value **cos** of a real argument returns a value in the range –1 to 1.

Error handling for these functions can be modified through **matherr** (or **_matherrl**).

See Also **acos, asin, atan, atan2, complex, matherr, sin, tan**

Example

```
#include <stdio.h>
#include <math.h>

int main(void)
{
```

```
   double result, x = 0.5;
   result = cos(x);
   printf("The cosine of %lf is %lf\n", x, result);
   return 0;
}
```

cosh, coshl

Function Calculates the hyperbolic cosine of a value.

Syntax *Real versions*:
#include <math.h>
double cosh(double *x*);
long double coshl(long double *x*);

Complex version:
#include <complex.h>
complex cosh(complex *x*);

	DOS	UNIX	Windows	ANSI C	C++ only
coshl	■		■		
Real ***cosh***	■	■	■	■	
Complex ***cosh***	■		■		■

Remarks **cosh** computes the hyperbolic cosine, $(e^x + e^{-x})/2$.

coshl is the long double version; it takes a long double argument and returns a long double result.

The complex hyperbolic cosine is defined by

cosh(*z*) = (**exp**(*z*) + **exp**(-*z*))/2

Return value **cosh** returns the hyperbolic cosine of the argument.

When the correct value would create an overflow, these functions return the value HUGE_VAL (**cosh** or _LHUGE_VAL (**coshl**) with the appropriate sign, and the global variable *errno* is set to ERANGE.

Error handling for these functions can be modified through the functions **matherr** and **_matherrl**.

See Also **acos, asin, atan, atan2, complex, cos, matherr, sin, sinh, tan, tanh**

Example

```
#include <stdio.h>
#include <math.h>

int main(void)
{
   double result, x = 0.5;
   result = cosh(x);
```

```
   printf("The hyperboic cosine of %lf is %lf\n", x, result);
   return 0;
}
```

country

Function Returns country-dependent information.

Syntax #include <dos.h>
struct COUNTRY *country(int *xcode*, struct country **cp*);

DOS	UNIX	Windows	ANSI C	C++ only
■		■		

Remarks **country** specifies how certain country-dependent data (such as dates, times, and currency) will be formatted. The values set by this function depend on the DOS version being used.

If *cp* has a value of –1, the current country is set to the value of *xcode*, which must be nonzero. Otherwise, the COUNTRY structure pointed to by *cp* is filled with the country-dependent information of the current country (if *xcode* is set to 0), or the country given by *xcode*.

The structure COUNTRY is defined as follows:

```
struct country {
   int co_date;              /* date format */
   char co_curr[5];          /* currency symbol */
   char co_thsep[2];         /* thousands separator */
   char co_desep[2];         /* decimal separator */
   char co_dtsep[2];         /* date separator */
   char co_tmsep[2];         /* time separator */
   char co_currstyle;        /* currency style */
   char co_digits;           /* significant digits in currency */
   char co_time;             /* time format */
   long co_case;             /* case map */
   char co_dasep[2];         /* data separator */
   char co_fill[10];         /* filler */
};
```

The date format in *co_date* is

- 0 for the U.S. style of month, day, year
- 1 for the European style of day, month, year
- 2 for the Japanese style of year, month, day

Currency display style is given by *co_currstyle* as follows:

C

0	Currency symbol precedes value with no spaces between the symbol and the number.
1	Currency symbol follows value with no spaces between the number and the symbol.
2	Currency symbol precedes value with a space after the symbol.
3	Currency symbol follows the number with a space before the symbol.

Return value On success, **country** returns the pointer argument *cp*. On error, it returns null.

Example

```
#include <dos.h>
#include <stdio.h>

#define USA 0

int main(void)
{
   struct COUNTRY country_info;
   country(USA, &country_info);
   printf("The currency symbol for the USA is: %s\n", country_info.co_curr);
   return 0;
}
```

cprintf

Function Writes formatted output to the screen.

Syntax #include <conio.h>
int cprintf(const char **format*[, *argument*, ...]);

DOS	UNIX	Windows	ANSI C	C++ only
■				

Remarks **cprintf** accepts a series of arguments, applies to each a format specifier contained in the format string pointed to by *format*, and outputs the formatted data directly to the current text window on the screen. There must be the same number of format specifiers as arguments.

*See **printf** for details on format specifiers.*

The string is written either directly to screen memory or by way of a BIOS call, depending on the value of the global variable *directvideo*.

Unlike **fprintf** and **printf**, **cprintf** does not translate linefeed characters (\n) into carriage-return/linefeed character pairs (\r\n).

Return value **cprintf** returns the number of characters output.

See also *directvideo* (global variable), **fprintf**, **printf**, **putch**, **sprintf**, **vprintf**

Example

```
#include <conio.h>

int main(void)
{
   clrscr();                      /* clear the screen */
   window(10, 10, 80, 25);        /* create a text window */
   cprintf("Hello world\r\n");    /* output some text in the window */
   getch();                       /* wait for a key */
   return 0;
}
```

cputs

Function Writes a string to the screen.

Syntax #include <conio.h>
int cputs(const char **str*);

DOS	UNIX	Windows	ANSI C	C++ only
■				

Remarks **cputs** writes the null-terminated string *str* to the current text window. It does not append a newline character.

The string is written either directly to screen memory or by way of a BIOS call, depending on the value of the global variable *directvideo*.

Unlike **puts**, **cputs** does not translate linefeed characters (\n) into carriage-return/linefeed character pairs (\r\n).

Return value **cputs** returns the last character printed.

See also **cgets**, *directvideo* (global variable), **fputs**, **putch**, **puts**

Example

```
#include <conio.h>

int main(void)
{
   clrscr();                 /* clear the screen */
   window(10, 10, 80, 25);   /* create a text window */
   /* icgoutput some text in the window */
   cputs("This is within the window\r\n");
   getch();                  /* wait for a key */
   return 0;
}
```

C

_creat, _dos_creat

Function Creates a new file or overwrites an existing one.

Syntax #include <dos.h>
int _creat(const char **path*, int *attrib*);
unsigned _dos_creat(const char **path*,int *attrib*,int **handlep*);

	DOS	UNIX	Windows	ANSI C	C++ only
_creat	■		■		
_dos_creat	■		■		

Remarks **_creat** and **_dos_creat** open the file specified by *path*. The file is always opened in binary mode. Upon successful file creation, the file pointer is set to the beginning of the file. **_dos_creat** stores the file handle in the location pointed to by *handlep*. The file is opened for both reading and writing.

If the file already exists, its size is reset to 0. (This is essentially the same as deleting the file and creating a new file with the same name.)

The *attrib* argument to **_creat** is an ORed combination of the one or more of following constants (defined in dos.h):

FA_RDONLY	Read-only attribute
FA_HIDDEN	Hidden file
FA_SYSTEM	System file

The *attrib* argument to **_dos_creat** is an ORed combination of one or more of the following constants (defined in dos.h):

_A_NORMAL	Normal file
_A_RDONLY	Read-only file
_A_HIDDEN	Hidden file
_A_SYSTEM	System file

Return value Upon successful completion, **_creat** returns the new file handle, a non-negative integer; otherwise, it returns –1.

Upon successful completion, **_dos_creat** returns 0.

If an error occurs, **_dos_creat** returns the DOS error code.

In the event of error, **_creat** and **_dos_creat**, the global variable *errno* is set to one of the following:

ENOENT	Path or file name not found
EMFILE	Too many open files

EACCES	Permission denied

See also **_chmod, chsize, _close, close, creat, creatnew, creattemp**

Example

```
#include <dos.h>
#include <string.h>
#include <stdio.h>
#include <io.h>

int main() {
    unsigned count;
    int handle;
    char buf[11] = "0123456789";

    /* Create a 10-byte file using _dos_creat. */
    if (_dos_creat("DUMMY.FIL", _A_NORMAL, &handle) != 0) {
        perror("Unable to _dos_creat DUMMY.FIL");
        return 1;
    }
    if (_dos_write(handle, buf, strlen(buf), &count) != 0) {
        perror("Unable to _dos_write to DUMMY.FIL");
        return 1;
    }
    _dos_close(handle);

    /* Create another 10-byte file using _creat. */
    if ((handle = _creat("DUMMY2.FIL", 0)) < 0) {
        perror("Unable to _create DUMMY2.FIL");
        return 1;
    }
    if (_write(handle, buf, strlen(buf)) < 0) {
        perror("Unable to _write to DUMMY2.FIL");
        return 1;
    }
    _close(handle);
    return 0;
}
```

creat

Function Creates a new file or overwrites an existing one.

Syntax #include <sys\stat.h>
int creat(const char **path*, int *amode*);

DOS	UNIX	Windows	ANSI C	C++ only
■	■	■		

C

Remarks **creat** creates a new file or prepares to rewrite an existing file given by *path*. *amode* applies only to newly created files.

A file created with **creat** is always created in the translation mode specified by the global variable *_fmode* (O_TEXT or O_BINARY).

If the file exists and the write attribute is set, **creat** truncates the file to a length of 0 bytes, leaving the file attributes unchanged. If the existing file has the read-only attribute set, the **creat** call fails and the file remains unchanged.

The **creat** call examines only the S_IWRITE bit of the access-mode word *amode*. If that bit is 1, the file can be is written to. If the bit is 0, the file is marked as read-only. All other DOS attributes are set to 0.

amode can be one of the following (defined in sys\stat.h):

Value of *amode*	Access permission
S_IWRITE	Permission to write
S_IREAD	Permission to read
S_IREAD | S_IWRITE	Permission to read and write

➡ In DOS, write permission implies read permission.

Return value Upon successful completion, **creat** returns the new file handle, a non-negative integer; otherwise, it returns –1.

In the event of error, the global variable *errno* is set to one of the following:

ENOENT	Path or file name not found
EMFILE	Too many open files
EACCES	Permission denied

See also **chmod**, **chsize**, **close**, **_creat**, **creatnew**, **creattemp**, **dup**, **dup2**, *_fmode* (global variable), **fopen**, **open**, **sopen**, **write**

Example

```
#include <sys\stat.h>
#include <process.h>
#include <string.h>
#include <stdio.h>
#include <fcntl.h>
#include <errno.h>
#include <io.h>

int main(void)
{
   int handle;
   char buf[] = "0123456789";
```

```
    /* create a binary file for reading and writing */
    if ((handle = _creat("DUMMY.FIL", 0)) < 0) {
       switch(errno) {
          case ENOENT: printf("Error: Path or file not found.\n");
                       break;
          case EMFILE: printf("Error: Too many open files.\n");
                       break;
          case EACCES: printf("Error: Permission denied.\n");
                       break;
          default:     printf("Error creating file.\n");
                       break;
       }
       exit(1);
    }

    /* write a string and NULL terminator into the file */
    write(handle, buf, strlen(buf)+1);

    /* close the file */
    close(handle);
    return 0;
}
```

creatnew

Function Creates a new file.

Syntax #include <dos.h>
int creatnew(const char **path*, int *mode*);

DOS	UNIX	Windows	ANSI C	C++ only
■		■		

Remarks **creatnew** is identical to **_creat** with one exception. If the file exists, **creatnew** returns an error and leaves the file untouched.

The *mode* argument to **creatnew** can be one of the following constants (defined in dos.h):

FA_RDONLY	Read-only attribute
FA_HIDDEN	Hidden file
FA_SYSTEM	System file

Return value Upon successful completion, **creat** returns the new file handle, a non-negative integer; otherwise, it returns –1.

In the event of error, the global variable *errno* is set to one of the following:

C

EEXIST	File already exists
ENOENT	Path or file name not found
EMFILE	Too many open files
EACCES	Permission denied

See also **close**, **_creat**, **creat**, **creattemp**, **dup**, *_fmode* (global variable), **open**

Example

```
#include <string.h>
#include <stdio.h>
#include <errno.h>
#include <dos.h>
#include <io.h>

int main(void)
{
   int handle;
   char buf[11] = "0123456789";

   /* attempt to create a file that doesn't already exist */
   handle = creatnew("DUMMY.FIL", 0);

   if (handle == -1)
      printf("DUMMY.FIL already exists.\n");
   else {
      printf("DUMMY.FIL successfully created.\n");
      write(handle, buf, strlen(buf));
      close(handle);
   }
   return 0;
}
```

creattemp

Function Creates a unique file in the directory associated with the path name.

Syntax #include <dos.h>
int creattemp(char **path*, int *attrib*);

DOS	UNIX	Windows	ANSI C	C++ only
■		■		

Remarks A file created with **creattemp** is always created in the translation mode specified by the global variable *_fmode* (O_TEXT or O_BINARY).

path is a path name ending with a backslash (\). A unique file name is selected in the directory given by *path*. The newly created file name is stored in the *path* string supplied. *path* should be long enough to hold the resulting file name. The file is not automatically deleted when the program terminates.

creattemp accepts *attrib*, a DOS attribute word. The file is always opened in binary mode. Upon successful file creation, the file pointer is set to the beginning of the file. The file is opened for both reading and writing.

The *attrib* argument to **creattemp** can be one of the following constants (defined in dos.h):

FA_RDONLY	Read-only attribute
FA_HIDDEN	Hidden file
FA_SYSTEM	System file

Return value Upon successful completion, the new file handle, a nonnegative integer, is returned; otherwise, –1 is returned.

In the event of error, the global variable *errno* is set to one of the following:

ENOENT	Path or file name not found
EMFILE	Too many open files
EACCES	Permission denied

See also **close**, **_creat**, **creat**, **creatnew**, **dup**, *_fmode* (global variable), **open**

Example

```
#include <string.h>
#include <stdio.h>
#include <io.h>

int main(void)
{
   int handle;
   char pathname[128];
   strcpy(pathname, "\\");

   /* create a unique file in the root directory */
   handle = creattemp(pathname, 0);
   printf("%s was the unique file created.\n", pathname);
   close(handle);
   return 0;
}
```

cscanf

Function Scans and formats input from the console.

Syntax #include <conio.h>
int cscanf(char **format*[, *address*, ...]);

DOS	UNIX	Windows	ANSI C	C++ only
■				

C

Remarks **cscanf** scans a series of input fields one character at a time, reading directly from the console. Then each field is formatted according to a format specifier passed to **cscanf** in the format string pointed to by *format*. Finally, **cscanf** stores the formatted input at an address passed to it as an argument following *format*, and echoes the input directly to the screen. There must be the same number of format specifiers and addresses as there are input fields.

*See **scanf** for details on format specifiers.*

cscanf might stop scanning a particular field before it reaches the normal end-of-field (whitespace) character, or it might terminate entirely for a number of reasons. See **scanf** for a discussion of possible causes.

Return value **cscanf** returns the number of input fields successfully scanned, converted, and stored; the return value does not include scanned fields that were not stored. If no fields were stored, the return value is 0.

If **cscanf** attempts to read at end-of-file , the return value is EOF.

See also **fscanf, getche, scanf, sscanf**

Example

```
#include <conio.h>

int main(void)
{
   char string[80];

   clrscr();                    /* clear the screen */
   cprintf("Enter a string:"); /* prompt the user for input */
   cscanf("%s", string);       /* read the input */

   /* display what was read */
   cprintf("\r\nThe string entered is: %s", string);
   return 0;
}
```

ctime

Function Converts date and time to a string.

Syntax #include <time.h>
char *ctime(const time_t **time*);

DOS	UNIX	Windows	ANSI C	C++ only
■	■	■	■	

Remarks **ctime** converts a time value pointed to by *time* (the value returned by the function **time**) into a 26-character string in the following form, terminating with a newline character and a null character:

```
Mon Nov 21 11:31:54 1983\n\0
```

All the fields have constant width.

Set the global long variable *timezone* to the difference in seconds between GMT and local standard time (in PST, *timezone* is 8×60×60). The global variable *daylight* is nonzero *if and only if* the standard U.S. daylight saving time conversion should be applied.

Return value **ctime** returns a pointer to the character string containing the date and time. The return value points to static data that is overwritten with each call to **ctime**.

See also **asctime**, *daylight* (global variable), **difftime**, **ftime**, **getdate**, **gmtime**, **localtime**, **settime**, **time**, *timezone* (global variable), **tzset**

Example

```
#include   <stdio.h>
#include   <time.h>

int main(void)
{
   time_t t;
   t = time(NULL);
   printf("Today's date and time:  %s\n", ctime(&t));
   return 0;
}
```

ctrlbrk

Function Sets control-break handler.

Syntax #include <dos.h>
void ctrlbrk(int (**handler*)(void));

DOS	UNIX	Windows	ANSI C	C++ only
■		■		

Remarks **ctrlbrk** sets a new control-break handler function pointed to by *handler*. The interrupt vector 0x23 is modified to call the named function.

ctrlbrk establishes a DOS interrupt handler that calls the named function; the named function is not called directly.

The handler function can perform any number of operations and system calls. The handler does not have to return; it can use **longjmp** to return to an arbitrary point in the program. The handler function returns 0 to abort the current program; any other value causes the program to resume execution.

Return value **ctrlbrk** returns nothing.

See also **getcbrk, signal**

Example

```
#include <stdio.h>
#include <dos.h>

int c_break(void)
{
   printf("Control-Break pressed. Program aborting ...\n");
   return(0);
}

void main(void)
{
   ctrlbrk(c_break);
   for(;;)
      printf("Looping... Press <Ctrl-Break> to quit:\n");
   }
```

delay

Function Suspends execution for an interval (milliseconds).

Syntax #include <dos.h>
void delay(unsigned *milliseconds*);

DOS	UNIX	Windows	ANSI C	C++ only
■				

Remarks With a call to **delay**, the current program is suspended from execution for the number of milliseconds specified by the argument *milliseconds*. It is no longer necessary to make a calibration call to delay before using it. **delay** is accurate to a millisecond.

Return value None.

See also **nosound, sleep, sound**

Example

```
/* emits a 440-Hz tone for 500 milliseconds */
#include <dos.h>

int main(void)
```

```
{
   sound(440);
   delay(500);
   nosound();
   return 0;
}
```

delline

Function Deletes line in text window.

Syntax #include <conio.h>
void delline(void);

DOS	UNIX	Windows	ANSI C	C++ only
■				

Remarks **delline** deletes the line containing the cursor and moves all lines below it one line up. **delline** operates within the currently active text window.

Return value None.

See also **clreol, clrscr, insline, window**

Example

```
#include <conio.h>

int main(void)
{
   clrscr();
   cprintf("The function DELLINE deletes the line containing the\r\n");
   cprintf("cursor and moves all lines below it one line up.\r\n");
   cprintf("DELLINE operates within the currently active text\r\n");
   cprintf("window.  Press any key to continue . . .");

   /* move cursor to the 2nd line, 1st column */
   gotoxy(1,2);
   getch();
   delline();
   getch();
   return 0;
}
```

detectgraph

Function Determines graphics driver and graphics mode to use by checking the hardware.

Syntax #include <graphics.h>
void far detectgraph(int far **graphdriver*, int far **graphmode*);

DOS	UNIX	Windows	ANSI C	C++ only
■				

Remarks **detectgraph** detects your system's graphics adapter and chooses the mode that provides the highest resolution for that adapter. If no graphics hardware is detected, **graphdriver* is set to grNotDetected (-2), and **graphresult** returns grNotDetected (-2).

**graphdriver* is an integer that specifies the graphics driver to be used. You can give it a value using a constant of the *graphics_drivers* enumeration type, defined in graphics.h and listed in the following table.

Table 2.1 detectgraph constants

***graphics_drivers* constant**	**Numeric value**
DETECT	0 (requests autodetection)
CGA	1
MCGA	2
EGA	3
EGA64	4
EGAMONO	5
IBM8514	6
HERCMONO	7
ATT400	8
VGA	9
PC3270	10

**graphmode* is an integer that specifies the initial graphics mode (unless **graphdriver* equals DETECT; in which case, **graphmode* is set to the highest resolution available for the detected driver). You can give **graphmode* a value using a constant of the *graphics_modes* enumeration type, defined in graphics.h and listed in the following table.

Table 2.2
Graphics drivers information

Graphics driver	*graphics_modes*	Value	Column × row	Palette	Pages
CGA	CGAC0	0	320 × 200	C0	1
	CGAC1	1	320 × 200	C1	1
	CGAC2	2	320 × 200	C2	1
	CGAC3	3	320 × 200	C3	1
	CGAHI	4	640 × 200	2 color	1
MCGA	MCGAC0	0	320 × 200	C0	1
	MCGAC1	1	320 × 200	C1	1
	MCGAC2	2	320 × 200	C2	1
	MCGAC3	3	320 × 200	C3	1
	MCGAMED	4	640 × 200	2 color	1
	MCGAHI	5	640 × 480	2 color	1
EGA	EGALO	0	640 × 200	16 color	4
	EGAHI	1	640 × 350	16 color	2
EGA64	EGA64LO	0	640 × 200	16 color	1
	EGA64HI	1	640 × 350	4 color	1
EGA-MONO	EGAMONOHI	3	640 × 350	2 color	1*
	EGAMONOHI	3	640 × 350	2 color	2**
HERC	HERCMONOHI	0	720 × 348	2 color	2
ATT400	ATT400C0	0	320 × 200	C0	1
	ATT400C1	1	320 × 200	C1	1
	ATT400C2	2	320 × 200	C2	1
	ATT400C3	3	320 × 200	C3	1
	ATT400MED	4	640 × 200	2 color	1
	ATT400HI	5	640 × 400	2 color	1
VGA	VGALO	0	640 × 200	16 color	2
	VGAMED	1	640 × 350	16 color	2
	VGAHI	2	640 × 480	16 color	1
PC3270	PC3270HI	0	720 × 350	2 color	1
IBM8514	IBM8514HI	0	640 × 480	256 color	
	IBM8514LO	0	1024 × 768	256 color	

* 64K on EGAMONO card
** 256K on EGAMONO card

Note: The main reason to call **detectgraph** directly is to override the graphics mode that **detectgraph** recommends to **initgraph**.

Return value None.

See also **graphresult, initgraph**

Example

```
#include <graphics.h>
#include <stdlib.h>
```

D

```
#include <stdio.h>
#include <conio.h>

/* the names of the various cards supported */
char *dname[] = { "requests detection",
                  "a CGA",
                  "an MCGA",
                  "an EGA",
                  "a 64K EGA",
                  "a monochrome EGA",
                  "an IBM 8514",
                  "a Hercules monochrome",
                  "an AT&T 6300 PC",
                  "a VGA",
                  "an IBM 3270 PC"
                };

int main(void)
{
   /* used to return detected hardware info. */
   int gdriver, gmode, errorcode;

   /* detect the graphics hardware available */
   detectgraph(&gdriver, &gmode);

   /* read result of detectgraph call */
   errorcode = graphresult();
   if (errorcode != grOk) {  /* an error occurred */
      printf("Graphics error: %s\n", grapherrormsg(errorcode));
      printf("Press any key to halt:");
      getch();
      exit(1);               /* terminate with an error code */
   }

   /* display the information detected */
   clrscr();
   printf("You have %s video display card.\n", dname[gdriver]);
   printf("Press any key to halt:");
   getch();
   return 0;
}
```

difftime

Function Computes the difference between two times.

Syntax #include <time.h>
double difftime(time_t *time2*, time_t *time1*);

DOS	UNIX	Windows	ANSI C	C++ only
■	■	■	■	

Remarks **difftime** calculates the elapsed time in seconds, from *time1* to *time2*.

Return value **difftime** returns the result of its calculation as a **double**.

See also **asctime**, **ctime**, *daylight* (global variable), **gmtime**, **localtime**, **time**, *timezone* (global variable)

Example

```
#include <time.h>
#include <stdio.h>
#include <dos.h>
#include <conio.h>

int main(void)
{
   time_t first, second;
   clrscr();
   first = time(NULL);          /* gets system time */
   delay(2000);                 /* waits 2000 millisecs or 2 secs */
   second = time(NULL);         /* gets system time again */
   printf("The difference is: %f seconds\n",difftime(second,first));
   getch();
   return 0;
}
```

disable, _disable, enable, _enable

Function Disables and enables interrupts.

Syntax #include <dos.h>
void disable(void);
void _disable(void);
void enable(void);
void _enable(void);

DOS	UNIX	Windows	ANSI C	C++ only
■		■		

Remarks These macros are designed to provide a programmer with flexible hardware interrupt control.

The **disable** and **_disable** macros disable interrupts. Only the NMI (non-maskable interrupt) is allowed from any external device.

The **enable** and **_enable** macros enable interrupts, allowing any device interrupts to occur.

Return value None.

See also **getvect**

Example

```
/* This is an interrupt service routine. You cannot compile this program with
   Test Stack Overflow turned on and get an executable file that operates
   correctly. */

#include <stdio.h>
#include <dos.h>
#include <conio.h>

#define INTR 0X1C  /* The clock tick interrupt */

#ifdef __cplusplus
    #define __CPPARGS ...
#else
    #define __CPPARGS
#endif

void interrupt (*oldhandler)(__CPPARGS);

int count=0;

void interrupt handler(__CPPARGS) /* if C++, need the the ellipsis */
{
   /* disable interrupts during the handling of the interrupt */
   _disable();
   /* increase the global counter */
   count++;
   /* reenable interrupts at the end of the handler */
   enable();
   /* call the old routine */
   oldhandler();
}

int main(void)
{
   /* save the old interrupt vector */
   oldhandler = _dos_getvect(INTR);

   /* install the new interrupt handler */
   _dos_setvect(INTR, handler);

   /* loop until the counter exceeds 20 */
   while (count < 20)
      printf("count is %d\n",count);

   /* reset the old interrupt handler */
   _dos_setvect(INTR, oldhandler);
```

```
   return 0;
}
```

div

Function Divides two integers, returning quotient and remainder.

Syntax #include <stdlib.h>
div_t div(int *numer*, int *denom*);

DOS	UNIX	Windows	ANSI C	C++ only
■		■	■	

Remarks **div** divides two integers and returns both the quotient and the remainder as a *div_t* type. *numer* and *denom* are the numerator and denominator, respectively. The *div_t* type is a structure of integers defined (with **typedef**) in stdlib.h as follows:

```
typedef struct {
   int  quot;       /* quotient */
   int  rem;        /* remainder */
} div_t;
```

Return value **div** returns a structure whose elements are *quot* (the quotient) and *rem* (the remainder).

See also **ldiv**

Example

```
#include <stdlib.h>
#include <stdio.h>

div_t x;

int main(void)
{
   x = div(10,3);
   printf("10 div 3 = %d remainder %d\n", x.quot, x.rem);
   return 0;
}
```

Program output

```
10 div 3 = 3 remainder 1
```

D

_dos_close

Function Closes a file.

Syntax #include <dos.h>
unsigned _dos_close(int *handle*);

DOS	UNIX	Windows	ANSI C	C++ only
■		■		

Remarks **_dos_close** closes the file associated with *handle*. *handle* is a file handle obtained from a **_dos_creat**, **_dos_creatnew**, or **_dos_open** call.

Return value Upon successful completion, **_dos_close** returns 0. Otherwise, it returns the DOS error code and the global variable *errno* is set to

EBADF Bad file number

See Also **_dos_creat**, **_dos_open**, **_dos_read**, **_dos_write**

Example

```
#include <dos.h>
#include <string.h>
#include <stdio.h>

int main(void)
{
   unsigned count;
   int handle;
   char buf[11] = "0123456789";

   /* create a file containing 10 bytes */
   if (_dos_creat("DUMMY.FIL", _A_NORMAL, &handle) != 0) {
      perror("Unable to create DUMMY.FIL");
      return 1;
   }
   if (_dos_write(handle, buf, strlen(buf), &count) != 0) {
      perror("Unable to write to DUMMY.FIL");
      return 1;
   }
   _dos_close(handle);   /* close the file */
   return 0;
}
```

_dos_creatnew

Function Creates a new file.

Syntax #include <dos.h>
unsigned _dos_creatnew(const char **path*, int *attrib*, int **handlep*);

DOS	UNIX	Windows	ANSI C	C++ only
■		■		

Remarks **_dos_creatnew** uses DOS function 0x5B to create and open the new file *path*. The file is given the access permission *attrib*, a DOS attribute word. The file is always opened in binary mode. Upon successful file creation, the file handle is stored in the location pointed to by *handlep*, and the file pointer is set to the beginning of the file. The file is opened for both reading and writing.

If the file already exists, **_dos_creatnew** returns an error and leaves the file untouched.

The *attrib* argument to **_dos_creatnew** is an OR combination of one or more of the following constants (defined in dos.h):

_A_NORMAL	Normal file
_A_RDONLY	Read-only file
_A_HIDDEN	Hidden file
_A_SYSTEM	System file

Return value Upon successful completion, **_dos_creatnew** returns 0. Otherwise, it returns the DOS error code, and the global variable *errno* is set to one of the following:

EEXIST	File already exists
ENOENT	Path or file name not found
EMFILE	Too many open files
EACCES	Permission denied

See Also **_dos_close**, **_dos_creat**, **_dos_getfileattr**, **_dos_setfileattr**

Example

```
#include <dos.h>
#include <string.h>
#include <stdio.h>

int main(void)
{
  unsigned count;
  int handle;
  char buf[11] = "0123456789";
```

```
   /* create a file containing 10 bytes */
   if (_dos_creatnew("DUMMY.FIL", _A_NORMAL, &handle) != 0) {
     perror("Unable to create DUMMY.FIL");
     return 1;
   }
   if (_dos_write(handle, buf, strlen(buf), &count) != 0) {
     perror("Unable to write to DUMMY.FIL");
     return 1;
   }
   /* close the file */
   _dos_close(handle);
   return 0;
}
```

dosexterr

Function Gets extended DOS error information.

Syntax #include <dos.h>
int dosexterr(struct DOSERROR **eblkp*);

DOS	UNIX	Windows	ANSI C	C++ only
■		■		

Remarks This function fills in the **DOSERROR** structure pointed to by *eblkp* with extended error information after a DOS call has failed. The structure is defined as follows:

```
struct  DOSERROR {
   int de_exterror;       /* extended error */
   char de_class;         /* error class */
   char de_action;        /* action */
   char de_locus;         /* error locus */
};
```

The values in this structure are obtained by way of DOS call 0x59. A *de_exterror* value of 0 indicates that the prior DOS call did not result in an error.

Return value **dosexterr** returns the value *de_exterror*.

Example

```
#include <stdio.h>
#include <dos.h>

int main(void)
{
   FILE *fp;
```

```
   struct DOSERROR info;
   fp = fopen("perror.dat","r");
   if (!fp) perror("Unable to open file for reading");
   dosexterr(&info);
   printf("Extended DOS error information:\n");
   printf("   Extended error:     %d\n",info.de_exterror);
   printf("            Class:     %x\n",info.de_class);
   printf("           Action:     %x\n",info.de_action);
   printf("      Error Locus:     %x\n",info.de_locus);
   return 0;
}
```

_dos_findfirst

Function Searches a disk directory.

Syntax #include <dos.h>
unsigned _dos_findfirst(const char **pathname*, int *attrib*,
struct find_t **ffblk*);

DOS	UNIX	Windows	ANSI C	C++ only
■		■		

Remarks **_dos_findfirst** begins a search of a disk directory by using the DOS function 0x4E.

pathname is a string with an optional drive specifier, path, and file name of the file to be found. The file name portion can contain wildcard match characters (such as ? or *). If a matching file is found, the **find_t** structure pointed to by *ffblk* is filled with the file-directory information.

The format of the **find_t** structure is as follows:

```
struct find_t {
   char reserved[21];      /* reserved by DOS */
   char attrib;            /* attribute found */
   int wr_time;            /* file time */
   int wr_date;            /* file date */
   long size;              /* file size */
   char name[13];          /* found file name */
};
```

attrib is a DOS file-attribute byte used in selecting eligible files for the search. *attrib* is an OR combination of one or more of the following constants (defined in dos.h):

_A_NORMAL   Normal file

_A_RDONLY	Read-only attribute
_A_HIDDEN	Hidden file
_A_SYSTEM	System file
_A_VOLID	Volume label
_A_SUBDIR	Directory
_A_ARCH	Archive

For more detailed information about these attributes, refer to your DOS reference manuals.

Note that *wr_time* and *wr_date* contain bit fields for referring to the file's date and time. The structure of these fields was established by DOS. Both are 16-bit structures divided into three fields.

***wr_time*:**

bits 0-4	The result of seconds divided by 2 (e.g., 10 here means 20 seconds)
bits 5-10	Minutes
bits 11-15	Hours

***wr_date*:**

bits 0-4	Day
bits 5-8	Month
bits 9-15	Years since 1980 (e.g., 9 here means 1989)

Return value **_dos_findfirst** returns 0 on successfully finding a file matching the search *pathname*. When no more files can be found, or if there is some error in the file name, the DOS error code is returned, and the global variable *errno* is set to

ENOENT Path or file name not found

See Also **_dos_findnext**

Example

```
#include <stdio.h>
#include <dos.h>

int main(void)
{
   struct find_t ffblk;
   int done;
   printf("Directory listing of *.*\n");
   done = _dos_findfirst("*.*",_A_NORMAL,&ffblk);
   while (!done) {
      printf("  %s\n", ffblk.name);
      done = _dos_findnext(&ffblk);
   }
   return 0;
}
```

Program output

```
Directory listing of *.*
  FINDFRST.C
  FINDFRST.OBJ
  FINDFRST.MAP
  FINDFRST.EXE
```

_dos_findnext

Function Continues **_dos_findfirst** search.

Syntax #include <dos.h>
unsigned _dos_findnext(struct find_t **ffblk*);

DOS	UNIX	Windows	ANSI C	C++ only
■		■		

Remarks **_dos_findnext** is used to fetch subsequent files that match the *pathname* given in **_dos_findfirst**. *ffblk* is the same block filled in by the **_dos_findfirst** call. This block contains necessary information for continuing the search. One file name for each call to **_dos_findnext** will be returned until no more files are found in the directory matching the *pathname*.

Return value **_dos_findnext** returns 0 on successfully finding a file matching the search *pathname*. When no more files can be found, or if there is some error in the file name, the DOS error code is returned, and the global variable *errno* is set to

ENOENT Path or file name not found

See Also **_dos_findfirst**

Example

```
#include <stdio.h>
#include <dos.h>

int main(void)
{
   struct find_t ffblk;
   int done;
   printf("Directory listing of *.*\n");
   done = _dos_findfirst("*.*",_A_NORMAL,&ffblk);
   while (!done) {
      printf("  %s\n", ffblk.name);
      done = _dos_findnext(&ffblk);
   }
```

```
   return 0;
}
```

Program output

```
Directory listing of *.*
  FINDFRST.C
  FINDFRST.OBJ
  FINDFRST.MAP
  FINDFRST.EXE
```

D

_dos_getdiskfree

Function Gets disk free space.

Syntax #include <dos.h>
unsigned _dos_getdiskfree(unsigned char *drive*, struct diskfree_t **dtable*);

DOS	UNIX	Windows	ANSI C	C++ only
■		■		

Remarks **_dos_getdiskfree** accepts a drive specifier in *drive* (0 for default, 1 for A, 2 for B, and so on) and fills in the **diskfree_t** structure pointed to by *dtable* with disk characteristics.

The **diskfree_t** structure is defined as follows:

```
struct diskfree_t {
   unsigned avail_clusters;     /* available clusters */
   unsigned total_clusters;     /* total clusters */
   unsigned bytes_per_sector;   /* bytes per sector */
   unsigned sectors_per_cluster;/* sectors per cluster */
};
```

Return value **_dos_getdiskfree** returns 0 if successful. Otherwise, it returns a non-zero value and and the global variable *errno* is set to

EINVAL	Invalid drive specified

See Also **getfat, getfatd**

Example

```
#include <stdio.h>
#include <dos.h>
#include <process.h>

int main(void)
{
  struct diskfree_t free;
```

```
   long avail;

   if (_dos_getdiskfree(0, &free) != 0) {
     printf("Error in _dos_getdiskfree() call\n");
     exit(1);
   }
   avail = (long) free.avail_clusters
         * (long) free.bytes_per_sector
         * (long) free.sectors_per_cluster;
   printf("The current drive has %ld bytes available\n", avail);
   return 0;
}
```

_dos_getdrive, _dos_setdrive

Function Gets and sets the current drive number.

Syntax #include <dos.h>
void _dos_getdrive(unsigned **drivep*);
void _dos_setdrive(unsigned *drivep*, unsigned **ndrives*);

DOS	UNIX	Windows	ANSI C	C++ only
■		■		

Remarks **_dos_getdrive** uses DOS function 0x19 to get the current drive number.

_dos_setdrive uses DOS function 0x0E to set the current drive. **_dos_setdrive** stores the total number of drives at the location pointed to by *ndrives*.

The drive numbers at the location pointed to by *drivep* are as follows: 1 for A, 2 for B, 3 for C, and so on.

Return value None. Use **_dos_getdrive** to verify that the current drive was changed successfully.

See Also **_getcwd**

Example

```
#include <stdio.h>
#include <dos.h>

int main(void)
{
   unsigned disk, maxdrives;

   /* Get the current drive. */
   _dos_getdrive(&disk);
   printf("The current drive is: %c\n", disk + 'A' - 1);
```

```
   /* Set current drive to C: */
   printf("Setting current drive to C:\n");
   _dos_setdrive(3, &maxdrives);
   printf("The number of logical drives is: %d\n", maxdrives);
   return 0;
}
```

D

_dos_getfileattr, _dos_setfileattr

Function Changes file access mode.

Syntax #include <dos.h>
int _dos_getfileattr(const char **path*, unsigned **attribp*);
int _dos_setfileattr(const char *path*, unsigned *attrib*);

DOS	UNIX	Windows	ANSI C	C++ only
■		■		

Remarks **_dos_getfileattr** fetches the DOS file attributes for the file *path*. The attributes are stored at the location pointed to by *attribp*.

_dos_setfileattr sets the DOS file attributes for the file *path* to the value *attrib*.

The DOS file attributes can be a OR combination of the following symbolic constants (defined in dos.h):

_A_RDONLY	Read-only attribute
_A_HIDDEN	Hidden file
_A_SYSTEM	System file
_A_VOLID	Volume label
_A_SUBDIR	Directory
_A_ARCH	Archive
_A_NORMAL	Normal file (no attribute bits set)

Return value Upon successful completion, **_dos_getfileattr** and **_dos_setfileattr** return 0. Otherwise, these functions return the DOS error code, and the global variable *errno* is set to the following:

ENOENT	Path or file name not found

See Also **chmod, stat**

Example

```
#include <stdio.h>
#include <dos.h>

int main(void)
```

```
{
   char filename[128];
   unsigned attrib;

   printf("Enter a file name:");
   scanf("%s", filename);
   if (_dos_getfileattr(filename,&attrib) != 0) {
      perror("Unable to obtain file attributes");
      return 1;
   }
   if (attrib & _A_RDONLY) {
      printf("%s currently read-only, making it read-write.\n", filename);
      attrib &= ~_A_RDONLY;
   }
   else {
      printf("%s currently read-write, making it read-only.\n", filename);
      attrib |= _A_RDONLY;
   }
   if (_dos_setfileattr(filename,attrib) != 0)
      perror("Unable to set file attributes");
   return 0;
}
```

_dos_getftime, _dos_setftime

Function Gets and sets file date and time.

Syntax #include <dos.h>
unsigned _dos_getftime(int *handle*, unsigned **datep*, unsigned **timep*);
unsigned _dos_setftime(int *handle*, unsigned *date*, unsigned *time*);

DOS	UNIX	Windows	ANSI C	C++ only
■		■		

Remarks **_dos_getftime** retrieves the file time and date for the disk file associated with the open *handle*. The file must have been previously opened using **_dos_open**, **_dos_creat**, or **_dos_creatnew**. **_dos_getftime** stores the date and time at the locations pointed to by *datep* and *timep*.

_dos_setftime sets the file's new date and time values as specified by *date* and *time*.

Note that the date and time values contain bit fields for referring to the file's date and time. The structure of these fields was established by DOS. Both are 16-bit structures divided into three fields.

D

Date:	
bits 0-4	Day
bits 5-8	Month
bits 9-15	Years since 1980 (e.g., 9 here means 1989)
Time:	
bits 0-4	The result of seconds divided by 2 (e.g., 10 here means 20 seconds)
bits 5-10	Minutes
bits 11-15	Hours

Return value **_dos_getftime** and **_dos_setftime** return 0 on success.

In the event of an error return, the DOS error code is returned and the global variable *errno* is set to the following:

EBADF	Bad file number

See Also **fstat, stat**

Example

```
#include <stdio.h>
#include <dos.h>

int main(void)
{
   FILE *stream;
   unsigned date, time;
   if ((stream = fopen("TEST.$$$", "w")) == NULL) {
      fprintf(stderr, "Cannot open output file.\n");
      return 1;
   }
   _dos_getftime(fileno(stream), &date, &time);
   printf("File year of TEST.$$$: %d\n",((date >> 9) & 0x7f) + 1980);
   date = (date & 0x1ff) | (21 << 9);
   _dos_setftime(fileno(stream), date, time);
   printf("Set file year to 2001.\n");
   fclose(stream);
   return 0;
}
```

_dos_gettime, _dos_settime

Function Gets and sets system time.

Syntax #include <dos.h>
void _dos_gettime(struct dostime_t **timep*);
unsigned _dos_settime(struct dostime_t **timep*);

DOS	UNIX	Windows	ANSI C	C++ only
■		■		

Remarks **_dos_gettime** fills in the **dostime_t** structure pointed to by *timep* with the system's current time.

_dos_settime sets the system time to the values in the **dostime_t** structure pointed to by *timep*.

The **dostime_t** structure is defined as follows:

```
struct dostime_t {
   unsigned char hour;     /* hours 0-23 */
   unsigned char minute;   /* minutes 0-59 */
   unsigned char second;   /* seconds 0-59 */
   unsigned char hsecond;  /* hundredths of seconds 0-99 */
};
```

Return value **_dos_gettime** does not return a value.

If **_dos_settime** is successful, it returns 0. Otherwise, it returns the DOS error code, and the global variable *errno* is set to the following:

EINVAL Invalid time

See Also **_dos_getdate, _dos_setdate, _dos_settime, stime, time**

Example

```
#include   <stdio.h>
#include   <dos.h>

int main(void)  /* Example for _dos_gettime. */
{
   struct dostime_t t;
   _dos_gettime(&t);
   printf("The current time is: %2d:%02d:%02d.%02d\n", t.hour, t.minute,
           t.second, t.hsecond);
   return 0;
}


#include <dos.h>
#include <process.h>
#include <stdio.h>

int main(void)  /* Example for _dos_settime. */
{
   struct dostime_t reset;
   reset.hour    = 17;
   reset.minute  = 0;
   reset.second  = 0;
   reset.hsecond = 0;
```

```
   printf("Setting time to 5 PM.\n");
   _dos_settime(&reset);
   system("time");
   return 0;
}
```


_dos_getvect

Function Gets interrupt vector.

Syntax #include <dos.h>
void interrupt(*_dos_getvect(unsigned *interruptno*)) ();

DOS	UNIX	Windows	ANSI C	C++ only
■		■		

Remarks Every processor of the 8086 family includes a set of interrupt vectors, numbered 0 to 255. The 4-byte value in each vector is actually an address, which is the location of an interrupt function.

_dos_getvect reads the value of the interrupt vector given by *interruptno* and returns that value as a (far) pointer to an interrupt function. The value of *interruptno* can be from 0 to 255.

Return value **_dos_getvect** returns the current 4-byte value stored in the interrupt vector named by *interruptno*.

See Also **_disable, _enable, _dos_setvect**

Example

```
#include <stdio.h>
#include <dos.h>

#ifdef __cplusplus
    #define __CPPARGS ...
#else
    #define __CPPARGS
#endif

void interrupt get_out(__CPPARGS);     /* interrupt prototype */
void interrupt (*oldfunc)(__CPPARGS); /* interrupt function pointer */

int looping = 1;

int main(void)
{
  puts("Press <Shift><PrtSc> to terminate");

  /* save the old interrupt */
  oldfunc  = _dos_getvect(5);
```

```
   /* install interrupt handler */
   _dos_setvect(5,get_out);

   while (looping);  /* do nothing */
   /* restore to original interrupt routine */
   _dos_setvect(5,oldfunc);
   puts("Success");
   return 0;
}

void interrupt get_out(__CPPARGS) {
   looping = 0;    /* change global var to get out of loop */
}
```

_dos_setvect

Function Sets interrupt vector entry.

Syntax #include <dos.h>
void _dos_setvect(unsigned *interruptno*, void interrupt (**isr*) ());

DOS	UNIX	Windows	ANSI C	C++ only
■		■		

Remarks Every processor of the 8086 family includes a set of interrupt vectors, numbered 0 to 255. The 4-byte value in each vector is actually an address, which is the location of an interrupt function.

_dos_setvect sets the value of the interrupt vector named by *interruptno* to a new value, *isr*, which is a far pointer containing the address of a new interrupt function. The address of a C routine can only be passed to *isr* if that routine is declared to be an interrupt routine.

➡ If you use the prototypes declared in dos.h, simply pass the address of an interrupt function to **_dos_setvect** in any memory model.

Return value None.

See Also **_dos_getvect**

Example

```
/* This is an interrupt service routine. You can NOT compile this program with
   Test Stack Overflow turned on and get an executable file which will operate
   correctly. */

#include <stdio.h>
#include <dos.h>
#include <conio.h>

#define INTR 0X1C  /* The clock tick interrupt */
```

```
#ifdef __cplusplus
   #define __CPPARGS ...
#else
   #define __CPPARGS
#endif

void interrupt ( *oldhandler)(__CPPARGS);

int count=0;

void interrupt handler(__CPPARGS)
{
   count++;       /* increase the global counter */
   oldhandler();  /* call the old routine */
}

int main(void)
{
   /* save the old interrupt vector */
   oldhandler = getvect(INTR);

   /* install the new interrupt handler */
   setvect(INTR, handler);

   /* loop until the counter exceeds 20 */
   while (count < 20)
      printf("count is %d\n",count);

   /* reset the old interrupt handler */
   setvect(INTR, oldhandler);
   return 0;
}
```

_dos_write

Function Writes to a file.

Syntax #include <dos.h>
unsigned _dos_write(int *handle*, void far **buf*,
unsigned *len*, unsigned **nwritten*);

DOS	UNIX	Windows	ANSI C	C++ only
■		■		

Remarks **_dos_write** uses DOS function 0x40 to write *len* bytes from the buffer pointed to by the far pointer *buf* to the file associated with *handle*.

_dos_write does not translate a linefeed character (LF) to a CR/LF pair because all its files are binary files.

The actual number of bytes written is stored at the location pointed to by *nwritten*. If the number of bytes actually written is less than that requested, the condition should be considered an error and probably indicates a full disk.

For disk files, writing always proceeds from the current file pointer. On devices, bytes are directly sent to the device.

Return value On successful completion, **_dos_read** returns 0. Otherwise, it returns the DOS error code and the global variable *errno* is set to one of the following:

EACCES	Permission denied
EBADF	Bad file number

See Also **_dos_open, _dos_creat, _dos_read**

Example

```
#include <dos.h>
#include <string.h>
#include <stdio.h>

int main(void)
{
   unsigned count;
   int handle;
   char buf[11] = "0123456789";

   /* create a file containing 10 bytes */
   if (_dos_creat("DUMMY.FIL", _A_NORMAL, &handle) != 0) {
      perror("Unable to create DUMMY.FIL");
      return 1;
   }
   if (_dos_write(handle, buf, strlen(buf), &count) != 0) {
      perror("Unable to write to DUMMY.FIL");
      return 1;
   }
   _dos_close(handle);   /* close the file */
   return 0;
}
```

dostounix

Function Converts date and time to UNIX time format.

Syntax #include <dos.h>
long dostounix(struct date **d*, struct time **t*);

DOS	UNIX	Windows	ANSI C	C++ only
■		■		

D

Remarks **dostounix** converts a date and time as returned from **getdate** and **gettime** into UNIX time format. *d* points to a **date** structure, and *t* points to a **time** structure containing valid DOS date and time information.

The date and time must not be earlier than or equal to Jan 1 1980 00:00:00.

Return value UNIX version of current date and time parameters: number of seconds since 00:00:00 on January 1, 1970 (GMT).

See also **unixtodos**

Example

```
#include <time.h>
#include <stddef.h>
#include <dos.h>
#include <stdio.h>

int main(void)
{
   time_t t;
   struct time d_time;
   struct date d_date;
   struct tm *local;
   getdate(&d_date);
   gettime(&d_time);
   t = dostounix(&d_date, &d_time);
   local = localtime(&t);
   printf("Time and Date: %s\n", asctime(local));
   return 0;
}
```

drawpoly

Function Draws the outline of a polygon.

Syntax #include <graphics.h>
void far drawpoly(int *numpoints*, int far **polypoints*);

DOS	UNIX	Windows	ANSI C	C++ only
■				

Remarks **drawpoly** draws a polygon with *numpoints* points, using the current line style and color.

**polypoints* points to a sequence of (*numpoints* × 2) integers. Each pair of integers gives the *x* and *y* coordinates of a point on the polygon.

➡ In order to draw a closed figure with *n* vertices, you must pass *n* + 1 coordinates to **drawpoly** where the *n*th coordinate is equal to the 0th.

Return value None.

See also **fillpoly, floodfill, graphresult, setwritemode**

Example

```
#include <graphics.h>
#include <stdlib.h>
#include <stdio.h>
#include <conio.h>

int main(void)
{
   /* request autodetection */
   int gdriver = DETECT, gmode, errorcode;
   int maxx, maxy;

   int poly[10];    /* our polygon array */

   /* initialize graphics and local variables */
   initgraph(&gdriver, &gmode, "");

   /* read result of initialization */
   errorcode = graphresult();
   if (errorcode != grOk){ /* an error occurred */
      printf("Graphics error: %s\n", grapherrormsg(errorcode));
      printf("Press any key to halt:");
      getch();
      exit(1);              /* terminate with an error code */
   }

   maxx = getmaxx();
   maxy = getmaxy();
   poly[0] = 20;            /* first vertex */
   poly[1] = maxy / 2;
   poly[2] = maxx - 20;     /* second vertex */
   poly[3] = 20;
   poly[4] = maxx - 50;     /* third vertex */
   poly[5] = maxy - 20;
   poly[6] = maxx / 2;      /* fourth vertex */
   poly[7] = maxy / 2;
   poly[8] = poly[0];       /* drawpoly doesn't automatically close */
   poly[9] = poly[1];       /* the polygon, so we close it */

   drawpoly(5, poly);    /* draw the polygon */

   /* clean up */
   getch();
   closegraph();
```

```
   return 0;
}
```


dup

Function Duplicates a file handle.

Syntax #include <io.h>
int dup(int *handle*);

DOS	UNIX	Windows	ANSI C	C++ only
■	■	■		

Remarks **dup** creates a new file handle that has the following in common with the original file handle:

- same open file or device
- same file pointer (that is, changing the file pointer of one changes the other)
- same access mode (read, write, read/write)

handle is a file handle obtained from a **_creat**, **creat**, **_open**, **open**, **dup**, or **dup2** call.

Return value Upon successful completion, **dup** returns the new file handle, a non-negative in teger; otherwise, **dup** returns –1.

In the event of error, the global variable *errno* is set to one of the following:

EMFILE	Too many open files
EBADF	Bad file number

See also **_close**, **close**, **_creat**, **creat**, **creatnew**, **creattemp**, **dup2**, **fopen**, **_open**, **open**

Example

```
#include <string.h>
#include <stdio.h>
#include <conio.h>
#include <io.h>

void flush(FILE *stream);

int main(void)
{
   FILE *fp;
   char msg[] = "This is a test";

   /* create a file */
```

```
    fp = fopen("DUMMY.FIL", "w");
    if (fp) {
       /* write some data to the file */
       fwrite(msg, strlen(msg), 1, fp);
       clrscr();
       printf("Press any key to flush DUMMY.FIL:");
       getch();

       /* flush the data to DUMMY.FIL without closing it */
       flush(fp);
       printf("\nFile was flushed, Press any key to quit:");
       getch();
    }
    else
       printf("Error opening file!\n");
    return 0;
}

void flush(FILE *stream)
{
   int duphandle;

   /* flush BC's internal buffer */
   fflush(stream);

   /* make a duplicate file handle */
   duphandle = dup(fileno(stream));

   /* close duplicate handle to flush DOS buffer */
   close(duphandle);
}
```

dup2

Function Duplicates a file handle (*oldhandle*) onto an existing file handle (*newhandle*).

Syntax #include <io.h>
int dup2(int *oldhandle*, int *newhandle*);

DOS	UNIX	Windows	ANSI C	C++ only
■	■	■		

Remarks **dup2** is not available on UNIX System III.

dup2 creates a new file handle that has the following in common with the original file handle:

- same open file or device

- same file pointer (that is, changing the file pointer of one changes the other)
- same access mode (read, write, read/write)

dup2 creates a new handle with the value of *newhandle*. If the file associated with *newhandle* is open when **dup2** is called, the file is closed.

newhandle and *oldhandle* are file handles obtained from a **creat**, **open**, **dup**, or **dup2** call.

Return value **dup2** returns 0 on successful completion, –1 otherwise.

In the event of error, the global variable *errno* is set to one of the following:

EMFILE	Too many open files
EBADF	Bad file number

See also **_close**, **close**, **_creat**, **creat**, **creatnew**, **creattemp**, **dup**, **fopen**, **_open**, **open**

Example

```
#include <sys\stat.h>
#include <string.h>
#include <fcntl.h>
#include <io.h>
#include <stdio.h>
#define STDOUT 1

int main(void)
{
   int fptr, oldstdout;
   char msg[] = "This is a test";

   /* create a file */
   fptr = open("DUMMY.FIL", O_CREAT | O_RDWR, S_IREAD | S_IWRITE);
   if (fptr) {
      /* create a duplicate handle for standard output */
      oldstdout = dup(STDOUT);

      /* redirect standard output to DUMMY.FIL by duplicating the */
      /* file handle onto the file handle for standard output */
      dup2(fptr, STDOUT);

      /* close the handle for DUMMY.FIL */
      close(fptr);

      /* this will be redirected into DUMMY.FIL */
      write(STDOUT, msg, strlen(msg));

      /* restore original standard output handle */
      dup2(oldstdout, STDOUT);

      /* close the duplicate handle for STDOUT */
      close(oldstdout);
   }
```

```
    else
        printf("Error opening file!\n");
    return 0;
}
```

ecvt

Function Converts a floating-point number to a string.

Syntax #include <stdlib.h>
char *ecvt(double *value*, int *ndig*, int **dec*, int **sign*);

DOS	UNIX	Windows	ANSI C	C++ only
■	■	■		

Remarks **ecvt** converts *value* to a null-terminated string of *ndig* digits, starting with the leftmost significant digit, and returns a pointer to the string. The position of the decimal point relative to the beginning of the string is stored indirectly through *dec* (a negative value for *dec* means that the decimal lies to the left of the returned digits). There is no decimal point in the string itself. If the sign of *value* is negative, the word pointed to by *sign* is nonzero; otherwise, it's 0. The low-order digit is rounded.

Return value The return value of **ecvt** points to static data for the string of digits whose content is overwritten by each call to **ecvt** and **fcvt**.

See also **fcvt, gcvt, sprintf**

Example

```
#include <stdlib.h>
#include <stdio.h>

int main(void)
{
   char *string;
   double value;
   int dec, sign, ndig = 10;
   value = 9.876;
   string = ecvt(value, ndig, &dec, &sign);
   printf("string = %s      dec = %d sign = %d\n", string, dec, sign);
   value = -123.45;
   ndig= 15;
   string = ecvt(value,ndig,&dec,&sign);
   printf("string = %s dec = %d sign = %d\n", string, dec, sign);
   value = 0.6789e5; /* scientific notation */
   ndig = 5;
   string = ecvt(value,ndig,&dec,&sign);
   printf("string = %s           dec = %d sign = %d\n", string, dec, sign);
```

```
    return 0;
}
```

ellipse

Function Draws an elliptical arc.

Syntax #include <graphics.h>
void far ellipse(int *x*, int *y*, int *stangle*, int *endangle*, int *xradius*, int *yradius*);

DOS	UNIX	Windows	ANSI C	C++ only
■				

Remarks **ellipse** draws an elliptical arc in the current drawing color with its center at (*x*,*y*) and the horizontal and vertical axes given by *xradius* and *yradius*, respectively. The ellipse travels from *stangle* to *endangle*. If *stangle* equals 0 and *endangle* equals 360, the call to **ellipse** draws a complete ellipse.

The angle for **ellipse** is reckoned counterclockwise, with 0 degrees at 3 o'clock, 90 degrees at 12 o'clock, and so on.

The *linestyle* parameter does not affect arcs, circles, ellipses, or pie slices. Only the *thickness* parameter is used.

Return value None.

See also **arc**, **circle**, **fillellipse**, **sector**

Example

```
#include <graphics.h>
#include <stdlib.h>
#include <stdio.h>
#include <conio.h>

int main(void)
{
   /* request autodetection */
   int gdriver = DETECT, gmode, errorcode;
   int midx, midy;
   int stangle = 0, endangle = 360;
   int xradius = 100, yradius = 50;

   /* initialize graphics and local variables */
   initgraph(&gdriver, &gmode, "");

   /* read result of initialization */
   errorcode = graphresult();
   if (errorcode != grOk) {  /* an error occurred */
      printf("Graphics error: %s\n", grapherrormsg(errorcode));
      printf("Press any key to halt:");
```

```
      getch();
      exit(1);              /* terminate with an error code */
   }

   midx = getmaxx() / 2;
   midy = getmaxy() / 2;
   setcolor(getmaxcolor());

   /* draw ellipse */
   ellipse(midx, midy, stangle, endangle, xradius, yradius);

   /* clean up */
   getch();
   closegraph();
   return 0;
}
```

__emit__

Function Inserts literal values directly into code.

Syntax #include <dos.h>
void __emit__(argument, ...);

DOS	UNIX	Windows	ANSI C	C++ only
■		■		

Description **__emit__** is an inline function that lets you insert literal values directly into object code as it is compiling. It is used to generate machine language instructions without using inline assembly language or an assembler.

Generally the arguments of an **__emit__** call are single-byte machine instructions. However, because of the capabilities of this function, more complex instructions, complete with references to C variables, can be constructed.

➡ You should only use this function if you are familiar with the machine language of the 80x86 processor family. You can use this function to place arbitrary bytes in the instruction code of a function; if any of these bytes are incorrect, the program misbehaves and can easily crash your machine. Borland C++ does not attempt to analyze your calls for correctness in any way. If you encode instructions that change machine registers or memory, Borland C++ will not be aware of it and might not properly preserve registers, as it would in many cases with inline assembly language (for example, it recognizes the usage of SI and DI registers in inline instructions). You are completely on your own with this function.

You must pass at least one argument to **__emit__**; any number can be given. The arguments to this function are not treated like any other function call arguments in the language. An argument passed to **__emit__** will not be converted in any way.

There are special restrictions on the form of the arguments to **__emit__**. Arguments must be in the form of expressions that can be used to initialize a static object. This means that integer and floating-point constants and the addresses of static objects can be used. The values of such expressions are written to the object code at the point of the call, exactly as if they were being used to initialize data. The address of a parameter or auto variable, plus or minus a constant offset, may also be used. For these arguments, the offset of the variable from BP is stored.

The number of bytes placed in the object code is determined from the type of the argument, except in the following cases:

- If a signed integer constant (i.e. 0x90) appears that fits within the range of 0 to 255, it is treated as if it were a character.
- If the address of an auto or parameter variable is used, a byte is written if the offset of the variable from BP is between –128 and 127; otherwise, a word is written.

Simple bytes are written as follows:

```
__emit__(0x90);
```

If you want a word written, but the value you are passing is under 255, simply cast it to unsigned as follows:

```
__emit__(0xB8, (unsigned)17);
```

or

```
__emit__(0xB8, 17u);
```

Two- or four-byte address values can be forced by casting an address to **void near** * or **void far** *, respectively.

Return value None.

Example

```
#include <dos.h>

int main(void)
{
/* emit code that generates a print screen via int 5 */
   __emit__(0xcd,0x05); /* INT 05h */
   return 0;
}
```

eof

Function Checks for end-of-file.

Syntax #include <io.h>
int eof(int *handle*);

DOS	UNIX	Windows	ANSI C	C++ only
■		■		

Remarks **eof** determines whether the file associated with *handle* has reached end-of-file.

Return value If the current position is end-of-file, **eof** returns the value 1; otherwise, it returns 0. A return value of –1 indicates an error; the global variable *errno* is set to

EBADF Bad file number

See also **clearerr, feof, ferror, perror**

Example

```
#include <process.h>
#include <string.h>
#include <stdio.h>
#include <io.h>

int main(void)
{
   FILE *temp_file;
   int handle;
   char msg[] = "This is a test", ch;

   /* create a unique temporary file */
   if ((temp_file = tmpfile()) == NULL) {
      perror("OPENING FILE:");
      exit(1);
   }

   /* get handle associated with file */
   handle = fileno(temp_file);

   /* write some data to the file */
   write(handle, msg, strlen(msg));

   /* seek to the beginning of the file */
   lseek(handle, 0L, SEEK_SET);

   /* reads chars from the file until EOF is hit */
   do {
      read(handle, &ch, 1);
      printf("%c", ch);
```

```
    } while (!eof(handle));

    /* close and remove the temporary file */
    fclose(temp_file);
    return 0;
}
```


execl, execle, execlp, execlpe, execv, execve, execvp, execvpe

Function Loads and runs other programs.

Syntax #include <process.h>
int execl(char **path*, char **arg0* **arg1*, ..., **argn*, NULL);
int execle(char **path*, char **arg0*, **arg1*, ..., **argn*, NULL, char ***env*);

int execlp(char **path*, char **arg0*,**arg1*, ..., **argn*, NULL);
int execlpe(char **path*, char **arg0*, **arg1*, ..., **argn*, NULL, char ***env*);

int execv(char **path*, char **argv[]*);
int execve(char **path*, char **argv[]*, char ***env*);

int execvp(char **path*, char **argv[]*);
int execvpe(char **path*, char **argv[]*, char ***env*);

DOS	UNIX	Windows	ANSI C	C++ only
■				

Remarks The functions in the **exec...** family load and run (execute) other programs, known as *child processes*. When an **exec...** call succeeds, the child process overlays the *parent process*. There must be sufficient memory available for loading and executing the child process.

path is the file name of the called child process. The **exec...** functions search for *path* using the standard DOS search algorithm:

- If no explicit extension is given, the functions search for the file as given. If the file is not found, they add .COM and search again. If that search is not successful, they add .EXE and search one last time.
- If an explicit extension or a period is given, the functions search for the file exactly as given.

The suffixes *l*, *v*, *p*, and *e* added to the **exec...** "family name" specify that the named function operate with certain capabilities.

p The function searches for the file in those directories specified by the DOS PATH environment variable (without the *p* suffix, the function searches only the current working directory). If the *path* parameter does not contain an explicit directory, the function searches first the current directory, then the directories set with the DOS PATH environment variable.

l The argument pointers (*arg0*, *arg1*, ..., *argn*) are passed as separate arguments. Typically, the *l* suffix is used when you know in advance the number of arguments to be passed.

v The argument pointers (*argv[0]* ..., *arg[n]*) are passed as an array of pointers. Typically, the *v* suffix is used when a variable number of arguments is to be passed.

e The argument *env* can be passed to the child process, letting you alter the environment for the child process. Without the *e* suffix, child processes inherit the environment of the parent process.

Each function in the **exec...** family *must* have one of the two argument-specifying suffixes (either *l* or *v*). The *path search* and *environment inheritance* suffixes (*p* and *e*) are optional.

For example,

- **execl** is an **exec...** function that takes separate arguments, searches only the root or current directory for the child, and passes on the parent's environment to the child.
- **execvpe** is an **exec...** function that takes an array of argument pointers, incorporates PATH in its search for the child process, and accepts the *env* argument for altering the child's environment.

The **exec...** functions must pass at least one argument to the child process (*arg0* or *argv[0]*); this argument is, by convention, a copy of *path*. (Using a different value for this 0th argument won't produce an error.)

Under DOS 3.x, *path* is available for the child process; under earlier versions of DOS, the child process cannot use the passed value of the 0th argument (*arg0* or *argv[0]*).

When the *l* suffix is used, *arg0* usually points to *path*, and *arg1*, ..., *argn* point to character strings that form the new list of arguments. A mandatory null following *argn* marks the end of the list.

When the *e* suffix is used, you pass a list of new environment settings through the argument *env*. This environment argument is an array of character pointers. Each element points to a null-terminated character string of the form

envvar = *value*

where *envvar* is the name of an environment variable, and *value* is the string value to which *envvar* is set. The last element in *env* is null. When *env* is null, the child inherits the parents' environment settings.

The combined length of *arg0* + *arg1* + ... + *argn* (or of *argv[0]* + *argv[1]* + ... + *argn[n]*), including space characters that separate the arguments, must be less than 128 bytes. Null terminators are not counted.

When an **exec...** function call is made, any open files remain open in the child process.

E

Return value If successful, the **exec...** functions do not return. On error, the **exec...** functions return –1, and the global variable *errno* is set to one of the following:

E2BIG	Arg list too long
EACCES	Permission denied
EMFILE	Too many open files
ENOENT	Path or file name not found
ENOEXEC	Exec format error
ENOMEM	Not enough core

See also **abort, atexit, _exit, exit, _fpreset, searchpath, spawn..., system**

Examples

```
#include <stdio.h>
#include <stdlib.h>

int main(int argc, char *argv[])
{
   int i;
   printf("Child running ...\n");
   printf("%s\n",getenv("PATH"));
   for(i = 0; i < argc; i++)
   printf("argv[%d]: %s\n", i, argv[i]);
   return 0;
}
```

Each function has its own example program.

```
#include <stdio.h>
#include <errno.h>
#include <dos.h>

int main(int argc, char *argv[])
{
   int loop;
   printf("%s running...\n\n", argv[0]);
   if (argc == 1) {    /* check for only one command-line parameter */
      printf("%s calling itself again...\n", argv[0]);
      execl(argv[0], argv[0], "ONE", "TWO", "THREE", NULL);
      perror("EXEC:");
```

```
      exit(1);
   }
   printf("%s called with arguments:\n", argv[0]);
   for (loop = 1; loop <= argc; loop++)
   puts(argv[loop]);    /* display all command-line parameters */
   return 0;
}
```

```
#include <process.h>
#include <stdlib.h>
#include <stdio.h>
#include <errno.h>
#include <dos.h>

int main(int argc, char *argv[], char *env[])
{
   int loop;
   char *new_env[] = { "TESTING", NULL };
   printf("%s running...\n\n", argv[0]);
   if (argc == 1) {     /* check for only one command-line parameter */
      printf("%s calling itself again...\n", argv[0]);
      execle(argv[0], argv[0], "ONE", "TWO", "THREE", NULL, new_env);
      perror("EXEC:");
      exit(1);
   }
   printf("%s called with arguments:\n", argv[0]);
   for (loop = 1; loop <= argc; loop++)
   puts(argv[loop]);    /* display all command-line parameters */

   /* display the first environment parameter */
   printf("value of env[0]: %s\n",env[0]);
   return 0;
}
```

```
#include <process.h>
#include <stdio.h>
#include <errno.h>

int main(int argc, char *argv[], char **envp)
{
   int i;
   printf("Command line arguments:\n");
   for (i=0; i < argc; ++i)
      printf("[%2d] %s\n", i, argv[i]);
   printf("About to exec child with arg1 arg2 ...\n");
   execlpe("CHILD.EXE", "CHILD.EXE", "arg1", "arg2", NULL, envp);
   perror("exec error");
   exit(1);
```

```
   return 0;
}
```

```
#include <process.h>
#include <stdio.h>
#include <errno.h>

int main(int argc, char *argv[], char **envp)
{
   int i;
   printf("Command line arguments:\n");
   for (i=0; i < argc; ++i)
      printf("[%2d] %s\n", i, argv[i]);
   printf("About to exec child with arg1 arg2 ...\n");
   execlpe("CHILD.EXE", "CHILD.EXE", "arg1", "arg2", NULL, envp);
   perror("exec error");
   return 1;
}
```

```
#include <process.h>
#include <stdio.h>
#include <errno.h>

void main(int argc, char *argv[])
{
   int i;
   printf("Command line arguments:\n");
   for (i=0; i<argc; i++)
      printf("[%2d] : %s\n", i, argv[i]);
   printf("About to exec child with arg1 arg2 ...\n");
   execv("CHILD.EXE", argv);
   perror("exec error");
   exit(1);
}
```

```
#include <process.h>
#include <stdio.h>
#include <errno.h>

void main(int argc, char *argv[], char **envp)
{
   int i;
   printf("Command line arguments:\n");
   for (i=0; i<argc; ++i)
      printf("[%2d] : %s\n", i, argv[i]);
   printf("About to exec child with arg1 arg2 ...\n");
   execve("CHILD.EXE", argv, envp);
   perror("exec error");
```

```
   exit(1);
}
```

```
#include <process.h>
#include <stdio.h>
#include <errno.h>

void main(int argc, char *argv[])
{
   int i;
   printf("Command line arguments:\n");
   for (i=0; i<argc; ++i)
      printf("[%2d] : %s\n", i, argv[i]);
   printf("About to exec child with arg1 arg2 ...\n");
   execvp("CHILD.EXE", argv);
   perror("exec error");
   exit(1);
}
```

```
#include <process.h>
#include <stdio.h>
#include <errno.h>

void main(int argc, char *argv[], char **envp)
{
   int i;
   printf("Command line arguments:\n");
   for (i=0; i<argc; ++i)
      printf("[%2d] : %s\n", i, argv[i]);
   printf("About to exec child with arg1 arg2 ...\n");
   execvpe("CHILD.EXE", argv, envp);
   perror("exec error");
   exit(1);
}
```

_exit

Function Terminates program.

Syntax# #include <stdlib.h>
void _exit(int *status*);

DOS	UNIX	Windows	ANSI C	C++ only
■	■	■		

Remarks **_exit** terminates execution without closing any files, flushing any output, or calling any exit functions.

The calling process uses *status* as the exit status of the process. Typically a value of 0 is used to indicate a normal exit, and a nonzero value indicates some error.

Return value None.

See also **abort, atexit, exec..., exit, spawn...**

Example

```
#include <stdlib.h>
#include <stdio.h>

void done(void);

int main(void)
{
   atexit(done);
   _exit(0);
   return 0;
}

void done()
{
   printf("hello\n");
}
```

E

exit

Function Terminates program.

Syntax #include <stdlib.h>
void exit(int *status*);

DOS	UNIX	Windows	ANSI C	C++ only
■	■	■	■	

Remarks **exit** terminates the calling process. Before termination, all files are closed, buffered output (waiting to be output) is written, and any registered "exit functions" (posted with **atexit**) are called.

status is provided for the calling process as the exit status of the process. Typically a value of 0 is used to indicate a normal exit, and a nonzero value indicates some error. It is set with one of the following

EXIT_SUCCESS Normal program termination.

EXIT_FAILURE	Abnormal program termination; signal to operating system that program has terminated with an error.

Return value None.

See also **abort, atexit, exec..., _exit, keep, signal, spawn...**

Example

```
#include <stdlib.h>
#include <conio.h>
#include <stdio.h>

int main(void)
{
   int status;
   printf("Enter either 1 or 2\n");
   status = getch();
   exit(status - '0');    /* sets DOS error level */
   return 0;              /* NOTE: This line is never reached */
}
```

exp, expl

Function Calculates the exponential *e* to the *x*.

Syntax

Real versions:
#include <math.h>
double exp(double *x*);
long double expl(long double *x*);

Complex version:
#include <complex.h>
complex exp(complex *x*);

	DOS	UNIX	Windows	ANSI C	C++ only
expl	■		■		
Real ***exp***	■	■	■	■	
Complex ***exp***	■		■		■

Remarks **exp** calculates the exponential function e^x.

expl is the long double version; it takes a long double argument and returns a long double result.

The complex exponential function is defined by

$$\exp(x + y\,i) = \exp(x)\,(\cos(y) + i\,\sin(y))$$

Return value **exp** returns e^x.

Sometimes the arguments passed to these functions produce results that overflow or are incalculable. When the correct value overflows, **exp** returns the value HUGE_VAL and **expl** returns _LHUGE_VAL. Results of excessively large magnitude will cause the global variable *errno* to be set to

ERANGE   Result out of range

On underflow, these functions return 0.0, and the global variable *errno* is not changed.

Error handling for these functions can be modified through the functions **matherr** and **_matherrl**.

See Also **frexp, ldexp, log, log10, matherr, pow, pow10, sqrt**

Example

```
#include <stdio.h>
#include <math.h>

int main(void)
{
   double result, x = 4.0;
   result = exp(x);
   printf("'e' raised to the power of %lf (e ^ %lf) = %lf\n", x, x, result);
   return 0;
}
```

fabs, fabsl

Function Returns the absolute value of a floating-point number.

Syntax #include <math.h>
double fabs(double *x*);
long double fabsl(long double *x*);

	DOS	UNIX	Windows	ANSI C	C++ only
fabs	■	■	■	■	
fabsl	■		■		

Remarks **fabs** calculates the absolute value of *x*, a double. **fabsl** is the long double version; it takes a long double argument and returns a long double result.

Return value **fabs** and **fabsl** return the absolute value of *x*.

See also **abs, cabs, labs**

Example

```
#include <stdio.h>
#include <math.h>

int main(void)
{
```

```
   float number = -1234.0;
   printf("number: %f  absolute value: %f\n", number, fabs(number));
   return 0;
}
```

farcalloc

Function Allocates memory from the far heap.

Syntax #include <alloc.h>
void far *farcalloc(unsigned long *nunits*, unsigned long *unitsz*);

DOS	UNIX	Windows	ANSI C	C++ only
■		■		

Remarks **farcalloc** allocates memory from the far heap for an array containing *nunits* elements, each *unitsz* bytes long.

For allocating from the far heap, note that

- all available RAM can be allocated.
- blocks larger than 64K can be allocated.
- far pointers (or huge pointers if blocks are larger than 64K) are used to access the allocated blocks.

In the compact, large, and huge memory models, **farcalloc** is similar, though not identical, to **calloc**. It takes **unsigned long** parameters, while **calloc** takes **unsigned** parameters.

A tiny model program cannot make use of **farcalloc**.

Return value **farcalloc** returns a pointer to the newly allocated block, or null if not enough space exists for the new block.

See also **calloc, farcoreleft, farfree, farmalloc, malloc**

Example

```
#include <stdio.h>
#include <alloc.h>
#include <string.h>
#include <dos.h>

int main(void)
{
   char far *fptr, *str = "Hello";

   /* allocate memory for the far pointer */
   fptr = (char far *) farcalloc(10, sizeof(char));

   /* copy "Hello" into allocated memory */
```

```
   /* Note: movedata is used because you might be in a small data model, in which
      case a normal string copy routine can not be used since it assumes the
      pointer size is near. */
   movedata(FP_SEG(str), FP_OFF(str),
            FP_SEG(fptr), FP_OFF(fptr),
            strlen(str)
            );

   /* display string (note the F modifier) */
   printf("Far string is: %Fs\n", fptr);

   /* free the memory */
   farfree(fptr);
   return 0;
}
```

F

farcoreleft

Function Returns a measure of unused memory in far heap.

Syntax #include <alloc.h>
unsigned long farcoreleft(void);

DOS	UNIX	Windows	ANSI C	C++ only
■				

Remarks **farcoreleft** returns a measure of the amount of unused memory in the far heap beyond the highest allocated block.

A tiny model program cannot make use of **farcoreleft**.

Return value **farcoreleft** returns the total amount of space left in the far heap, between the highest allocated block and the end of available memory.

See also **coreleft, farcalloc, farmalloc**

Example

```
#include <stdio.h>
#include <alloc.h>

int main(void)
{
   printf("The difference between the highest allocated block in the far\n");
   printf("heap and the top of the far heap is: %lu bytes\n", farcoreleft());
   return 0;
}
```

farfree

Function Frees a block from far heap.

Syntax #include <alloc.h>
void farfree(void far * *block*);

DOS	UNIX	Windows	ANSI C	C++ only
■		■		

Remarks **farfree** releases a block of memory previously allocated from the far heap.

A tiny model program cannot make use of **farfree**.

In the small and medium memory models, blocks allocated by **farmalloc** cannot be freed with normal **free**, and blocks allocated with **malloc** cannot be freed with **farfree**. In these models, the two heaps are completely distinct.

Return value None.

See also **farcalloc**, **farmalloc**

Example

```
#include <stdio.h>
#include <alloc.h>
#include <string.h>
#include <dos.h>

int main(void)
{
   char far *fptr, *str = "Hello";

   /* allocate memory for the far pointer */
   fptr = (char far *) farcalloc(10, sizeof(char));

   /* copy "Hello" into allocated memory */
   /* Note: movedata is used because you might be in a small data model, in which
      case a normal string copy routine can't be used since it assumes the
      pointer size is near. */
   movedata(FP_SEG(str), FP_OFF(str),
            FP_SEG(fptr), FP_OFF(fptr),
            strlen(str));

   /* display string (note the F modifier) */
   printf("Far string is: %Fs\n", fptr);

   /* free the memory */
   farfree(fptr);
   return 0;
}
```

farheapcheck

Function Checks and verifies the far heap.

Syntax #include <alloc.h>
int farheapcheck(void);

DOS	UNIX	Windows	ANSI C	C++ only
■				

F

Remarks **farheapcheck** walks through the far heap and examines each block, checking its pointers, size, and other critical attributes.

Return value The return value is less than zero for an error and greater than zero for success.

_HEAPEMPTY is returned if there is no heap (value 1).
_HEAPOK is returned if the heap is verified (value 2).
_HEAPCORRUPT is returned if the heap has been corrupted (value –1).

See also **heapcheck**

Example

```
#include <stdio.h>
#include <alloc.h>

#define NUM_PTRS  10
#define NUM_BYTES 16

int main(void)
{
char far *array[ NUM_PTRS ];
int i;

   for( i = 0; i < NUM_PTRS; i++ )
      array[ i ] = (char far *) farmalloc( NUM_BYTES );

   for( i = 0; i < NUM_PTRS; i += 2 )
      farfree( array[ i ] );

   if( farheapcheck() == _HEAPCORRUPT )
      printf( "Heap is corrupted.\n" );
   else
      printf( "Heap is OK.\n" );
   return 0;
}
```

farheapcheckfree

Function Checks the free blocks on the far heap for a constant value.

Syntax #include <alloc.h>
int farheapcheckfree(unsigned int fillvalue);

DOS	UNIX	Windows	ANSI C	C++ only
■				

Return value The return value is less than zero for an error and greater than zero for success.

_HEAPEMPTY is returned if there is no heap (value 1).
_HEAPOK is returned if the heap is accurate (value 2).
_HEAPCORRUPT is returned if the heap has been corrupted (value –1).
_BADVALUE is returned if a value other than the fill value was found (value –3).

See also **farheapfillfree, heapcheckfree**

Example

```
#include <mem.h>
#include <stdio.h>
#include <alloc.h>

#define NUM_PTRS  10
#define NUM_BYTES 16

int main(void)
{
   char far *array[NUM_PTRS];
   int i, j, res;

   for (i = 0; i < NUM_PTRS; i++)
      if ((array[i] = (char far *) farmalloc(NUM_BYTES)) == NULL) {
         printf("No memory for allocation\n");
         return 1;
      }

   for (i = 0; i < NUM_PTRS; i += 2)
      farfree(array[i]);

   if(farheapfillfree(1) < 0) {
      printf("Heap corrupted.\n");
      return 1;
   }

   for (i = 1; i < NUM_PTRS; i += 2)
      for (j = 0; j < NUM_BYTES; j++)
         array[i][j] = 0;

   res = farheapcheckfree(1);
   if (res < 0)
      switch(res) {
         case _HEAPCORRUPT:
```

```
            printf("Heap corrupted.\n");
            return 1;
         case _BADVALUE:
            printf("Bad value in free space.\n");
            return 1;
         default:
            printf("Unknown error.\n");
            return 1;
      }
   printf("Test successful.\n");
   return 0;
}
```

F

farheapchecknode

Function Checks and verifies a single node on the far heap.

Syntax #include <alloc.h>
int farheapchecknode(void *node);

DOS	UNIX	Windows	ANSI C	C++ only
■				

Remarks If a node has been freed and **farheapchecknode** is called with a pointer to the freed block, **farheapchecknode** can return _BADNODE rather than the expected _FREEENTRY. This is because adjacent free blocks on the heap are merged, and the block in question no longer exists.

Return value The return value is less than zero for an error and greater than zero for success.

_HEAPEMPTY is returned if there is no heap (value 1).
_HEAPCORRUPT is returned if the heap has been corrupted (value –1).
_BADNODE is returned if the node could not be found (value –2).
_FREEENTRY is returned if the node is a free block (value 3).
_USEDENTRY is returned if the node is a used block (value 4).

See also **heapchecknode**

Example

```
#include <stdio.h>
#include <alloc.h>

#define NUM_PTRS  10
#define NUM_BYTES 16

int main(void)
{
```

```
   char far *array[ NUM_PTRS ];
   int i;

   for( i = 0; i < NUM_PTRS; i++ )
      array[ i ] = (char far *) farmalloc( NUM_BYTES );
   for( i = 0; i < NUM_PTRS; i += 2 )
      farfree( array[ i ] );
   for( i = 0; i < NUM_PTRS; i++ ) {
      printf( "Node %2d ", i );
      switch( farheapchecknode( array[ i ] )) {
         case _HEAPEMPTY:
            printf("No heap.\n" );
            break;
         case _HEAPCORRUPT:
            printf("Heap corrupt.\n" );
            break;
         case _BADNODE:
            printf("Bad node.\n" );
            break;
         case _FREEENTRY:
            printf("Free entry.\n" );
            break;
         case _USEDENTRY:
            printf("Used entry.\n" );
            break;
         default:
            printf("Unknown return code.\n");
            break;
         }
      }
   return 0;
}
```

farheapfillfree

Function Fills the free blocks on the far heap with a constant value.

Syntax #include <alloc.h>
int farheapfillfree(unsigned int fillvalue);

DOS	UNIX	Windows	ANSI C	C++ only
■				

Return value The return value is less than zero for an error and greater than zero for success.

_HEAPEMPTY is returned if there is no heap (value 1).

_HEAPOK is returned if the heap is accurate (value 2).
_HEAPCORRUPT is returned if the heap has been corrupted (value –1).

See also **farheapcheckfree, heapfillfree**

Example

```
#include <mem.h>
#include <stdio.h>
#include <alloc.h>

#define NUM_PTRS  10
#define NUM_BYTES 16

int main(void)
{
   char far *array[NUM_PTRS];
   int i, j, res;

   for (i = 0; i < NUM_PTRS; i++)
      if ((array[i] = (char far *) farmalloc(NUM_BYTES)) == NULL){
         printf("No memory for allocation\n");
         return 1;
      }
   for (i = 0; i < NUM_PTRS; i += 2)
      farfree(array[i]);
   if(farheapfillfree(1) < 0) {
      printf("Heap corrupted.\n");
      return 1;
   }
   for (i = 1; i < NUM_PTRS; i += 2)
      for (j = 0; j < NUM_BYTES; j++)
         array[i][j] = 0;

   res = farheapcheckfree(1);
   if (res < 0)
      switch(res) {
         case _HEAPCORRUPT:
            printf("Heap corrupted.\n");
            return 1;
         case _BADVALUE:
            printf("Bad value in free space.\n");
            return 1;
         default:
            printf("Unknown error.\n");
            return 1;
      }
   printf("Test successful.\n");
   return 0;
}
```

farheapwalk

Function **farheapwalk** is used to "walk" through the far heap node by node.

Syntax

```
#include <alloc.h>
int farheapwalk(struct farheapinfo *hi);
```

DOS	UNIX	Windows	ANSI C	C++ only
■				

Remarks **farheapwalk** assumes the heap is correct. Use **farheapcheck** to verify the heap before using **farheapwalk**. _HEAPOK is returned with the last block on the heap. _HEAPEND will be returned on the next call to **farheapwalk**.

farheapwalk receives a pointer to a structure of type *heapinfo* (defined in alloc.h). For the first call to **farheapwalk**, set the hi.ptr field to null. **farheapwalk** returns with hi.ptr containing the address of the first block. hi.size holds the size of the block in bytes. hi.in_use is a flag that's set if the block is currently in use.

Return value _HEAPEMPTY is returned if there is no heap (value 1).
_HEAPOK is returned if the heapinfo block contains valid data (value 2).
_HEAPEND is returned if the end of the heap has been reached (value 5).

See also **heapwalk**

Example

```
#include <stdio.h>
#include <alloc.h>

#define NUM_PTRS  10
#define NUM_BYTES 16

int main( void )
{
   struct farheapinfo hi;
   char far *array[ NUM_PTRS ];
   int i;

   for( i = 0; i < NUM_PTRS; i++ )
      array[ i ] = (char far *) farmalloc( NUM_BYTES );

   for( i = 0; i < NUM_PTRS; i += 2 )
      farfree( array[ i ] );

   hi.ptr = NULL;
   printf( "   Size   Status\n" );
   printf( "   ----   ------\n" );
   while( farheapwalk( &hi ) == _HEAPOK )
      printf( "%7u    %s\n", hi.size, hi.in_use ? "used" : "free" );
}
```

farmalloc

Function Allocates from far heap.

Syntax #include <alloc.h>
void far *farmalloc(unsigned long *nbytes*);

DOS	UNIX	Windows	ANSI C	C++ only
■		■		

F

Remarks **farmalloc** allocates a block of memory *nbytes* bytes long from the far heap.

For allocating from the far heap, note that

- all available RAM can be allocated.
- blocks larger than 64K can be allocated.
- far pointers are used to access the allocated blocks.

In the compact, large, and huge memory models, **farmalloc** is similar though not identical to **malloc**. It takes **unsigned long** parameters, while **malloc** takes **unsigned** parameters.

A tiny model program cannot make use of **farmalloc**.

Return value **farmalloc** returns a pointer to the newly allocated block, or null if not enough space exists for the new block.

See also **farcalloc, farcoreleft, farfree, farrealloc, malloc**

Example

```
#include <stdio.h>
#include <alloc.h>
#include <string.h>
#include <dos.h>

int main(void)
{
   char far *fptr, *str = "Hello";

   /* allocate memory for the far pointer */
   fptr = (char far *) farmalloc(10);

   /* copy "Hello" into allocated memory */
   /* movedata is used because we might be in a small data model, in which case a
     normal string copy routine can not be used since it assumes the pointer size
     is near. */
   movedata(FP_SEG(str), FP_OFF(str),
            FP_SEG(fptr), FP_OFF(fptr),
            strlen(str));

   /* display string (note the F modifier) */
   printf("Far string is: %Fs\n", fptr);
```

```
   /* free the memory */
   farfree(fptr);
   return 0;
}
```

farrealloc

Function Adjusts allocated block in far heap.

Syntax #include <alloc.h>
void far *farrealloc(void far **oldblock*, unsigned long *nbytes*);

DOS	UNIX	Windows	ANSI C	C++ only
■		■		

Remarks **farrealloc** adjusts the size of the allocated block to *nbytes*, copying the contents to a new location, if necessary.

For allocating from the far heap, note that

- all available RAM can be allocated.
- blocks larger than 64K can be allocated.
- far pointers are used to access the allocated blocks.

A tiny model program cannot make use of **farrealloc**.

Return value **farrealloc** returns the address of the reallocated block, which might be different than the address of the original block. If the block cannot be reallocated, **farrealloc** returns null.

See also **farmalloc, realloc**

Example

```
#include <stdio.h>
#include <alloc.h>

int main(void)
{
   char far *fptr;
   char far *newptr;

   fptr = (char far *) farmalloc(16);
   printf("First address: %Fp\n", fptr);

   /* We use a second pointer, newptr, so that in the case of farrealloc()
      returning NULL, our original pointer is not set to NULL. */

   newptr = (char far *) farrealloc(fptr,64);
   printf("New address  : %Fp\n", newptr);
   if (newptr != NULL)
```

```
      farfree(newptr);
   return 0;
}
```

fclose

Function Closes a stream.

Syntax #include <stdio.h>
int fclose(FILE **stream*);

DOS	UNIX	Windows	ANSI C	C++ only
■	■	■	■	

Remarks **fclose** closes the named stream. All buffers associated with the stream are flushed before closing. System-allocated buffers are freed upon closing. Buffers assigned with **setbuf** or **setvbuf** are not automatically freed. (But if **setvbuf** is passed null for the buffer pointer, it *will* free it upon close.)

Return value **fclose** returns 0 on success. It returns EOF if any errors were detected.

See also **close, fcloseall, fdopen, fflush, flushall, fopen, freopen**

Example

```
#include <string.h>
#include <stdio.h>

int main(void)
{
   FILE *fp;
   char buf[11] = "0123456789";

   /* create a file containing 10 bytes */
   fp = fopen("DUMMY.FIL", "w");
   if (fp) {
      fwrite(&buf, strlen(buf), 1, fp);
      fclose(fp);        /* close the file */
   }
   else
      printf("Unable to open file!\n");
   return 0;
}
```

fcloseall

Function Closes open streams.

Syntax #include <stdio.h>
int fcloseall(void);

DOS	UNIX	Windows	ANSI C	C++ only
■	■	■		

Remarks **fcloseall** closes all open streams except stdin, stdout, stdprn, stderr, and stdaux.

Return value **fcloseall** returns the total number of streams it closed. It returns EOF if any errors were detected.

See also **fclose, fdopen, flushall, fopen, freopen**

Example

```
#include <stdio.h>

int main(void)
{
   int streams_closed;

   /* open two streams */
   fopen("DUMMY.ONE", "w");
   fopen("DUMMY.TWO", "w");

   /* close the open streams */
   streams_closed = fcloseall();
   if (streams_closed == EOF)
      perror("Error");         /* issue an error message */
   else         /* print result of fcloseall() function */
      printf("%d streams were closed.\n", streams_closed);
   return 0;
}
```

fcvt

Function Converts a floating-point number to a string.

Syntax #include <stdlib.h>
char *fcvt(double *value*, int *ndig*, int **dec*, int **sign*);

DOS	UNIX	Windows	ANSI C	C++ only
■	■	■		

Remarks **fcvt** converts *value* to a null-terminated string digits, starting with the leftmost significant digit, with *ndig* digits to the right of the decimal point. **fcvt** then returns a pointer to the string. The position of the decimal point relative to the beginning of the string is stored indirectly through *dec* (a negative value for *dec* means to the left of the returned digits). There is no decimal point in the string itself. If the sign of *value* is negative, the word pointed to by *sign* is nonzero; otherwise, it is 0.

The correct digit has been rounded for the number of digits to the right of the decimal point specified by *ndig*.

Return value The return value of **fcvt** points to static data whose content is overwritten by each call to **fcvt** and **ecvt**.

See also **ecvt, gcvt, sprintf**

Example

```
#include <stdlib.h>
#include <stdio.h>

int main(void)
{
   char *str;
   double num;
   int dec, sign, ndig = 5;

   /* a regular number */
   num = 9.876;
   str = fcvt(num, ndig, &dec, &sign);
   printf("string = %10s decimal place = %d sign = %d\n", str, dec, sign);

   /* a negative number */
   num = -123.45;
   str = fcvt(num, ndig, &dec, &sign);
   printf("string = %10s decimal place = %d sign = %d\n", str, dec, sign);

   /* scientific notation */
   num = 0.678e5;
   str = fcvt(num, ndig, &dec, &sign);
   printf("string = %10s  decimal place= %d  sign = %d\n", str, dec, sign);
   return 0;
}
```

fdopen

Function Associates a stream with a file handle.

Syntax #include <stdio.h>
FILE *fdopen(int *handle*, char **type*);

DOS	UNIX	Windows	ANSI C	C++ only
■	■	■		

Remarks **fdopen** associates a stream with a file handle obtained from **creat**, **dup**, **dup2**, or **open**. The type of stream must match the mode of the open *handle*.

The *type* string used in a call to **fdopen** is one of the following values:

- *r* Open for reading only.
- *w* Create for writing.
- *a* Append; open for writing at end-of-file or create for writing if the file does not exist.
- *r+* Open an existing file for update (reading and writing).
- *w+* Create a new file for update.
- *a+* Open for append; open (or create if the file does not exist) for update at the end of the file.

To specify that a given file is being opened or created in text mode, append a *t* to the value of the *type* string (*rt*, *w+t*, and so on); similarly, to specify binary mode, append a *b* to the *type* string (*wb*, *a+b*, and so on).

If a *t* or *b* is not given in the *type* string, the mode is governed by the global variable *_fmode*. If *_fmode* is set to O_BINARY, files will be opened in binary mode. If *_fmode* is set to O_TEXT, they will be opened in text mode. These O_... constants are defined in fcntl.h.

When a file is opened for update, both input and output can be done on the resulting stream. However, output cannot be directly followed by input without an intervening **fseek** or **rewind**, and input cannot be directly followed by output without an intervening **fseek**, **rewind**, or an input that encounters end-of-file.

Return value On successful completion, **fdopen** returns a pointer to the newly opened stream. In the event of error, it returns null.

See also **fclose**, **fopen**, **freopen**, **open**

Example

```
#include <sys\stat.h>
#include <stdio.h>
#include <fcntl.h>
#include <io.h>

int main(void)
{
```

```
   int handle;
   FILE *stream;

   /* open a file */
   handle = open("DUMMY.FIL", O_CREAT, S_IREAD | S_IWRITE);

   /* now turn the handle into a stream */
   stream = fdopen(handle, "w");
   if (stream == NULL)
      printf("fdopen failed\n");
   else {
      fprintf(stream, "Hello world\n");
      fclose(stream);
   }
   return 0;
}
```

F

feof

Function Detects end-of-file on a stream.

Syntax #include <stdio.h>
int feof(FILE **stream*);

DOS	UNIX	Windows	ANSI C	C++ only
■	■	■	■	

Remarks **feof** is a macro that tests the given stream for an end-of-file indicator. Once the indicator is set, read operations on the file return the indicator until **rewind** is called, or the file is closed.

The end-of-file indicator is reset with each input operation.

Return value **feof** returns nonzero if an end-of-file indicator was detected on the last input operation on the named stream, and 0 if end-of-file has not been reached.

See also **clearerr**, **eof**, **ferror**, **perror**

Example

```
#include <stdio.h>

int main(void)
{
   FILE *stream;

   stream = fopen("DUMMY.FIL", "r");  /* open a file for reading */
   fgetc(stream);        /* read a character from the file */
   if (feof(stream))     /* check for EOF */
      printf("We have reached end-of-file\n");
```

```
   fclose(stream);      /* close the file */
   return 0;
}
```

ferror

Function Detects errors on stream.

Syntax #include <stdio.h>
int ferror(FILE **stream*);

DOS	UNIX	Windows	ANSI C	C++ only
■	■	■	■	

Remarks **ferror** is a macro that tests the given stream for a read or write error. If the stream's error indicator has been set, it remains set until **clearerr** or **rewind** is called, or until the stream is closed.

Return value **ferror** returns nonzero if an error was detected on the named stream.

See also **clearerr, eof, feof, fopen, gets, perror**

Example

```
#include <stdio.h>

int main(void)
{
   FILE *stream;

   /* open a file for writing */
   stream = fopen("DUMMY.FIL", "w");

   /* force an error condition by attempting to read */
   (void) getc(stream);
   if (ferror(stream)) {     /* test for error on the stream */
      /* display an error message */
      printf("Error reading from DUMMY.FIL\n");

      /* reset the error and EOF indicators */
      clearerr(stream);
   }
   fclose(stream);
   return 0;
}
```

fflush

Function Flushes a stream.

Syntax #include <stdio.h>
int fflush(FILE **stream*);

DOS	UNIX	Windows	ANSI C	C++ only
■	■	■	■	

F

Remarks If the given stream has buffered output, **fflush** writes the output for *stream* to the associated file.

The stream remains open after **fflush** has executed. **fflush** has no effect on an unbuffered stream.

Return value **fflush** returns 0 on success. It returns EOF if any errors were detected.

See also **fclose, flushall, setbuf, setvbuf**

Example

```
#include <string.h>
#include <stdio.h>
#include <conio.h>
#include <io.h>

void flush(FILE *stream);

int main(void)
{
   FILE *stream;
   char msg[] = "This is a test";

   /* create a file */
   stream = fopen("DUMMY.FIL", "w");

   /* write some data to the file */
   fwrite(msg, strlen(msg), 1, stream);
   clrscr();
   printf("Press any key to flush DUMMY.FIL:");
   getch();

   /* flush the data to DUMMY.FIL without closing it */
   flush(stream);
   printf("\nFile was flushed, Press any key to quit:");
   getch();
   return 0;
}

void flush(FILE *stream) {
   int duphandle;

   /* flush the stream's internal buffer */
   fflush(stream);

   /* make a duplicate file handle */
   duphandle = dup(fileno(stream));
```

```
   /* close the duplicate handle to flush the DOS buffer */
   close(duphandle);
}
```

fgetc

Function Gets character from stream.

Syntax #include <stdio.h>
int fgetc(FILE **stream*);

DOS	UNIX	Windows	ANSI C	C++ only
■	■	■	■	

Remarks **fgetc** returns the next character on the named input stream.

Return value On success, **fgetc** returns the character read, after converting it to an **int** without sign extension. On end-of-file or error, it returns EOF.

See also **fgetchar, fputc, getc, getch, getchar, getche, ungetc, ungetch**

Example

```
#include <string.h>
#include <stdio.h>
#include <conio.h>

int main(void)
{
   FILE *stream;
   char string[] = "This is a test", ch;

   /* open a file for update */
   stream = fopen("DUMMY.FIL", "w+");

   /* write a string into the file */
   fwrite(string, strlen(string), 1, stream);

   /* seek to the beginning of the file */
   fseek(stream, 0, SEEK_SET);
   do {
      ch = fgetc(stream);    /* read a char from the file */
      putch(ch);             /* display the character */
   }
   while (ch != EOF);
   fclose(stream);
   return 0;
}
```

fgetchar

Function Gets character from stdin.

Syntax #include <stdio.h>
int fgetchar(void);

DOS	UNIX	Windows	ANSI C	C++ only
■	■	■		

Remarks **fgetchar** returns the next character from stdin. It is defined as **fgetc**(*stdin*).

Return value On success, **fgetchar** returns the character read, after converting it to an **int** without sign extension. On end-of-file or error, it returns EOF.

See also **fgetc, fputchar, getchar**

Example

```
#include <stdio.h>

int main(void)
{
   char ch;

   /* prompt the user for input */
   printf("Enter a character followed by <Enter>: ");

   /* read the character from stdin */
   ch = fgetchar();

   /* display what was read */
   printf("The character read is: '%c'\n", ch);
   return 0;
}
```

fgetpos

Function Gets the current file pointer.

Syntax #include <stdio.h>
int fgetpos(FILE **stream*, fpos_t **pos*);

DOS	UNIX	Windows	ANSI C	C++ only
■		■	■	

Remarks **fgetpos** stores the position of the file pointer associated with the given stream in the location pointed to by *pos*. The exact value is a magic cookie; in other words, it is irrelevant to your purposes.

The type *fpos_t* is defined in stdio.h as `typedef long fpos_t;`.

Return value On success, **fgetpos** returns 0. On failure, it returns a nonzero value and sets the global variable *errno* to EBADF or EINVAL.

See also **fseek, fsetpos, ftell, tell**

Example

```
#include <string.h>
#include <stdio.h>

int main(void)
{
   FILE *stream;
   char string[] = "This is a test";
   fpos_t filepos;

   /* open a file for update */
   stream = fopen("DUMMY.FIL", "w+");

   /* write a string into the file */
   fwrite(string, strlen(string), 1, stream);

   /* report the file pointer position */
   fgetpos(stream, &filepos);
   printf("The file pointer is at byte %ld\n", filepos);
   fclose(stream);

   return 0;
}
```

fgets

Function Gets a string from a stream.

Syntax #include <stdio.h>
char *fgets(char **s*, int *n*, FILE **stream*);

DOS	UNIX	Windows	ANSI C	C++ only
■	■	■	■	

Remarks **fgets** reads characters from *stream* into the string *s*. The function stops reading when it reads either *n* – 1 characters or a newline character, whichever comes first. **fgets** retains the newline character at the end of *s*. A null byte is appended to *s* to mark the end of the string.

Return value On success, **fgets** returns the string pointed to by *s*; it returns null on end-of-file or error.

See also **cgets, fputs, gets**

Example

```
#include <string.h>
#include <stdio.h>

int main(void)
{
   FILE *stream;
   char string[] = "This is a test";
   char msg[20];

   /* open a file for update */
   stream = fopen("DUMMY.FIL", "w+");

   /* write a string into the file */
   fwrite(string, strlen(string), 1, stream);

   /* seek to the start of the file */
   fseek(stream, 0, SEEK_SET);

   /* read a string from the file */
   fgets(msg, strlen(string)+1, stream);

   /* display the string */
   printf("%s", msg);
   fclose(stream);

   return 0;
}
```

filelength

Function Gets file size in bytes.

Syntax #include <io.h>
long filelength(int *handle*);

DOS	UNIX	Windows	ANSI C	C++ only
■		■		

Remarks **filelength** returns the length (in bytes) of the file associated with *handle*.

Return value On success, **filelength** returns a **long** value, the file length in bytes. On error, it returns –1 and the global variable *errno* is set to

EBADF Bad file number

See also **fopen, lseek, open**

Example

```
#include <stdio.h>
#include <io.h>
#include <fcntl.h>
#include <sys\stat.h>
#include <string.h>

int main(void)
{
   int handle;
   char buf[11] = "0123456789";

   /* create a file containing 10 bytes */
   handle = open("DUMMY.FIL", O_RDWR|O_CREAT|O_TRUNC, S_IREAD|S_IWRITE);
   write(handle, buf, strlen(buf));

   /* display the size of the file */
   printf("file length in bytes: %ld\n", filelength(handle));

   /* close the file */
   close(handle);
   return 0;
}
```

fileno

Function Gets file handle.

Syntax #include <stdio.h>
int fileno(FILE **stream*);

DOS	UNIX	Windows	ANSI C	C++ only
■	■	■		

Remarks **fileno** is a macro that returns the file handle for the given stream. If *stream* has more than one handle, **fileno** returns the handle assigned to the stream when it was first opened.

Return value **fileno** returns the integer file handle associated with *stream*.

See also **fdopen, fopen, freopen**

Example

```
#include <stdio.h>

int main(void)
{
   FILE *stream;
   int handle;

   /* create a file */
```

```
   stream = fopen("DUMMY.FIL", "w");

   /* obtain the file handle associated with the stream */
   handle = fileno(stream);

   /* display the handle number */
   printf("handle number: %d\n", handle);

   /* close the file */
   fclose(stream);
   return 0;
}
```

F

fillellipse

Function Draws and fills an ellipse.

Syntax #include <graphics.h>
void far fillellipse(int *x*, int *y*, int *xradius*, int *yradius*);

DOS	UNIX	Windows	ANSI C	C++ only
■				

Remarks Draws an ellipse using (*x*,*y*) as a center point and *xradius* and *yradius* as the horizontal and vertical axes, and fills it with the current fill color and fill pattern.

Return value None.

See also **arc, circle, ellipse, pieslice**

Example

```
#include <graphics.h>
#include <stdlib.h>
#include <stdio.h>
#include <conio.h>

int main(void)
{
   /* request autodetection */
   int gdriver = DETECT, gmode, errorcode;
   int midx, midy, i;
   int xradius = 100, yradius = 50;

   /* initialize graphics and local variables */
   initgraph(&gdriver, &gmode, "");

   /* read result of initialization */
   errorcode = graphresult();
   if (errorcode != grOk) {  /* an error occurred */
      printf("Graphics error: %s\n", grapherrormsg(errorcode));
```

```
      printf("Press any key to halt:");
      getch();
      exit(1);               /* terminate with an error code */
   }

   midx = getmaxx() / 2;
   midy = getmaxy() / 2;

   /* loop through the fill patterns */
   for (i = EMPTY_FILL; i < USER_FILL; i++) {
      /* set fill pattern */
      setfillstyle(i, getmaxcolor());

      /* draw a filled ellipse */
      fillellipse(midx, midy, xradius, yradius);
      getch();
   }

   /* clean up */
   closegraph();
   return 0;
}
```

fillpoly

Function Draws and fills a polygon.

Syntax #include <graphics.h>
void far fillpoly(int *numpoints*, int far **polypoints*);

DOS	UNIX	Windows	ANSI C	C++ only
■				

Remarks **fillpoly** draws the outline of a polygon with *numpoints* points in the current line style and color (just as **drawpoly** does), then fills the polygon using the current fill pattern and fill color.

polypoints points to a sequence of (*numpoints* × 2) integers. Each pair of integers gives the *x* and *y* coordinates of a point on the polygon.

Return value None.

See also **drawpoly, floodfill, graphresult, setfillstyle**

Example

```
#include <graphics.h>
#include <stdlib.h>
#include <stdio.h>
#include <conio.h>

int main(void)
```

```
{
   /* request autodetection */
   int gdriver = DETECT, gmode, errorcode;
   int i, maxx, maxy;

   /* our polygon array */
   int poly[8];

   /* initialize graphics and local variables */
   initgraph(&gdriver, &gmode, "");

   /* read result of initialization */
   errorcode = graphresult();
   if (errorcode != grOk) {  /* an error occurred */
      printf("Graphics error: %s\n", grapherrormsg(errorcode));
      printf("Press any key to halt:");
      getch();
      exit(1);               /* terminate with an error code */
   }

   maxx = getmaxx();
   maxy = getmaxy();

   poly[0] = 20;             /* first vertex */
   poly[1] = maxy / 2;
   poly[2] = maxx - 20;      /* second vertex */
   poly[3] = 20;
   poly[4] = maxx - 50;      /* third vertex */
   poly[5] = maxy - 20;
   poly[6] = maxx / 2;       /* fourth, fillpoly automatically */
   poly[7] = maxy / 2;       /* closes the polygon */

   /* loop through the fill patterns */
   for (i=EMPTY_FILL; i<USER_FILL; i++) {
      /* set fill pattern */
      setfillstyle(i, getmaxcolor());

      /* draw a filled polygon */
      fillpoly(4, poly);
      getch();
   }

   /* clean up */
   closegraph();
   return 0;
}
```

findfirst

Function Searches a disk directory.

Syntax

#include <dir.h>
#include <dos.h>
int findfirst(const char **pathname*, struct ffblk **ffblk*, int *attrib*);

DOS	UNIX	Windows	ANSI C	C++ only
■		■		

Remarks

findfirst begins a search of a disk directory by using the DOS system call 0x4E.

pathname is a string with an optional drive specifier, path, and file name of the file to be found. The file name portion can contain wildcard match characters (such as ? or *). If a matching file is found, the **ffblk** structure is filled with the file-directory information.

The format of the structure **ffblk** is as follows:

```
struct ffblk {
   char ff_reserved[21];      /* reserved by DOS */
   char ff_attrib;            /* attribute found */
   int ff_ftime;              /* file time */
   int ff_fdate;              /* file date */
   long ff_fsize;             /* file size */
   char ff_name[13];          /* found file name */
};
```

attrib is a DOS file-attribute byte used in selecting eligible files for the search. *attrib* can be one of the following constants defined in dos.h:

FA_RDONLY	Read-only attribute
FA_HIDDEN	Hidden file
FA_SYSTEM	System file
FA_LABEL	Volume label
FA_DIREC	Directory
FA_ARCH	Archive

For more detailed information about these attributes, refer to your DOS reference manuals.

Note that *ff_ftime* and *ff_fdate* contain bit fields for referring to the current date and time. The structure of these fields was established by MS-DOS. Both are 16-bit structures divided into three fields.

***ff_ftime*:**

bits 0 to 4	The result of seconds divided by 2 (e.g., 10 here means 20 seconds)
bits 5 to 10	Minutes

bits 11 to 15	Hours

ff_fdate:

bits 0-4	Day
bits 5-8	Month
bits 9-15	Years since 1980 (e.g., 9 here means 1989)

The structure **ftime** declared in io.h uses time and date bit fields similar in structure to *ff_ftime*, and *ff_fdate*. See **getftime** or **setftime** for examples.

Return value **findfirst** returns 0 on successfully finding a file matching the search *pathname*. When no more files can be found, or if there is some error in the file name, –1 is returned, and the global variable *errno* is set to

ENOENT	Path or file name not found

and *doserno* is set to one of the following:

ENOENT	Path or file name not found
ENMFILE	No more files

See also **findnext**

Example

```
#include <stdio.h>
#include <dir.h>

int main(void)
{
   struct ffblk ffblk;
   int done;
   printf("Directory listing of *.*\n");
   done = findfirst("*.*",&ffblk,0);
   while (!done) {
      printf("  %s\n", ffblk.ff_name);
      done = findnext(&ffblk);
   }
   return 0;
}
```

Program output

```
Directory listing of *.*
   FINDFRST.C
   FINDFRST.OBJ
   FINDFRST.EXE
```

findnext

Function Continues **findfirst** search.

Syntax #include <dir.h>
int findnext(struct ffblk **ffblk*);

DOS	UNIX	Windows	ANSI C	C++ only
■		■		

Remarks **findnext** is used to fetch subsequent files that match the *pathname* given in **findfirst**. *ffblk* is the same block filled in by the **findfirst** call. This block contains necessary information for continuing the search. One file name for each call to **findnext** will be returned until no more files are found in the directory matching the *pathname*.

Return value **findnext** returns 0 on successfully finding a file matching the search *pathname*. When no more files can be found, or if there is some error in the file name, –1 is returned, and the global variable *errno* is set to

ENOENT	Path or file name not found

and *doserno* is set to one of the following:

ENOENT	Path or file...
ENMFILE	No more files

See also **findfirst**

Example

```
#include <stdio.h>
#include <dir.h>

int main(void)
{
   struct ffblk ffblk;
   int done;
   printf("Directory listing of *.*\n");
   done = findfirst("*.*",&ffblk,0);
   while (!done) {
      printf("  %s\n", ffblk.ff_name);
      done = findnext(&ffblk);
   }
   return 0;
}
```

Program output

```
Directory listing of *.*
   FINDFRST.C
   FINDFRST.OBJ
   FINDFRST.EXE
```

F

floodfill

Function Flood-fills a bounded region.

Syntax #include <graphics.h>
void far floodfill(int *x*, int *y*, int *border*);

DOS	UNIX	Windows	ANSI C	C++ only
■				

Remarks **floodfill** fills an enclosed area on bitmap devices. (*x*,*y*) is a "seed point" within the enclosed area to be filled. The area bounded by the color *border* is flooded with the current fill pattern and fill color. If the seed point is within an enclosed area, the inside will be filled. If the seed is outside the enclosed area, the exterior will be filled.

Use **fillpoly** instead of **floodfill** whenever possible so that you can maintain code compatibility with future versions.

floodfill does not work with the IBM-8514 driver.

Return value If an error occurs while flooding a region, **graphresult** returns a value of –7.

See also **drawpoly**, **fillpoly**, **graphresult**, **setcolor**, **setfillstyle**

Example

```
#include <graphics.h>
#include <stdlib.h>
#include <stdio.h>
#include <conio.h>

int main(void)
{
   /* request autodetection */
   int gdriver = DETECT, gmode, errorcode;
   int maxx, maxy;

   /* initialize graphics and local variables */
   initgraph(&gdriver, &gmode, "");

   /* read result of initialization */
```

```
    errorcode = graphresult();
    if (errorcode != grOk) {  /* an error occurred */
       printf("Graphics error: %s\n", grapherrormsg(errorcode));
       printf("Press any key to halt:");
       getch();
       exit(1);                /* terminate with an error code */
    }

    maxx = getmaxx();
    maxy = getmaxy();

    /* select drawing color */
    setcolor(getmaxcolor());


    /* select fill color */
    setfillstyle(SOLID_FILL, getmaxcolor());

    /* draw a border around the screen */
    rectangle(0, 0, maxx, maxy);

    /* draw some circles */
    circle(maxx / 3, maxy /2, 50);
    circle(maxx / 2, 20, 100);
    circle(maxx-20, maxy-50, 75);
    circle(20, maxy-20, 25);

    /* wait for a key */
    getch();

    /* fill in bounded region */
    floodfill(2, 2, getmaxcolor());

    /* clean up */
    getch();
    closegraph();
    return 0;
}
```

floor, floorl

Function Rounds down.

Syntax #include <math.h>
double floor(double *x*);
long double floorl(long double *x*);

	DOS	UNIX	Windows	ANSI C	C++ only
floor	■	■	■	■	
floorl	■		■		

Remarks **floor** finds the largest integer not greater than *x*.
floorl is the long double version; it takes a long double argument and returns a long double result.

Return value **floor** returns the integer found as a double.
floorl returns the integer found as a long double.

See also **ceil, fmod**

Example

```
#include <stdio.h>
#include <math.h>

int main(void)
{
   double number = 123.54, down, up;

   down = floor(number);
   up = ceil(number);
   printf("original number     %10.2lf\n", number);
   printf("number rounded down %10.2lf\n", down);
   printf("number rounded up   %10.2lf\n", up);
   return 0;
}
```


flushall

Function Flushes all streams.

Syntax #include <stdio.h>
int flushall(void);

DOS	UNIX	Windows	ANSI C	C++ only
■	■	■		

Remarks **flushall** clears all buffers associated with open input streams, and writes all buffers associated with open output streams to their respective files. Any read operation following **flushall** reads new data into the buffers from the input files.

Streams stay open after **flushall** executes.

Return value **flushall** returns an integer, the number of open input and output streams.

See also **fclose, fcloseall, fflush**

Example

```
#include <stdio.h>

int main(void)
```

```
{
   FILE *stream;

   /* create a file */
   stream = fopen("DUMMY.FIL", "w");

   /* flush all open streams */
   printf("%d streams were flushed.\n", flushall());

   /* close the file */
   fclose(stream);
   return 0;
}
```

_fmemccpy

See **memccpy**.

_fmemchr

See **memchr**.

_fmemcmp

See **memcmp**.

_fmemcpy

See **memcpy**.

_fmemicmp

See **memicmp**.

_fmemset

See **memset**.

F

fmod, fmodl

Function Calculates x modulo y, the remainder of x/y.

Syntax
#include <math.h>
double fmod(double *x*, double *y*);
long double fmodl(long double *x*, long double *y*);

	DOS	UNIX	Windows	ANSI C	C++ only
fmod	■	■	■	■	
fmodl	■		■		

Remarks **fmod** calculates x modulo y (the remainder f, where $x = ay + f$ for some integer a and $0 \le f < y$).
fmodl is the long double version; it takes long double arguments and returns a long double result.

Return value **fmod** and **fmodl** return the remainder f, where $x = ay + f$ (as described). Where y = 0, **fmod** and **fmodl** return 0.

See also **ceil, floor, modf**

Example

```
#include <stdio.h>
#include <math.h>

int main(void)
{
   double x = 5.0, y = 2.0;
   double result;
   result = fmod(x,y);
   printf("The remainder of (%lf / %lf) is %lf\n", x, y, result);
   return 0;
}
```

Program output

```
The remainder of 5.0 / 2.0 is 1.0.
```

fnmerge

Function Builds a path from component parts.

Syntax #include <dir.h>

void fnmerge(char **path*, const char **drive*, const char **dir*,
const char **name*, const char **ext*);

DOS	UNIX	Windows	ANSI C	C++ only
■		■		

Remarks **fnmerge** makes a path name from its components. The new path name is

```
X:\DIR\SUBDIR\NAME.EXT
```

where

drive = `X:`
dir = `\DIR\SUBDIR\`
name = `NAME`
ext = `.EXT`

fnmerge assumes there is enough space in *path* for the constructed path name. The maximum constructed length is MAXPATH. MAXPATH is defined in dir.h.

fnmerge and **fnsplit** are invertible; if you split a given *path* with **fnsplit**, then merge the resultant components with **fnmerge**, you end up with *path*.

Return value None.

See also **fnsplit**

Example

```
#include <string.h>
#include <stdio.h>
#include <dir.h>

int main(void)
{
   char s[MAXPATH];
   char drive[MAXDRIVE];
   char dir[MAXDIR];
   char file[MAXFILE];
   char ext[MAXEXT];
   getcwd(s,MAXPATH);              /* get current working directory */
   strcat(s,"\\");                 /* append a trailing \ character */
   fnsplit(s,drive,dir,file,ext); /* split the string to separate elems */
   strcpy(file,"DATA");
   strcpy(ext,".TXT");
   fnmerge(s,drive,dir,file,ext); /* merge everything into one string */
   puts(s);                        /* display resulting string */
   return 0;
}
```

fnsplit

Function Splits a full path name into its components.

Syntax #include <dir.h>
int fnsplit(const char **path*, char **drive*, char **dir*, char **name*, char **ext*);

DOS	UNIX	Windows	ANSI C	C++ only
■		■		

Remarks **fnsplit** takes a file's full path name (*path*) as a string in the form

X:\DIR\SUBDIR\NAME.EXT

and splits *path* into its four components. It then stores those components in the strings pointed to by *drive*, *dir*, *name*, and *ext*. (All five components must be passed, but any of them can be a null, which means the corresponding component will be parsed but not stored.)

The maximum sizes for these strings are given by the constants MAXDRIVE, MAXDIR, MAXPATH, MAXFILE, and MAXEXT (defined in dir.h), and each size includes space for the null-terminator.

Constant	Max	String
MAXPATH	(80)	*path*
MAXDRIVE	(3)	*drive*; includes colon (:)
MAXDIR	(66)	*dir*; includes leading and trailing backslashes (\)
MAXFILE	(9)	*name*
MAXEXT	(5)	*ext*; includes leading dot (.)

fnsplit assumes that there is enough space to store each non-null component.

When **fnsplit** splits *path*, it treats the punctuation as follows:

- *drive* includes the colon (C:, A:, and so on).
- *dir* includes the leading and trailing backslashes (\BC\include\, \source\, and so on).
- *name* includes the file name.
- *ext* includes the dot preceding the extension (.C, .EXE, and so on).

fnmerge and **fnsplit** are invertible; if you split a given *path* with **fnsplit**, then merge the resultant components with **fnmerge**, you end up with *path*.

Return value **fnsplit** returns an integer (composed of five flags, defined in dir.h) indicating which of the full path name components were present in *path*; these flags and the components they represent are

EXTENSION	An extension
FILENAME	A file name
DIRECTORY	A directory (and possibly subdirectories)
DRIVE	A drive specification (see dir.h)
WILDCARDS	Wildcards (* or ?)

See also **fnmerge**

Example

```
#include <stdlib.h>
#include <stdio.h>
#include <dir.h>

int main(void)
{
   char *s;
   char drive[MAXDRIVE];
   char dir[MAXDIR];
   char file[MAXFILE];
   char ext[MAXEXT];
   int flags;

   /* get comspec environment parameter */
   s = getenv("COMSPEC");
   flags = fnsplit(s,drive,dir,file,ext);
   printf("Command processor info:\n");
   if(flags & DRIVE)
     printf("\tdrive: %s\n",drive);
   if(flags & DIRECTORY)
     printf("\tdirectory: %s\n",dir);
   if(flags & FILENAME)
     printf("\tfile: %s\n",file);
   if(flags & EXTENSION)
     printf("\textension: %s\n",ext);
   return 0;
}
```

fopen

Function Opens a stream.

Syntax #include <stdio.h>
FILE *fopen(const char **filename*, const char **mode*);

DOS	UNIX	Windows	ANSI C	C++ only
■	■	■	■	

Remarks **fopen** opens the file named by *filename* and associates a stream with it. **fopen** returns a pointer to be used to identify the stream in subsequent operations.

The *mode* string used in calls to **fopen** is one of the following values:

Mode	Description
r	Open for reading only.
w	Create for writing. If a file by that name already exists, it will be overwritten.
a	Append; open for writing at end of file, or create for writing if the file does not exist.
r+	Open an existing file for update (reading and writing).
w+	Create a new file for update (reading and writing). If a file by that name already exists, it will be overwritten.
a+	Open for append; open for update at the end of the file, or create if the file does not exist.

To specify that a given file is being opened or created in text mode, append a *t* to the *mode* string (*rt*, *w+t*, and so on). Similarly, to specify binary mode, append a *b* to the *mode* string (*wb*, *a+b*, and so on). **fopen** also allows the *t* or *b* to be inserted between the letter and the + character in the mode string; for example, *rt+* is equivalent to *r+t*.

If a *t* or *b* is not given in the *mode* string, the mode is governed by the global variable *_fmode*. If *_fmode* is set to O_BINARY, files are opened in binary mode. If *_fmode* is set to O_TEXT, they are opened in text mode. These O_... constants are defined in fcntl.h.

When a file is opened for update, both input and output can be done on the resulting stream. However, output cannot be followed directly by input without an intervening **fseek** or **rewind**, and input cannot be directly followed by output without an intervening **fseek**, **rewind**, or an input that encounters end-of-file.

Return value On successful completion, **fopen** returns a pointer to the newly opened stream. In the event of error, it returns null.

See also **creat**, **dup**, **fclose**, **fdopen** **ferror**, *_fmode* (global variable), **fread**, **freopen**, **fseek**, **fwrite**, **open**, **rewind**, **setbuf**, **setmode**

Example

```
/* program to create backup of the AUTOEXEC.BAT file */
```

```
#include <stdio.h>

int main(void)
{
   FILE *in, *out;
   if ((in = fopen("\\AUTOEXEC.BAT", "rt")) == NULL) {
      fprintf(stderr, "Cannot open input file.\n");
      return 1;
   }
   if ((out = fopen("\\AUTOEXEC.BAK", "wt")) == NULL) {
      fprintf(stderr, "Cannot open output file.\n");
      return 1;
   }
   while (!feof(in))
      fputc(fgetc(in), out);
   fclose(in);
   fclose(out);
   return 0;
}
```

FP_OFF, FP_SEG

Function Gets a far address offset or segment.

Syntax #include <dos.h>
unsigned FP_OFF(void far **p*);
unsigned FP_SEG(void far **p*);

DOS	UNIX	Windows	ANSI C	C++ only
■		■		

Remarks The **FP_OFF** macro can be used to get or set the offset of the far pointer **p*.

FP_SEG is a macro that gets or sets the segment value of the far pointer **p*.

Return value **FP_OFF** returns an **unsigned** integer value representing an offset value.

FP_SEG returns an **unsigned** integer representing a segment value.

See also **MK_FP, movedata, segread**

Example

```
#include <dos.h>
#include <stdio.h>
#include <graphics.h>

/* FP_OFF */

int fp_off(void)
```

F

```
{
   char *str = "fpoff.c";

   printf("The offset of this file name in memory\
     is: %Fp\n", FP_OFF(str));

   return 0;
}

/* FP_SEG */

int fp_seg(void)
{
   char *filename = "fpseg.c";

   printf("The segment of this file in memory\
     is: %Fp\n", FP_SEG(filename));

   return(0);
}

/* MK_FP */

int main(void)
{
   int gd, gm, i;
   unsigned int far *screen;

   detectgraph(&gd, &gm);
   if (gd == HERCMONO)
  screen = (unsigned int *) MK_FP(0xB000, 0);
   else
  screen = (unsigned int *) MK_FP(0xB800, 0);
   for (i=0; i<26; i++)
      screen[i] = 0x0700 + ('a' + i);
   return 0;
}
```

_fpreset

Function Reinitializes floating-point math package.

Syntax #include <float.h>
void _fpreset(void);

DOS	UNIX	Windows	ANSI C	C++ only
■		■		

Remarks **_fpreset** reinitializes the floating-point math package. This function is usually used in conjunction with **system** or the **exec...** or **spawn...** functions.

Under DOS, if an 80x87 coprocessor is used in a program, a child process (executed by **system** or by an **exec...** or **spawn...** function) might alter the parent process's floating-point state.

If you use an 80x87, take the following precautions:

- Do not call **system** or an **exec...** or **spawn...** function while a floating-point expression is being evaluated.
- Call **_fpreset** to reset the floating-point state after using **system**, **exec...**, or **spawn...** if there is *any* chance that the child process performed a floating-point operation with the 80x87.

Return value None.

See also **_clear87**, **_control87**, **exec...**, **spawn...**, **_status87**, **system**

Example

```
#include <stdio.h>
#include <float.h>
#include <setjmp.h>
#include <signal.h>
#include <process.h>
#include <conio.h>

#ifdef __cplusplus
    typedef void (*fptr)(int);
#else
    typedef void (*fptr)();
#endif

jmp_buf reenter;

/* define a handler for trapping floating
   point errors */
void float_trap(int sig)
{
   printf("Trapping floating point error,");
   printf("signal is %d\n",sig);
   printf("Press a key to continue\n");
   getch();
   /* Reset the 8087 chip or emulator to clear any extraneous garbage. */
   _fpreset();
   /* return to the problem spot */
   longjmp(reenter, -1);
}

int main(void)
```

```
{
   float one = 3.14, two = 0.0;

   /* Install signal handler for floating point exception. */
   signal(SIGFPE, (fptr)float_trap);
   printf("Generating a math error,");
   printf("press a key\n");
   getch();
   if (setjmp(reenter) == 0)
      one /= two;
   printf("Returned from signal trap\n");
   return 0;
}
```

F

fprintf

Function Writes formatted output to a stream.

Syntax #include <stdio.h>
int fprintf(FILE *_stream_, const char *_format_[, argument, ...]);

DOS	UNIX	Windows	ANSI C	C++ only
■	■	■	■	

Remarks **fprintf** accepts a series of arguments, applies to each a format specifier contained in the format string pointed to by _format_, and outputs the formatted data to a stream. There must be the same number of format specifiers as arguments.

*See **printf** for details on format specifiers.*

Return value **fprintf** returns the number of bytes output. In the event of error, it returns EOF.

See also **cprintf, fscanf, printf, putc, sprintf**

Example

```
#include <stdio.h>

int main(void)
{
   FILE *stream;
   int i = 100;
   char c = 'C';
   float f = 1.234;

   stream = fopen("DUMMY.FIL", "w+");    /* open a file for update */
   fprintf(stream, "%d %c %f", i, c, f); /* write some data to the file */
   fclose(stream);   /* close the file */
   return 0;
}
```

fputc

Function Puts a character on a stream.

Syntax #include <stdio.h>
int fputc(int *c*, FILE **stream*);

DOS	UNIX	Windows	ANSI C	C++ only
■	■	■	■	

Remarks **fputc** outputs character *c* to the named stream.

Return value On success, **fputc** returns the character *c*. On error, it returns EOF.

See also **fgetc**, **putc**

Example

```
#include <stdio.h>

int main(void)
{
   char msg[] = "Hello world";
   int i = 0;
   while (msg[i]) {
      fputc(msg[i], stdout);
      i++;
   }
   return 0;
}
```

fputchar

Function Outputs a character on stdout.

Syntax #include <stdio.h>
int fputchar(int *c*);

DOS	UNIX	Windows	ANSI C	C++ only
■	■	■		

Remarks **fputchar** outputs character *c* to stdout. **fputchar**(*c*) is the same as **fputc**(*c, stdout*).

Return value On success, **fputchar** returns the character *c*. On error, it returns EOF.

See also **fgetchar**, **putchar**

Example

```
#include <stdio.h>
```

```
int main(void)
{
   char msg[] = "This is a test\n";
   int i = 0;
   while (msg[i]) {
      fputchar(msg[i]);
      i++;
   }
   return 0;
}
```

F

fputs

Function Outputs a string on a stream.

Syntax #include <stdio.h>
int fputs(const char **s*, FILE **stream*);

DOS	UNIX	Windows	ANSI C	C++ only
■	■	■	■	

Remarks **fputs** copies the null-terminated string *s* to the given output stream; it does not append a newline character, and the terminating null character is not copied.

Return value On successful completion, **fputs** returns a non-negative value. Otherwise, it returns a value of EOF.

See also **fgets**, **gets**, **puts**

Example

```
#include <stdio.h>

int main(void)
{
   /* write a string to standard output */
   fputs("Hello world\n", stdout);
   return 0;
}
```

fread

Function Reads data from a stream.

Syntax #include <stdio.h>
size_t fread(void **ptr*, size_t *size*, size_t *n*, FILE **stream*);

DOS	UNIX	Windows	ANSI C	C++ only
■	■	■	■	

Remarks **fread** reads *n* items of data, each of length *size* bytes, from the given input stream into a block pointed to by *ptr*.

The total number of bytes read is ($n \times size$).

Return value On successful completion, **fread** returns the number of items (not bytes) actually read. It returns a short count (possibly 0) on end-of-file or error.

See also **fopen, fwrite, printf, read**

Example

```
#include <string.h>
#include <stdio.h>

int main(void)
{
   FILE *stream;
   char msg[] = "this is a test";
   char buf[20];
   if ((stream = fopen("DUMMY.FIL", "w+")) == NULL) {
      fprintf(stderr, "Cannot open output file.\n");
      return 1;
   }
   /* write some data to the file */
   fwrite(msg, strlen(msg)+1, 1, stream);

   /* seek to the beginning of the file */
   fseek(stream, SEEK_SET, 0);

   /* read the data and display it */
   fread(buf, strlen(msg)+1, 1, stream);
   printf("%s\n", buf);
   fclose(stream);
   return 0;
}
```

free

Function Frees allocated block.

Syntax #include <alloc.h>
void free(void **block*);

DOS	UNIX	Windows	ANSI C	C++ only
■	■	■	■	

Remarks **free** deallocates a memory block allocated by a previous call to **calloc**, **malloc**, or **realloc**.

Return value None.

See also **calloc**, **freemem**, **malloc**, **realloc**, **strdup**

Example

```
#include <string.h>
#include <stdio.h>
#include <alloc.h>

int main(void)
{
   char *str;

   /* allocate memory for string */
   str = (char *) malloc(10);

   /* copy "Hello" to string */
   strcpy(str, "Hello");

   /* display string */
   printf("String is %s\n", str);

   /* free memory */
   free(str);
   return 0;
}
```


freemem, _dos_freemem

Function Frees a previously allocated DOS memory block.

Syntax #include <dos.h>
int freemem(unsigned *segx*);
unsigned _dos_freemem(unsigned *segx*);

DOS	UNIX	Windows	ANSI C	C++ only
■				

Remarks **freemem** frees a memory block allocated by a previous call to **allocmem**. **_dos_freemem** frees a memory block allocated by a previous call to **_dos_allocmem**. *segx* is the segment address of that block.

Return value **freemem** and **_dos_freemem** return 0 on success.

In the event of error, **freemem** returns –1 and sets *errno*.

In the event of error, **_dos_freemem** returns the DOS error code and sets *errno*.

In the event of error, these functions set global variable *errno* to

ENOMEM	Insufficient memory

See also **allocmem, _dos_allocmem, free**

Example

```
#include <dos.h>
#include <alloc.h>
#include <stdio.h>

int main(void) /* Example for freemem. */
{
   unsigned int size, segp;
   int stat;
   size = 64;          /* allocmem requests blocks in 16 byte chunks,
                          64 of these is 1024 bytes of memory */
   stat = allocmem(size, &segp);
   if (stat == -1)
      printf("Allocated memory at segment: %x\n", segp);
   else
      printf("Failed: maximum number of paragraphs available is %u\n", stat);
   freemem(segp);
   return 0;
}
```

Example 2

```
#include <dos.h>
#include <stdio.h>

int main(void)  /* Example for _dos_freemem. */
{
   unsigned int size, segp, err, maxb;
   size = 64; /* (64 x 16) = 1024 bytes */
   err = _dos_allocmem(size, &segp);
   if (err == 0)
      printf("Allocated memory at segment: %x\n", segp);
   else {
      perror("Unable to allocate block");
      printf("Maximum no. of paragraphs available is %u\n", segp);
      return 1;
   }
   if (_dos_setblock(size * 2, segp, &maxb) == 0)
      printf("Expanded memory block at segment: %X\n", segp);
   else {
      perror("Unable to expand block");
      printf("Maximum no. of paragraphs available is %u\n", maxb);
   }
   _dos_freemem(segp);
```

```
    return 0;
}
```

freopen

Function Associates a new file with an open stream.

Syntax #include <stdio.h>
FILE *freopen(const char **filename*, const char **mode*, FILE **stream*);

DOS	UNIX	Windows	ANSI C	C++ only
■	■	■	■	

Remarks **freopen** substitutes the named file in place of the open stream. It closes *stream*, regardless of whether the open succeeds. **freopen** is useful for changing the file attached to stdin, stdout, or stderr.

The *mode* string used in calls to **fopen** is one of the following values:

r Open for reading only.

w Create for writing.

a Append; open for writing at end-of-file, or create for writing if the file does not exist.

r+ Open an existing file for update (reading and writing).

w+ Create a new file for update.

a+ Open for append; open (or create if the file does not exist) for update at the end of the file.

To specify that a given file is being opened or created in text mode, append a *t* to the *mode* string (*rt*, *w+t*, and so on); similarly, to specify binary mode, append a *b* to the *mode* string (*wb*, *a+b*, and so on).

If a *t* or *b* is not given in the *mode* string, the mode is governed by the global variable *_fmode*. If *_fmode* is set to O_BINARY, files are opened in binary mode. If *_fmode* is set to O_TEXT, they are opened in text mode. These O_... constants are defined in fcntl.h.

When a file is opened for update, both input and output can be done on the resulting stream. However, output cannot be directly followed by input without an intervening **fseek** or **rewind**, and input cannot be directly followed by output without an intervening **fseek**, **rewind**, or an input that encounters end-of-file.

Return value On successful completion, **freopen** returns the argument *stream*. In the event of error, it returns null.

See also **fclose, fdopen, fopen, open, setmode**

Example

```
#include <stdio.h>

int main(void)
{
   /* redirect standard output to a file */
   if (freopen("OUTPUT.FIL", "w", stdout) == NULL)
      fprintf(stderr, "error redirecting stdout\n");

   /* this output will go to a file */
   printf("This will go into a file.");

   /* close the standard output stream */
   fclose(stdout);
   return 0;
}
```

frexp, frexpl

Function Splits a number into mantissa and exponent.

Syntax #include <math.h>
double frexp(double *x*, int **exponent*);
long double frexpl(long double *x*, int **exponent*);

	DOS	UNIX	Windows	ANSI C	C++ only
frexp	■	■	■	■	
frexpl	■		■		

Remarks **frexp** calculates the mantissa *m* (a double greater than or equal to 0.5 and less than 1) and the integer value *n*, such that *x* (the original double value) equals $m \times 2^n$. **frexp** stores *n* in the integer that *exponent* points to. **frexpl** is the long double version; it takes a long double argument for *x* and returns a long double result.

Return value **frexp** and **frexpl** return the mantissa *m*.

Error handling for these routines can be modified through the functions **matherr** and **_matherrl**.

See also **exp, ldexp**

Example

```
#include <math.h>
#include <stdio.h>
```

```
int main(void)
{
   double mantissa, number = 8.0;
   int exponent;
   mantissa = frexp(number, &exponent);
   printf("The number %lf is %lf times two to the power of %d\n", number,
          mantissa, exponent);
   return 0;
}
```

F

fscanf

Function Scans and formats input from a stream.

Syntax #include <stdio.h>
int fscanf(FILE **stream*, const char **format*[, *address*, ...]);

DOS	UNIX	Windows	ANSI C	C++ only
■	■	■	■	

Remarks **fscanf** scans a series of input fields, one character at a time, reading from a stream. Then each field is formatted according to a format specifier passed to **fscanf** in the format string pointed to by *format*. Finally, **fscanf** stores the formatted input at an address passed to it as an argument following *format*. The number of format specifiers and addresses must be the same as the number of input fields.

*See **scanf** for details on format specifiers.*

fscanf can stop scanning a particular field before it reaches the normal end-of-field character (whitespace), or it can terminate entirely for a number of reasons. See **scanf** for a discussion of possible causes.

Return value **fscanf** returns the number of input fields successfully scanned, converted, and stored; the return value does not include scanned fields that were not stored.

If **fscanf** attempts to read at end-of-file, the return value is EOF. If no fields were stored, the return value is 0.

See also **atof, cscanf, fprintf, printf, scanf, sscanf, vfscanf, vscanf, vsscanf**

Example

```
#include <stdlib.h>
#include <stdio.h>

int main(void)
{
   int i;
   printf("Input an integer: ");
```

```
    /* read an integer from the standard input stream */
    if (fscanf(stdin, "%d", &i))
       printf("The integer read was: %i\n", i);
    else {
       fprintf(stderr, "Error reading an integer from stdin.\n");
       exit(1);
    }
    return 0;
}
```

fseek

Function Repositions a file pointer on a stream.

Syntax #include <stdio.h>
int fseek(FILE **stream*, long *offset*, int *whence*);

DOS	UNIX	Windows	ANSI C	C++ only
■	■	■	■	

Remarks **fseek** sets the file pointer associated with *stream* to a new position that is *offset* bytes from the file location given by *whence*. For text mode streams, *offset* should be 0 or a value returned by **ftell**.

whence must be one of the values 0, 1, or 2, which represent three symbolic constants (defined in stdio.h) as follows:

whence		File location
SEEK_SET	(0)	File beginning
SEEK_CUR	(1)	Current file pointer position
SEEK_END	(2)	End-of-file

fseek discards any character pushed back using **ungetc**.

fseek is used with stream I/O; for file handle I/O, use **lseek**.

After **fseek**, the next operation on an update file can be either input or output.

Return value **fseek** returns 0 if the pointer is successfully moved and a nonzero on failure.

➡ **fseek** can return a zero, indicating that the pointer has been moved successfully, when in fact it has not been. This is because DOS, which actually resets the pointer, does not verify the setting. **fseek** returns an error code only on an unopened file or device.

See also **fgetpos, fopen, fsetpos, ftell, lseek, rewind, setbuf, tell**

Example

```
#include <stdio.h>

long filesize(FILE *stream);

int main(void)
{
   FILE *stream;
   stream = fopen("MYFILE.TXT", "w+");
   fprintf(stream, "This is a test");
   printf("Filesize of MYFILE.TXT is %ld bytes\n", filesize(stream));
   fclose(stream);
   return 0;
}

long filesize(FILE *stream) {
   long curpos, length;

   /* save the current location in the file */
   curpos = ftell(stream);

   /* seek to the end of the file */
   fseek(stream, 0L, SEEK_END);

   /* get the current offset into the file */
   length = ftell(stream);

   /* restore saved cursor position */
   fseek(stream, curpos, SEEK_SET);
   return length;
}
```

fsetpos

Function Positions the file pointer of a stream.

Syntax #include <stdio.h>
int fsetpos(FILE **stream*, const fpos_t **pos*);

DOS	UNIX	Windows	ANSI C	C++ only
■		■	■	

Remarks **fsetpos** sets the file pointer associated with *stream* to a new position. The new position is the value obtained by a previous call to **fgetpos** on that stream. It also clears the end-of-file indicator on the file that *stream* points to and undoes any effects of **ungetc** on that file. After a call to **fsetpos**, the next operation on the file can be input or output.

Return value On success, **fsetpos** returns 0. On failure, it returns a nonzero value and also sets the global variable *errno* to a nonzero value.

See also **fgetpos, fseek, ftell**

Example

```
#include <stdlib.h>
#include <stdio.h>

void showpos(FILE *stream);

int main(void)
{
   FILE *stream;
   fpos_t filepos;

   /* open a file for update */
   stream = fopen("DUMMY.FIL", "w+");

   /* save the file pointer position */
   fgetpos(stream, &filepos);

   /* write some data to the file */
   fprintf(stream, "This is a test");

   /* show the current file position */
   showpos(stream);

   /* set a new file position and display it */
   if (fsetpos(stream, &filepos) == 0)
      showpos(stream);
   else {
      fprintf(stderr, "Error setting file pointer.\n");
      exit(1);
   }

   /* close the file */
   fclose(stream);
   return 0;
}

void showpos(FILE *stream) {
   fpos_t pos;

   /* display the current file pointer position of a stream */
   fgetpos(stream, &pos);
   printf("File position: %ld\n", pos);
}
```

_fsopen

Function Opens a stream with file sharing.

Syntax #include <stdio.h>
#include <share.h>
FILE *_fsopen(const char **filename*, const char **mode*, int *shflg*);

DOS	UNIX	Windows	ANSI C	C++ only
■		■		

F

Remarks **_fsopen** opens the file named by *filename* and associates a stream with it. **_fsopen** returns a pointer to be used to identify the stream in subsequent operations.

The *mode* string used in calls to **_fsopen** is one of the following values:

Mode	Description
r	Open for reading only.
w	Create for writing. If a file by that name already exists, it will be overwritten.
a	Append; open for writing at end of file, or create for writing if the file does not exist.
r+	Open an existing file for update (reading and writing).
w+	Create a new file for update (reading and writing). If a file by that name already exists, it will be overwritten.
a+	Open for append; open for update at the end of the file, or create if the file does not exist.

To specify that a given file is being opened or created in text mode, append a *t* to the *mode* string (*rt*, *w+t*, and so on). Similarly, to specify binary mode, append a *b* to the *mode* string (*wb*, *a+b*, and so on). **_fsopen** also allows the *t* or *b* to be inserted between the letter and the + character in the mode string; for example, *rt+* is equivalent to *r+t*.

If a *t* or *b* is not given in the *mode* string, the mode is governed by the global variable *_fmode*. If *_fmode* is set to O_BINARY, files are opened in binary mode. If *_fmode* is set to O_TEXT, they are opened in text mode. These O_... constants are defined in fcntl.h.

When a file is opened for update, both input and output can be done on the resulting stream. However, output cannot be followed directly by input without an intervening **fseek** or **rewind**, and input cannot be directly followed by output without an intervening **fseek**, **rewind**, or an input that encounters end-of-file.

shflag specifies the type of file-sharing allowed on the file *filename*. The file-sharing flags are ignored if the DOS SHARE command has not been run. Symbolic constants for *shflag* are defined in share.h.

Value of *shflag*	What it does
SH_COMPAT	Sets compatibility mode
SH_DENYRW	Denies read/write access
SH_DENYWR	Denies write access
SH_DENYRD	Denies read access
SH_DENYNONE	Permits read/write access
SH_DENYNO	Permits read/write access

Return value On successful completion, **_fsopen** returns a pointer to the newly opened stream. In the event of error, it returns null.

See also **creat**, **_dos_open**, **dup**, **fclose**, **fdopen**, **ferror**, *_fmode* (global variable), **fopen**, **fread**, **freopen**, **fseek**, **fwrite**, **open**, **rewind**, **setbuf**, **setmode**, **sopen**

Example

```
#include <io.h>
#include <process.h>
#include <share.h>
#include <stdio.h>

int main(void)
{
   FILE *f;
   int status;
   f = _fsopen("c:\\test.$$$", "r", SH_DENYNO);
   if (f == NULL) {
     printf("_fsopen failed\n");
     exit(1);
   }
   status = access("c:\\test.$$$", 6);
   if (status == 0)
     printf("read/write access allowed\n");
   else
     printf("read/write access not allowed\n");
   fclose(f);
   return 0;
}
```

fstat, stat

Function Gets open file information.

Syntax #include <sys\stat.h>
int fstat(int *handle*, struct stat **statbuf*);

int stat(char **path*, struct *stat* **statbuf*);

DOS	UNIX	Windows	ANSI C	C++ only
■	■	■		

Remarks **fstat** stores information in the **stat** structure about the open file or directory associated with *handle*.

stat stores information about a given file or directory in the **stat** structure.

statbuf points to the **stat** structure (defined in sys\stat.h). That structure contains the following fields:

- *st_mode* Bit mask giving information about the open file's mode
- *st_dev* Drive number of disk containing the file, or file handle if the file is on a device
- *st_rdev* Same as *st_dev*
- *st_nlink* Set to the integer constant 1
- *st_size* Size of the open file in bytes
- *st_atime* Most recent time the open file was modified
- *st_mtime* Same as *st_atime*
- *st_ctime* Same as *st_atime*

The **stat** structure contains three more fields not mentioned here. They contain values that are not meaningful under DOS.

The bit mask that gives information about the mode of the open file includes the following bits:

One of the following bits will be set

- S_IFCHR If *handle* refers to a device.
- S_IFREG If an ordinary file is referred to by *handle*.

One or both of the following bits will be set

- S_IWRITE If user has permission to write to file.
- S_IREAD If user has permission to read to file.

The bit mask also includes the read/write bits; these are set according to the file's permission mode.

Return value **fstat** and **stat** return 0 if they successfully retrieved the information about the open file. On error (failure to get the information), these functions return –1 and set the global variable *errno* to

EBADF	Bad file handle

See also **access, chmod**

Example

```
#include <stdio.h>
#include <io.h>
#include <stdlib.h>
#include <fcntl.h>
#include <sys\stat.h>

struct stat statbuf;

void pstat(void)
{
    if (statbuf.st_mode & S_IWRITE)
        printf("File is writable\n");
    if (statbuf.st_mode & S_IREAD)
        printf("File is readable\n");
    if (statbuf.st_mode & S_IFREG)
        printf("File is a regular file\n");
    if (statbuf.st_mode & S_IFCHR)
        printf("File is a character device\n");
    if (statbuf.st_mode & S_IFDIR)
        printf("File is a directory\n");
}

void main(int argc, char **argv) {
    char *infilename;
    int infile;

    if (argc != 2) {
        printf("Usage: fstatest filename\n");
        exit(1);
    }
    infilename = argv[1];

    if ((infile = open(infilename,O_RDONLY)) == -1)
        perror("Unable to open file for reading");
    else {
        if (fstat(infile,&statbuf) != 0) {
            perror("Unable to fstat");
            exit(1);
        }
        close(infile);
        printf("Results of fstat:\n");
        pstat();
    }

    if (stat(infilename,&statbuf) != 0)
        perror("Unable to stat");
    else {
```

```
        printf("Results of stat:\n");
        pstat();
    }
    exit(0);
}
```


_fstr*

See **strcat**, **strchr**, **strcspn**, **strdup**, **stricmp**, **strlen**, **strlwr**, **strncat**, **strncmp**, **strncpy**, **strnicmp**, **strnset**, **strpbrk**, **strrchr**, **strrev**, **strset**, **strspn**, **strstr**, **strtok**, and **strupr** for descriptions of the far versions of each of these functions.

ftell

Function Returns the current file pointer.

Syntax #include <stdio.h>
long int ftell(FILE **stream*);

DOS	UNIX	Windows	ANSI C	C++ only
■	■	■	■	

Remarks **ftell** returns the current file pointer for *stream*. The offset is measured in bytes from the beginning of the file (if the file is binary).

The value returned by **ftell** can be used in a subsequent call to **fseek**.

Return value **ftell** returns the current file pointer position on success. It returns –1L on error and sets the global variable *errno* to a positive value.

See also **fgetpos**, **fseek**, **fsetpos**, **lseek**, **rewind**, **tell**

Example

```
#include <stdio.h>

int main(void)
{
   FILE *stream;
   stream = fopen("MYFILE.TXT", "w+");
   fprintf(stream, "This is a test");
   printf("The file pointer is at byte %ld\n", ftell(stream));
   fclose(stream);
   return 0;
}
```

ftime

Function Stores current time in **timeb** structure.

Syntax #include <sys\timeb.h>
void ftime(struct timeb **buf*)

DOS	UNIX	Windows	ANSI C	C++ only
■	■	■		

Remarks On UNIX platforms, **ftime** is only available on System V systems.

ftime determines the current time and fills in the fields in the **timeb** structure pointed to by *buf*. The **timeb** structure contains four fields: *time, millitm, timezone,* and *dstflag*:

```
struct timeb {
   long time ;
   short millitm ;
   short timezone ;

   short dstflag ;
};
```

- *time* provides the time in seconds since 00:00:00 Greenwich mean time (GMT), January 1, 1970.
- *millitm* is the fractional part of a second in milliseconds.
- *timezone* is the difference in minutes between GMT and the local time. This value is computed going west from GMT. **ftime** gets this field from the global variable *timezone,* which is set by **tzset**.
- *dstflag* is used to indicate whether daylight saving time will be taken into account during time calculations.

ftime calls **tzset**. Therefore, it isn't necessary to call **tzset** explicitly when you use **ftime**.

Return value None.

See also **asctime, ctime, gmtime, localtime, stime, time, tzset**

Example

```
#include <stdio.h>
#include <stdlib.h>
#include <time.h>
#include <sys\timeb.h>

/* pacific standard & daylight savings */
char *tzstr = "TZ=PST8PDT";

int main(void)
```

```
{
   struct timeb t;
   putenv(tzstr);
   tzset();
   ftime(&t);
   printf("Seconds since 1/1/1970 GMT: %ld\n", t.time);
   printf("Thousandths of a second: %d\n", t.millitm);
   printf("Difference between local time and GMT: %d\n", t.timezone);
   printf("Daylight savings in effect (1) not (0): %d\n", t.dstflag);
   return 0;
}
```


_fullpath

Function Convert a path name from relative to absolute.

Syntax #include <stdlib.h>
char * _fullpath(char **buffer*, const char **path*, int *buflen*);

DOS	UNIX	Windows	ANSI C	C++ only
■		■		

Remarks **_fullpath** converts the relative path name in *path* to an absolute path name that is stored in the array of characters pointed to by *buffer*. The maximum number of characters that can be stored at *buffer* is *buflen*. The function returns NULL if the buffer isn't big enough to store the absolute path name, or if the path contains an invalid drive letter.

If *buffer* is NULL, the **_fullpath** allocates a buffer of up to _MAX_PATH characters. This buffer should be freed using **free** when it is no longer needed. _MAX_PATH is defined in stdlib.h

Return value If successful, the **_fullpath** function returns a pointer to the buffer containing the absolute path name. Otherwise, it returns NULL.

See also **_makepath, _splitpath**

Example

```
#include <stdio.h>
#include <stdlib.h>

void main(int argc, char *argv[])
{
char buf[_MAX_PATH];
    for ( ; argc; argv++, argc--) {
        if (_fullpath(buf, argv[0], _MAX_PATH) == NULL)
            printf("Unable to obtain full path of %s\n",argv[0]);
        else
```

```
            printf("Full path of %s is %s\n",argv[0],buf);
    }
}
```

fwrite

Function Writes to a stream.

Syntax #include <stdio.h>
size_t fwrite(const void **ptr*, size_t *size*, size_t *n*, FILE **stream*);

DOS	UNIX	Windows	ANSI C	C++ only
■	■	■	■	

Remarks **fwrite** appends *n* items of data, each of length *size* bytes, to the given output file. The data written begins at *ptr*.

The total number of bytes written is ($n \times size$).

ptr in the declarations is a pointer to any object.

Return value On successful completion, **fwrite** returns the number of items (not bytes) actually written. It returns a short count on error.

See also **fopen, fread**

Example

```
#include <stdio.h>

struct mystruct
{
  int i;
  char ch;
};

int main(void)
{
   FILE *stream;
   struct mystruct s;

   /* open file TEST.$$$ */
   if ((stream = fopen("TEST.$$$", "wb")) == NULL) {
      fprintf(stderr, "Cannot open output file.\n");
      return 1;
   }
   s.i = 0;
   s.ch = 'A';
   fwrite(&s, sizeof(s), 1, stream); /* write struct s to file */
   fclose(stream);                   /* close file */
```

```
    return 0;
}
```

gcvt

F

Function Converts floating-point number to a string.

Syntax #include <stdlib.h>
char *gcvt(double *value*, int *ndec*, char **buf*);

DOS	UNIX	Windows	ANSI C	C++ only
■	■	■		

Remarks **gcvt** converts *value* to a null-terminated ASCII string and stores the string in *buf*. It produces *ndec* significant digits in FORTRAN F format, if possible; otherwise, it returns the value in the **printf** E format (ready for printing). It might suppress trailing zeros.

Return value **gcvt** returns the address of the string pointed to by *buf*.

See also **ecvt, fcvt, sprintf**

Example

```
#include <stdlib.h>
#include <stdio.h>

int main(void)
{
   char str[25];
   double num;
   int sig = 5; /* significant digits */

   /* a regular number */
   num = 9.876;
   gcvt(num, sig, str);
   printf("string = %s\n", str);

   /* a negative number */
   num = -123.4567;
   gcvt(num, sig, str);
   printf("string = %s\n", str);

   /* scientific notation */
   num = 0.678e5;
   gcvt(num, sig, str);
   printf("string = %s\n", str);
   return(0);
}
```

geninterrupt

Function Generates a software interrupt.

Syntax #include <dos.h>
void geninterrupt(int *intr_num*);

DOS	UNIX	Windows	ANSI C	C++ only
■		■		

Remarks The **geninterrupt** macro triggers a software trap for the interrupt given by *intr_num*. The state of all registers after the call depends on the interrupt called.

➡ Interrupts can leave registers used by C in unpredictable states.

Return value None.

See also **bdos, bdosptr, disable, enable, getvect, int86, int86x, intdos, intdosx, intr**

Example

```
#include <conio.h>
#include <dos.h>

void writechar(char ch);  /* function prototype */

int main(void)
{
   clrscr();
   gotoxy(80,25);
   writechar('*');
   getch();
   return 0;
}

/* outputs a character at the current cursor position */
/* using the video BIOS to avoid scrolling of the screen */
/* when writing to location (80,25) */

void writechar(char ch) {
   struct text_info ti;
   gettextinfo(&ti);      /* grab current text settings */
   _AH = 9;               /* interrupt 0x10 sub-function 9 */
   _AL = ch;              /* character to be output */
   _BH = 0;               /* video page */
   _BL = ti.attribute;    /* video attribute */
   _CX = 1;               /* repetition factor */
   geninterrupt(0x10);    /* output the char */
}
```

G

getarccoords

Function Gets coordinates of the last call to **arc**.

Syntax #include <graphics.h>
void far getarccoords(struct arccoordstype far **arccoords*);

DOS	UNIX	Windows	ANSI C	C++ only
■				

Remarks **getarccoords** fills in the **arccoordstype** structure pointed to by *arccoords* with information about the last call to **arc**. The **arccoordstype** structure is defined in graphics.h as follows:

```
struct arccoordstype {
   int x, y;
   int xstart, ystart, xend, yend;
};
```

The members of this structure are used to specify the center point (*x*,*y*), the starting position (*xstart*, *ystart*), and the ending position (*xend*, *yend*) of the arc. These values are useful if you need to make a line meet at the end of an arc.

Return value None.

See also **arc, fillellipse, sector**

Example

```
#include <graphics.h>
#include <stdlib.h>
#include <stdio.h>
#include <conio.h>

int main(void)
{
   /* request autodetection */
   int gdriver = DETECT, gmode, errorcode;
   struct arccoordstype arcinfo;
   int midx, midy;
   int stangle = 45, endangle = 270;
   char sstr[80], estr[80];

   /* initialize graphics and local variables */
   initgraph(&gdriver, &gmode, "");

   /* read result of initialization */
   errorcode = graphresult();
```

```
   if (errorcode != grOk) {  /* an error occurred */
      printf("Graphics error: %s\n", grapherrormsg(errorcode));
      printf("Press any key to halt:");
      getch();
      exit(1);               /* terminate with an error code */
   }

   midx = getmaxx() / 2;
   midy = getmaxy() / 2;

   /* draw arc and get coordinates */
   setcolor(getmaxcolor());
   arc(midx, midy, stangle, endangle, 100);
   getarccoords(&arcinfo);

   /* convert arc information into strings */
   sprintf(sstr, "*- (%d, %d)", arcinfo.xstart, arcinfo.ystart);
   sprintf(estr, "*- (%d, %d)", arcinfo.xend, arcinfo.yend);

   /* output the arc information */
   outtextxy(arcinfo.xstart, arcinfo.ystart, sstr);
   outtextxy(arcinfo.xend, arcinfo.yend, estr);

   /* clean up */
   getch();

   closegraph();
   return 0;
}
```

getaspectratio

Function Retrieves the current graphics mode's aspect ratio.

Syntax #include <graphics.h>
void far getaspectratio(int far **xasp*, int far **yasp*);

DOS	UNIX	Windows	ANSI C	C++ only
■				

Remarks The *y* aspect factor, **yasp*, is normalized to 10,000. On all graphics adapters except the VGA, **xasp* (the *x* aspect factor) is less than **yasp* because the pixels are taller than they are wide. On the VGA, which has "square" pixels, **xasp* equals **yasp*. In general, the relationship between **yasp* and **xasp* can be stated as

**yasp* = 10,000
**xasp* <= 10,000

getaspectratio gets the values in **xasp* and **yasp*.

Return value None.

See also **arc, circle, ellipse, fillellipse, pieslice, sector, setaspectratio**

Example

```
#include <graphics.h>
#include <stdlib.h>
#include <stdio.h>
#include <conio.h>

main()
{
   /* request autodetection */
   int gdriver = DETECT, gmode, errorcode;
   int xasp, yasp, midx, midy;


   /* initialize graphics and local variables */
   initgraph(&gdriver, &gmode, "");

   /* read result of initialization */
   errorcode = graphresult();
   if (errorcode != grOk) {  /* an error occurred */
      printf("Graphics error: %s\n", grapherrormsg(errorcode));
      printf("Press any key to halt:");
      getch();
      exit(1);               /* terminate with an error code */
   }

   midx = getmaxx() / 2;
   midy = getmaxy() / 2;
   setcolor(getmaxcolor());

   /* get current aspect ratio settings */
   getaspectratio(&xasp, &yasp);

   /* draw normal circle */
   circle(midx, midy, 100);
   getch();

   /* draw wide circle */
   cleardevice();
   setaspectratio(xasp/2, yasp);
   circle(midx, midy, 100);
   getch();

   /* draw narrow circle */
   cleardevice();
   setaspectratio(xasp, yasp/2);
   circle(midx, midy, 100);

   /* clean up */
```

```
    getch();
    closegraph();
    return 0;
}
```

getbkcolor

Function Returns the current background color.

Syntax #include <graphics.h>
int far getbkcolor(void);

DOS	UNIX	Windows	ANSI C	C++ only
■				

Remarks **getbkcolor** returns the current background color. (See the table under **setbkcolor** for details.)

Return value **getbkcolor** returns the current background color.

See also **getcolor, getmaxcolor, getpalette, setbkcolor**

Example

```
#include <graphics.h>
#include <stdlib.h>
#include <string.h>
#include <stdio.h>
#include <conio.h>

int main(void)
{
   /* request autodetection */
   int gdriver = DETECT, gmode, errorcode;
   int bkcolor, midx, midy;
   char bkname[35];

   /* initialize graphics and local variables */
   initgraph(&gdriver, &gmode, "");

   /* read result of initialization */
   errorcode = graphresult();
   if (errorcode != grOk) {  /* an error occurred */
      printf("Graphics error: %s\n", grapherrormsg(errorcode));
      printf("Press any key to halt:");
      getch();
      exit(1);               /* terminate with an error code */
   }

   midx = getmaxx() / 2;
   midy = getmaxy() / 2;
```

```
   setcolor(getmaxcolor());

   /* for centering text on the display */
   settextjustify(CENTER_TEXT, CENTER_TEXT);

   /* get the current background color */
   bkcolor = getbkcolor();

   /* convert color value into a string */
   itoa(bkcolor, bkname, 10);
   strcat(bkname, " is the current background color.");


   /* display a message */
   outtextxy(midx, midy, bkname);

   /* clean up */
   getch();
   closegraph();
   return 0;
}
```

getc

Function Gets character from stream.

Syntax #include <stdio.h>
int getc(FILE **stream*);

DOS	UNIX	Windows	ANSI C	C++ only
■	■	■	■	

Remarks **getc** is a macro that returns the next character on the given input stream and increments the stream's file pointer to point to the next character.

Return value On success, **getc** returns the character read, after converting it to an **int** without sign extension. On end-of-file or error, it returns EOF.

See also **fgetc, getch, getchar, getche, gets, putc, putchar, ungetc**

Example

```
#include <stdio.h>

int main(void)
{
   char ch;
   printf("Input a character:");

   /* read a character from the standard input stream */
   ch = getc(stdin);
   printf("The character input was: '%c'\n", ch);
```

```
   return 0;
}
```

getcbrk

Function Gets control-break setting.

Syntax #include <dos.h>
int getcbrk(void);

DOS	UNIX	Windows	ANSI C	C++ only
■		■		

Remarks **getcbrk** uses the DOS system call 0x33 to return the current setting of control-break checking.

Return value **getcbrk** returns 0 if control-break checking is off, or 1 if checking is on.

See also **ctrlbrk, setcbrk**

Example

```
#include <stdio.h>
#include <dos.h>

int main(void)
{
   if (getcbrk())
      printf("Cntrl-brk flag is on\n");
   else
      printf("Cntrl-brk flag is off\n");
   return 0;
}
```

getch

Function Gets character from keyboard, does not echo to screen.

Syntax #include <conio.h>
int getch(void);

DOS	UNIX	Windows	ANSI C	C++ only
■				

Remarks **getch** reads a single character directly from the keyboard, without echoing to the screen.

Return value **getch** returns the character read from the keyboard.

See also **cgets, cscanf, fgetc, getc, getchar, getche, getpass, kbhit, putch, ungetch**

Example

```
#include <conio.h>
#include <stdio.h>

int main(void)
{
   int c;
   int extended = 0;
   c = getch();
   if (!c)
      extended = getch();
   if (extended)
      printf("The character is extended\n");
   else
      printf("The character isn't extended\n");

   return 0;
}
```


getchar

Function Gets character from stdin.

Syntax #include <stdio.h>
int getchar(void);

DOS	UNIX	Windows	ANSI C	C++ only
■	■		■	

Remarks **getchar** is a macro that returns the next character on the named input stream stdin. It is defined to be **getc**(*stdin*).

Return value On success, **getchar** returns the character read, after converting it to an **int** without sign extension. On end-of-file or error, it returns EOF.

See also **fgetc, fgetchar, getc, getch, getche, gets, putc, putchar, scanf, ungetc**

Example

```
#include <stdio.h>

int main(void)
{
   int c;

   /* Note that getchar reads from stdin and is line buffered; */
   /* this means it will not return until you press <ENTER> */
   while ((c = getchar()) != '\n')
      printf("%c", c);
```

```
    return 0;
}
```

getche

Function Gets character from the keyboard, echoes to screen.

Syntax #include <conio.h>
int getche(void);

DOS	UNIX	Windows	ANSI C	C++ only
■				

Remarks **getche** reads a single character from the keyboard and echoes it to the current text window, using direct video or BIOS.

Return value **getche** returns the character read from the keyboard.

See also **cgets**, **cscanf**, **fgetc**, **getc**, **getch**, **getchar**, **kbhit**, **putch**, **ungetch**

Example

```
#include <stdio.h>
#include <conio.h>

int main(void)
{
   char ch;
   printf("Input a character:");
   ch = getche();
   printf("\nYou input a '%c'\n", ch);
   return 0;
}
```

getcolor

Function Returns the current drawing color.

Syntax #include <graphics.h>
int far getcolor(void);

DOS	UNIX	Windows	ANSI C	C++ only
■				

Remarks **getcolor** returns the current drawing color.

The drawing color is the value to which pixels are set when lines and so on are drawn. For example, in CGAC0 mode, the palette contains four colors: the background color, light green, light red, and yellow. In this mode, if **getcolor** returns 1, the current drawing color is light green.

Return value **getcolor** returns the current drawing color.

See also **getbkcolor, getmaxcolor, getpalette, setcolor**

Example

```
#include <graphics.h>
#include <stdlib.h>
#include <string.h>
#include <stdio.h>
#include <conio.h>

int main(void)
{
   /* request autodetection */
   int gdriver = DETECT, gmode, errorcode;
   int color, midx, midy;
   char colname[35];

   /* initialize graphics and local variables */
   initgraph(&gdriver, &gmode, "");

   /* read result of initialization */
   errorcode = graphresult();
   if (errorcode != grOk) {  /* an error occurred */
      printf("Graphics error: %s\n", grapherrormsg(errorcode));
      printf("Press any key to halt:");
      getch();
      exit(1);               /* terminate with an error code */
   }

   midx = getmaxx() / 2;
   midy = getmaxy() / 2;
   setcolor(getmaxcolor());

   /* for centering text on the display */
   settextjustify(CENTER_TEXT, CENTER_TEXT);

   /* get the current drawing color */
   color = getcolor();

   /* convert color value into a string */
   itoa(color, colname, 10);
   strcat(colname, " is the current drawing color.");

   /* display a message */
   outtextxy(midx, midy, colname);

   /* clean up */
   getch();
   closegraph();
```

```
   return 0;
}
```

getcurdir

Function Gets current directory for specified drive.

Syntax #include <dir.h>
int getcurdir(int *drive*, char **directory*);

DOS	UNIX	Windows	ANSI C	C++ only
■		■		

Remarks **getcurdir** gets the name of the current working directory for the drive indicated by *drive*.

drive specifies a drive number (0 for default, 1 for A, and so on).

directory points to an area of memory of length MAXDIR where the null-terminated directory name will be placed. The name does not contain the drive specification and does not begin with a backslash.

Return value **getcurdir** returns 0 on success or –1 in the event of error.

See also **chdir**, **getcwd**, **getdisk**, **mkdir**, **rmdir**

getcwd

Function Gets current working directory.

Syntax #include <dir.h>
char *getcwd(char **buf*, int *buflen*);

DOS	UNIX	Windows	ANSI C	C++ only
■		■		

Remarks **getcwd** gets the full path name (including the drive) of the current working directory, up to *buflen* bytes long and stores it in *buf*. If the full path name length (including the null terminator) is longer than *buflen* bytes, an error occurs.

If *buf* is null, a buffer *buflen* bytes long is allocated for you with **malloc**. You can later free the allocated buffer by passing the return value of **getcwd** to the function **free**.

Return value **getcwd** returns the following values:

- If *buf* is not null on input, **getcwd** returns *buf* on success, null on error.
- If *buf* is null on input, **getcwd** returns a pointer to the allocated buffer.

In the event of an error return, the global variable *errno* is set to one of the following:

ENODEV	No such device
ENOMEM	Not enough core
ERANGE	Result out of range

G

See also **chdir, getcurdir, _getdcwd, getdisk, mkdir, rmdir**

Example

```
#include <stdio.h>
#include <dir.h>

int main(void)
{
   char buffer[MAXPATH];
   getcwd(buffer, MAXPATH);
   printf("The current directory is: %s\n", buffer);
   return 0;
}
```

getdate, _dos_getdate, _dos_setdate, setdate

Function Gets and sets system date.

Syntax
#include <dos.h>
void getdate(struct date **datep*);
void _dos_getdate(struct dosdate_t **datep*);
void setdate(struct date **datep*);
unsigned _dos_setdate(struct dosdate_t **datep*);

DOS	UNIX	Windows	ANSI C	C++ only
■		■		

Remarks **getdate** fills in the **date** structure (pointed to by *datep*) with the system's current date.

setdate sets the system date (month, day, and year) to that in the **date** structure pointed to by *datep*.

The **date** structure is defined as follows:

```
struct date {
```

```
      int da_year;     /* current year */
      char da_day;     /* day of the month */
      char da_mon;     /* month (1 = Jan) */
   };
```

_dos_getdate fills in the **dosdate_t** structure (pointed to by *datep*) with the system's current date.

The **dosdate_t** structure is defined as follows:

```
   struct dosdate_t {
      unsigned char day;        /* 1-31 */
      unsigned char month;      /* 1-12 */
      unsigned int  year;       /* 1980 - 2099 */
      unsigned char dayofweek; /* 0 - 6 (0=Sunday) */
   };
```

Return value **_dos_getdate, getdate**, and **setdate**, do not return a value.

If the date is set successfully, **_dos_setdate** returns 0. Otherwise, it returns a non-zero value and the global variable *errno* is set to the following:

EINVAL   Invalid date

See also **ctime, gettime, settime**

Example

```
#include <dos.h>
#include <process.h>
#include <stdio.h>

int main(void)
{
   struct dosdate_t reset;
   reset.year  = 2001;
   reset.day   = 1;
   reset.month = 1;
   printf("Setting date to 1/1/2001.\n");
   _dos_setdate(&reset);
   _dos_getdate(&reset);
   printf("The new year is: %d\n", reset.year);
   printf("The new day is: %d\n", reset.day);
   printf("The new month is: %d\n", reset.month);
   return 0;
}
```

_getdcwd

Function Gets current directory for specified drive.

Syntax #include <direct.h>
char * _getdcwd(int *drive*, char **buffer*, int *buflen*);

DOS	UNIX	Windows	ANSI C	C++ only
■		■		

Remarks **_getdcwd** gets the full path name of the working directory of the specified drive (including the drive name), up to *buflen* bytes long, and stores it in *buffer*. If the full path name length (including the null-terminator) is longer than *buflen*, an error occurs. The *drive* is 0 for the default drive, 1=A, 2=B, etc.

If *buffer* is NULL, **_getdcwd** will allocate a buffer at least *buflen* bytes long. You can later free the allocated buffer by passing the **_getdcwd** return value to the **free** function.

Return value If successful, **_getdcwd** returns a pointer to the buffer containing the current directory for the specified drive. Otherwise it returns NULL, and sets the global variable *errno* to one of the following:

ENOMEM	Not enough memory to allocate a buffer (*buffer* is NULL)
ERANGE	Directory name longer than *buflen* (*buffer* is not NULL)

See also **chdir, getcwd, _getdrive, mkdir, rmdir**

Example

```
#include <direct.h>
#include <stdio.h>

void main()
{
   char buf[65];
   if (_getdcwd(3, buf, sizeof(buf)) == NULL)
      perror("Unable to get current directory of drive C");
   else
      printf("Current directory of drive C is %s\n",buf);
}
```

getdefaultpalette

Function Returns the palette definition structure.

Syntax #include <graphics.h>
struct palettetype *far getdefaultpalette(void);

DOS	UNIX	Windows	ANSI C	C++ only
■				

Remarks **getdefaultpalette** finds the **palettetype** structure that contains the palette initialized by the driver during **initgraph**.

Return value **getdefaultpalette** returns a pointer to the default palette set up by the current driver when that driver was initialized.

See also **getpalette, initgraph**

Example

```
#include <graphics.h>
#include <stdlib.h>
#include <stdio.h>
#include <conio.h>

int main(void)
{
   /* request autodetection */
   int gdriver = DETECT, gmode, errorcode;

   /* far pointer to palette structure */
   struct palettetype far *pal = NULL;
   int i;

   /* initialize graphics and local variables */
   initgraph(&gdriver, &gmode, "");

   /* read result of initialization */
   errorcode = graphresult();
   if (errorcode != grOk) {  /* an error occurred */
      printf("Graphics error: %s\n", grapherrormsg(errorcode));
      printf("Press any key to halt:");
      getch();
      exit(1);               /* terminate with an error code */
   }

   /* return a pointer to the default palette */
   pal = getdefaultpalette();
   for (i=0; i<pal->size; i++) {
      printf("colors[%d] = %d\n", i, pal->colors[i]);
      getch();
   }

   /* clean up */
   getch();
   closegraph();
   return 0;
}
```

getdfree

Function Gets disk free space.

Syntax #include <dos.h>
void getdfree(unsigned char *drive*, struct dfree **dtable*);

DOS	UNIX	Windows	ANSI C	C++ only
■		■		

G

Remarks **getdfree** accepts a drive specifier in *drive* (0 for default, 1 for A, and so on) and fills the **dfree** structure pointed to by *dtable* with disk attributes.

The **dfree** structure is defined as follows:

```
struct dfree {
   unsigned df_avail;      /* available clusters */
   unsigned df_total;      /* total clusters */
   unsigned df_bsec;       /* bytes per sector */
   unsigned df_sclus;      /* sectors per cluster */
};
```

Return value **getdfree** returns no value. In the event of an error, *df_sclus* in the **dfree** structure is set to 0xFFFF.

See also **getfat, getfatd**

Example

```
#include <stdio.h>
#include <stdlib.h>
#include <dir.h>
#include <dos.h>
int main(void)
{
   struct dfree free;
   long avail;
   int drive;
   drive = getdisk();
   getdfree(drive+1, &free);
   if (free.df_sclus == 0xFFFF) {
      printf("Error in getdfree() call\n");
      exit(1);
   }
   avail = (long) free.df_avail * (long) free.df_bsec * (long) free.df_sclus;
   printf("Drive %c: has %ld bytes available\n", 'A' + drive, avail);
   return 0;
}
```

getdisk, setdisk

Function Gets or set the current drive number.

Syntax #include <dir.h>
int getdisk(void);
int setdisk(int *drive*);

DOS	UNIX	Windows	ANSI C	C++ only
■		■		

Remarks **getdisk** gets the current drive number. It returns an integer: 0 for A, 1 for B, 2 for C, and so on (equivalent to DOS function 0x19).

setdisk sets the current drive to the one associated with *drive*: 0 for A, 1 for B, 2 for C, and so on (equivalent to DOS call 0x0E).

Return value **getdisk** returns the current drive number.
setdisk returns the total number of drives available.

See also **getcurdir**, **getcwd**

Example

```
#include <stdio.h>
#include <dir.h>

int main(void)
{
   int disk, maxdrives = setdisk(2);
   disk = getdisk() + 'A';
   printf("\nThe number of logical drives is:%d\n", maxdrives);
   printf("The current drive is: %c\n", disk);
   return 0;
}
```

_getdrive

Function Gets current drive number.

Syntax #include <direct.h>
int _getdrive(void);

DOS	UNIX	Windows	ANSI C	C++ only
■		■		

Remarks **_getdrive** uses DOS function 0x19 to get the current drive number. It returns an integer: 1 for A, 2 for B, 2 for 3, and so on.

Return value **_getdrive** returns the current drive number.

See also **_dos_getdrive, _dos_setdrive, _getdcwd**

Example

```
#include <stdio.h>
#include <direct.h>

int main(void)
{
   int disk;
   disk = _getdrive() + 'A' - 1;
   printf("The current drive is: %c\n", disk);
   return 0;
}
```


getdrivername

Function Returns a pointer to a string containing the name of the current graphics driver.

Syntax #include <graphics.h>
char *far getdrivername(void);

DOS	UNIX	Windows	ANSI C	C++ only
■				

Remarks After a call to **initgraph**, **getdrivername** returns the name of the driver that is currently loaded.

Return value **getdrivername** returns a pointer to a string with the name of the currently loaded graphics driver.

See also **initgraph**

Example

```
#include <graphics.h>
#include <stdlib.h>
#include <stdio.h>
#include <conio.h>

int main()
{
   /* request autodetection */
   int gdriver = DETECT, gmode, errorcode;

   /* stores the device driver name */
   char *drivername;

   /* initialize graphics and local variables */
   initgraph(&gdriver, &gmode, "");
```

```
   /* read result of initialization */
   errorcode = graphresult();
   if (errorcode != grOk) { /* an error occurred */
      printf("Graphics error: %s\n", grapherrormsg(errorcode));
      printf("Press any key to halt:");
      getch();
      exit(1);               /* terminate with an error code */
   }
   setcolor(getmaxcolor());

   /* get the name of the device driver in use */
   drivername = getdrivername();

   /* for centering text onscreen */
   settextjustify(CENTER_TEXT, CENTER_TEXT);

   /* output the name of the driver */
   outtextxy(getmaxx() / 2, getmaxy() / 2, drivername);

   /* clean up */
   getch();
   closegraph();
   return 0;
}
```

getdta

Function Gets disk transfer address.

Syntax #include <dos.h>
char far *getdta(void);

DOS	UNIX	Windows	ANSI C	C++ only
■		■		

Remarks **getdta** returns the current setting of the disk transfer address (DTA).

In the small and medium memory models, it's assumed the segment is the current data segment. If you use C exclusively, this will be the case, but assembly routines can set the DTA to any hardware address.

In the compact, large, or huge memory models, the address returned by **getdta** is the correct hardware address and can be located outside the program.

Return value **getdta** returns a far pointer to the current DTA.

See also **fcb** (structure), **setdta**

Example

```
#include <dos.h>
#include <stdio.h>

int main(void)
{
   char far *dta;
   dta = getdta();
   printf("The current disk transfer address is: %Fp\n", dta);
   return 0;
}
```

G

getenv

Function Gets a string from environment.

Syntax #include <stdlib.h>
char *getenv(const char **name*);

DOS	UNIX	Windows	ANSI C	C++ only
■	■	■	■	

Remarks **getenv** returns the value of a specified variable. On DOS, *name* must be uppercase. On other systems, *name* can be either uppercase or lowercase. *name* must not include the equal sign (**=**). If the specified environment variable does not exist, **getenv** returns a NULL pointer.

Return value On success, **getenv** returns the value associated with *name*. If the specified *name* is not defined in the environment, **getenv** returns a NULL pointer.

➡ Environment entries must not be changed directly. If you want to change an environment value, you must use **putenv**.

See also *environ* (global variable), **getpsp**, **putenv**

Example

```
#include <stdlib.h>
#include <stdio.h>

int main(void)
{
   char *s;

/* get the comspec environment parameter */
   s=getenv("COMSPEC");

/* display comspec parameter */
   printf("Command processor: %s\n",s);
   return 0;
}
```

getfat

Function Gets file allocation table information for given drive.

Syntax #include <dos.h>
void getfat(unsigned char *drive*, struct fatinfo **dtable*);

DOS	UNIX	Windows	ANSI C	C++ only
■		■		

Remarks **getfat** gets information from the file allocation table (FAT) for the drive specified by *drive* (0 for default, 1 for A, 2 for B, and so on). *dtable* points to the **fatinfo** structure to be filled in. The **fatinfo** structure filled in by **getfat** is defined as follows:

```
struct fatinfo {
   char fi_sclus;          /* sectors per cluster */
   char fi_fatid;          /* the FAT id byte */
   unsigned fi_nclus;      /* number of clusters */
   int fi_bysec;           /* bytes per sector */
};
```

Return value None.

See also **getdfree, getfatd**

Example

```
#include <stdio.h>
#include <conio.h>
#include <dos.h>

int main()
{
   struct fatinfo diskinfo;
   int flag = 0;
   printf("Please insert a diskette in drive 'A'\n");
   getch();
   getfat(1, &diskinfo); /* get drive information */
   printf("\nDrive A: is ");
   switch((unsigned char) diskinfo.fi_fatid) {
      case 0xFD: printf("a 360K low density\n");
                 break;
      case 0xF9: printf("a 1.2 Meg 5-1/4\" or 720 K 3-1/2\"\n");
                 break;
      case 0xF0: printf("1.44 Meg 3-1/2\"\n");
                 break;
      default:   printf("unformatted\n");
                 flag = 1;
   }
```

```
   if (!flag) {
      printf("sectors per cluster: %5d\n", diskinfo.fi_sclus);
      printf("number of clusters:  %5d\n", diskinfo.fi_nclus);
      printf("bytes per sector:    %5d\n", diskinfo.fi_bysec);
   }
   return 0;
}
```

getfatd

G

Function Gets file allocation table information.

Syntax #include <dos.h>
void getfatd(struct fatinfo **dtable*);

DOS	UNIX	Windows	ANSI C	C++ only
■		■		

Remarks **getfatd** gets information from the file allocation table (FAT) of the default drive. *dtable* points to the **fatinfo** structure to be filled in. The **fatinfo** structure filled in by **getfatd** is defined as follows:

```
struct fatinfo {
   char fi_sclus;      /* sectors per cluster */
   char fi_fatid;      /* the FAT id byte */
   int fi_nclus;       /* number of clusters */
   int fi_bysec;       /* bytes per sector */
};
```

Return value None.

See also **getdfree, getfat**

Example

```
#include <stdio.h>
#include <dos.h>
int main()
{
   struct fatinfo diskinfo;
   /* get default drive information */
   getfatd(&diskinfo);
   printf("\nDefault Drive:\n");
   printf("sectors per cluster: %5d\n",diskinfo.fi_sclus);
   printf("FAT ID byte:         %5X\n",diskinfo.fi_fatid & 0xFF);
   printf("number of clusters   %5d\n",diskinfo.fi_nclus);
   printf("bytes per sector     %5d\n",diskinfo.fi_bysec);
   return 0;
}
```

getfillpattern

Function Copies a user-defined fill pattern into memory.

Syntax #include <graphics.h>
void far getfillpattern(char far **pattern*);

DOS	UNIX	Windows	ANSI C	C++ only
■				

Remarks **getfillpattern** copies the user-defined fill pattern, as set by **setfillpattern**, into the 8-byte area pointed to by *pattern*.

pattern is a pointer to a sequence of 8 bytes, with each byte corresponding to 8 pixels in the pattern. Whenever a bit in a pattern byte is set to 1, the corresponding pixel will be plotted. For example, the following user-defined fill pattern represents a checkerboard:

```
char checkboard[8] = {
   0xAA, 0x55, 0xAA, 0x55, 0xAA, 0x55, 0xAA, 0x55
};
```

Return value None.

See also **getfillsettings, setfillpattern**

Example

```
#include <graphics.h>
#include <stdlib.h>
#include <stdio.h>
#include <conio.h>

int main(void)
{
   /* request autodetection */
   int gdriver = DETECT, gmode, errorcode;
   int maxx, maxy;
   char pattern[8] = {0x00, 0x70, 0x20, 0x27, 0x25, 0x27, 0x04, 0x04};

   /* initialize graphics and local variables */
   initgraph(&gdriver, &gmode, "");

   /* read result of initialization */
   errorcode = graphresult();
   if (errorcode != grOk) {  /* an error occurred */
      printf("Graphics error: %s\n", grapherrormsg(errorcode));
      printf("Press any key to halt:");
      getch();
```

```
      exit(1);                /* terminate with an error code */
   }

   maxx = getmaxx();
   maxy = getmaxy();
   setcolor(getmaxcolor());

   /* select a user-defined fill pattern */
   setfillpattern(pattern, getmaxcolor());

   /* fill the screen with the pattern */
   bar(0, 0, maxx, maxy);
   getch();

   /* get the current user-defined fill pattern */
   getfillpattern(pattern);


   /* alter the pattern we grabbed */
   pattern[4] -= 1;
   pattern[5] -= 3;
   pattern[6] += 3;
   pattern[7] -= 4;

   /* select our new pattern */
   setfillpattern(pattern, getmaxcolor());

   /* fill the screen with the new pattern */
   bar(0, 0, maxx, maxy);

   /* clean up */
   getch();
   closegraph();
   return 0;
}
```

G

getfillsettings

Function Gets information about current fill pattern and color.

Syntax #include <graphics.h>
void far getfillsettings(struct fillsettingstype far **fillinfo*);

DOS	UNIX	Windows	ANSI C	C++ only
■				

Remarks **getfillsettings** fills in the **fillsettingstype** structure pointed to by *fillinfo* with information about the current fill pattern and fill color. The **fillsettingstype** structure is defined in graphics.h as follows:

```
struct fillsettingstype {
   int pattern;           /* current fill pattern */
   int color;             /* current fill color */
};
```

The functions **bar**, **bar3d**, **fillpoly**, **floodfill**, and **pieslice** all fill an area with the current fill pattern in the current fill color. There are 11 predefined fill pattern styles (such as solid, crosshatch, dotted, and so on). Symbolic names for the predefined patterns are provided by the enumerated type *fill_patterns* in graphics.h (see the following table). In addition, you can define your own fill pattern.

If *pattern* equals 12 (USER_FILL), then a user-defined fill pattern is being used; otherwise, *pattern* gives the number of a predefined pattern.

The enumerated type *fill_patterns*, defined in graphics.h, gives names for the predefined fill patterns, plus an indicator for a user-defined pattern.

Name	Value	Description
EMPTY_FILL	0	Fill with background color
SOLID_FILL	1	Solid fill
LINE_FILL	2	Fill with ——
LTSLASH_FILL	3	Fill with ///
SLASH_FILL	4	Fill with ///, thick lines
BKSLASH_FILL	5	Fill with \\\, thick lines
LTBKSLASH_FILL	6	Fill with \\\
HATCH_FILL	7	Light hatch fill
XHATCH_FILL	8	Heavy crosshatch fill
INTERLEAVE_FILL	9	Interleaving line fill
WIDE_DOT_FILL	10	Widely spaced dot fill
CLOSE_DOT_FILL	11	Closely spaced dot fill
USER_FILL	12	User-defined fill pattern

All but EMPTY_FILL fill with the current fill color; EMPTY_FILL uses the current background color.

Return value None.

See also **getfillpattern**, **setfillpattern**, **setfillstyle**

Example

```
#include <graphics.h>
#include <stdlib.h>
#include <stdio.h>
#include <conio.h>

/* the names of the fill styles supported */
char *fname[] = { "EMPTY_FILL", "SOLID_FILL", "LINE_FILL", "LTSLASH_FILL",
                  "SLASH_FILL", "BKSLASH_FILL", "LTBKSLASH_FILL", "HATCH_FILL",
                  "XHATCH_FILL", "INTERLEAVE_FILL", "WIDE_DOT_FILL",
                  "CLOSE_DOT_FILL", "USER_FILL" };
```

```
int main(void)
{
   /* request autodetection */
   int gdriver = DETECT, gmode, errorcode;
   struct fillsettingstype fillinfo;
   int midx, midy;
   char patstr[40], colstr[40];

   /* initialize graphics and local variables */
   initgraph(&gdriver, &gmode, "");

   /* read result of initialization */
   errorcode = graphresult();
   if (errorcode != grOk) {  /* an error occurred */
      printf("Graphics error: %s\n", grapherrormsg(errorcode));
      printf("Press any key to halt:");
      getch();
      exit(1);               /* terminate with an error code */
   }

   midx = getmaxx() / 2;
   midy = getmaxy() / 2;

   /* get info about current fill pattern and color */
   getfillsettings(&fillinfo);

   /* convert fill information into strings */
   sprintf(patstr, "%s is the fill style.", fname[fillinfo.pattern]);
   sprintf(colstr, "%d is the fill color.", fillinfo.color);

   /* display the information */
   settextjustify(CENTER_TEXT, CENTER_TEXT);
   outtextxy(midx, midy, patstr);
   outtextxy(midx, midy+2*textheight("W"), colstr);

   /* clean up */
   getch();
   closegraph();
   return 0;
}
```

getftime, setftime

Function Gets and set the file date and time.

Syntax #include <io.h>
int getftime(int *handle*, struct ftime **ftimep*);
int setftime(int *handle*, struct ftime **ftimep*);

DOS	UNIX	Windows	ANSI C	C++ only
■		■		

Remarks **getftime** retrieves the file time and date for the disk file associated with the open *handle*. The **ftime** structure pointed to by *ftimep* is filled in with the file's time and date.

setftime sets the file date and time of the disk file associated with the open *handle* to the date and time in the **ftime** structure pointed to by *ftimep*. The file must not be written to after the **setftime** call or the changed information will be lost.

The **ftime** structure is defined as follows:

```
struct ftime {
   unsigned ft_tsec: 5;        /* two seconds */
   unsigned ft_min: 6;         /* minutes */
   unsigned ft_hour: 5;        /* hours */
   unsigned ft_day: 5;         /* days */
   unsigned ft_month: 4;       /* months */
   unsigned ft_year: 7;        /* year - 1980*/
};
```

Return value **getftime** and **setftime** return 0 on success.

In the event of an error return, –1 is returned and the global variable *errno* is set to one of the following:

EINVFNC	Invalid function number
EBADF	Bad file number

See also **fflush, open, setftime**

Example

```
#include <stdio.h>
#include <io.h>

int main()
{
   FILE *stream;
   struct ftime ft;

   printf("Creating new file TEST.$$$\n");
   if ((stream = fopen("TEST.$$$", "wt")) == NULL) {
      printf("Cannot open output file.\n");
      return 1;
   }
   if (getftime(fileno(stream), &ft) != 0) {
      perror("Unable to get file time");
      return 1;
   }
```

```
    printf("File time: %02u:%02u:%02u\n",
           ft.ft_hour, ft.ft_min, ft.ft_tsec * 2);
    printf("File date: %02u/%02u/%04u\n",
           ft.ft_month, ft.ft_day, ft.ft_year+1980);
    printf("Setting file year to 2001.\n");
    ft.ft_year = 2001 - 1980;
    if (setftime(fileno(stream), &ft) != 0)
       perror("Unable to set file time");
    fclose(stream);
    return 0;
}
```

G

getgraphmode

Function Returns the current graphics mode.

Syntax #include <graphics.h>
int far getgraphmode(void);

DOS	UNIX	Windows	ANSI C	C++ only
■				

Remarks Your program must make a successful call to **initgraph** before calling **getgraphmode**.

The enumeration *graphics_mode*, defined in graphics.h, gives names for the predefined graphics modes. For a table listing these enumeration values, refer to the description for **initgraph**.

Return value **getgraphmode** returns the graphics mode set by **initgraph** or **setgraphmode**.

See also **getmoderange, restorecrtmode, setgraphmode**

Example

```
#include <graphics.h>
#include <stdlib.h>
#include <stdio.h>
#include <conio.h>

int main(void)
{
    /* request autodetection */
    int gdriver = DETECT, gmode, errorcode;
    int midx, midy, mode;
    char numname[80], modename[80];

    /* initialize graphics and local variables */
    initgraph(&gdriver, &gmode, "");
```

```
   /* read result of initialization */
   errorcode = graphresult();
   if (errorcode != grOk) {  /* an error occurred */
      printf("Graphics error: %s\n", grapherrormsg(errorcode));
      printf("Press any key to halt:");
      getch();
      exit(1);               /* terminate with an error code */
   }

   midx = getmaxx() / 2;
   midy = getmaxy() / 2;

   /* get mode number and name strings */
   mode = getgraphmode();
   sprintf(numname, "%d is the current mode number.", mode);
   sprintf(modename, "%s is the current graphics mode.", getmodename(mode));

   /* display the information */
   settextjustify(CENTER_TEXT, CENTER_TEXT);
   outtextxy(midx, midy, numname);
   outtextxy(midx, midy+2*textheight("W"), modename);

   /* clean up */
   getch();
   closegraph();
   return 0;
}
```

getimage

Function Saves a bit image of the specified region into memory.

Syntax #include <graphics.h>
void far getimage(int *left*, int *top*, int *right*, int *bottom*, void far **bitmap*);

DOS	UNIX	Windows	ANSI C	C++ only
■				

Remarks **getimage** copies an image from the screen to memory.

left, *top*, *right*, and *bottom* define the screen area to which the rectangle is copied. *bitmap* points to the area in memory where the bit image is stored. The first two words of this area are used for the width and height of the rectangle; the remainder holds the image itself.

Return value None.

See also **imagesize, putimage, putpixel**

Example

```
#include <graphics.h>
#include <stdlib.h>
#include <stdio.h>
#include <conio.h>
#include <alloc.h>

void save_screen(void far *buf[4]);
void restore_screen(void far *buf[4]);

int maxx, maxy;
int main(void)
{
   int gdriver=DETECT, gmode, errorcode;
   void far *ptr[4];

   /* autodetect the graphics driver and mode */
   initgraph(&gdriver, &gmode, "");
   errorcode = graphresult();  /* check for any errors */
   if (errorcode != grOk) {
      printf("Graphics error: %s\n", grapherrormsg(errorcode));
      printf("Press any key to halt:");
      getch();
      exit(1);
   }

   maxx = getmaxx();
   maxy = getmaxy();

   /* draw an image on the screen */
   rectangle(0, 0, maxx, maxy);
   line(0, 0, maxx, maxy);
   line(0, maxy, maxx, 0);
   save_screen(ptr);              /* save the current screen */
   getch();                       /* pause screen */
   cleardevice();                 /* clear screen */
   restore_screen(ptr);           /* restore the screen */
   getch();                       /* pause screen */
   closegraph();
   return 0;
}

void save_screen(void far *buf[4])
{
   unsigned size;
   int ystart=0, yend, yincr, block;
   yincr = (maxy+1) / 4;
   yend = yincr;

   /* get byte size of image */
   size = imagesize(0, ystart, maxx, yend);
   for (block=0; block<=3; block++) {
```

```
      if ((buf[block] = farmalloc(size)) == NULL) {
         closegraph();
         printf("Error: not enough heap space in save_screen().\n");
         exit(1);
      }
      getimage(0, ystart, maxx, yend, buf[block]);
      ystart = yend + 1;
      yend += yincr + 1;
   }
}

void restore_screen(void far *buf[4])
{
   int ystart=0, yend, yincr, block;
   yincr = (maxy+1) / 4;
   yend = yincr;
   for (block=0; block<=3; block++) {
      putimage(0, ystart, buf[block], COPY_PUT);
      farfree(buf[block]);
      ystart = yend + 1;

      yend += yincr + 1;
   }
}
```

getlinesettings

Function Gets the current line style, pattern, and thickness.

Syntax #include <graphics.h>
void far getlinesettings(struct linesettingstype far **lineinfo*);

DOS	UNIX	Windows	ANSI C	C++ only
■				

Remarks **getlinesettings** fills a **linesettingstype** structure pointed to by *lineinfo* with information about the current line style, pattern, and thickness.

The **linesettingstype** structure is defined in graphics.h as follows:

```
struct linesettingstype {
   int linestyle;
   unsigned upattern;
   int thickness;
};
```

linestyle specifies in which style subsequent lines will be drawn (such as solid, dotted, centered, dashed). The enumeration *line_styles*, defined in graphics.h, gives names to these operators:

Name	Value	Description
SOLID_LINE	0	Solid line
DOTTED_LINE	1	Dotted line
CENTER_LINE	2	Centered line
DASHED_LINE	3	Dashed line
USERBIT_LINE	4	User-defined line style

thickness specifies whether the width of subsequent lines drawn will be normal or thick.

Name	Value	Description
NORM_WIDTH	1	1 pixel wide
THICK_WIDTH	3	3 pixels wide

upattern is a 16-bit pattern that applies only if *linestyle* is USERBIT_LINE (4). In that case, whenever a bit in the pattern word is 1, the corresponding pixel in the line is drawn in the current drawing color. For example, a solid line corresponds to a *upattern* of 0xFFFF (all pixels drawn), while a dashed line can correspond to a *upattern* of 0x3333 or 0x0F0F. If the *linestyle* parameter to **setlinestyle** is not USERBIT_LINE (!=4), the *upattern* parameter must still be supplied but is ignored.

Return value None.

See also **setlinestyle**

Example

```
#include <graphics.h>
#include <stdlib.h>
#include <stdio.h>
#include <conio.h>

/* the names of the line styles supported */
char *lname[] = { "SOLID_LINE", "DOTTED_LINE", "CENTER_LINE", "DASHED_LINE",
                  "USERBIT_LINE" };

int main(void)
{
   /* request autodetection */
   int gdriver = DETECT, gmode, errorcode;
   struct linesettingstype lineinfo;
   int midx, midy;
   char lstyle[80], lpattern[80], lwidth[80];
```

```
   /* initialize graphics and local variables */
   initgraph(&gdriver, &gmode, "");

   /* read result of initialization */
   errorcode = graphresult();
   if (errorcode != grOk) {  /* an error occurred */
      printf("Graphics error: %s\n", grapherrormsg(errorcode));
      printf("Press any key to halt:");
      getch();
      exit(1);               /* terminate with an error code */
   }

   midx = getmaxx() / 2;
   midy = getmaxy() / 2;

   /* get information about current line settings */
   getlinesettings(&lineinfo);

   /* convert line information into strings */
   sprintf(lstyle, "%s is the line style.", lname[lineinfo.linestyle]);
   sprintf(lpattern, "0x%X is the user-defined line pattern.",
           lineinfo.upattern);
   sprintf(lwidth, "%d is the line thickness.", lineinfo.thickness);

   /* display the information */
   settextjustify(CENTER_TEXT, CENTER_TEXT);
   outtextxy(midx, midy, lstyle);
   outtextxy(midx, midy+2*textheight("W"), lpattern);
   outtextxy(midx, midy+4*textheight("W"), lwidth);

   /* clean up */
   getch();
   closegraph();
   return 0;
}
```

getmaxcolor

Function Returns maximum color value that can be passed to the **setcolor** function.

Syntax #include <graphics.h>
int far getmaxcolor(void);

DOS	UNIX	Windows	ANSI C	C++ only
▪				

Remarks **getmaxcolor** returns the highest valid color value for the current graphics driver and mode that can be passed to **setcolor**.

For example, on a 256K EGA, **getmaxcolor** always returns 15, which means that any call to **setcolor** with a value from 0 to 15 is valid. On a CGA in high-resolution mode or on a Hercules monochrome adapter, **getmaxcolor** returns a value of 1.

Return value **getmaxcolor** returns the highest available color value.

See also **getbkcolor, getcolor, getpalette, getpalettesize, setcolor**

Example

```
#include <graphics.h>
#include <stdlib.h>
#include <stdio.h>
#include <conio.h>

int main(void)
{
   /* request autodetection */
   int gdriver = DETECT, gmode, errorcode;
   int midx, midy;
   char colstr[80];

   /* initialize graphics and local variables */
   initgraph(&gdriver, &gmode, "");

   /* read result of initialization */
   errorcode = graphresult();
   if (errorcode != grOk) {  /* an error occurred */
      printf("Graphics error: %s\n", grapherrormsg(errorcode));
      printf("Press any key to halt:");
      getch();
      exit(1);               /* terminate with an error code */
   }

   midx = getmaxx() / 2;
   midy = getmaxy() / 2;

   /* grab the color info. and convert it to a string */
   sprintf(colstr, "This mode supports colors 0..%d", getmaxcolor());

   /* display the information */
   settextjustify(CENTER_TEXT, CENTER_TEXT);
   outtextxy(midx, midy, colstr);

   /* clean up */
   getch();
   closegraph();
   return 0;
}
```

G

getmaxmode

Function Returns the maximum mode number for the current driver.

Syntax #include <graphics.h>
int far getmaxmode(void);

DOS	UNIX	Windows	ANSI C	C++ only
■				

Remarks **getmaxmode** lets you find out the maximum mode number for the currently loaded driver, directly from the driver. This gives it an advantage over **getmoderange**, which works for Borland drivers only. The minimum mode is 0.

Return value **getmaxmode** returns the maximum mode number for the current driver.

See also **getmodename, getmoderange**

Example

```
#include <graphics.h>
#include <stdlib.h>
#include <stdio.h>
#include <conio.h>

int main(void)
{
   /* request autodetection */
   int gdriver = DETECT, gmode, errorcode;
   int midx, midy;
   char modestr[80];

   /* initialize graphics and local variables */
   initgraph(&gdriver, &gmode, "");

   /* read result of initialization */
   errorcode = graphresult();
   if (errorcode != grOk) {  /* an error occurred */
      printf("Graphics error: %s\n", grapherrormsg(errorcode));
      printf("Press any key to halt:");
      getch();
      exit(1);               /* terminate with an error code */
   }

   midx = getmaxx() / 2;
   midy = getmaxy() / 2;

   /* grab the mode info. and convert it to a string */
   sprintf(modestr, "This driver supports modes 0..%d", getmaxmode());

   /* display the information */
```

```
    settextjustify(CENTER_TEXT, CENTER_TEXT);
    outtextxy(midx, midy, modestr);

    /* clean up */
    getch();
    closegraph();
    return 0;
}
```

G

getmaxx

Function Returns maximum *x* screen coordinate.

Syntax #include <graphics.h>
int far getmaxx(void);

DOS	UNIX	Windows	ANSI C	C++ only
■				

Remarks **getmaxx** returns the maximum (screen-relative) *x* value for the current graphics driver and mode.

For example, on a CGA in 320×200 mode, **getmaxx** returns 319. **getmaxx** is invaluable for centering, determining the boundaries of a region onscreen, and so on.

Return value **getmaxx** returns the maximum *x* screen coordinate.

See also **getmaxy**, **getx**

Example

```
#include <graphics.h>
#include <stdlib.h>
#include <stdio.h>
#include <conio.h>

int main(void)
{
   /* request autodetection */
   int gdriver = DETECT, gmode, errorcode;
   int midx, midy;
   char xrange[80], yrange[80];

   /* initialize graphics and local variables */
   initgraph(&gdriver, &gmode, "");

   /* read result of initialization */
   errorcode = graphresult();
   if (errorcode != grOk) {   /* an error occurred */
```

```
      printf("Graphics error: %s\n", grapherrormsg(errorcode));
      printf("Press any key to halt:");
      getch();
      exit(1);             /* terminate with an error code */
   }

   midx = getmaxx() / 2;
   midy = getmaxy() / 2;

   /* convert max resolution values to strings */
   sprintf(xrange, "X values range from 0..%d", getmaxx());
   sprintf(yrange, "Y values range from 0..%d", getmaxy());

   /* display the information */
   settextjustify(CENTER_TEXT, CENTER_TEXT);
   outtextxy(midx, midy, xrange);
   outtextxy(midx, midy + textheight("W"), yrange);

   /* clean up */
   getch();
   closegraph();
   return 0;
}
```

getmaxy

Function Returns maximum *y* screen coordinate.

Syntax #include <graphics.h>
int far getmaxy(void);

DOS	UNIX	Windows	ANSI C	C++ only
■				

Remarks **getmaxy** returns the maximum (screen-relative) *y* value for the current graphics driver and mode.

For example, on a CGA in 320×200 mode, **getmaxy** returns 199. **getmaxy** is invaluable for centering, determining the boundaries of a region onscreen, and so on.

Return value **getmaxy** returns the maximum *y* screen coordinate.

See also **getmaxx, getx, gety**

Example

```
#include <graphics.h>
#include <stdlib.h>
#include <stdio.h>
#include <conio.h>
```

```
int main(void)
{
  /* request autodetection */
  int gdriver = DETECT, gmode, errorcode;
  int midx, midy;
  char xrange[80], yrange[80];

  /* initialize graphics and local variables */
  initgraph(&gdriver, &gmode, "");

  /* read result of initialization */
  errorcode = graphresult();
  if (errorcode != grOk) {     /* an error occurred */
     printf("Graphics error: %s\n", grapherrormsg(errorcode));
     printf("Press any key to halt:");
     getch();
     exit(1);                /* terminate with an error code */
  }

  midx = getmaxx() / 2;
  midy = getmaxy() / 2;

  /* convert max resolution values into strings */
  sprintf(xrange, "X values range from 0..%d", getmaxx());
  sprintf(yrange, "Y values range from 0..%d", getmaxy());

  /* display the information */
  settextjustify(CENTER_TEXT, CENTER_TEXT);
  outtextxy(midx, midy, xrange);
  outtextxy(midx, midy+textheight("W"), yrange);

  /* clean up */
  getch();
  closegraph();
  return 0;
}
```


getmodename

Function Returns a pointer to a string containing the name of a specified graphics mode.

Syntax #include <graphics.h>
char *far getmodename(int *mode_number*);

DOS	UNIX	Windows	ANSI C	C++ only
■				

Remarks **getmodename** accepts a graphics mode number as input and returns a string containing the name of the corresponding graphics mode. The mode names are embedded in each driver. The return values ("320×200 CGA P1," "640×200 CGA", and so on) are useful for building menus or displaying status.

Return value **getmodename** returns a pointer to a string with the name of the graphics mode.

See also **getmaxmode, getmoderange**

Example

```
#include <graphics.h>
#include <stdlib.h>
#include <stdio.h>
#include <conio.h>

int main(void)
{
   /* request autodetection */
   int gdriver = DETECT, gmode, errorcode;
   int midx, midy, mode;
   char numname[80], modename[80];

   /* initialize graphics and local variables */
   initgraph(&gdriver, &gmode, "");

   /* read result of initialization */
   errorcode = graphresult();
   if (errorcode != grOk) {  /* an error occurred */
      printf("Graphics error: %s\n", grapherrormsg(errorcode));
      printf("Press any key to halt:");
      getch();
      exit(1);               /* terminate with an error code */
   }
   midx = getmaxx() / 2;
   midy = getmaxy() / 2;

   /* get mode number and name strings */
   mode = getgraphmode();
   sprintf(numname, "%d is the current mode number.", mode);
   sprintf(modename, "%s is the current graphics mode.", getmodename(mode));

   /* display the information */
   settextjustify(CENTER_TEXT, CENTER_TEXT);
   outtextxy(midx, midy, numname);
   outtextxy(midx, midy+2*textheight("W"), modename);

   /* clean up */
   getch();
   closegraph();
```

```
    return 0;
}
```

getmoderange

Function Gets the range of modes for a given graphics driver.

Syntax #include <graphics.h>
void far getmoderange(int *graphdriver*, int far **lomode*, int far **himode*);

DOS	UNIX	Windows	ANSI C	C++ only
■				

G

Remarks **getmoderange** gets the range of valid graphics modes for the given graphics driver, *graphdriver*. The lowest permissible mode value is returned in **lomode*, and the highest permissible value is **himode*. If *graphdriver* specifies an invalid graphics driver, both **lomode* and **himode* are set to –1. If the value of *graphdriver* is –1, the currently loaded driver modes are given.

Return value None.

See also **getgraphmode, getmaxmode, getmodename, initgraph, setgraphmode**

Example

```
#include <graphics.h>
#include <stdlib.h>
#include <stdio.h>
#include <conio.h>

int main(void)
{
   /* request autodetection */
   int gdriver = DETECT, gmode, errorcode;
   int midx, midy;
   int low, high;
   char mrange[80];

   /* initialize graphics and local variables */
   initgraph(&gdriver, &gmode, "");

   /* read result of initialization */
   errorcode = graphresult();
   if (errorcode != grOk) {  /* an error occurred */
         printf("Graphics error: %s\n", grapherrormsg(errorcode));
         printf("Press any key to halt:");
         getch();
         exit(1);             /* terminate with an error code */
   }
```

```
    midx = getmaxx() / 2;
    midy = getmaxy() / 2;

    /* get the mode range for this driver */
    getmoderange(gdriver, &low, &high);

    /* convert mode range info. into strings */
    sprintf(mrange, "This driver supports modes %d..%d", low, high);

    /* display the information */
    settextjustify(CENTER_TEXT, CENTER_TEXT);
    outtextxy(midx, midy, mrange);

    /* clean up */
    getch();
    closegraph();
    return 0;
}
```

getpalette

Function Gets information about the current palette.

Syntax #include <graphics.h>
void far getpalette(struct palettetype far **palette*);

DOS	UNIX	Windows	ANSI C	C++ only
■				

Remarks **getpalette** fills the **palettetype** structure pointed to by *palette* with information about the current palette's size and colors.

The MAXCOLORS constant and the **palettetype** structure used by **getpalette** are defined in graphics.h as follows:

```
#define MAXCOLORS  15

struct palettetype {
   unsigned char size;
   signed char colors[MAXCOLORS + 1];
};
```

size gives the number of colors in the palette for the current graphics driver in the current mode.

colors is an array of *size* bytes containing the actual raw color numbers for each entry in the palette.

➡ **getpalette** cannot be used with the IBM-8514 driver.

Return value None.

See also **getbkcolor, getcolor, getdefaultpalette, getmaxcolor, setallpalette, setpalette**

Example

```
#include <graphics.h>
#include <stdlib.h>
#include <stdio.h>
#include <conio.h>

int main()
{
   /* request autodetection */
   int gdriver = DETECT, gmode, errorcode;
   struct palettetype pal;
   char psize[80], pval[20];
   int i, ht;
   int y = 10;

   /* initialize graphics and local variables */
   initgraph(&gdriver, &gmode, "");

   /* read result of initialization */
   errorcode = graphresult();
   if (errorcode != grOk) {  /* an error occurred */
      printf("Graphics error: %s\n", grapherrormsg(errorcode));
      printf("Press any key to halt:");
      getch();
      exit(1);               /* terminate with an error code */
   }

   /* grab a copy of the palette */
   getpalette(&pal);

   /* convert palette info into strings */
   sprintf(psize, "The palette has %d modifiable entries.", pal.size);

   /* display the information */
   outtextxy(0, y, psize);
   if (pal.size != 0) {
      ht = textheight("W");
      y += 2*ht;
      outtextxy(0, y, "Here are the current values:");
      y += 2*ht;
      for (i=0; i<pal.size; i++, y+=ht) {
         sprintf(pval, "palette[%02d]: 0x%02X", i, pal.colors[i]);
         outtextxy(0, y, pval);
      }
   }

   /* clean up */
```

```
   getch();
   closegraph();
   return 0;
}
```

getpalettesize

Function Returns size of palette color lookup table.

Syntax #include <graphics.h>
int far getpalettesize(void);

DOS	UNIX	Windows	ANSI C	C++ only
■				

Remarks **getpalettesize** is used to determine how many palette entries can be set for the current graphics mode. For example, the EGA in color mode returns 16.

Return value **getpalettesize** returns the number of palette entries in the current palette.

See also **setpalette, setallpalette**

Example

```
#include <graphics.h>
#include <stdlib.h>
#include <stdio.h>
#include <conio.h>

int main()
{
   /* request autodetection */
   int gdriver = DETECT, gmode, errorcode;
   int midx, midy;
   char psize[80];

   /* initialize graphics and local variables */
   initgraph(&gdriver, &gmode, "");

   /* read result of initialization */
   errorcode = graphresult();
   if (errorcode != grOk) {  /* an error occurred */
      printf("Graphics error: %s\n", grapherrormsg(errorcode));
      printf("Press any key to halt:");
      getch();
      exit(1);              /* terminate with an error code */
   }

   midx = getmaxx() / 2;
   midy = getmaxy() / 2;
```

```
    /* convert palette size info into string */
    sprintf(psize, "The palette has %d modifiable entries.", getpalettesize());

    /* display the information */
    settextjustify(CENTER_TEXT, CENTER_TEXT);
    outtextxy(midx, midy, psize);

    /* clean up */
    getch();
    closegraph();
    return 0;
}
```

G

getpass

Function Reads a password.

Syntax #include <conio.h>
char *getpass(const char **prompt*);

DOS	UNIX	Windows	ANSI C	C++ only
■	■			

Remarks **getpass** reads a password from the system console, after prompting with the null-terminated string *prompt* and disabling the echo. A pointer is returned to a null-terminated string of up to eight characters (not counting the null-terminator).

Return value The return value is a pointer to a static string, which is overwritten with each call.

See also **getch**

Example

```
#include <conio.h>

int main()
{
   char *password;
   password = getpass("Input a password:");
   cprintf("The password is: %s\r\n", password);
   return 0;
}
```

getpid

Function Gets the process ID of a program.

Syntax #include <process.h>
unsigned getpid(void)

DOS	UNIX	Windows	ANSI C	C++ only
■	■	■		

Remarks A process ID uniquely identifies a program. The concept is borrowed from multitasking operating systems like UNIX, where each process is associated with a unique process number.

Return value **getpid** returns the segment value of a program's PSP.

See also **getpsp**, *_psp* (global variable)

Example

```
#include <stdio.h>
#include <process.h>

int main()
{
   printf("This program's process identification number (PID) "
          "number is %X\n", getpid());
   printf("Note: under DOS it is the PSP segment\n");
   return 0;
}
```

getpixel

Function Gets the color of a specified pixel.

Syntax #include <graphics.h>
unsigned far getpixel(int *x*, int *y*);

DOS	UNIX	Windows	ANSI C	C++ only
■				

Remarks **getpixel** gets the color of the pixel located at (*x*,*y*).

Return value **getpixel** returns the color of the given pixel.

See also **getimage, putpixel**

Example

```
#include <graphics.h>
#include <stdlib.h>
#include <stdio.h>
#include <conio.h>
#include <dos.h>
```

```
#define PIXEL_COUNT 1000
#define DELAY_TIME  100  /* in milliseconds */

int main(void)
{
   /* request autodetection */
   int gdriver = DETECT, gmode, errorcode;
   int i, x, y, color, maxx, maxy, maxcolor, seed;

   /* initialize graphics and local variables */
   initgraph(&gdriver, &gmode, "");

   /* read result of initialization */
   errorcode = graphresult();
   if (errorcode != grOk) {  /* an error occurred */
      printf("Graphics error: %s\n", grapherrormsg(errorcode));
      printf("Press any key to halt:");
      getch();
      exit(1);               /* terminate with an error code */
   }

   maxx = getmaxx() + 1;
   maxy = getmaxy() + 1;
   maxcolor = getmaxcolor() + 1;
   while (!kbhit()) {
      seed = random(32767);  /* seed the random number generator */
      srand(seed);
      for (i=0; i<PIXEL_COUNT; i++) {
         x = random(maxx);
         y = random(maxy);
         color = random(maxcolor);
         putpixel(x, y, color);
      }
      delay(DELAY_TIME);
      srand(seed);
      for (i=0; i<PIXEL_COUNT; i++) {
         x = random(maxx);
         y = random(maxy);
         color = random(maxcolor);
         if (color == getpixel(x, y))
            putpixel(x, y, 0);
      }
   }

   /* clean up */
   getch();
   closegraph();
   return 0;
}
```

G

getpsp

Function Gets the program segment prefix.

Syntax #include <dos.h>
unsigned getpsp(void);

DOS	UNIX	Windows	ANSI C	C++ only
■		■		

Remarks **getpsp** gets the segment address of the program segment prefix (PSP) using DOS call 0x62.

Return value **getpsp** returns the address of the Program Segment Prefix (PSP).

See also **getenv**, *_psp* (global variable)

Example

```
#include <stdio.h>
#include <dos.h>

int main(void)
{
   static char command[128];
   char far *cp;
   int len, i;
   printf("The program segment prefix is: %x\n", getpsp());

   /* _psp is preset to the segment of the Program Segment Prefix (PSP).
     The remainder of the command line is located at offset 0x80
     from the start of PSP. Try passing this program arguments. */
   cp = MK_FP(_psp, 0x80);
   len = *cp;
   for (i = 0; i < len; i++)
      command[i] = cp[i+1];
   printf("Command line: %s\n", command);
   return 0;
}
```

gets

Function Gets a string from stdin.

Syntax #include <stdio.h>
char *gets(char *s);

DOS	UNIX	Windows	ANSI C	C++ only
■	■		■	

Remarks **gets** collects a string of characters terminated by a new line from the standard input stream stdin and puts it into *s*. The new line is replaced by a null character (\0) in *s*.

gets allows input strings to contain certain whitespace characters (spaces, tabs). **gets** returns when it encounters a new line; everything up to the new line is copied into *s*.

Return value On success, **gets** returns the string argument *s*; it returns null on end-of-file or error.

See also **cgets, ferror, fgets, fopen, fputs, fread, getc, puts, scanf**

Example

```
#include <stdio.h>

int main(void)
{
   char string[80];
   printf("Input a string:");
   gets(string);
   printf("The string input was: %s\n", string);
   return 0;
}
```

G

gettext

Function Copies text from text mode screen to memory.

Syntax #include <conio.h>
int gettext(int *left*, int *top*, int *right*, int *bottom*, void **destin*);

DOS	UNIX	Windows	ANSI C	C++ only
■				

Remarks **gettext** stores the contents of an onscreen text rectangle defined by *left*, *top*, *right*, and *bottom* into the area of memory pointed to by *destin*.

All coordinates are absolute screen coordinates, not window-relative. The upper left corner is (1,1).

gettext reads the contents of the rectangle into memory sequentially from left to right and top to bottom.

Each position onscreen takes 2 bytes of memory: The first byte is the character in the cell, and the second is the cell's video attribute. The space required for a rectangle *w* columns wide by *h* rows high is defined as *bytes* = (*h* rows) × (*w* columns) × 2

Return value **gettext** returns 1 if the operation succeeds. It returns 0 if it fails (for example, if you gave coordinates outside the range of the current screen mode).

See also **movetext, puttext**

Example

```
#include <conio.h>

char buffer[4096];

int main(void)
{
   int i;
   clrscr();
   for (i = 0; i <= 20; i++)
      cprintf("Line #%d\r\n", i);
   gettext(1, 1, 80, 25, buffer);
   gotoxy(1, 25);
   cprintf("Press any key to clear screen...");
   getch();
   clrscr();
   gotoxy(1, 25);
   cprintf("Press any key to restore screen...");
   getch();
   puttext(1, 1, 80, 25, buffer);
   gotoxy(1, 25);
   cprintf("Press any key to quit...");
   getch();
   return 0;
}
```

gettextinfo

Function Gets text mode video information.

Syntax #include <conio.h>
void gettextinfo(struct text_info **r*);

DOS	UNIX	Windows	ANSI C	C++ only
■				

Remarks **gettextinfo** fills in the **text_info** structure pointed to by *r* with the current text video information.

The **text_info** structure is defined in conio.h as follows:

```
struct text_info {
   unsigned char winleft;         /* left window coordinate */
   unsigned char wintop;          /* top window coordinate */
   unsigned char winright;        /* right window coordinate */
   unsigned char winbottom;       /* bottom window coordinate */
   unsigned char attribute;       /* text attribute */
   unsigned char normattr;        /* normal attribute */
   unsigned char currmode;        /* BW40, BW80, C40, C80, or C4350 */
   unsigned char screenheight;    /* text screen's height */
   unsigned char screenwidth;     /* text screen's width */
   unsigned char curx;            /* x-coordinate in current window */
   unsigned char cury;            /* y-coordinate in current window */
};
```

G

Return value **gettextinfo** returns nothing; the results are returned in the structure pointed to by *r*.

See also **textattr, textbackground, textcolor, textmode, wherex, wherey, window**

Example

```
#include <conio.h>

int main(void)
{
   struct text_info ti;
   gettextinfo(&ti);
   cprintf("window left      %2d\r\n",ti.winleft);
   cprintf("window top       %2d\r\n",ti.wintop);
   cprintf("window right     %2d\r\n",ti.winright);
   cprintf("window bottom    %2d\r\n",ti.winbottom);
   cprintf("attribute        %2d\r\n",ti.attribute);
   cprintf("normal attribute %2d\r\n",ti.normattr);
   cprintf("current mode     %2d\r\n",ti.currmode);
   cprintf("screen height    %2d\r\n",ti.screenheight);
   cprintf("screen width     %2d\r\n",ti.screenwidth);
   cprintf("current x        %2d\r\n",ti.curx);
   cprintf("current y        %2d\r\n",ti.cury);
   return 0;
}
```

gettextsettings

Function Gets information about the current graphics text font.

Syntax #include <graphics.h>
void far gettextsettings(struct textsettingstype far **texttypeinfo*);

DOS	UNIX	Windows	ANSI C	C++ only
■				

Remarks **gettextsettings** fills the **textsettingstype** structure pointed to by *textinfo* with information about the current text font, direction, size, and justification.

The **textsettingstype** structure used by **gettextsettings** is defined in graphics.h as follows:

```
struct textsettingstype {
   int font;
   int direction;
   int charsize;
   int horiz;
   int vert;
};
```

See **settextstyle** for a description of these fields.

Return value None.

See also **outtext**, **outtextxy**, **registerbgifont**, **settextjustify**, **settextstyle**, **setusercharsize**, **textheight**, **textwidth**

Example

```
#include <graphics.h>
#include <stdlib.h>
#include <stdio.h>
#include <conio.h>

/* the names of the supported fonts */
char *font[] = { "DEFAULT_FONT", "TRIPLEX_FONT", "SMALL_FONT", "SANS_SERIF_FONT",
                 "GOTHIC_FONT" };

/* the names of the text directions supported */
char *dir[] = { "HORIZ_DIR", "VERT_DIR" };

/* horizontal text justifications supported */
char *hjust[] = { "LEFT_TEXT", "CENTER_TEXT", "RIGHT_TEXT" };

/* vertical text justifications supported */
char *vjust[] = { "BOTTOM_TEXT", "CENTER_TEXT", "TOP_TEXT" };

int main(void)
{
   /* request autodetection */
   int gdriver = DETECT, gmode, errorcode;
   struct textsettingstype textinfo;
   int midx, midy, ht;
   char fontstr[80], dirstr[80], sizestr[80];
```

```
   char hjuststr[80], vjuststr[80];

   /* initialize graphics and local variables */
   initgraph(&gdriver, &gmode, "");

   /* read result of initialization */
   errorcode = graphresult();
   if (errorcode != grOk) {  /* an error occurred */
      printf("Graphics error: %s\n", grapherrormsg(errorcode));
      printf("Press any key to halt:");
      getch();
      exit(1);               /* terminate with an error code */
   }

   midx = getmaxx() / 2;
   midy = getmaxy() / 2;

   /* get information about current text settings */
   gettextsettings(&textinfo);

   /* convert text information into strings */
   sprintf(fontstr, "%s is the text style.", font[textinfo.font]);
   sprintf(dirstr, "%s is the text direction.", dir[textinfo.direction]);
   sprintf(sizestr, "%d is the text size.", textinfo.charsize);
   sprintf(hjuststr, "%s is the horizontal justification.",
           hjust[textinfo.horiz]);
   sprintf(vjuststr, "%s is the vertical justification.", vjust[textinfo.vert]);

   /* display the information */
   ht = textheight("W");
   settextjustify(CENTER_TEXT, CENTER_TEXT);
   outtextxy(midx, midy, fontstr);
   outtextxy(midx, midy+2*ht, dirstr);
   outtextxy(midx, midy+4*ht, sizestr);
   outtextxy(midx, midy+6*ht, hjuststr);
   outtextxy(midx, midy+8*ht, vjuststr);

   /* clean up */
   getch();
   closegraph();
   return 0;
}
```

gettime, settime

Function Gets and sets the system time.

Syntax #include <dos.h>
void gettime(struct time **timep*);
void settime(struct time **timep*);

DOS	UNIX	Windows	ANSI C	C++ only
■		■		

Remarks **gettime** fills in the **time** structure pointed to by *timep* with the system's current time.

settime sets the system time to the values in the **time** structure pointed to by *timep*.

The **time** structure is defined as follows:

```
struct time {
   unsigned char ti_min;      /* minutes */
   unsigned char ti_hour;     /* hours */
   unsigned char ti_hund;     /* hundredths of seconds */
   unsigned char ti_sec;      /* seconds */
};
```

Return value None.

See also **_dos_gettime, _dos_settime, getdate, setdate, stime, time**

Example

```
#include <stdio.h>
#include <dos.h>

int main(void)
{
   struct  time t;
   gettime(&t);
   printf("The current minute is: %d\n", t.ti_min);
   printf("The current hour is: %d\n", t.ti_hour);
   printf("The current hundredth of a second is: %d\n", t.ti_hund);
   printf("The current second is: %d\n", t.ti_sec);

   /* add 1 to minutes struct element, then call settime */
   t.ti_min++;
   settime(&t);
   return 0;
}
```

getvect, setvect

Function Gets and sets interrupt vector.

Syntax #include <dos.h>
void interrupt(*getvect(int *interruptno*)) ();
void setvect(int *interruptno*, void interrupt (**isr*) ());

DOS	UNIX	Windows	ANSI C	C++ only
■		■		

Remarks Every processor of the 8086 family includes a set of interrupt vectors, numbered 0 to 255. The 4-byte value in each vector is actually an address, which is the location of an interrupt function.

getvect reads the value of the interrupt vector given by *interruptno* and returns that value as a (far) pointer to an interrupt function. The value of *interruptno* can be from 0 to 255.

setvect sets the value of the interrupt vector named by *interruptno* to a new value, *isr*, which is a far pointer containing the address of a new interrupt function. The address of a C routine can only be passed to *isr* if that routine is declared to be an interrupt routine.

If you use the prototypes declared in dos.h, simply pass the address of an interrupt function to **setvect** in any memory model.

Return value **getvect** returns the current 4-byte value stored in the interrupt vector named by *interruptno*.

setvect does not return a value.

See also **disable, _dos_getvect, _dos_setvect, enable, geninterrupt**

Example

```
#include <stdio.h>
#include <dos.h>

#ifdef __cplusplus
    #define __CPPARGS ...
#else
    #define __CPPARGS
#endif

void interrupt get_out(__CPPARGS);     /* interrupt prototype */
void interrupt (*oldfunc)(__CPPARGS); /* interrupt function pointer */

int looping = 1;

int main(void)
{
   puts("Press <Shift><Prt Sc> to terminate");

   /* save the old interrupt */
   oldfunc  = getvect(5);

   /* install interrupt handler */
   setvect(5,get_out);

   /* do nothing */
  while (looping);
```

```
   /* restore to original interrupt routine */
   setvect(5,oldfunc);

   puts("Success");
   return 0;
}

void interrupt get_out(__CPPARGS)
{
   looping = 0; /* change global variable to get out of loop */
}
```

getverify

Function Returns the state of the DOS verify flag.

Syntax #include <dos.h>
int getverify(void);

DOS	UNIX	Windows	ANSI C	C++ only
■		■		

Remarks **getverify** gets the current state of the verify flag.

The verify flag controls output to the disk. When verify is off, writes are not verified; when verify is on, all disk writes are verified to ensure proper writing of the data.

Return value **getverify** returns the current state of the verify flag, either 0 or 1.

- A return of 0 = verify flag off.
- A return of 1 = verify flag on.

See also **setverify**

Example

```
#include <stdio.h>
#include <dos.h>

int main(void)
{
   if (getverify())
      printf("DOS verify flag is on\n");
   else
      printf("DOS verify flag is off\n");
   return 0;
}
```

getviewsettings

Function Gets information about the current viewport.

Syntax #include <graphics.h>
void far getviewsettings(struct viewporttype far **viewport*);

DOS	UNIX	Windows	ANSI C	C++ only
■				

Remarks **getviewsettings** fills the **viewporttype** structure pointed to by *viewport* with information about the current viewport.

The **viewporttype** structure used by **getviewport** is defined in graphics.h as follows:

```
struct viewporttype {
   int left, top, right, bottom;
   int clip;
};
```

Return value None.

See also **clearviewport, getx, gety, setviewport**

Example

```
#include <graphics.h>
#include <stdlib.h>
#include <stdio.h>
#include <conio.h>

char *clip[] = { "OFF", "ON" };

int main(void)
{
   /* request autodetection */
   int gdriver = DETECT, gmode, errorcode;
   struct viewporttype viewinfo;
   int midx, midy, ht;
   char topstr[80], botstr[80], clipstr[80];

   /* initialize graphics and local variables */
   initgraph(&gdriver, &gmode, "");

   /* read result of initialization */
   errorcode = graphresult();
   if (errorcode != grOk) {  /* an error occurred */
      printf("Graphics error: %s\n", grapherrormsg(errorcode));
      printf("Press any key to halt:");
```

```
      getch();
      exit(1);              /* terminate with an error code */
   }

   midx = getmaxx() / 2;
   midy = getmaxy() / 2;

   /* get information about current viewport */
   getviewsettings(&viewinfo);

   /* convert text information into strings */
   sprintf(topstr, "(%d, %d) is the upper left viewport corner.", viewinfo.left,
          viewinfo.top);
   sprintf(botstr, "(%d, %d) is the lower right viewport corner.",
          viewinfo.right, viewinfo.bottom);
   sprintf(clipstr, "Clipping is turned %s.", clip[viewinfo.clip]);

   /* display the information */
   settextjustify(CENTER_TEXT, CENTER_TEXT);
   ht = textheight("W");
   outtextxy(midx, midy, topstr);
   outtextxy(midx, midy+2*ht, botstr);
   outtextxy(midx, midy+4*ht, clipstr);

   /* clean up */
   getch();
   closegraph();
   return 0;
}
```

getw

Function Gets integer from stream.

Syntax #include <stdio.h>
int getw(FILE **stream*);

DOS	UNIX	Windows	ANSI C	C++ only
■	■	■		

Remarks **getw** returns the next integer in the named input stream. It assumes no special alignment in the file.

getw should not be used when the stream is opened in text mode.

Return value **getw** returns the next integer on the input stream. On end-of-file or error, **getw** returns EOF. Because EOF is a legitimate value for **getw** to return, **feof** or **ferror** should be used to detect end-of-file or error.

See also putw

Example

```
#include <stdio.h>
#include <stdlib.h>

#define FNAME "test.$$$"

int main(void)
{
   FILE *fp;
   int word;

   /* place the word in a file */
   fp = fopen(FNAME, "wb");
   if (fp == NULL) {
      printf("Error opening file %s\n", FNAME);
      exit(1);
   }

   word = 94;
   putw(word,fp);
   if (ferror(fp))
       printf("Error writing to file\n");
   else
       printf("Successful write\n");
   fclose(fp);

   /* reopen the file */
   fp = fopen(FNAME, "rb");
   if (fp == NULL) {
      printf("Error opening file %s\n", FNAME);
      exit(1);
   }

   /* extract the word */
   word = getw(fp);
   if (ferror(fp))
       printf("Error reading file\n");
   else
       printf("Successful read: word = %d\n", word);

   /* clean up */
   fclose(fp);
   unlink(FNAME);
   return 0;
}
```

G

getx

Function Returns the current graphics position's x-coordinate.

Syntax #include <graphics.h>
int far getx(void);

DOS	UNIX	Windows	ANSI C	C++ only
■				

Remarks **getx** finds the current graphics position's x-coordinate. The value is viewport-relative.

Return value **getx** returns the x-coordinate of the current position.

See also **getmaxx, getmaxy, getviewsettings, gety, moveto**

Example

```
#include <graphics.h>
#include <stdlib.h>
#include <stdio.h>
#include <conio.h>

int main(void)
{
   /* request autodetection */
   int gdriver = DETECT, gmode, errorcode;
   char msg[80];

   /* initialize graphics and local variables */
   initgraph(&gdriver, &gmode, "");

   /* read result of initialization */
   errorcode = graphresult();
   if (errorcode != grOk) {  /* an error occurred */
      printf("Graphics error: %s\n", grapherrormsg(errorcode));
      printf("Press any key to halt:");
      getch();
      exit(1);               /* terminate with an error code */
   }

   /* move to the screen center point */
   moveto(getmaxx() / 2, getmaxy() / 2);

   /* create a message string */
   sprintf(msg, "<-(%d, %d) is the here.", getx(), gety());

   /* display the message */
   outtext(msg);

   /* clean up */
   getch();
```

```
    closegraph();
    return 0;
}
```

gety

Function Returns the current graphics position's y-coordinate.

Syntax #include <graphics.h>
int far gety(void);

DOS	UNIX	Windows	ANSI C	C++ only
■				

Remarks **gety** returns the current graphics position's y-coordinate. The value is viewport-relative.

Return value **gety** returns the y-coordinate of the current position.

See also **getmaxx, getmaxy, getviewsettings, getx, moveto**

Example

```
#include <graphics.h>
#include <stdlib.h>
#include <stdio.h>
#include <conio.h>

int main(void)
{
   /* request autodetection */
   int gdriver = DETECT, gmode, errorcode;
   char msg[80];

   /* initialize graphics and local variables */
   initgraph(&gdriver, &gmode, "");

   /* read result of initialization */
   errorcode = graphresult();
   if (errorcode != grOk) {   /* an error occurred */
      printf("Graphics error: %s\n", grapherrormsg(errorcode));
      printf("Press any key to halt:");
      getch();
      exit(1);               /* terminate with an error code */
   }

   /* move to the screen center point */
   moveto(getmaxx() / 2, getmaxy() / 2);

   /* create a message string */
   sprintf(msg, "<-(%d, %d) is the here.", getx(), gety());
```

```
    /* display the message */
    outtext(msg);

    /* clean up */
    getch();
    closegraph();
    return 0;
}
```

gmtime

Function Converts date and time to Greenwich mean time (GMT).

Syntax #include <time.h>
struct tm *gmtime(const time_t **timer*);

DOS	UNIX	Windows	ANSI C	C++ only
■	■	■	■	

Remarks **gmtime** accepts the address of a value returned by **time** and returns a pointer to the structure of type **tm** containing the broken-down time. **gmtime** converts directly to GMT.

The global long variable *timezone* should be set to the difference in seconds between GMT and local standard time (in PST, *timezone* is 8×60×60). The global variable *daylight* should be set to nonzero *only if* the standard U.S. daylight saving time conversion should be applied.

The **tm** structure declaration from the time.h include file is

```
struct tm {
   int tm_sec;      /* Seconds */
   int tm_min;      /* Minutes */
   int tm_hour;     /* Hour (0 - 23) */
   int tm_mday;     /* Day of month (1 - 31) */
   int tm_mon;      /* Month (0 - 11) */
   int tm_year;     /* Year (calender year minus 1900) */
   int tm_wday;     /* Weekday (0 - 6; Sunday is 0) */
   int tm_yday;     /* Day of year (0 -365) */
   int tm_isdst;    /* Nonzero if daylight saving time is in effect. */
};
```

These quantities give the time on a 24-hour clock, day of month (1 to 31), month (0 to 11), weekday (Sunday equals 0), year – 1900, day of year (0 to 365), and a flag that is nonzero if daylight saving time is in effect.

Return value **gmtime** returns a pointer to the structure containing the broken-down time. This structure is a static that is overwritten with each call.

See also **asctime, ctime, ftime, localtime, stime, time, tzset**

Example

```
#include <stdio.h>
#include <stdlib.h>
#include <time.h>
#include <dos.h>

/* pacific standard & daylight savings time */
char *tzstr = "TZ=PST8PDT";

int main(void)
{
   time_t t;
   struct tm *gmt, *area;
   putenv(tzstr);
   tzset();
   t = time(NULL);
   area = localtime(&t);
   printf("Local time is: %s", asctime(area));
   gmt = gmtime(&t);
   printf("GMT is:        %s", asctime(gmt));

   return 0;
}
```

G

gotoxy

Function Positions cursor in text window.

Syntax #include <conio.h>
void gotoxy(int *x*, int *y*);

DOS	UNIX	Windows	ANSI C	C++ only
■				

Remarks **gotoxy** moves the cursor to the given position in the current text window. If the coordinates are in any way invalid, the call to **gotoxy** is ignored. An example of this is a call to **gotoxy**(40,30), when (35,25) is the bottom right position in the window.

Return value None.

See also **wherex, wherey, window**

Example

```
#include <conio.h>
```

```
int main(void)
{
   clrscr();
   gotoxy(35, 12);
   cprintf("Hello world");
   getch();
   return 0;
}
```

graphdefaults

Function Resets all graphics settings to their defaults.

Syntax #include <graphics.h>
void far graphdefaults(void);

DOS	UNIX	Windows	ANSI C	C++ only
■				

Remarks **graphdefaults** resets all graphics settings to their defaults:

- sets the viewport to the entire screen.
- moves the current position to (0,0).
- sets the default palette colors, background color, and drawing color.
- sets the default fill style and pattern.
- sets the default text font and justification.

Return value None.

See also **initgraph, setgraphmode**

Example

```
#include <graphics.h>
#include <stdlib.h>
#include <stdio.h>
#include <conio.h>

int main(void)
{
   /* request autodetection */
   int gdriver = DETECT, gmode, errorcode;
   int maxx, maxy;

   /* initialize graphics and local variables */
   initgraph(&gdriver, &gmode, "");

   /* read result of initialization */
   errorcode = graphresult();
```

```
   if (errorcode != grOk) {  /* an error occurred */
      printf("Graphics error: %s\n", grapherrormsg(errorcode));
      printf("Press any key to halt:");
      getch();
      exit(1);              /* terminate with an error code */
   }

   maxx = getmaxx();
   maxy = getmaxy();

   /* output line with nondefault settings */
   setlinestyle(DOTTED_LINE, 0, 3);
   line(0, 0, maxx, maxy);
   outtextxy(maxx/2, maxy/3, "Before default values are restored.");
   getch();

   /* restore default values for everything */
   graphdefaults();

   /* clear the screen */
   cleardevice();


   /* output line with default settings */
   line(0, 0, maxx, maxy);
   outtextxy(maxx/2, maxy/3, "After restoring default values.");

   /* clean up */
   getch();
   closegraph();
   return 0;
}
```

G

grapherrormsg

Function Returns a pointer to an error message string.

Syntax #include <graphics.h>
char * far grapherrormsg(int *errorcode*);

DOS	UNIX	Windows	ANSI C	C++ only
■				

Remarks **grapherrormsg** returns a pointer to the error message string associated with *errorcode*, the value returned by **graphresult**.

Refer to the entry for *errno* in Chapter 3 ("Global variables") for a list of error messages and mnemonics.

Return value **grapherrormsg** returns a pointer to an error message string.

See also **graphresult**

Example

```
#include <graphics.h>
#include <stdlib.h>
#include <stdio.h>
#include <conio.h>

#define NONSENSE -50

int main(void)
{
   /* force an error to occur */
   int gdriver = NONSENSE, gmode, errorcode;

   /* initialize graphics mode */
   initgraph(&gdriver, &gmode, "");

   /* read result of initialization */
   errorcode = graphresult();

   /* if an error occurred, then output descriptive error message */
   if (errorcode != grOk) {
      printf("Graphics error: %s\n", grapherrormsg(errorcode));
      printf("Press any key to halt:");
      getch();
      exit(1);               /* terminate with an error code */
   }

   /* draw a line */
   line(0, 0, getmaxx(), getmaxy());

   /* clean up */
   getch();
   closegraph();
   return 0;
}
```

_graphfreemem

Function User hook into graphics memory deallocation.

Syntax #include <graphics.h>
void far _graphfreemem(void far **ptr*, unsigned *size*);

DOS	UNIX	Windows	ANSI C	C++ only
■				

Remarks The graphics library calls **_graphfreemem** to release memory previously allocated through **_graphgetmem**. You can choose to control the graphics library memory management by simply defining your own version of **_graphfreemem** (you must declare it exactly as shown in the declaration). The default version of this routine merely calls **free**.

Return value None.

See also **_graphgetmem, setgraphbufsize**

G

Example

```
#include <graphics.h>
#include <stdlib.h>
#include <stdio.h>
#include <conio.h>
#include <alloc.h>

int main(void)
{
   /* request autodetection */
   int gdriver = DETECT, gmode, errorcode, midx, midy;

   /* clear the text screen */
   clrscr();
   printf("Press any key to initialize graphics mode:");
   getch();
   clrscr();

   /* initialize graphics and local variables */
   initgraph(&gdriver, &gmode, "");

   /* read result of initialization */
   errorcode = graphresult();
   if (errorcode != grOk) {  /* an error occurred */
      printf("Graphics error: %s\n", grapherrormsg(errorcode));
      printf("Press any key to halt:");
      getch();
      exit(1);               /* terminate with an error code */
   }

   midx = getmaxx() / 2;
   midy = getmaxy() / 2;

   /* display a message */
   settextjustify(CENTER_TEXT, CENTER_TEXT);
   outtextxy(midx, midy, "Press any key to exit graphics mode:");

   /* clean up */
   getch();
   closegraph();
   return 0;
}
```

```
/* called by the graphics kernel to allocate memory */
void far * far _graphgetmem(unsigned size) {
   printf("_graphgetmem called to allocate %d bytes.\n", size);
   printf("hit any key:");
   getch();
   printf("\n");

   /* allocate memory from far heap */
   return farmalloc(size);
}

/* called by the graphics kernel to free memory */
void far _graphfreemem(void far *ptr, unsigned size) {
   printf("_graphfreemem called to free %d bytes.\n", size);
   printf("hit any key:");
   getch();
   printf("\n");

   /* free ptr from far heap */
   farfree(ptr);
}
```

_graphgetmem

Function User hook into graphics memory allocation.

Syntax #include <graphics.h>
void far * far _graphgetmem(unsigned *size*);

DOS	UNIX	Windows	ANSI C	C++ only
▪				

Remarks Routines in the graphics library (not the user program) normally call **_graphgetmem** to allocate memory for internal buffers, graphics drivers, and character sets. You can choose to control the memory management of the graphics library by defining your own version of **_graphgetmem** (you must declare it exactly as shown in the declaration). The default version of this routine merely calls **malloc**.

Return value None.

See also **_graphfreemem, initgraph, setgraphbufsize**

Example

```
#include <graphics.h>
#include <stdlib.h>
#include <stdio.h>
#include <conio.h>
#include <alloc.h>
```

```
int main(void)
{
   /* request autodetection */
   int gdriver = DETECT, gmode, errorcode, midx, midy;

   /* clear the text screen */
   clrscr();
   printf("Press any key to initialize graphics mode:");
   getch();
   clrscr();

   /* initialize graphics and local variables */
   initgraph(&gdriver, &gmode, "");

   /* read result of initialization */
   errorcode = graphresult();
   if (errorcode != grOk) {  /* an error occurred */
      printf("Graphics error: %s\n", grapherrormsg(errorcode));
      printf("Press any key to halt:");
      getch();
      exit(1);               /* terminate with an error code */
   }

   midx = getmaxx() / 2;
   midy = getmaxy() / 2;

   /* display a message */
   settextjustify(CENTER_TEXT, CENTER_TEXT);
   outtextxy(midx, midy, "Press any key to exit graphics mode:");

   /* clean up */
   getch();
   closegraph();
   return 0;
}

/* called by the graphics kernel to allocate memory */
void far * far _graphgetmem(unsigned size) {
   printf("_graphgetmem called to allocate %d bytes.\n", size);
   printf("hit any key:");
   getch();
   printf("\n");

   /* allocate memory from far heap */
   return farmalloc(size);
}

/* called by the graphics kernel to free memory */
void far _graphfreemem(void far *ptr, unsigned size) {
   printf("_graphfreemem called to free %d bytes.\n", size);
   printf("hit any key:");
   getch();
```

G

```
   printf("\n");

   /* free ptr from far heap */
   farfree(ptr);
}
```

graphresult

Function Returns an error code for the last unsuccessful graphics operation.

Syntax #include <graphics.h>
int far graphresult(void);

DOS	UNIX	Windows	ANSI C	C++ only
■				

Remarks **graphresult** returns the error code for the last graphics operation that reported an error and resets the error level to grOk.

The following table lists the error codes returned by **graphresult**. The enumerated type *graph_errors* defines the errors in this table. *graph_errors* is declared in graphics.h.

Error code	*graphics_errors* constant	Corresponding error message string
0	grOk	No error
–1	grNoInitGraph	(BGI) graphics not installed (use **initgraph**)
–2	grNotDetected	Graphics hardware not detected
–3	grFileNotFound	Device driver file not found
–4	grInvalidDriver	Invalid device driver file
–5	grNoLoadMem	Not enough memory to load driver
–6	grNoScanMem	Out of memory in scan fill
–7	grNoFloodMem	Out of memory in flood fill
–8	grFontNotFound	Font file not found
–9	igrNoFontMem	Not enough memory to load font
–10	grInvalidMode	Invalid graphics mode for selected driver
–11	grError	Graphics error
–12	grIOerror	Graphics I/O error
–13	grInvalidFont	Invalid font file
–14	grInvalidFontNum	Invalid font number
–15	grInvalidDeviceNum	Invalid device number
–18	grInvalidVersion	Invalid version number

Note that the variable maintained by **graphresult** is reset to 0 after **graphresult** has been called. Therefore, you should store the value of **graphresult** into a temporary variable and then test it.

Return value **graphresult** returns the current graphics error number, an integer in the range –15 to 0; **grapherrormsg** returns a pointer to a string associated with the value returned by **graphresult**.

See also **detectgraph, drawpoly, fillpoly, floodfill, grapherrormsg, initgraph, pieslice, registerbgidriver, registerbgifont, setallpalette, setcolor, setfillstyle, setgraphmode, setlinestyle, setpalette, settextjustify, settextstyle, setusercharsize, setviewport, setvisualpage**

Example

```
#include <graphics.h>
#include <stdlib.h>
#include <stdio.h>
#include <conio.h>

int main(void)
{
   /* request autodetection */
   int gdriver = DETECT, gmode, errorcode;

   /* initialize graphics and local variables */
   initgraph(&gdriver, &gmode, "");

   /* read result of initialization */
   errorcode = graphresult();

   if (errorcode != grOk) {  /* an error occurred */
      printf("Graphics error: %s\n", grapherrormsg(errorcode));
      printf("Press any key to halt:");
      getch();
      exit(1);               /* terminate with an error code */
   }

   /* draw a line */
   line(0, 0, getmaxx(), getmaxy());

   /* clean up */
   getch();
   closegraph();
   return 0;
}
```

harderr, hardresume, hardretn

Function Establishes and handles hardware errors.

Syntax
```
#include <dos.h>
void harderr(int (*handler)());
void hardresume(int axret);
void hardretn(int retn);
```

DOS	UNIX	Windows	ANSI C	C++ only
■				

Remarks The error handler established by **harderr** can call **hardresume** to return to DOS. The return value of the *rescode* (result code) of **hardresume** contains an abort (2), retry (1), or ignore (0) indicator. The abort is accomplished by invoking DOS interrupt 0x23, the control-break interrupt.

The error handler established by **harderr** can return directly to the application program by calling **hardretn**. The returned value is whatever value you passed to **hardretn**.

harderr establishes a hardware error handler for the current program. This error handler is invoked whenever an interrupt 0x24 occurs. (See your DOS reference manuals for a discussion of the interrupt.)

The function pointed to by *handler* is called when such an interrupt occurs. The handler function is called with the following arguments:

```
handler(int errval, int ax, int bp, int si);
```

errval is the error code set in the DI register by DOS. *ax*, *bp*, and *si* are the values DOS sets for the AX, BP, and SI registers, respectively.

- *ax* indicates whether a disk error or other device error was encountered. If *ax* is nonnegative, a disk error was encountered; otherwise, the error was a device error. For a disk error, *ax* ANDed with 0x00FF gives the failing drive number (0 equals A, 1 equals B, and so on).
- *bp* and *si* together point to the device driver header of the failing driver. *bp* contains the segment address, and *si* the offset.

The function pointed to by *handler* is not called directly. **harderr** establishes a DOS interrupt handler that calls the function.

The handler can issue DOS calls 1 through 0xC; any other DOS call corrupts DOS. In particular, any of the C standard I/O or UNIX-emulation I/O calls *cannot* be used.

The handler must return 0 for ignore, 1 for retry, and 2 for abort.

Return Value None.

See also **peek, poke**

Example

```
/* This program will trap disk errors and prompt the user for action. Try running
   it with no disk in drive A: to invoke its functions.
*/

#include <stdio.h>
#include <conio.h>
#include <dos.h>

#define IGNORE  0
#define RETRY   1
#define ABORT   2

int buf[500];

/* Define the error messages for trapping disk problems. */
static char *err_msg[] = {
    "write protect",
    "unknown unit",
    "drive not ready",
    "unknown command",
    "data error (CRC)",
    "bad request",
    "seek error",
    "unknown media type",
    "sector not found",
    "printer out of paper",
    "write fault",
    "read fault",
    "general failure",
    "reserved",
    "reserved",
    "invalid disk change"
};

error_win(char *msg)
{
   int retval;
   cputs(msg);

/* Prompt for user to press a key to abort, retry, ignore. */
   while(1) {
      retval= getch();
```

H

```
        if (retval == 'a' || retval == 'A') {
            retval = ABORT;
            break;
        }
    if (retval == 'r' || retval == 'R') {
        retval = RETRY;
        break;
    }
    if (retval == 'i' || retval == 'I')
    {
        retval = IGNORE;
        break;
    }
    }

    return(retval);
}

/*
pragma warn -par reduces warnings which occur
due to the non use of the parameters errval,
bp and si to the handler.
*/
#pragma warn -par

int handler(int errval,int ax,int bp,int si)
{
    static char msg[80];
    unsigned di;
    int drive;
    int errorno;

    di= _DI;
/*
if this is not a disk error then it was
another device having trouble
*/

    if (ax < 0)
    {
        /* report the error */
        error_win("Device error");
        /* and return to the program directly requesting abort */
        hardretn(ABORT);
    }
/* otherwise it was a disk error */
    drive = ax & 0x00FF;
    errorno = di & 0x00FF;
/* report which error it was */
    sprintf(msg, "Error: %s on drive %c\r\nA)bort, R)etry, I)gnore: ",
```

```
        err_msg[errorno], 'A' + drive);
/*
return to the program via dos interrupt 0x23 with abort, retry,
or ignore as input by the user.
*/
   hardresume(error_win(msg));
   return ABORT;
}
#pragma warn +par

int main(void)
{
/*
install our handler on the hardware problem interrupt
*/
   harderr(handler);
   clrscr();
   printf("Make sure there is no disk in drive A:\n");
   printf("Press any key ....\n");
   getch();
   printf("Trying to access drive A:\n");
   printf("fopen returned %p\n",fopen("A:temp.dat", "w"));
   return 0;
}
```


_harderr

Function Establishes a hardware error handler.

Syntax #include <dos.h>
void _harderr(int (far **handler*)());

DOS	UNIX	Windows	ANSI C	C++ only
■				

Remarks **_harderr** establishes a hardware error handler for the current program. This error handler is invoked whenever an interrupt 0x24 occurs. (See your DOS reference manuals for a discussion of the interrupt.)

The function pointed to by *handler* is called when such an interrupt occurs. The handler function is called with the following arguments:

```
void far handler(unsigned deverr, unsigned errval, unsigned far *devhdr);
```

- *deverr* is the device error code (passed to the handler by DOS in the AX register).
- *errval* is the error code (passed to the handler by DOS in the DI register).

- *devhdr* a far pointer to the driver header of the device that caused the error (passed to the handler by DOS in the BP:SI register pair).

The handler should use these arguments instead of referring directly to the CPU registers.

deverr indicates whether a disk error or other device error was encountered. If bit 15 of *deverr* is 0, a disk error was encountered. Otherwise, the error was a device error. For a disk error, *deverr* ANDed with 0x00FF give the failing drive number (0 equals A, 1 equals B, and so on).

The function pointed to by *handler* is not called directly. **_harderr** establishes a DOS interrupt handler that calls the function.

The handler can issue DOS calls 1 through 0xC; any other DOS call corrupts DOS. In particular, any of the C standard I/O or UNIX-emulation I/O calls *cannot* be used.

The handler does not return a value, and it must exit using **_hardretn** or **_hardresume**.

Return Value None.

See also **_hardresume, _hardretn**

Example

```
/* This program traps disk errors and prompts the user for action. */
/* Try running it with no disk in drive A to invoke its functions. */

#include <stdio.h>
#include <ctype.h>
#include <dos.h>
#include <fcntl.h>

int buf[500];

/* Define the error messages for trapping disk problems. */
static char *err_msg[] =
{
  "write protect",   "unknown unit",
  "drive not ready", "unknown command",
  "data error (CRC)","bad request",
  "seek error",      "unknown media type",
  "sector not found","printer out of paper",
  "write fault",     "read fault",
  "general failure", "reserved",
  "reserved",        "invalid disk change"
};

static void mesg(char *s)
{
```

```
   while (*s)
      bdos(2,*s++,0);
}

static int getkey(void)
{
   return (bdos(7, 0, 0) & 0xff);
}

error_win(char *msg)
{
   int c;

   /* Prompt user to press a key to abort, retry, ignore, fail. */
   while(1) {
      mesg(msg);
      c = tolower(getkey());
      mesg("\r\n");
      switch (c) {
         case 'a':
            return (_HARDERR_ABORT);
         case 'r':
            return (_HARDERR_RETRY);
         case 'i':
            return (_HARDERR_IGNORE);
         case 'f':
            return (_HARDERR_FAIL);
      }
   }
}

/* Pragma warn -par reduces warnings which occur due to the nonuse of the
   parameter devhdr */
#pragma warn -par

void far handler(unsigned deverr, unsigned errval,
                 unsigned far *devhdr)
{
   static char msg[80];
   int drive, errorno;

   /* If this not disk error then another device having trouble. */
   if (deverr & 0x8000) {
      error_win("Device error"); /* report the error */
      /* return to the program directly requesting abort */
      _hardretn(5);              /* 5 = DOS "access denied" error */
   }
   drive = deverr & 0x00FF;      /* otherwise it was disk error */
   errorno = errval & 0x00FF;

   /* report which error it was */
```

H

```
   sprintf(msg, "Error: %s on drive %c\r\nA)bort, R)etry,
           I)gnore, F)ail: ",
           err_msg[errorno], 'A' + drive);

   /* Return to program via dos interrupt 0x23 with abort, retry or ignore as
      input by the user */
   _hardresume(error_win(msg));
}

#pragma warn +par

int main(void)
{
   int handle;

   /* Install our handler on the hardware problem interrupt. */
   _harderr(handler);
   printf("Make sure there is no disk in drive A:\n");
   printf("Press any key ....\n");
   getkey();
   printf("Trying to access drive A:\n");
   printf("_dos_open returned 0x%x\n",
          _dos_open("A:temp.dat", O_RDONLY, &handle));
   return 0;
}
```

_hardresume

Function Hardware error handler.

Syntax #include <dos.h>
void _hardresume(int *rescode*);

DOS	UNIX	Windows	ANSI C	C++ only
■				

Remarks The error handler established by **_harderr** can call **_hardresume** to return to DOS. The return value of the *rescode* (result code) of **_hardresume** contains one of the following values:

_HARDERR_ABORT	Abort the program by invoking DOS interrupt 0x23, the control-break interrupt.
_HARDERR_IGNORE	Ignore the error.
_HARDERR_RETRY	Retry the operation.
_HARDERR_FAIL	Fail the operation.

Return Value The **_hardresume** function does not return a value, and does not return to the caller.

See also **_harderr**, **_hardretn**

Example See the example for **_harderr**.

_hardretn

Function Hardware error handler.

Syntax
```
#include <dos.h>
void _hardretn(int retn);
```

DOS	UNIX	Windows	ANSI C	C++ only
■				

Remarks The error handler established by **_harderr** can return directly to the application program by calling **_hardretn**.

If the DOS function that caused the error is less than 0x38, and it is a function that can indicate an error condition, then **_hardretn** will return to the application program with the AL register set to 0xFF. The *retn* argument is ignored for all DOS functions less than 0x38.

If the DOS function is greater than or equal to 0x38, the *retn* argument should be a DOS error code; it is returned to the application program in the AX register. The carry flag is also set to indicate to the application that the operation resulted in an error.

Return Value The **_hardresume** function does not return a value, and does not return to the caller.

See also **_harderr**, **_hardresume**

Example See the example for **_harderr**.

heapcheck

Function Checks and verifies the heap.

Syntax
```
#include <alloc.h>
int heapcheck(void);
```

DOS	UNIX	Windows	ANSI C	C++ only
■				

Remarks **heapcheck** walks through the heap and examines each block checking its pointers, size, and other critical attributes. In the large data models, **heapcheck** maps to **farheapcheck**.

Return Value The return value is less than zero for an error and greater than zero for success. The return values and their meaning is as follows:

_HEAPEMPTY	no heap (value 1).
_HEAPOK	heap is verified (value 2).
_HEAPCORRUPT	heap has been corrupted (value –1).

See also **farheapcheck**

Example

```
#include <stdio.h>
#include <alloc.h>

#define NUM_PTRS  10
#define NUM_BYTES 16

int main(void)
{
   char *array[ NUM_PTRS ];
   int i;

   for( i = 0; i < NUM_PTRS; i++ )
      array[ i ] = (char *) malloc( NUM_BYTES );
   for( i = 0; i < NUM_PTRS; i += 2 )
      free( array[ i ] );
   if( heapcheck() == _HEAPCORRUPT )
      printf( "Heap is corrupted.\n" );
   else
      printf( "Heap is OK.\n" );
   return 0;
}
```

heapcheckfree

Function Checks the free blocks on the heap for a constant value.

Syntax #include <alloc.h>
int heapcheckfree(unsigned int fillvalue);

DOS	UNIX	Windows	ANSI C	C++ only
■				

Return Value The return value is less then zero for an error and greater than zero for success. The return values and their meaning is as follows:

_HEAPEMPTY	no heap (value 1).
_HEAPOK	heap is accurate (value 2).
_HEAPCORRUPT	heap has been corrupted (value –1).
_BADVALUE	a value other than the fill value was found (value –3).

See also **farheapcheckfree**

Example

```
#include <stdio.h>
#include <alloc.h>
#include <mem.h>

#define NUM_PTRS  10
#define NUM_BYTES 16

int main(void)
{
   char *array[ NUM_PTRS ];
   int i, res;

   for( i = 0; i < NUM_PTRS; i++ )
      array[ i ] = (char *) malloc( NUM_BYTES );
   for( i = 0; i < NUM_PTRS; i += 2 )
      free( array[ i ] );
   if( heapfillfree( 1 ) < 0 ) {
      printf( "Heap corrupted.\n" );
      return 1;
   }
   for( i = 1; i < NUM_PTRS; i += 2 )
      memset( array[ i ], 0, NUM_BYTES );
   res = heapcheckfree( 1 );
   if( res < 0 )
      switch( res ) {
         case _HEAPCORRUPT:
              printf( "Heap corrupted.\n" );
              return 1;
         case _BADVALUE:
              printf( "Bad value in free space.\n" );
              return 1;
         default:
              printf( "Unknown error.\n" );
              return 1;
      }
   printf( "Test successful.\n" );
   return 0;
}
```

heapchecknode

Function Checks and verifies a single node on the heap.

Syntax #include <alloc.h>
int heapchecknode(void *node);

DOS	UNIX	Windows	ANSI C	C++ only
■				

Remarks If a node has been freed and **heapchecknode** is called with a pointer to the freed block, **heapchecknode** can return _BADNODE rather than the expected _FREEENTRY. This is because adjacent free blocks on the heap are merged, and the block in question no longer exists.

Return Value The return value is less than zero for an error and greater than zero for success. The return values and their meaning is as follows:

_HEAPEMPTY	no heap (value 1).
_HEAPCORRUPT	heap has been corrupted (value –1).
_BADNODE	node could not be found (value –2).
_FREEENTRY	node is a free block (value 3).
_USEDENTRY	node is a used block (value 4).

See also **farheapchecknode**

Example

```
#include <stdio.h>
#include <alloc.h>

#define NUM_PTRS  10
#define NUM_BYTES 16

int main(void)
{
   char *array[ NUM_PTRS ];
   int i;

   for( i = 0; i < NUM_PTRS; i++ )
      array[ i ] = (char *) malloc( NUM_BYTES );
   for( i = 0; i < NUM_PTRS; i += 2 )
      free( array[ i ] );
   for( i = 0; i < NUM_PTRS; i++ ) {
      printf( "Node %2d ", i );
      switch( heapchecknode( array[ i ] ) ) {
         case _HEAPEMPTY:
              printf( "No heap.\n" );
              break;
         case _HEAPCORRUPT:
              printf( "Heap corrupt.\n" );
```

```
                break;
            case _BADNODE:
                printf( "Bad node.\n" );
                break;
            case _FREEENTRY:
                printf( "Free entry.\n" );
                break;
            case _USEDENTRY:
                printf( "Used entry.\n" );
                break;
            default:
                printf( "Unknown return code.\n" );
                 break;
        }
    }
    return 0;
}
```


heapfillfree

Function Fills the free blocks on the heap with a constant value.

Syntax #include <alloc.h>
int heapfillfree(unsigned int fillvalue);

DOS	UNIX	Windows	ANSI C	C++ only
■				

Return Value The return value is less than zero for an error and greater than zero for success. The return values and their meaning is as follows:

_HEAPEMPTY	no heap (value 1).
_HEAPOK	heap is accurate (value 2).
_HEAPCORRUPT	heap has been corrupted (value –1).

See also **farheapfillfree**

Example

```
#include <stdio.h>
#include <alloc.h>
#include <mem.h>

#define NUM_PTRS  10
#define NUM_BYTES 16

int main(void)
{
   char *array[ NUM_PTRS ];
   int i, res;
```

```
    for( i = 0; i < NUM_PTRS; i++ )
       array[ i ] = (char *) malloc( NUM_BYTES );
    for( i = 0; i < NUM_PTRS; i += 2 )
       free( array[ i ] );
    if( heapfillfree( 1 ) < 0 ) {
       printf( "Heap corrupted.\n" );
       return 1;
    }
    for( i = 1; i < NUM_PTRS; i += 2 )
       memset( array[ i ], 0, NUM_BYTES );
    res = heapcheckfree( 1 );
    if( res < 0 )
       switch( res ) {
          case _HEAPCORRUPT:
                printf( "Heap corrupted.\n" );
                return 1;
          case _BADVALUE:
                printf( "Bad value in free space.\n" );
                return 1;
          default:
                printf( "Unknown error.\n" );
                return 1;
       }
    printf( "Test successful.\n" );
    return 0;
}
```

heapwalk

Function **heapwalk** is used to "walk" through the heap, node by node.

Syntax #include <alloc.h>
int heapwalk(struct heapinfo *hi);

DOS	UNIX	Windows	ANSI C	C++ only
■				

Remarks **heapwalk** assumes the heap is correct. Use **heapcheck** to verify the heap before using **heapwalk**. _HEAPOK is returned with the last block on the heap. _HEAPEND will be returned on the next call to **heapwalk**.

heapwalk receives a pointer to a structure of type *heapinfo* (declared in alloc.h). For the first call to **heapwalk**, set the hi.ptr field to null. **heapwalk** returns with hi.ptr containing the address of the first block. hi.size holds the size of the block in bytes. hi.in_use is a flag that's set if the block is currently in use.

Return Value The return values and their meaning is as follows:

_HEAPEMPTY	no heap (value 1).
_HEAPOK	*heapinfo* block contains valid data (value 2).
_HEAPEND	end of the heap has been reached (value 5).

See also **farheapwalk**

Example

```
#include <stdio.h>
#include <alloc.h>

#define NUM_PTRS  10
#define NUM_BYTES 16

int main( void )
{
   struct heapinfo hi;
   char *array[ NUM_PTRS ];
   int i;

   for( i = 0; i < NUM_PTRS; i++ )
      array[ i ] = (char *) malloc( NUM_BYTES );
   for( i = 0; i < NUM_PTRS; i += 2 )
      free( array[ i ] );

   hi.ptr = NULL;
   printf( "   Size   Status\n" );
   printf( "   ----   ------\n" );
   while( heapwalk( &hi ) == _HEAPOK )
   printf( "%7u    %s\n", hi.size, hi.in_use ? "used" : "free" );
   return 0;
}
```

H

highvideo

Function Selects high-intensity characters.

Syntax #include <conio.h>
void highvideo(void);

DOS	UNIX	Windows	ANSI C	C++ only
■				

Remarks **highvideo** selects high-intensity characters by setting the high-intensity bit of the currently selected foreground color.

This function does not affect any characters currently on the screen, but does affect those displayed by functions (such as **cprintf**) that perform direct video, text mode output *after* **highvideo** is called.

Return Value None.

See also **cprintf, cputs, gettextinfo, lowvideo, normvideo, textattr, textcolor**

Example

```
#include <conio.h>

int main(void)
{
   clrscr();
   lowvideo();
   cprintf("Low Intensity text\r\n");
   highvideo();
   gotoxy(1,2);
   cprintf("High Intensity Text\r\n");
   return 0;
}
```

hypot, hypotl

Function Calculates hypotenuse of a right triangle.

Syntax #include <math.h>
double hypot(double *x*, double *y*);
long double hypotl(long double *x*, long double *y*);

	DOS	UNIX	Windows	ANSI C	C++ only
hypot	■	■	■		
hypotl	■		■		

Remarks **hypot** calculates the value *z* where

$$z^2 = x^2 + y^2$$

and

$$z >= 0$$

This is equivalent to the length of the hypotenuse of a right triangle, if the lengths of the two sides are *x* and *y*.

hyptol is the long double version; it takes long double arguments and returns a long double result.

Return Value On success, these functions return *z*, a double (**hypot**) or a long double) (**hypotl**). On error (such as an overflow), they set the global variable *errno* to

ERANGE   Result out of range

and return the value HUGE_VAL (**hypot**) or _LHUGE_VAL) (**hypotl**).

Error handling for these routines can be modified through the functions **matherr** and **_matherrl**.

Example

```
#include <stdio.h>
#include <math.h>

int main(void)
{
   double result, x = 3.0, y = 4.0;

   result = hypot(x, y);
   printf("The hypotenuse is: %lf\n", result);
   return 0;
}
```

H

imag

Function Returns the imaginary part of a complex number.

Syntax #include <complex.h>
double imag(complex *x*);

DOS	UNIX	Windows	ANSI C	C++ only
■		■		■

Remarks The data associated to a complex number consists of two floating-point (double) numbers. **imag** returns the one considered to be the imaginary part.

Return Value The imaginary part of the complex number.

See also **complex**, **conj**, **real**

Example

```
#include <complex.h>

int main(void)
{
   double x = 3.1, y = 4.2;
   complex z = complex(x,y);
   cout << "z = " << z << "\n";
   cout << "  has real part = " << real(z) << "\n";
```

```
    cout << "  and imaginary real part = " << imag(z) << "\n";
    cout << "z has complex conjugate = " << conj(z) << "\n";
    return 0;
}
```

imagesize

Function Returns the number of bytes required to store a bit image.

Syntax #include <graphics.h>
unsigned far imagesize(int *left*, int *top*, int *right*, int *bottom*);

DOS	UNIX	Windows	ANSI C	C++ only
■				

Remarks **imagesize** determines the size of the memory area required to store a bit image. If the size required for the selected image is greater than or equal to 64K – 1 bytes, **imagesize** returns 0xFFFF (-1).

Return Value **imagesize** returns the size of the required memory area in bytes.

See also **getimage**, **putimage**

Example

```
#include <graphics.h>
#include <stdlib.h>
#include <stdio.h>
#include <conio.h>

#define ARROW_SIZE 10

void draw_arrow(int x, int y);

int main(void)
{
   /* request autodetection */
   int gdriver = DETECT, gmode, errorcode;
   void *arrow;
   int x, y, maxx;
   unsigned int size;

   /* initialize graphics and local variables */
   initgraph(&gdriver, &gmode, "");

   /* read result of initialization */
   errorcode = graphresult();
   if (errorcode != grOk) {  /* an error occurred */
      printf("Graphics error: %s\n", grapherrormsg(errorcode));
      printf("Press any key to halt:");
      getch();
```

```
      exit(1);               /* terminate with an error code */
   }

   maxx = getmaxx();
   x = 0;
   y = getmaxy() / 2;

   /* draw the image to be grabbed */
   draw_arrow(x, y);

   /* calculate the size of the image */
   size = imagesize(x, y-ARROW_SIZE, x+(4*ARROW_SIZE), y+ARROW_SIZE);

   /* allocate memory to hold the image */
   arrow = malloc(size);

   /* grab the image */
   getimage(x, y-ARROW_SIZE, x+(4*ARROW_SIZE), y+ARROW_SIZE, arrow);

   /* repeat until a key is pressed */
   while (!kbhit()) {
      /* erase old image */
      putimage(x, y-ARROW_SIZE, arrow, XOR_PUT);
      x += ARROW_SIZE;
      if (x >= maxx)
          x = 0;

      /* plot new image */
      putimage(x, y-ARROW_SIZE, arrow, XOR_PUT);
   }

   /* clean up */
   free(arrow);
   closegraph();
   return 0;
}

void draw_arrow(int x, int y)
{
   /* draw an arrow on the screen */
   moveto(x, y);
   linerel(4*ARROW_SIZE, 0);
   linerel(-2*ARROW_SIZE, -1*ARROW_SIZE);
   linerel(0, 2*ARROW_SIZE);
   linerel(2*ARROW_SIZE, -1*ARROW_SIZE);
}
```

I-J

initgraph

Function Initializes the graphics system.

Syntax
#include <graphics.h>
void far initgraph(int far **graphdriver*, int far **graphmode*,
char far **pathtodriver*);

DOS	UNIX	Windows	ANSI C	C++ only
■				

Remarks
initgraph initializes the graphics system by loading a graphics driver from disk (or validating a registered driver), and putting the system into graphics mode.

To start the graphics system, first call the **initgraph** function. **initgraph** loads the graphics driver and puts the system into graphics mode. You can tell **initgraph** to use a particular graphics driver and mode, or to autodetect the attached video adapter at run time and pick the corresponding driver.

If you tell **initgraph** to autodetect, it calls **detectgraph** to select a graphics driver and mode. **initgraph** also resets all graphics settings to their defaults (current position, palette, color, viewport, and so on) and resets **graphresult** to 0.

Normally, **initgraph** loads a graphics driver by allocating memory for the driver (through **_graphgetmem**), then loading the appropriate .BGI file from disk. As an alternative to this dynamic loading scheme, you can link a graphics driver file (or several of them) directly into your executable program file. See UTIL.DOC (included with your distribution disks) for more information on BGIOBJ.

pathtodriver specifies the directory path where **initgraph** looks for graphics drivers. **initgraph** first looks in the path specified in *pathtodriver*, then (if they're not there) in the current directory. Accordingly, if *pathtodriver* is null, the driver files (*.BGI) must be in the current directory. This is also the path **settextstyle** searches for the stroked character font files (*.CHR).

**graphdriver* is an integer that specifies the graphics driver to be used. You can give it a value using a constant of the *graphics_drivers* enumeration type, defined in graphics.h and listed in Table 2.3.

Table 2.3
Graphics drivers constants

graphics_drivers constant	Numeric value
DETECT	0 (requests autodetection)
CGA	1
MCGA	2
EGA	3
EGA64	4
EGAMONO	5
IBM8514	6
HERCMONO	7
ATT400	8
VGA	9
PC3270	10

graphmode* is an integer that specifies the initial graphics mode (unless **graphdriver* equals DETECT; in which case, **graphmode* is set by **initgraph to the highest resolution available for the detected driver). You can give **graphmode* a value using a constant of the *graphics_modes* enumeration type, defined in graphics.h and listed in Table 2.5.

graphdriver and *graphmode* must be set to valid values from tables 2.3 and 2.5, or you'll get unpredictable results. The exception is *graphdriver* = DETECT.

In Table 2.5, the **Palette** listings C0, C1, C2, and C3 refer to the four predefined four-color palettes available on CGA (and compatible) systems. You can select the background color (entry #0) in each of these palettes, but the other colors are fixed. These palettes are described in greater detail in Chapter 11, "Video functions" in the *Programmer's Guide* (in the section titled "Color control," toward the end of the chapter) and summarized in Table 2.4.

Table 2.4
Color palettes

	Color assigned to pixel value		
Palette number	**1**	**2**	**3**
0	LIGHTGREEN	LIGHTRED	YELLOW
1	LIGHTCYAN	LIGHTMAGENTA	WHITE
2	GREEN	RED	BROWN
3	CYAN	MAGENTA	LIGHTGRAY

After a call to **initgraph**, **graphdriver* is set to the current graphics driver, and **graphmode* is set to the current graphics mode.

Table 2.5
Graphics modes

Graphics driver	*graphics_modes*	Value	Column ×row	Palette	Pages
CGA	CGAC0	0	320×200	C0	1
	CGAC1	1	320×200	C1	1
	CGAC2	2	320×200	C2	1
	CGAC3	3	320×200	C3	1
	CGAHI	4	640×200	2 color	1
MCGA	MCGAC0	0	320×200	C0	1
	MCGAC1	1	320×200	C1	1
	MCGAC2	2	320×200	C2	1
	MCGAC3	3	320×200	C3	1
	MCGAMED	4	640×200	2 color	1
	MCGAHI	5	640×480	2 color	1
EGA	EGALO	0	640×200	16 color	4
	EGAHI	1	640×350	16 color	2
EGA64	EGA64LO	0	640×200	16 color	1
	EGA64HI	1	640×350	4 color	1
EGA-MONO	EGAMONOHI	3	640×350	2 color	1*
	EGAMONOHI	3	640×350	2 color	2**
HERC	HERCMONOHI	0	720×348	2 color	2
ATT400	ATT400C0	0	320×200	C0	1
	ATT400C1	1	320×200	C1	1
	ATT400C2	2	320×200	C2	1
	ATT400C3	3	320×200	C3	1
	ATT400MED	4	640×200	2 color	1
	ATT400HI	5	640×400	2 color	1
VGA	VGALO	0	640×200	16 color	2
	VGAMED	1	640×350	16 color	2
	VGAHI	2	640×480	16 color	1
PC3270	PC3270HI	0	720×350	2 color	1
IBM8514	IBM8514HI	1	1024×768	256 color	
	IBM8514LO	0	640×480	256 color	

* 64K on EGAMONO card
** 256K on EGAMONO card

Return Value **initgraph** always sets the internal error code; on success, it sets the code to 0. If an error occurred, **graphdriver* is set to –2, –3, –4, or –5, and **graphresult** returns the same value as listed here:

grNotDetected	–2	Cannot detect a graphics card
grFileNotFound	–3	Cannot find driver file
grInvalidDriver	–4	Invalid driver
grNoLoadMem	–5	Insufficient memory to load driver

See also **closegraph**, **detectgraph**, **getdefaultpalette**, **getdrivername**, **getgraphmode**, **getmoderange**, **graphdefaults**, **_graphgetmem**, **graphresult**, **installuserdriver**, **registerbgidriver**, **registerbgifont**, **restorecrtmode**, **setgraphbufsize**, **setgraphmode**

Example

```
#include <graphics.h>
#include <stdlib.h>
#include <stdio.h>
#include <conio.h>

int main(void)
{
   /* request autodetection */
   int gdriver = DETECT, gmode, errorcode;

   /* initialize graphics mode */
   initgraph(&gdriver, &gmode, "");

   /* read result of initialization */
   errorcode = graphresult();

   if (errorcode != grOk)     /* an error occurred */
   {
      printf("Graphics error: %s\n", grapherrormsg(errorcode));
      printf("Press any key to halt:");
      getch();
      exit(1);                /* return with error code */
   }

   /* draw a line */
   line(0, 0, getmaxx(), getmaxy());

   /* clean up */
   getch();
   closegraph();
   return 0;
}
```

inp

Function Reads a byte from a hardware port.

Syntax #include <conio.h>
int inp(unsigned *portid*);

DOS	UNIX	Windows	ANSI C	C++ only
■		■		

Remarks **inp** is a macro that reads a byte from the input port specified by *portid*.

If **inp** is called when conio.h has been included, it will be treated as a macro that expands to inline code. If you don't include conio.h, or if you do include conio.h and **#undef** the macro **inp**, you get the **inp** function.

Return Value **inp** returns the value read.

See also **inpw, outp, outpw**

Example

```
#include <stdio.h>
#include <conio.h>

int main(void)
{
   int result;
   unsigned port = 0;
   result = inp(port);
   printf("Byte read from port %d = 0x%X\n", port, result);
   return 0;
}
```

inport

Function Reads a word from a hardware port.

Syntax #include <dos.h>
int inport(int *portid*);

DOS	UNIX	Windows	ANSI C	C++ only
■		■		

Remarks **inport** works just like the 80x86 instruction **IN**. It reads the low byte of a word from the input port specified by *portid*; it reads the high byte from *portid* + 1.

Return Value **inport** returns the value read.

See also **inportb, outport, outportb**

Example

```
#include <stdio.h>
#include <dos.h>

int main(void)
{
   int result;
   int port = 0;
   result = inport(port);
```

```
    printf("Word read from port %d = 0x%X\n", port, result);
    return 0;
}
```

inportb

Function Reads a byte from a hardware port.

Syntax #include <dos.h>
unsigned char inportb(int *portid*);

DOS	UNIX	Windows	ANSI C	C++ only
■		■		

Remarks **inportb** is a macro that reads a byte from the input port specified by *portid*.

If **inportb** is called when dos.h has been included, it will be treated as a macro that expands to inline code. If you don't include dos.h, or if you do include dos.h and **#undef** the macro **inportb**, you get the **inportb** function.

Return Value **inportb** returns the value read.

See also **inport**, **outport**, **outportb**

Example

```
#include <stdio.h>
#include <dos.h>

int main(void)
{
    unsigned char result;
    int port = 0;
    result = inportb(port);
    printf("Byte read from port %d = 0x%X\n", port, result);
    return 0;
}
```

inpw

Function Reads a word from a hardware port.

Syntax #include <conio.h>
unsigned inpw(unsigned *portid*);

DOS	UNIX	Windows	ANSI C	C++ only
■		■		

Remarks **inpw** is a macro that reads a 16-bit word from the inport port specified by *portid*. It reads the low byte of the word from *portid*, and the high byte from *portid* + 1.

If **inpw** is called when conio.h has been included, it will be treated as a macro that expands to inline code. If you don't include conio.h, or if you do include conio.h and **#undef** the macro **inpw**, you get the **inpw** function.

Return Value **inpw** returns the value read.

See also **inp, outp, outpw**

Example

```
#include <stdio.h>
#include <conio.h>

int main(void)
{
   unsigned result;
   unsigned port = 0;
   result = inpw(port);
   printf("Word read from port %d = 0x%X\n", port, result);
   return 0;
}
```

insline

Function Inserts a blank line in the text window.

Syntax #include <conio.h>
void insline(void);

DOS	UNIX	Windows	ANSI C	C++ only
■				

Remarks **insline** inserts an empty line in the text window at the cursor position using the current text background color. All lines below the empty one move down one line, and the bottom line scrolls off the bottom of the window.

insline is used in text mode.

Return Value None.

See also **clreol, delline, window**

Example

```
#include <conio.h>

int main(void)
```

```
{
   clrscr();
   cprintf("INSLINE inserts an empty line in the text window\r\n");
   cprintf("at the cursor position using the current text\r\n");
   cprintf("background color.  All lines below the empty one\r\n");
   cprintf("move down one line and the bottom line scrolls\r\n");
   cprintf("off the bottom of the window.\r\n");
   cprintf("\r\nPress any key to continue:");
   gotoxy(1, 3);
   getch();
   insline();
   getch();
   return 0;
}
```


installuserdriver

Function Installs a vendor-added device driver to the BGI device driver table.

Syntax #include <graphics.h>
int far installuserdriver(char far **name*, int huge (**detect*)(void));

DOS	UNIX	Windows	ANSI C	C++ only
■				

Remarks **installuserdriver** allows you to add a vendor-added device driver to the BGI internal table. The *name* parameter is the name of the new device driver file (.BGI), and the *detect* parameter is a pointer to an optional autodetect function that can accompany the new driver. This autodetect function takes no parameters and returns an integer value.

There are two ways to use this vendor-supplied driver. Let's assume you have a new video card called the Spiffy Graphics Array (SGA) and that the SGA manufacturer provided you with a BGI device driver (SGA.BGI). The easiest way to use this driver is to install it by calling **installuserdriver** and then passing the return value (the assigned driver number) directly to **initgraph**.

The other, more general way to use this driver is to link in an autodetect function that will be called by **initgraph** as part of its hardware-detection logic (presumably, the manufacturer of the SGA gave you this autodetect function). When you install the driver (by calling **installuserdriver**), you pass the address of this function, along with the device driver's file name.

After you install the device driver file name and the SGA autodetect function, call **initgraph** and let it go through its normal autodetection process. Before **initgraph** calls its built-in autodetection function (**detectgraph**), it first calls the SGA autodetect function. If the SGA autodetect function doesn't find the SGA hardware, it returns a value of –11 (grError), and **initgraph** proceeds with its normal hardware detection logic (which can include calling any other vendor-supplied autodetection functions in the order in which they were "installed"). If, however, the autodetect function determines that an SGA is present, it returns a non-negative mode number; then **initgraph** locates and loads SGA.BGI, puts the hardware into the default graphics mode recommended by the autodetect function, and finally returns control to your program.

You can install up to ten drivers at one time.

Return Value The value returned by **installuserdriver** is the driver number parameter you would pass to **initgraph** in order to select the newly installed driver manually.

See also **initgraph**, **registerbgidriver**

Example

```
#include <graphics.h>
#include <stdlib.h>
#include <stdio.h>
#include <conio.h>

/* function prototypes */
int huge detectEGA(void);
void checkerrors(void);
int main(void)
{
   int gdriver, gmode;

   /* install a user written device driver */
   gdriver = installuserdriver("EGA", detectEGA);

   /* must force use of detection routine */
   gdriver = DETECT;

   /* check for any installation errors */
   checkerrors();

   /* initialize graphics and local variables */
   initgraph(&gdriver, &gmode, "");

   /* check for any initialization errors */
   checkerrors();

   /* draw a line */
   line(0, 0, getmaxx(), getmaxy());

   /* clean up */
   getch();
   closegraph();
```

```
   return 0;
}

/* detects EGA or VGA cards */
int huge detectEGA(void)
{
   int driver, mode, sugmode = 0;
   detectgraph(&driver, &mode);
   if ((driver == EGA) || (driver == VGA))
      return sugmode;       /* return suggested video mode number */
   else
      return grError;       /* return an error code */
}

/* check for and report any graphics errors */
void checkerrors(void)
{
   int errorcode;

   /* read result of last graphics operation */
   errorcode = graphresult();
   if (errorcode != grOk) {
      printf("Graphics error: %s\n", grapherrormsg(errorcode));
      printf("Press any key to halt:");
      getch();
      exit(1);
   }
}
```


installuserfont

Function Loads a font file (.CHR) that is not built into the BGI system.

Syntax #include <graphics.h>
int far installuserfont(char far **name*);

DOS	UNIX	Windows	ANSI C	C++ only
■				

Remarks *name* is a path name to a font file containing a stroked font. Up to twenty fonts can be installed at one time.

Return Value **installuserfont** returns a font ID number that can then be passed to **settextstyle** to select the corresponding font. If the internal font table is full, a value of –11 (grError) is returned.

See also **settextstyle**

Example

```
#include <graphics.h>
#include <stdlib.h>
#include <stdio.h>
#include <conio.h>

/* function prototype */
void checkerrors(void);
int main(void)
{
   /* request autodetection */
   int gdriver = DETECT, gmode;
   int userfont;
   int midx, midy;

   /* initialize graphics and local variables */
   initgraph(&gdriver, &gmode, "");

   midx = getmaxx() / 2;
   midy = getmaxy() / 2;

   /* check for any initialization errors */
   checkerrors();

   /* install a user-defined font file */
   userfont = installuserfont("USER.CHR");

   /* check for any installation errors */
   checkerrors();

   /* select the user font */
   settextstyle(userfont, HORIZ_DIR, 4);

   /* output some text */
   outtextxy(midx, midy, "Testing!");

   /* clean up */
   getch();
   closegraph();
   return 0;
}

/* check for and report any graphics errors */
void checkerrors(void)
{
   int errorcode;

   /* read result of last graphics operation */
   errorcode = graphresult();
   if (errorcode != grOk) {
      printf("Graphics error: %s\n", grapherrormsg(errorcode));
      printf("Press any key to halt:");
      getch();
```

```
        exit(1);
    }
}
```

int86

Function General 8086 software interrupt.

Syntax #include <dos.h>
int int86(int *intno*, union REGS **inregs*, union REGS **outregs*);

DOS	UNIX	Windows	ANSI C	C++ only
■		■		

Remarks **int86** executes an 8086 software interrupt specified by the argument *intno*. Before executing the software interrupt, it copies register values from *inregs* into the registers.

After the software interrupt returns, **int86** copies the current register values to *outregs*, copies the status of the carry flag to the *x.cflag* field in *outregs*, and copies the value of the 8086 flags register to the *x.flags* field in *outregs*. If the carry flag is set, it usually indicates that an error has occurred.

Note that *inregs* can point to the same structure that *outregs* points to.

Return Value **int86** returns the value of AX after completion of the software interrupt. If the carry flag is set (`outregs -> x.cflag != 0`), indicating an error, this function sets the global variable *_doserrno* to the error code.

See also **bdos**, **bdosptr**, **geninterrupt**, **int86x**, **intdos**, **intdosx**, **intr**

Example

```
#include <stdio.h>
#include <conio.h>
#include <dos.h>

#define VIDEO 0x10

void movetoxy(int x, int y)
{
   union REGS regs;
   regs.h.ah = 2;                /* set cursor postion */
   regs.h.dh = y;
   regs.h.dl = x;
   regs.h.bh = 0;                /* video page 0 */
   int86(VIDEO, &regs, &regs);
}
```

```
int main(void)
{
   clrscr();
   movetoxy(35, 10);
   printf("Hello\n");
   return 0;
}
```

int86x

Function General 8086 software interrupt interface.

Syntax #include <dos.h>
int int86x(int *intno*, union REGS **inregs*, union REGS **outregs*,
struct SREGS **segregs*);

DOS	UNIX	Windows	ANSI C	C++ only
■		■		

Remarks **int86x** executes an 8086 software interrupt specified by the argument *intno*. Before executing the software interrupt, it copies register values from *inregs* into the registers.

In addition, **int86x** copies the *segregs ->ds* and *segregs ->es* values into the corresponding registers before executing the software interrupt. This feature allows programs that use far pointers or a large data memory model to specify which segment is to be used for the software interrupt.

After the software interrupt returns, **int86x** copies the current register values to *outregs*, the status of the carry flag to the x.cflag field in *outregs*, and the value of the 8086 flags register to the x.flags field in *outregs*. In addition, **int86x** restores DS and sets the *segregs ->es* and *segregs ->ds* fields to the values of the corresponding segment registers. If the carry flag is set, it usually indicates that an error has occurred.

int86x lets you invoke an 8086 software interrupt that takes a value of DS different from the default data segment, and/or takes an argument in ES.

Note that *inregs* can point to the same structure that *outregs* points to.

Return Value **int86x** returns the value of AX after completion of the software interrupt. If the carry flag is set (`outregs -> x.cflag != 0`), indicating an error, this function sets the global variable *_doserrno* to the error code.

See also **bdos, bdosptr, geninterrupt, intdos, intdosx, int86, intr, segread**

Example

```
#include <dos.h>
```

```
#include <process.h>
#include <stdio.h>

int main(void)
{
   char filename[80];
   union REGS inregs, outregs;
   struct SREGS segregs;
   printf("Enter file name: ");
   gets(filename);
   inregs.h.ah = 0x43;
   inregs.h.al = 0;
   inregs.x.dx = FP_OFF(filename);
   segregs.ds = FP_SEG(filename);
   int86x(0x21, &inregs, &outregs, &segregs);
   printf("File attribute: %X\n", outregs.x.cx);
   return 0;
}
```


intdos

Function General DOS interrupt interface.

Syntax #include <dos.h>
int intdos(union REGS *inregs*, union REGS *outregs*);

DOS	UNIX	Windows	ANSI C	C++ only
■		■		

Remarks **intdos** executes DOS interrupt 0x21 to invoke a specified DOS function. The value of *inregs -> h.ah* specifies the DOS function to be invoked.

After the interrupt 0x21 returns, **intdos** copies the current register values to *outregs*, copies the status of the carry flag to the *x.cflag* field in *outregs*, and copies the value of the 8086 flags register to the *x.flags* field in *outregs*. If the carry flag is set, it indicates that an error has occurred.

Note that *inregs* can point to the same structure that *outregs* points to.

Return Value **intdos** returns the value of AX after completion of the DOS function call. If the carry flag is set (`outregs -> x.cflag != 0`), indicating an error, it sets the global variable *_doserrno* to the error code.

See also **bdos**, **bdosptr**, **geninterrupt**, **int86**, **int86x**, **intdosx**, **intr**

Example

```
#include <stdio.h>
#include <dos.h>
```

```
/* deletes file name; returns 0 on success, nonzero on failure */
int delete_file(char near *filename)
{
   union REGS regs;
   int ret;
   regs.h.ah = 0x41;                              /* delete file */
   regs.x.dx = (unsigned) filename;
   ret = intdos(&regs, &regs);

   /* if carry flag is set, there was an error */
   return(regs.x.cflag ? ret : 0);
}

int main(void)
{
   int err;
   err = delete_file("NOTEXIST.$$$");
   if (!err)
      printf("Able to delete NOTEXIST.$$$\n");
   else
      printf("Not able to delete NOTEXIST.$$$\n");
   return 0;
}
```

intdosx

Function General DOS interrupt interface.

Syntax #include <dos.h>
int intdosx(union REGS **inregs*, union REGS **outregs*,
struct SREGS **segregs*);

DOS	UNIX	Windows	ANSI C	C++ only
■		■		

Remarks **intdosx** executes DOS interrupt 0x21 to invoke a specified DOS function. The value of *inregs -> h.ah* specifies the DOS function to be invoked.

In addition, **intdosx** copies the *segregs ->ds* and *segregs ->es* values into the corresponding registers before invoking the DOS function. This feature allows programs that use far pointers or a large data memory model to specify which segment is to be used for the function execution.

After the interrupt 0x21 returns, **intdosx** copies the current register values to *outregs*, copies the status of the carry flag to the x.cflag field in *outregs*, and copies the value of the 8086 flags register to the x.flags field in *outregs*. In addition, **intdosx** sets the *segregs ->es* and *segregs ->ds* fields to the values of the corresponding segment registers and then restores DS. If the carry flag is set, it indicates that an error occurred.

intdosx lets you invoke a DOS function that takes a value of DS different from the default data segment and/or takes an argument in ES.

Note that *inregs* can point to the same structure that *outregs* points to.

Return Value **intdosx** returns the value of AX after completion of the DOS function call. If the carry flag is set (`outregs -> x.cflag != 0`), indicating an error, it sets the global variable *_doserrno* to the error code.

See also **bdos, bdosptr, geninterrupt, int86, int86x, intdos, intr, segread**

Example

```
#include <stdio.h>
#include <dos.h>

/* deletes file name; returns 0 on success, nonzero on failure */
int delete_file(char far *filename)
{
   union REGS regs; struct SREGS sregs;
   int ret;
   regs.h.ah = 0x41;                            /* delete file */
   regs.x.dx = FP_OFF(filename);
   sregs.ds = FP_SEG(filename);
   ret = intdosx(&regs, &regs, &sregs);

   /* if carry flag is set, there was an error */
   return(regs.x.cflag ? ret : 0);
}

int main(void)
{
   int err;
   err = delete_file("NOTEXIST.$$$");
   if (!err)
      printf("Able to delete NOTEXIST.$$$\n");
   else
      printf("Not Able to delete NOTEXIST.$$$\n");
   return 0;
}
```

intr

Function Alternate 8086 software interrupt interface.

Syntax #include <dos.h>
void *intr*(int *intno*, struct REGPACK **preg*);

DOS	UNIX	Windows	ANSI C	C++ only
■		■		

Remarks The **intr** function is an alternate interface for executing software interrupts. It generates an 8086 software interrupt specified by the argument *intno*.

intr copies register values from the **REGPACK** structure **preg* into the registers before executing the software interrupt. After the software interrupt completes, **intr** copies the current register values into **preg*, including the flags.

The arguments passed to **intr** are as follows:

intno Interrupt number to be executed

preg Address of a structure containing

(a) the input registers before the interrupt call
(b) the value of the registers after the interrupt call

The **REGPACK** structure (defined in dos.h) has the following format:

```
struct  REGPACK {
   unsigned  r_ax, r_bx, r_cx, r_dx;
   unsigned  r_bp, r_si, r_di, r_ds, r_es, r_flags;
};
```

Return Value No value is returned. The **REGPACK** structure **preg* contains the value of the registers after the interrupt call.

See also **geninterrupt, int86, int86x, intdos, intdosx**

Example

```
#include <stdio.h>
#include <string.h>
#include <dir.h>
#include <dos.h>
#define CF 1  /* Carry flag */

int main(void)
{
   char directory[80];
   struct REGPACK reg;
   printf("Enter directory to change to: ");
   gets(directory);
   reg.r_ax = 0x3B << 8;            /* shift 3Bh into  AH */
   reg.r_dx = FP_OFF(directory);
   reg.r_ds = FP_SEG(directory);
   intr(0x21, &reg);
   if (reg.r_flags & CF)
```

```
        printf("Directory change failed\n");
    getcwd(directory, 80);
    printf("The current directory is: %s\n", directory);
    return 0;
}
```

ioctl

Function Controls I/0 device.

Syntax #include <io.h>
int ioctl(int *handle*, int *func* [, void *argdx, int argcx]);

DOS	UNIX	Windows	ANSI C	C++ only
■	■	■		

Remarks **ioctl** is available on UNIX systems, but not with these parameters or functionality. UNIX version 7 and System III differ from each other in their use of **ioctl**. **ioctl** calls are not portable to UNIX and are rarely portable across DOS machines.

DOS 3.0 extends **ioctl** with *func* values of 8 and 11.

This is a direct interface to the DOS call 0x44 (IOCTL).

The exact function depends on the value of *func* as follows:

- 0 Get device information.
- 1 Set device information (in *argdx*).
- 2 Read *argcx* bytes into the address pointed to by *argdx*.
- 3 Write *argcx* bytes from the address pointed to by *argdx*.
- 4 Same as 2 except *handle* is treated as a drive number (0 equals default, 1 equals A, and so on).
- 5 Same as 3 except *handle* is a drive number (0 equals default, 1 equals A, and so on).
- 6 Get input status.
- 7 Get output status.
- 8 Test removability; DOS 3.0 only.
- 11 Set sharing conflict retry count; DOS 3.0 only.

ioctl can be used to get information about device channels. Regular files can also be used, but only *func* values 0, 6, and 7 are defined for them. All other calls return an EINVAL error for files.

See the documentation for system call 0x44 in your DOS reference manuals for detailed information on argument or return values.

The arguments *argdx* and *argcx* are optional.

ioctl provides a direct interface to DOS device drivers for special functions. As a result, the exact behavior of this function varies across different vendors' hardware and in different devices. Also, several vendors do not follow the interfaces described here. Refer to the vendor BIOS documentation for exact use of **ioctl**.

Return Value For *func* 0 or 1, the return value is the device information (DX of the IOCTL call).

For *func* values of 2 through 5, the return value is the number of bytes actually transferred.

For *func* values of 6 or 7, the return value is the device status.

In any event, if an error is detected, a value of –1 is returned, and the global variable *errno* is set to one of the following:

EINVAL	Invalid argument
EBADF	Bad file number
EINVDAT	Invalid data

Example

```
#include <stdio.h>
#include <dir.h>
#include <io.h>

int main(void)
{
   int stat;

   /* use func 8 to determine if the default drive is removable */
   stat = ioctl(0, 8, 0, 0);
   if (!stat)
      printf("Drive %c is removable.\n", getdisk() + 'A');
   else
      printf("Drive %c is not removable.\n", getdisk() + 'A');
   return 0;
}
```

isalnum

Function Character classification macro.

Syntax #include <ctype.h>
int isalnum(int *c*);

DOS	UNIX	Windows	ANSI C	C++ only
■	■	■	■	

Remarks **isalnum** is a macro that classifies ASCII-coded integer values by table lookup. It is a predicate returning nonzero for true and 0 for false. It is defined only when **isascii**(*c*) is true or *c* is EOF.

You can make this macro available as a function by undefining (**#undef**) it.

Return Value **isalnum** returns nonzero if *c* is a letter (*A* to *Z* or *a* to *z*) or a digit (0 to 9).

Example

```
#include <ctype.h>
#include <stdio.h>

int main(void)
{
   char c = 'C';
   if (isalnum(c))
      printf("%c is alphanumeric\n",c);
   else
      printf("%c isn't alphanumeric\n",c);
   return 0;
}
```


isalpha

Function Character classification macro.

Syntax #include <ctype.h>
int isalpha(int *c*);

DOS	UNIX	Windows	ANSI C	C++ only
■	■	■	■	

Remarks **isalpha** is a macro that classifies ASCII-coded integer values by table lookup. It is a predicate returning nonzero for true and 0 for false. It is defined only when **isascii**(*c*) is true or *c* is EOF.

You can make this macro available as a function by undefining (**#undef**) it.

Return Value **isalpha** returns nonzero if *c* is a letter (*A* to *Z* or *a* to *z*).

Example

```
#include <ctype.h>
#include <stdio.h>

int main(void)
{
   char c = 'C';
```

```
    if (isalpha(c))
       printf("%c is alphabetic\n",c);
    else
       printf("%c isn't alphabetic\n",c);

    return 0;
}
```

isascii

Function Character classification macro.

Syntax #include <ctype.h>
int isascii(int *c*);

DOS	UNIX	Windows	ANSI C	C++ only
■	■	■		

Remarks **isascii** is a macro that classifies ASCII-coded integer values by table lookup. It is a predicate returning nonzero for true and 0 for false.

isascii is defined on all integer values.

Return Value **isascii** returns nonzero if the low order byte of *c* is in the range 0 to 127 (0x00-0x7F).

Example

```
#include <ctype.h>
#include <stdio.h>

int main(void)
{
   char c = 'C';
   if (isascii(c))
      printf("%c is ascii\n",c);
   else
      printf("%c isn't ascii\n",c);

   return 0;
}
```

isatty

Function Checks for device type.

Syntax #include <io.h>
int isatty(int *handle*);

DOS	UNIX	Windows	ANSI C	C++ only
■	■	■		

Remarks **isatty** determines whether *handle* is associated with any one of the following character devices:

- a terminal
- a console
- a printer
- a serial port

Return Value If the device is a character device, **isatty** returns a nonzero integer. If it is not such a device, **isatty** returns 0.

Example

```
#include <stdio.h>
#include <io.h>

int main(void)
{
   int handle;
   handle = fileno(stdprn);
   if (isatty(handle))
      printf("Handle %d is a device type\n", handle);
   else
      printf("Handle %d isn't a device type\n", handle);
   return 0;
}
```

iscntrl

Function Character classification macro.

Syntax #include <ctype.h>
int iscntrl(int *c*);

DOS	UNIX	Windows	ANSI C	C++ only
■	■	■	■	

Remarks **iscntrl** is a macro that classifies ASCII-coded integer values by table lookup. It is a predicate returning nonzero for true and 0 for false. It is defined only when **isascii**(*c*) is true or *c* is EOF.

You can make this macro available as a function by undefining (**#undef**) it.

Return Value **iscntrl** returns nonzero if *c* is a delete character or ordinary control character (0x7F or 0x00 to 0x1F).

Example

```
#include <ctype.h>
#include <stdio.h>

int main(void)
{
   char c = 'C';
   if (iscntrl(c))
      printf("%c is a control character\n",c);
   else
      printf("%c isn't a control character\n",c);
   return 0;
}
```

isdigit

Function Character classification macro.

Syntax #include <ctype.h>
int isdigit(int *c*);

DOS	UNIX	Windows	ANSI C	C++ only
■	■	■	■	

Remarks **isdigit** is a macro that classifies ASCII-coded integer values by table lookup. It is a predicate returning nonzero for true and 0 for false. It is defined only when **isascii**(*c*) is true or *c* is EOF.

You can make this macro available as a function by undefining (#**undef**) it.

Return Value **isdigit** returns nonzero if *c* is a digit (0 to 9).

Example

```
#include <ctype.h>
#include <stdio.h>

int main(void)
{
   char c = 'C';
   if (isdigit(c))
      printf("%c is a digit\n",c);
   else
      printf("%c isn't a digit\n",c);
   return 0;
}
```

isgraph

Function Character classification macro.

Syntax #include <ctype.h>
int isgraph(int *c*);

DOS	UNIX	Windows	ANSI C	C++ only
■	■	■	■	

Remarks **isgraph** is a macro that classifies ASCII-coded integer values by table lookup. It is a predicate returning nonzero for true and 0 for false. It is defined only when **isascii**(*c*) is true or *c* is EOF.

You can make this macro available as a function by undefining (**#undef**) it.

Return Value **isgraph** returns nonzero if *c* is a printing character, like **isprint**, except that a space character is excluded.

Example

```
#include <ctype.h>
#include <stdio.h>

int main(void)
{
   char c = 'C';
   if (isgraph(c))
      printf("%c is a graphic character\n",c);
   else
      printf("%c isn't a graphic character\n",c);

   return 0;
}
```

islower

Function Character classification macro.

Syntax #include <ctype.h>
int islower(int *c*);

DOS	UNIX	Windows	ANSI C	C++ only
■	■	■	■	

Remarks **islower** is a macro that classifies ASCII-coded integer values by table lookup. It is a predicate returning nonzero for true and 0 for false. It is defined only when **isascii**(*c*) is true or *c* is EOF.

You can make this macro available as a function by undefining (**#undef**) it.

Return Value **islower** returns nonzero if *c* is a lowercase letter (*a* to *z*).

Example

```
#include <ctype.h>
#include <stdio.h>

int main(void)
{
   char c = 'C';

   if (islower(c))
      printf("%c is lower case\n",c);
   else
      printf("%c isn't lower case\n",c);
   return 0;
}
```

isprint

Function Character classification macro.

Syntax #include <ctype.h>
int isprint(int *c*);

DOS	UNIX	Windows	ANSI C	C++ only
▪	▪	▪	▪	

Remarks **isprint** is a macro that classifies ASCII-coded integer values by table lookup. It is a predicate returning nonzero for true and 0 for false. It is defined only when **isascii**(*c*) is true or *c* is EOF.

You can make this macro available as a function by undefining (**#undef**) it.

Return Value **isprint** returns nonzero if *c* is a printing character (0x20 to 0x7E).

Example

```
#include <ctype.h>
#include <stdio.h>

int main(void)
{
   char c = 'C';
   if (isprint(c))
      printf("%c is a printable character\n",c);
   else
```

```
      printf("%c isn't a printable character\n",c);
   return 0;
}
```

ispunct

Function Character classification macro.

Syntax #include <ctype.h>
int ispunct(int *c*);

DOS	UNIX	Windows	ANSI C	C++ only
■	■	■	■	

Remarks **ispunct** is a macro that classifies ASCII-coded integer values by table lookup. It is a predicate returning nonzero for true and 0 for false. It is defined only when **isascii**(*c*) is true or *c* is EOF.

You can make this macro available as a function by undefining (**#undef**) it.

Return Value **ispunct** returns nonzero if *c* is a punctuation character (**iscntrl** or **isspace**).

Example

```
#include <ctype.h>
#include <stdio.h>

int main(void)
{
   char c = 'C';
   if (ispunct(c))
      printf("%c is a punctuation character\n",c);
   else
      printf("%c isn't a punctuation character\n",c);
   return 0;
}
```

isspace

Function Character classification macro.

Syntax #include <ctype.h>
int isspace(int *c*);

DOS	UNIX	Windows	ANSI C	C++ only
■	■	■	■	

Remarks **isspace** is a macro that classifies ASCII-coded integer values by table lookup. It is a predicate returning nonzero for true and 0 for false. It is defined only when **isascii**(*c*) is true or *c* is EOF.

You can make this macro available as a function by undefining (#**undef**) it.

Return Value **isspace** returns nonzero if *c* is a space, tab, carriage return, new line, vertical tab, or formfeed (0x09 to 0x0D, 0x20).

Example

```
#include <ctype.h>
#include <stdio.h>

int main(void)
{
   char c = 'C';
   if (isspace(c))
      printf("%c is white space\n",c);
   else
      printf("%c isn't white space\n",c);
   return 0;
}
```

isupper

Function Character classification macro.

Syntax #include <ctype.h>
int isupper(int *c*);

DOS	UNIX	Windows	ANSI C	C++ only
■	■	■	■	

Remarks **isupper** is a macro that classifies ASCII-coded integer values by table lookup. It is a predicate returning nonzero for true and 0 for false. It is defined only when **isascii**(*c*) is true or *c* is EOF.

You can make this macro available as a function by undefining (#**undef**) it.

Return Value **isupper** returns nonzero if *c* is an uppercase letter (*A* to *Z*).

Example

```
#include <ctype.h>
#include <stdio.h>

int main(void)
{
   char c = 'C';
   if (isupper(c))
      printf("%c is upper case\n",c);
```

```
   else
      printf("%c isn't upper case\n",c);
   return 0;
}
```

isxdigit

Function Character classification macro.

Syntax #include <ctype.h>
int isxdigit(int *c*);

DOS	UNIX	Windows	ANSI C	C++ only
■	■	■	■	

Remarks **isxdigit** is a macro that classifies ASCII-coded integer values by table lookup. It is a predicate returning nonzero for true and 0 for false. It is defined only when **isascii**(*c*) is true or *c* is EOF.

You can make this macro available as a function by undefining (**#undef**) it.

Return Value **isxdigit** returns nonzero if *c* is a hexadecimal digit (0 to 9, *A to F, a to f*).

Example

```
#include <ctype.h>
#include <stdio.h>

int main(void)
{
   char c = 'C';
   if (isxdigit(c))
      printf("%c is hexadecimal\n",c);
   else
      printf("%c isn't hexadecimal\n",c);
   return 0;
}
```

itoa

Function Converts an integer to a string.

Syntax #include <stdlib.h>
char *itoa(int *value*, char **string*, int *radix*);

DOS	UNIX	Windows	ANSI C	C++ only
■		■		

Remarks **itoa** converts *value* to a null-terminated string and stores the result in *string*. With **itoa**, *value* is an integer.

radix specifies the base to be used in converting *value*; it must be between 2 and 36, inclusive. If *value* is negative and *radix* is 10, the first character of *string* is the minus sign (–).

➡ The space allocated for *string* must be large enough to hold the returned string, including the terminating null character (\0). **itoa** can return up to 17 bytes.

Return Value **itoa** returns a pointer to *string*.

See also **ltoa**, **ultoa**

Example

```
#include <stdlib.h>
#include <stdio.h>

int main(void)
{
   int number = 12345;
   char string[25];
   itoa(number, string, 10);
   printf("integer = %d string = %s\n", number, string);
   return 0;
}
```

kbhit

Function Checks for currently available keystrokes.

Syntax #include <conio.h>
int kbhit(void);

DOS	UNIX	Windows	ANSI C	C++ only
■				

Remarks **kbhit** checks to see if a keystroke is currently available. Any available keystrokes can be retrieved with **getch** or **getche**.

Return Value If a keystroke is available, **kbhit** returns a nonzero value. Otherwise, it returns 0.

See also **getch**, **getche**

Example

```
#include <conio.h>

int main(void)
```

```
{
   cprintf("Press any key to continue:");
   while (!kbhit()) /* do nothing */ ;
   cprintf("\r\nA key was pressed...\r\n");
   return 0;
}
```

keep, _dos_keep

Function Exits and remains resident.

Syntax #include <dos.h>
void keep(unsigned char *status*, unsigned *size*);
void _dos_keep(unsigned char *status*, unsigned *size*);

DOS	UNIX	Windows	ANSI C	C++ only
■				

Remarks **keep** and **_dos_keep** return to DOS with the exit status in *status*. The current program remains resident, however. The program is set to *size* paragraphs in length, and the remainder of the memory of the program is freed.

keep and **_dos_keep** can be used when installing TSR programs. **keep** and **_dos_keep** use DOS function 0x31.

Before **_dos_keep** exits, it calls any registered "exit functions" (posted with **atexit**), flushes file buffers, and restores interrupt vectors modified by the startup code.

Return Value None.

See also **abort, exit**

Example

```
/* This is an interrupt service routine. You can NOT compile this program with
   Test Stack Overflow turned on and get an executable file which will operate
   correctly. Due to the nature of this function the formula used to compute the
   number of paragraphs may not necessarily work in all cases. Use with care!
   Terminate Stay Resident (TSR) programs are complex and no other support for
   them is provided. Refer to the MS-DOS technical documentation for more
   information. */

#include <dos.h>
   /* The clock tick interrupt */
#define INTR 0x1C
   /* Screen attribute (blue on grey) */
#define ATTR 0x7900
```

```
#ifdef __cplusplus
    #define __CPPARGS ...
#else
    #define __CPPARGS
#endif

/* Reduce heaplength and stacklength to make a smaller program in memory. */
extern unsigned _heaplen = 1024;
extern unsigned _stklen  = 512;

void interrupt ( *oldhandler)(__CPPARGS);

typedef unsigned int (far *s_arrayptr);

void interrupt handler(__CPPARGS)
{
   s_arrayptr screen[80];
   static int count;

   /* For a color screen the video memory is at B800:0000.
      For a monochrome system use B000:000.
   */
   screen[0] = (s_arrayptr) MK_FP(0xB800,0);

   /* increase the counter and keep it within 0 to 9 */
   count++;
   count %= 10;

   /* put the number on the screen */
   screen[0][79] = count + '0' + ATTR;

   /* call the old interrupt handler */
   oldhandler();
}

int main(void)
{

   /* Get the address of the current clock tick interrupt */
   oldhandler = getvect(INTR);

   /* install the new interrupt handler */
   setvect(INTR, handler);

   /* _psp is the starting address of the program in memory. The top of the stack
      is the end of the program. Using _SS and _SP together we can get the end of
      the stack. You may want to allow a bit of safety space to insure that
      enough room is being allocated ie:
      (_SS + ((_SP + safety space)/16) - _psp)
   */
   keep(0, (_SS + (_SP/16) - _psp));
   return 0;
}
```

Example 2

```
/* NOTE: This is an interrupt service routine. You CANNOT compile this program
   with Test Stack Overflow turned on and get an executable file which will
   operate correctly. Due to the nature of this function the formula used to
   compute the number of paragraphs may not necessarily work in all cases. Use
   with care! Terminate Stay Resident (TSR) programs are complex and no other
   support for them is provided. Refer to the MS-DOS technical documentation for
   more information. */

#include <dos.h>
   /* The clock tick interrupt */
#define INTR 0x1C
   /* Screen attribute (blue on grey) */
#define ATTR 0x7900

#ifdef __cplusplus
    #define __CPPARGS ...
#else
    #define __CPPARGS
#endif

/* Reduce heaplength and stacklength to make a smaller program in memory */
extern unsigned _heaplen = 1024;
extern unsigned _stklen  = 512;

void interrupt ( *oldhandler)(__CPPARGS);

typedef unsigned int (far *s_arrayptr);

void interrupt handler(__CPPARGS)
{
   s_arrayptr screen[80];
   static int count;

/* For a color screen the video memory is at B800:0000.
   For a monochrome system use B000:000 */
   screen[0] = (s_arrayptr) MK_FP(0xB800,0);

/* Increase the counter and keep it within 0 to 9. */
   count++;
   count %= 10;

/* Put the number on the screen. */
   screen[0][79] = count + '0' + ATTR;

/* Call the old interrupt handler. */
   oldhandler();
}

int main(void)
{
/* Get the address of the current clock tick interrupt. */
   oldhandler = _dos_getvect(INTR);

/* install the new interrupt handler */
```

```
   _dos_setvect(INTR, handler);

/* _psp is the starting address of the program in memory. The top of the stack is
   the end of the program. Using _SS and _SP together we can get the end of the
   stack. You may want to allow a bit of safety space to insure that enough room
   is being allocated ie:
   (_SS + ((_SP + safety space)/16) - _psp) */

   _dos_keep(0, (_SS + (_SP/16) - _psp));
   return 0;
}
```

labs

Function Gives long absolute value.

Syntax #include <math.h>
long int labs(long int *x*);

DOS	UNIX	Windows	ANSI C	C++ only
■	■	■	■	

Remarks **labs** computes the absolute value of the parameter *x*.

Return Value **labs** returns the absolute value of *x*.

See also **abs, cabs, fabs**

Example

```
#include <stdio.h>
#include <math.h>

int main(void)
{
   long result;
   long x = -12345678L;
   result= labs(x);
   printf("number: %ld abs value: %ld\n", x, result);
   return 0;
}
```

ldexp, ldexpl

Function Calculates $x \times 2^{exp}$.

Syntax #include <math.h>
double ldexp(double *x*, int *exp*);
long double ldexpl(long double *x*, int *exp*);

	DOS	UNIX	Windows	ANSI C	C++ only
ldexp	■	■	■	■	
ldexpl	■		■		

Remarks **ldexp** calculates the double value $x \times 2^{exp}$.
lexpl is the long double version; it takes a long double argument for *x* and returns a long double result.

Return Value On success, **ldexp** (or **ldexpl**) returns the value it calculated, $x \times 2^{exp}$.

Error handling for these routines can be modified through the functions **matherr** and **_matherrl**.

See also **exp, frexp, modf**

Example

```
#include <stdio.h>
#include <math.h>

int main(void)
{
   double value, x = 2;

   /* ldexp raises 2 by a power of 3 then multiplies the result by 2 */
   value = ldexp(x,3);
   printf("The ldexp value is: %lf\n", value);
   return 0;
}
```

K-M

ldiv

Function Divides two **long**s, returning quotient and remainder.

Syntax #include <stdlib.h>
ldiv_t ldiv(long int *numer*, long int *denom*);

DOS	UNIX	Windows	ANSI C	C++ only
■		■	■	

Remarks **ldiv** divides two **long**s and returns both the quotient and the remainder as an *ldiv_t* type. *numer* and *denom* are the numerator and denominator, respectively. The *ldiv_t* type is a structure of **long**s defined (with **typedef**) in stdlib.h as follows:

```
typedef struct {
   long int quot;       /* quotient */
   long int rem;        /* remainder */
```

```
} ldiv_t;
```

Return Value **ldiv** returns a structure whose elements are *quot* (the quotient) and *rem* (the remainder).

See also **div**

Example

```
#include <stdlib.h>
#include <stdio.h>

int main(void)
{
   ldiv_t lx;
   lx = ldiv(100000L, 30000L);
   printf("100000 div 30000 = %ld remainder %ld\n", lx.quot, lx.rem);
   return 0;
}
```

lfind

Function Performs a linear search.

Syntax #include <stdlib.h>
void *lfind(const void **key*, const void **base*, size_t **num*, size_t *width*,
int (**fcmp*)(const void *, const void *));

DOS	UNIX	Windows	ANSI C	C++ only
■	■	■		

Remarks **lfind** makes a linear search for the value of *key* in an array of sequential records. It uses a user-defined comparison routine (*fcmp*).

The array is described as having **num* records that are *width* bytes wide, and begins at the memory location pointed to by *base*.

Return Value **lfind** returns the address of the first entry in the table that matches the search key. If no match is found, **lfind** returns null. The comparison routine must return 0 if **elem1* == **elem2*, and nonzero otherwise (*elem1* and *elem2* are its two parameters).

See also **bsearch**, **lsearch**, **qsort**

Example

```
#include <stdio.h>
#include <stdlib.h>

int compare(int *x, int *y)
{
   return( *x - *y );
}
```

```
int main(void)
{
   int array[5] = {35, 87, 46, 99, 12};
   size_t nelem = 5;
   int key = 99;
   int *result;

   result = (int *) lfind(&key, array, &nelem,
                          sizeof(int),
                          (int(*)(const void *,const void *))compare);
   if (result)
      printf("Number %d found\n",key);
   else
      printf("Number %d not found\n",key);
   return 0;
}
```


line

Function Draws a line between two specified points.

Syntax #include <graphics.h>
void far line(int *x1*, int *y1*, int *x2*, int *y2*);

DOS	UNIX	Windows	ANSI C	C++ only
■				

Remarks **line** draws a line in the current color, using the current line style and thickness between the two points specified, (*x1*,*y1*) and (*x2*,*y2*), without updating the current position (CP).

Return Value None.

See also **getlinesettings, linerel, lineto, setcolor, setlinestyle, setwritemode**

Example

```
#include <graphics.h>
#include <stdlib.h>
#include <stdio.h>
#include <conio.h>

int main(void)
{
   /* request autodetection */
   int gdriver = DETECT, gmode, errorcode;
   int xmax, ymax;

   /* initialize graphics and local variables */
   initgraph(&gdriver, &gmode, "");
```

```
   /* read result of initialization */
   errorcode = graphresult();

   if (errorcode != grOk) { /* an error occurred */
      printf("Graphics error: %s\n", grapherrormsg(errorcode));
      printf("Press any key to halt:");
      getch();
      exit(1);
   }

   setcolor(getmaxcolor());
   xmax = getmaxx();
   ymax = getmaxy();

   /* draw a diagonal line */
   line(0, 0, xmax, ymax);

   /* clean up */
   getch();
   closegraph();
   return 0;
}
```

linerel

Function Draws a line a relative distance from the current position (CP).

Syntax #include <graphics.h>
void far linerel(int *dx*, int *dy*);

DOS	UNIX	Windows	ANSI C	C++ only
■				

Remarks **linerel** draws a line from the CP to a point that is a relative distance (*dx*,*dy*) from the CP. The CP is advanced by (*dx*,*dy*).

Return Value None.

See also **getlinesettings, line, lineto, setcolor, setlinestyle, setwritemode**

Example

```
#include <graphics.h>
#include <stdlib.h>
#include <stdio.h>
#include <conio.h>

int main(void)
{
   /* request autodetection */
   int gdriver = DETECT, gmode, errorcode;
```

```
   char msg[80];

   /* initialize graphics and local variables */
   initgraph(&gdriver, &gmode, "");

   /* read result of initialization */
   errorcode = graphresult();
   if (errorcode != grOk) {
      printf("Graphics error: %s\n", grapherrormsg(errorcode));
      printf("Press any key to halt:");
      getch();
      exit(1);
   }

   /* move the CP to location (20,30) */
   moveto(20,30);

   /* create and output a message at (20,30) */
   sprintf(msg, " (%d, %d)", getx(), gety());
   outtextxy(20,30, msg);

   /* draw line to a point a relative distance away from current CP */
   linerel(100, 100);

   /* create and output a message at CP */
   sprintf(msg, " (%d, %d)", getx(), gety());
   outtext(msg);

   /* clean up */
   getch();
   closegraph();
   return 0;
}
```

K-M

lineto

Function Draws a line from the current position (CP) to (*x*,*y*).

Syntax #include <graphics.h>
void far lineto(int *x*, int *y*);

DOS	UNIX	Windows	ANSI C	C++ only
■				

Remarks **lineto** draws a line from the CP to (*x*,*y*), then moves the CP to (*x*,*y*).

Return Value None.

See also **getlinesettings, line, linerel, setcolor, setlinestyle, setvisualpage, setwritemode**

Example

```
#include <graphics.h>
#include <stdlib.h>
#include <stdio.h>
#include <conio.h>

int main(void)
{
   /* request autodetection */
   int gdriver = DETECT, gmode, errorcode;
   char msg[80];

   /* initialize graphics and local variables */
   initgraph(&gdriver, &gmode, "");

   /* read result of initialization */
   errorcode = graphresult();
   if (errorcode != grOk) {
      printf("Graphics error: %s\n", grapherrormsg(errorcode));
      printf("Press any key to halt:");
      getch();
      exit(1);
   }

   /* move the CP to location (20,30) */
   moveto(20, 30);

   /* create and output a message at (20,30) */
   sprintf(msg, " (%d, %d)", getx(), gety());
   outtextxy(20,30, msg);

   /* draw a line to (100,100) */
   lineto(100, 100);

   /* create and output a message at CP */
   sprintf(msg, " (%d, %d)", getx(), gety());
   outtext(msg);

   /* clean up */
   getch();
   closegraph();
   return 0;
}
```

localeconv

Function Returns a pointer to the current locale structure.

Syntax #include <locale.h>
struct lconv *localeconv(void);

DOS	UNIX	Windows	ANSI C	C++ only
■		■	■	

Remarks This function sets up country-specific monetary and other numeric formats. However, Borland C++ currently only supports locale C.

Return Value Returns a pointer to the current locale structure. See locale.h for details.

See also **setlocale**

Example

```
#include <locale.h>
#include <stdio.h>

int main(void)
{
   struct lconv ll;
   struct lconv *conv = &ll;

   /* read the locality conversion structure */
   conv = localeconv();

   /* display the structure */
   printf("Decimal Point                    : %s\n", conv->decimal_point);
   printf("Thousands Separator              : %s\n", conv->thousands_sep);
   printf("Grouping                         : %s\n", conv->grouping);
   printf("International Currency symbol  : %s\n", conv->int_curr_symbol);
   printf("$ thousands separator            : %s\n", conv->mon_thousands_sep);
   printf("$ grouping                       : %s\n", conv->mon_grouping);
   printf("Positive sign                    : %s\n", conv->positive_sign);
   printf("Negative sign                    : %s\n", conv->negative_sign);
   printf("International fraction digits  : %d\n", conv->int_frac_digits);
   printf("Fraction digits                  : %d\n", conv->frac_digits);
   printf("Positive $ symbol precedes       : %d\n", conv->p_cs_precedes);
   printf("Positive sign space separation : %d\n", conv->p_sep_by_space);
   printf("Negative $ symbol precedes       : %d\n", conv->n_cs_precedes);
   printf("Negative sign space separation : %d\n", conv->n_sep_by_space);
   printf("Positive sign position           : %d\n", conv->p_sign_posn);
   printf("Negative sign position           : %d\n", conv->n_sign_posn);
   return 0;
}
```

localtime

Function Converts date and time to a structure.

Syntax #include <time.h>
struct tm *localtime(const time_t *timer);

DOS	UNIX	Windows	ANSI C	C++ only
■	■	■	■	

Remarks **localtime** accepts the address of a value returned by **time** and returns a pointer to the structure of type *tm* containing the broken-down time. It corrects for the time zone and possible daylight saving time.

The global long variable *timezone* should be set to the difference in seconds between GMT and local standard time (in PST, *timezone* is 8×60×60). The global variable *daylight* should be set to nonzero *only if* the standard U.S. daylight saving time conversion should be applied.

The **tm** structure declaration from the time.h include file follows:

```
struct tm {
   int tm_sec;
   int tm_min;
   int tm_hour;
   int tm_mday;
   int tm_mon;
   int tm_year;
   int tm_wday;
   int tm_yday;
   int tm_isdst;
};
```

These quantities give the time on a 24-hour clock, day of month (1 to 31), month (0 to 11), weekday (Sunday equals 0), year – 1900, day of year (0 to 365), and a flag that is nonzero if daylight saving time is in effect.

Return Value **localtime** returns a pointer to the structure containing the broken-down time. This structure is a static that is overwritten with each call.

See also **asctime, ctime, ftime, gmtime, stime, time, tzset**

Example

```
#include <time.h>
#include <stdio.h>
#include <dos.h>

int main(void)
{
   time_t timer;
   struct tm *tblock;

   /* gets time of day */
   timer = time(NULL);

   /* converts date/time to a structure */
   tblock = localtime(&timer);
   printf("Local time is: %s", asctime(tblock));
```

```
    return 0;
}
```

lock

Function Sets file-sharing locks.

Syntax #include <io.h>
int lock(int *handle*, long *offset*, long *length*);

DOS	UNIX	Windows	ANSI C	C++ only
■		■		

Remarks **lock** provides an interface to the DOS 3.x file-sharing mechanism. SHARE.EXE must be loaded before using **lock**.

lock can be placed on arbitrary, nonoverlapping regions of any file. A program attempting to read or write into a locked region will retry the operation three times. If all three retries fail, the call fails with an error.

Return Value **lock** returns 0 on success. On error, **lock** returns –1 and sets the global variable *errno* to

EACCES Locking violation

See also **open, sopen, unlock**

Example

```
#include <io.h>
#include <fcntl.h>
#include <sys\stat.h>
#include <process.h>
#include <share.h>
#include <stdio.h>

int main(void)
{
   int handle, status;
   long length;

   /* must have DOS SHARE.EXE loaded for file locking to function */
   handle = sopen("c:\\autoexec.bat", O_RDONLY,SH_DENYNO,S_IREAD);
   if (handle < 0) {
      printf("sopen failed\n");
      exit(1);
   }
   length = filelength(handle);
   status = lock(handle,0L,length/2);
   if (status == 0)
```

```
      printf("lock succeeded\n");
   else
      printf("lock failed\n");
   status = unlock(handle,0L,length/2);
   if (status == 0)
      printf("unlock succeeded\n");
   else
      printf("unlock failed\n");
   close(handle);
   return 0;
}
```

locking

Function Sets or resets file-sharing locks.

Syntax #include <io.h>
#include <sys\locking.h>
int locking(int *handle*, int *cmd*, long *length*);

DOS	UNIX	Windows	ANSI C	C++ only
■		■		

Remarks **locking** provides an interface to the file-sharing mechanism of DOS 3.0 or later. SHARE.EXE must be loaded before using **locking**. The file to be locked or unlocked is the open file specified by *handle*. The region to be locked or unlocked starts at the current file position, and is *length* bytes long.

Locks can be placed on arbitrary, nonoverlapping regions of any file. A program attempting to read or write into a locked region will retry the operation three times. If all three retries fail, the call fails with an error.

The *cmd* specifies the action to be taken (the values are defined in sys\locking.h):

LK_LOCK	Lock the region. If the lock is unsuccessful, try once a second for 10 seconds before giving up.
LK_RLCK	Same as LK_LOCK.
LK_NBLCK	Lock the region. If the lock if unsuccessful, give up immediately.
LK_NBRLCK	Same as LK_NBLCK.

LK_UNLCK	Unlock the region, which must have been previously locked.

Return Value On successful operations, **locking** returns 0. Otherwise, it returns –1, and the global variable *errno* is set to one of the following:

EBADF	Bad file number
EACCESS	File already locked or unlocked
EDEADLOCK	File cannot be locked after 10 retries (*cmd* is LK_LOCK or LK_RLCK)
EINVAL	Invalid *cmd*, or SHARE.EXE not loaded

See also **_fsopen, open, sopen**

Example

```
#include <io.h>
#include <fcntl.h>
#include <process.h>
#include <share.h>
#include <stdio.h>
#include <sys\locking.h>

int main(void)
{
   int handle, status;
   long length;

   /* must have DOS SHARE.EXE loaded for file locking to function */
   handle = sopen("c:\\autoexec.bat", O_RDONLY,SH_DENYNO);
   if (handle < 0) {
      printf("sopen failed\n");
      exit(1);
   }
   length = filelength(handle);
   status = locking(handle,LK_LOCK,length/2);
   if (status == 0)
      printf("lock succeeded\n");
   else
      perror("lock failed");
   status = locking(handle,LK_UNLCK,length/2);
   if (status == 0)
      printf("unlock succeeded\n");
   else
      perror("unlock failed");
   close(handle);
   return 0;
}
```

K-M

log, logl

Function Calculates the natural logarithm of *x*.

Syntax

Real versions:
#include <math.h>
double log(double *x*);
long double logl(long double *x*);

Complex version:
#include <complex.h>
complex log(complex *x*);

	DOS	UNIX	Windows	ANSI C	C++ only
logl	■		■		
Real ***log***	■	■	■	■	
Complex ***log***	■		■		■

Remarks **log** calculates the natural logarithm of *x*.

logl is the long double version; it takes a long double argument and returns a long double result.

The complex natural logarithm is defined by

$$\log(z) = \log(\text{abs}(z)) + i\ \arg(z)$$

Return Value On success, **log** and **logl** return the value calculated, *ln*(*x*).

If the argument *x* passed to these functions is real and less than 0, the global variable *errno* is set to

EDOM Domain error

If *x* is 0, the functions return the value negative HUGE_VAL (**log**) or negative _LHUGE_VAL (**logl**), and set *errno* to ERANGE.

Error handling for these routines can be modified through the functions **matherr** and **_matherrl**.

See also **complex, exp, log10, sqrt**

Example

```
#include <math.h>
#include <stdio.h>

int main(void)
{
   double result, x = 8.6872;
   result = log(x);
   printf("The natural log of %lf is %lf\n", x, result);
   return 0;
}
```

log10, log10l

Function Calculates $\log_{10}(x)$.

Syntax

Real versions:
#include <math.h>
double log10(double *x*);
long double log10l(long double *x*);

Complex version:
#include <complex.h>
complex log10(complex *x*);

	DOS	UNIX	Windows	ANSI C	C++ only
log10l	■		■		
Real ***log10***	■	■	■	■	
Complex ***log10***	■		■		■

Remarks **log10** calculates the base 10 logarithm of *x*.
log10l is the long double version; it takes a long double argument and returns a long double result.

The complex common logarithm is defined by

log10(z) = log(z) / log(10)

Return Value On success, **log10** (or **log10l**) returns the value calculated, $log_{10}(x)$.

If the argument *x* passed to these functions is real and less than 0, the global variable *errno* is set to

EDOM Domain error

If *x* is 0, these functions return the value negative HUGE_VAL (**log10**) or _LHUGE_VAL (**log10l**).

Error handling for these routines can be modified through the functions **matherr** and **_matherrl**.

See also **complex, exp, log**

Example

```
#include <math.h>
#include <stdio.h>

int main(void)
{
   double result, x = 800.6872;
   result = log10(x);
   printf("The common log of %lf is %lf\n", x, result);
   return 0;
}
```

longjmp

Function Performs nonlocal goto.

Syntax #include <setjmp.h>
void longjmp(jmp_buf *jmpb*, int *retval*);

DOS	UNIX	Windows	ANSI C	C++ only
■	■	■	■	

Remarks A call to **longjmp** restores the task state captured by the last call to **setjmp** with the argument *jmpb*. It then returns in such a way that **setjmp** appears to have returned with the value *retval*.

A task state is

- all segment registers (CS, DS, ES, SS)
- register variables (SI, DI)
- stack pointer (SP)
- frame base pointer (BP)
- flags

A task state is complete enough that **setjmp** and **longjmp** can be used to implement coroutines.

setjmp must be called before **longjmp**. The routine that called **setjmp** and set up *jmpb* must still be active and cannot have returned before the **longjmp** is called. If this happens, the results are unpredictable.

longjmp cannot pass the value 0; if 0 is passed in *retval*, **longjmp** will substitute 1.

➡ You can't use **setjmp** and **longjmp** for implementing coroutines if your program is overlaid. Normally, **setjmp** and **longjmp** save and restore all the registers needed for coroutines, but the overlay manager needs to keep track of stack contents and assumes there is only one stack. When you implement coroutines there are usually either two stacks or two partitions of one stack, and the overlay manager will not track them properly.

You can have background tasks which run with their own stacks or sections of stack, but you must ensure that the background tasks do not invoke any overlaid code, and you must not use the overlay versions of **setjmp** or **longjmp** to switch to and from background.

Return Value None.

See also **ctrlbrk**, **setjmp**, **signal**

Example

```
#include <stdio.h>
#include <setjmp.h>
#include <stdlib.h>

void subroutine(jmp_buf);

int main(void)
{
   int value;
   jmp_buf jumper;
   value = setjmp(jumper);
   if (value != 0) {
      printf("Longjmp with value %d\n", value);
      exit(value);
   }
   printf("About to call subroutine ... \n");
   subroutine(jumper);
   return 0;
}

void subroutine(jmp_buf jumper) {
   longjmp(jumper,1);
}
```

Program output

```
About to call subroutine ...
Longjmp with value 1
```


lowvideo

Function Selects low-intensity characters.

Syntax #include <conio.h>
void lowvideo(void);

DOS	UNIX	Windows	ANSI C	C++ only
■				

Remarks **lowvideo** selects low-intensity characters by clearing the high-intensity bit of the currently selected foreground color.

This function does not affect any characters currently on the screen, only those displayed by functions that perform text mode, direct console output *after* this function is called.

Return Value None.

See also **highvideo, normvideo, textattr, textcolor**

Example

```
#include <conio.h>

int main(void)
{
   clrscr();
   highvideo();
   cprintf("High Intesity Text\r\n");
   lowvideo();
   gotoxy(1,2);
   cprintf("Low Intensity Text\r\n");
   return 0;
}
```

_lrotl

Function Rotates an **unsigned long** integer value to the left.

Syntax #include <stdlib.h>
unsigned long _lrotl(unsigned long *val*, int *count*);

DOS	UNIX	Windows	ANSI C	C++ only
■		■		

Remarks **_lrotl** rotates the given *val* to the left *count* bits; *val* is an **unsigned long**.

Return Value **_lrotl** returns the value of *val* left-rotated *count* bits.

See also **_lrotr, _rotl, _rotr**

Example

```
#include <stdlib.h>
#include <stdio.h>

/* function prototypes */

int lrotl_example(void);
int lrotr_example(void);

/* lrotl example */
int lrotl_example(void)
{
   unsigned long result;
   unsigned long value = 100;

   result = _lrotl(value,1);
   printf("The value %lu rotated left"
          " one bit is: %lu\n", value, result);
   return 0;
```

```
}

/* lrotr example */
int lrotr_example(void)
{
   unsigned long result;
   unsigned long value = 100;

   result = _lrotr(value,1);
   printf("The value %lu rotated right"
          " one bit is: %lu\n", value, result);
   return 0;
}

int main(void)
{
   lrotl_example();
   lrotr_example();
   return 0;
}
```

K-M

_lrotr

Function Rotates an **unsigned long** integer value to the right.

Syntax #include <stdlib.h>
unsigned long _lrotr(unsigned long *val*, int *count*);

DOS	UNIX	Windows	ANSI C	C++ only
■		■		

Remarks **_lrotr** rotates the given *val* to the right *count* bits; *val* is an **unsigned long**.

Return Value **_lrotr** returns the value of *val* right-rotated *count* bits.

See also **_lrotl, _rotl, _rotr**

Example

```
#include <stdlib.h>
#include <stdio.h>

int main(void)
{
   unsigned long result;
   unsigned long value = 100;
   result = _lrotr(value,1);
      printf("The value %lu rotated right one bit is: %lu\n", value, result);
   return 0;
}
```

lsearch

Function Performs a linear search.

Syntax #include <stdlib.h>
void *lsearch(const void **key*, void **base*, size_t **num*, size_t *width*,
int (**fcmp*)(const void *, const void *));

DOS	UNIX	Windows	ANSI C	C++ only
■	■	■		

Remarks **lsearch** searches a table for information. Because this is a linear search, the table entries do not need to be sorted before a call to **lsearch**. If the item that *key* points to is not in the table, **lsearch** appends that item to the table.

- *base* points to the base (0th element) of the search table.
- *num* points to an integer containing the number of entries in the table.
- *width* contains the number of bytes in each entry.
- *key* points to the item to be searched for (the *search key*).

The argument *fcmp* points to a user-written comparison routine, which compares two items and returns a value based on the comparison.

To search the table, **lsearch** makes repeated calls to the routine whose address is passed in *fcmp*.

On each call to the comparison routine, **lsearch** passes two arguments: *key*, a pointer to the item being searched for, and *elem*, a pointer to the element of *base* being compared.

fcmp is free to interpret the search key and the table entries in any way.

Return Value **lsearch** returns the address of the first entry in the table that matches the search key.

If the search key is not identical to **elem*, *fcmp* returns a nonzero integer. If the search key is identical to **elem*, *fcmp* returns 0.

See also **bsearch, lfind, qsort**

Example

```
#include <stdlib.h>
#include <stdio.h>
#include <string.h>              /* for strcmp declaration */

/* initialize number of colors */
char *colors[10] = { "Red", "Blue", "Green" };
int ncolors = 3;

int colorscmp(char **arg1, char **arg2) {
```

```
   return(strcmp(*arg1, *arg2));
}

int addelem(char *key) {
   int oldn = ncolors;
   lsearch(key, colors, (size_t *) &ncolors, sizeof(char *), (int(*)
           (const void *, const void *)) colorscmp);
   return(ncolors == oldn);
}

int main(void)
{
   int i;
   char *key = "Purple";
   if (addelem(key))
      printf("%s already in colors table\n", key);
   else {
      strcpy(colors[ncolors-1],key);
      printf("%s added to colors table\n", key);
   }
   printf("The colors:\n");
   for (i = 0; i < ncolors; i++)
      printf("%s\n", colors[i]);
   return 0;
}
```


lseek

Function Moves file pointer.

Syntax #include <io.h>
long lseek(int *handle*, long *offset*, int *fromwhere*);

DOS	UNIX	Windows	ANSI C	C++ only
■	■	■		

Remarks **lseek** sets the file pointer associated with *handle* to a new position *offset* bytes beyond the file location given by *fromwhere*. It is a good idea to set *fromwhere* using one of three symbolic constants (defined in io.h) instead of a specific number. The constants are

fromwhere		**File location**
SEEK_SET	(0)	File beginning
SEEK_CUR	(1)	Current file pointer position
SEEK_END	(2)	End-of-file

Return Value **lseek** returns the offset of the pointer's new position measured in bytes from the file beginning. **lseek** returns –1L on error, and the global variable *errno* is set to one of the following:

EBADF	Bad file number
EINVAL	Invalid argument

On devices incapable of seeking (such as terminals and printers), the return value is undefined.

See also **filelength, fseek, ftell, getc, open, sopen, ungetc, _write, write**

Example

```
#include <sys\stat.h>
#include <string.h>
#include <stdio.h>
#include <fcntl.h>
#include <io.h>

int main(void)
{
   int handle;
   char msg[] = "This is a test";
   char ch;

   /* create a file */
   handle = open("TEST.$$$", O_CREAT | O_RDWR, S_IREAD | S_IWRITE);

   /* write some data to the file */
   write(handle, msg, strlen(msg));

   /* seek to the begining of the file */
   lseek(handle, 0L, SEEK_SET);

   /* reads chars from the file until EOF */
   do {
      read(handle, &ch, 1);
      printf("%c", ch);
   }
   while (!eof(handle));
   close(handle);

   return 0;
}
```

ltoa

Function Converts a **long** to a string.

Syntax #include <stdlib.h>

char *ltoa(long *value*, char **string*, int *radix*);

DOS	UNIX	Windows	ANSI C	C++ only
■		■		

Remarks **ltoa** converts *value* to a null-terminated string and stores the result in *string*. *value* is a long integer.

radix specifies the base to be used in converting *value*; it must be between 2 and 36, inclusive. If *value* is negative and *radix* is 10, the first character of *string* is the minus sign (–).

The space allocated for *string* must be large enough to hold the returned string, including the terminating null character (\0). **ltoa** can return up to 33 bytes.

Return Value **ltoa** returns a pointer to *string*.

See also **itoa, ultoa**

Example

```
#include <stdlib.h>
#include <stdio.h>

int main(void)
{
   char string[25];
   long value = 123456789L;
   ltoa(value,string,10);
   printf("number = %ld  string = %s\n", value, string);
   return 0;
}
```

_makepath

Function Builds a path from component parts.

Syntax #include <stdlib.h>
void _makepath(char **path*, const char **drive*, const char **dir*, const char **name*, const char **ext*);

DOS	UNIX	Windows	ANSI C	C++ only
■		■		

Remarks **_makepath** makes a path name from its components. The new path name is

```
X:\DIR\SUBDIR\NAME.EXT
```

where

drive = X:
dir = \DIR\SUBDIR\
name = NAME
ext = .EXT

If *drive* is empty or NULL, no drive is inserted in the path name. If it is missing a trailing colon (:), a colon is inserted in the path name.

If *dir* is empty or NULL, no directory is inserted in the path name. If it is missing a trailing slash (\ or /), a backslash is inserted in the path name.

If *name* is empty or NULL, no filename is inserted in the path name.

If *ext* is empty or NULL, no extension is inserted in the path name. If it is missing a leading period (.), a period is inserted in the path name.

_makepath assumes there is enough space in *path* for the constructed path name. The maximum constructed length is _MAX_PATH. _MAX_PATH is defined in stdlib.h. **_makepath** and **_splitpath** are invertible; if you split a given *path* with **_splitpath**, then merge the resultant components with **_makepath**, you end up with *path*.

Return Value None.

See also **_fullpath**, **_splitpath**

Example

```
#include <dir.h>
#include <string.h>
#include <stdio.h>
#include <stdlib.h>

int main(void)
{
   char s[_MAX_PATH];
   char drive[_MAX_DRIVE];
   char dir[_MAX_DIR];
   char file[_MAX_FNAME];
   char ext[_MAX_EXT];

   getcwd(s,_MAX_PATH);            /* get current working directory */
   if (s[strlen(s)-1] != '\\')
      strcat(s,"\\");              /* append a trailing \ character */
   _splitpath(s,drive,dir,file,ext); /* split the string to separate elems */
   strcpy(file,"DATA");
   strcpy(ext,".TXT");
   _makepath(s,drive,dir,file,ext); /* merge everything into one string */
   puts(s);                        /* display resulting string */
   return 0;
}
```

malloc

Function Allocates main memory.

Syntax #include <stdlib.h> or #include<alloc.h>
void *malloc(size_t *size*);

DOS	UNIX	Windows	ANSI C	C++ only
■	■	■	■	

Remarks **malloc** allocates a block of *size* bytes from the memory heap. It allows a program to allocate memory explicitly as it's needed, and in the exact amounts needed.

The heap is used for dynamic allocation of variable-sized blocks of memory. Many data structures, such as trees and lists, naturally employ heap memory allocation.

All the space between the end of the data segment and the top of the program stack is available for use in the small data models, except for a small margin immediately before the top of the stack. This margin is intended to allow the application some room to make the stack larger, in addition to a small amount needed by DOS.

In the large data models, all the space beyond the program stack to the end of available memory is available for the heap.

Return Value On success, **malloc** returns a pointer to the newly allocated block of memory. If not enough space exists for the new block, it returns null. The contents of the block are left unchanged. If the argument *size* == 0, **malloc** returns null.

See also **allocmem**, **calloc**, **coreleft**, **farcalloc**, **farmalloc**, **free**, **realloc**

Example

```
#include <stdio.h>
#include <string.h>
#include <alloc.h>
#include <process.h>

int main(void)
{
   char *str;

   /* allocate memory for string */
   if ((str = (char *) malloc(10)) == NULL) {
      printf("Not enough memory to allocate buffer\n");
```

```
      exit(1);  /* terminate program if out of memory */
   }
   /* copy "Hello" into string */
   strcpy(str, "Hello");

   /* display string */
   printf("String is %s\n", str);

   /* free memory */
   free(str);
   return 0;
}
```

matherr, _matherrl

Function User-modifiable math error handler.

Syntax #include <math.h>
int matherr(struct exception **e*);
int _matherrl(struct _exceptionl **e*);

DOS	UNIX	Windows	ANSI C	C++ only
■		■		

Remarks **matherr** is called when an error is generated by the math library.

_matherrl is the long double version; it is called when an error is generated by the long double math functions.

matherr and **_matherrl** each serve as a user hook (a function that can be customized by the user) that you can replace by writing your own math error handling routine — see the following example of a user-defined **matherr** implementation.

matherr and **_matherrl** are useful for trapping domain and range errors caused by the math functions. They do not trap floating-point exceptions, such as division by zero. See **signal** for trapping such errors.

You can define your own **matherr** or **_matherrl** routine to be a custom error handler (such as one that catches and resolves certain types of errors); this customized function overrides the default version in the C library. The customized **matherr** or **_matherrl** should return 0 if it fails to resolve the error, or nonzero if the error is resolved. When **matherr** or **_matherrl** return nonzero, no error message is printed and the global variable *errno* is not changed.

Here are the **exception** and **_exceptionl** structures (defined in math.h):

```
struct exception {
   int    type;
   char   *Function;
   double arg1, arg2, retval;
};

struct _exceptionl {
   int    type;
   char   *Function;
   long double arg1, arg2, retval;
};
```

The members of the **exception** and **_exceptionl** structures are shown in the following table:

Member	What it is (or represents)
type	The type of mathematical error that occurred; an enum type defined in the typedef *_mexcep* (see definition after this list).
name	A pointer to a null-terminated string holding the *name* of the math library function that resulted in an error.
arg1, *arg2*	The arguments (passed to the function *name* points to) that caused the error; if only one argument was passed to the function, it is stored in *arg1*.
retval	The default return value for **matherr** (or **_matherrl**); you can modify this value.

The **typedef** *_mexcep*, also defined in math.h, enumerates the following symbolic constants representing possible mathematical errors:

Symbolic constant	Mathematical error
DOMAIN	Argument was not in domain of function, such as **log**(-1).
SING	Argument would result in a singularity, such as **pow**(0, –2).
OVERFLOW	Argument would produce a function result greater than DBL_MAX (or LDBL_MAX), such as **exp**(1000).
UNDERFLOW	Argument would produce a function result less than DBL_MIN (or LDBL_MIN), such as **exp**(-1000).
TLOSS	Argument would produce function result with total loss of significant digits, such as **sin**(10e70).

The macros DBL_MAX, DBL_MIN, LDBL_MAX, and LDBL_MIN are defined in float.h.

The source code to the default **matherr** and **_matherrl** is on the Borland C++ distribution disks.

The UNIX-style **matherr** and **_matherrl** default behavior (printing a message and terminating) is not ANSI compatible. If you desire a UNIX-style version of these routines, use MATHERR.C and MATHERRL.C provided on the Borland C++ distribution disks.

Return Value The default return value for **matherr** and **_matherrl** is 1 if the error is UNDERFLOW or TLOSS, 0 otherwise. **matherr** and **_matherrl** can also modify *e –> retval*, which propagates back to the original caller.

When **matherr** and **_matherrl** return 0 (indicating that they were not able to resolve the error), the global variable *errno* is set to 0 and an error message is printed.

When **matherr** and **_matherrl** return nonzero (indicating that they were able to resolve the error), the global variable *errno* is not set and no messages are printed.

Example

```
#include <math.h>
#include <string.h>
#include <stdio.h>

int matherr(struct exception *a)
{
   if (a->type == DOMAIN)
      if (!strcmp(a->name,"sqrt")) {
         a->retval = sqrt(-(a->arg1));
      return 1;
      }
   return 0;
}

int main(void)
{
   double x = -2.0, y;
   y = sqrt(x);
   printf("Matherr corrected value: %lf\n",y);
   return 0;
}
```

max

Function Returns the larger of two values.

Syntax #include <stdlib.h>
(type) max(*a*, *b*);

DOS	UNIX	Windows	ANSI C	C++ only
■		■		

Remarks This macro compares two values and returns the larger of the two. Both arguments and the macro declaration must be of the same type.

Return Value **max** returns the larger of two values.

See also **min**

Example

```
#include <stdlib.h>
#include <stdio.h>

int main(void)
{
   int x = 5, y = 6, z;
   z = max(x, y);
   printf("The larger number is %d\n", z);
   return 0;
}
```

Program output

```
The larger number is 6
```


mblen

Function Determines the length of a multibyte character.

Syntax #include <stdlib.h>
int mblen(const char **s*, size_t *n*);

DOS	UNIX	Windows	ANSI C	C++ only
■		■	■	

Remarks If *s* is not NULL, **mblen** determines the multibyte character pointed to by *s*. The maximum number of bytes examined is specified by *n*.

The behavior of **mblen** is affected by the setting of LC_CTYPE category of the current locale.

Return Value If *s* is null, **mblen** returns a nonzero value if multibyte characters have state-dependent encodings. Otherwise, **mblen** returns zero.

If *s* is not null, **mblen** returns the following:

zero   if *s* points to the null character;

–1 if the next *n* bytes do not comprise a valid multibyte character;
the number of bytes that comprise a valid multibyte charter.

See also **mbtowc, mbstowc, setlocale**

mbstowcs

Function Converts a multibyte string to a wchar_t array.

Syntax #include <stdlib.h>
size_t mbstowcs(wchar_t **pwcs*, const char **s*, size_t *n*);

DOS	UNIX	Windows	ANSI C	C++ only
■		■	■	

Remarks The function converts the multibyte string *s* into the array pointed to by *pwcs*. No more than *n* values are stored in the array. If an invalid multibyte sequence is encountered, **mbstowcs** returns (size_t) –1.

The *pwcs* array will not be terminated with a zero value if **mbstowcs** returns *n*.

Return Value If an invalid multibyte sequence is encountered, **mbstowcs** returns (size_t) –1. Otherwise, the function returns the number of array elements modified, not including the terminating code, if any.

See also **mblen, mbstowc, setlocale**

mbtowc

Function Converts a multibyte character to wchar_t code.

Syntax #include <stdlib.h>
int mbtowc(wchar_t **pwc*, const char **s*, size_t *n*);

DOS	UNIX	Windows	ANSI C	C++ only
■		■	■	

Remarks If *s* is not null, **mbtowc** determines the number of bytes that comprise the multibyte character pointed to by *s*. **mbtowc** then determines the value of the type wchar_t that corresponds to that multibyte character. If there is a successful match between wchar_t and the multibyte character, and *pwc* is not null, the wchar_t value is stored in the array pointed to by *pwc*. At most *n* characters are examined.

Return Value When *s* points to an invalid multibyte character, –1 is returned. When *s* points to the NULL character, zero is returned. Otherwise, **mbtowc** returns the number of bytes that comprise the converted multibyte character.

The return value will never exceed MB_CUR_MAX or the value of *n*.

See also **mblen, mbstowcs, setlocale**

memccpy, _fmemccpy

Function Copies a block of *n* bytes.

Syntax #include <mem.h>
Near version: void *memccpy(void **dest*, const void **src*, int *c*, size_t *n*);
Far version: void far * far _fmemccpy(void far **dest*, const void far **src*, int *c*, size_t *n*)

	DOS	UNIX	Windows	ANSI C	C++ only
Near version	■	■	■		
Far version	■		■		

Remarks **memccpy** is available on UNIX System V systems.

memccpy copies a block of *n* bytes from *src* to *dest*. The copying stops as soon as either of the following occurs:

- The character *c* is first copied into *dest*.
- *n* bytes have been copied into *dest*.

Return Value **memccpy** returns a pointer to the byte in *dest* immediately following *c*, if *c* was copied; otherwise, **memccpy** returns null.

See also **memcpy, memmove, memset**

Example

```
#include <string.h>
#include <stdio.h>

int main(void)
{
   char *src = "This is the source string", dest[50], *ptr;

   ptr = (char *) memccpy(dest, src, 'c', strlen(src));

   if (ptr) {
      *ptr = '\0';
      printf("The character was found: %s\n", dest);
   }
```

```
      else
         printf("The character wasn't found\n");
      return 0;
   }
```

memchr, _fmemchr

Function Searches *n* bytes for character *c*.

Syntax #include <mem.h>
Near version: void *memchr(const void **s*, int *c*, size_t *n*);
Far version: void far * far _fmemchr(const void far **s*, int *c*, size_t *n*);

	DOS	UNIX	Windows	ANSI C	C++ only
Near version	■	■	■	■	
Far version	■		■		

Remarks **memchr** is available on UNIX System V systems.

memchr searches the first *n* bytes of the block pointed to by *s* for character *c*.

Return Value On success, **memchr** returns a pointer to the first occurrence of *c* in *s*; otherwise, it returns null.

Example

```
#include <string.h>
#include <stdio.h>

int main(void)
{
   char str[17], *ptr;

   strcpy(str, "This is a string");
   ptr = (char *) memchr(str, 'r', strlen(str));
   if (ptr)
      printf("The character 'r' is at"
             " position: %d\n", ptr - str);
   else
      printf("The character was not found\n");
   return 0;
}
```

memcmp, _fmemcmp

Function Compares two blocks for a length of exactly *n* bytes.

Syntax #include <mem.h>
Near version: int memcmp(const void **s1*, const void **s2*, size_t *n*);
Far version: int far _fmemcmp(const void far **s1*, const void far **s2*, size_t *n*)

	DOS	UNIX	Windows	ANSI C	C++ only
Near version	■	■	■	■	
Far version	■		■		

Remarks **memcmp** is available on UNIX System V systems.

memcmp compares the first *n* bytes of the blocks *s1* and *s2* as **unsigned chars**.

Return Value Because it compares bytes as **unsigned chars**, **memcmp** returns a value

< 0 if *s1* is less than *s2*
= 0 if *s1* is the same as *s2*
> 0 if *s1* is greater than *s2*

For example,

```
memcmp("\xFF", "\x7F", 1)
```

returns a value greater than 0.

See also **memicmp**

Example

```
#include <stdio.h>
#include <string.h>

int main(void)
{
   char *buf1 = "aaa";
   char *buf2 = "bbb";
   char *buf3 = "ccc";
   int stat;
   stat = memcmp(buf2, buf1, strlen(buf2));
   if (stat > 0)
      printf("buffer 2 is greater than buffer 1\n");
   else
      printf("buffer 2 is less than buffer 1\n");
   stat = memcmp(buf2, buf3, strlen(buf2));
   if (stat > 0)
      printf("buffer 2 is greater than buffer 3\n");
   else
      printf("buffer 2 is less than buffer 3\n");
   return 0;
}
```

K-M

memcpy, _fmemcpy

Function Copies a block of *n* bytes.

Syntax #include <mem.h>
Near version: void *memcpy(void **dest*, const void **src*, size_t *n*);
Far version: void far *far _fmemcpy(void far **dest*, const void far **src*, size_t *n*);

	DOS	UNIX	Windows	ANSI C	C++ only
Near version	■	■	■	■	
Far version	■		■		

Remarks **memcpy** is available on UNIX System V systems.

memcpy copies a block of *n* bytes from *src* to *dest*. If *src* and *dest* overlap, the behavior of **memcpy** is undefined.

Return Value **memcpy** returns *dest*.

See also **memccpy, memmove, memset, movedata, movmem**

Example

```
#include <stdio.h>
#include <string.h>

int main(void)
{
   char src[] = "******************************";
   char dest[] = "abcdefghijlkmnopqrstuvwxyz0123456709";
   char *ptr;

   printf("destination before memcpy: %s\n", dest);
   ptr = (char *) memcpy(dest, src, strlen(src));
   if (ptr)
      printf("destination after memcpy: %s\n", dest);
   else
      printf("memcpy failed\n");
   return 0;
}
```

memicmp, _fmemicmp

Function Compares *n* bytes of two character arrays, ignoring case.

Syntax #include <mem.h>
Near version: int memicmp(const void **s1*, const void **s2*, size_t *n*);

Far version: int far _fmemicmp(const void far **s1*, const void far **s2*, size_t *n*)

	DOS	UNIX	Windows	ANSI C	C++ only
Near version	■	■	■		
Far version	■		■		

Remarks **memicmp** is available on UNIX System V systems.

memicmp compares the first *n* bytes of the blocks *s1* and *s2*, ignoring character case (upper or lower).

Return Value **memicmp** returns a value

< 0 if *s1* is less than *s2*
= 0 if *s1* is the same as *s2*
> 0 if *s1* is greater than *s2*

See also **memcmp**

Example

```
#include <stdio.h>
#include <string.h>

int main(void)
{
   char *buf1 = "ABCDE123";
   char *buf2 = "abcde456";
   int stat;
   stat = memicmp(buf1, buf2, 5);
   printf("The strings to position 5 are ");
   if (stat)
      printf("not ");
   printf("the same\n");
   return 0;
}
```

memmove

Function Copies a block of *n* bytes.

Syntax #include <mem.h>
void *memmove(void **dest*, const void **src*, size_t *n*);

DOS	UNIX	Windows	ANSI C	C++ only
■	■	■	■	

Remarks **memmove** is available on UNIX System V systems.

memmove copies a block of *n* bytes from *src* to *dest*. Even when the source and destination blocks overlap, bytes in the overlapping locations are copied correctly.

Return Value **memmove** returns *dest*.

See also **memccpy, memcpy, movmem**

Example

```
#include <string.h>
#include <stdio.h>

int main(void)
{
   char *dest = "abcdefghijklmnopqrstuvwxyz0123456789";
   char *src = "******************************";
   printf("destination prior to memmove: %s\n", dest);
   memmove(dest, src, 26);
   printf("destination after memmove:    %s\n", dest);
   return 0;
}
```

memset, _fmemset

Function Sets *n* bytes of a block of memory to byte *c*.

Syntax #include <mem.h>
Near version: void *memset(void **s*, int *c*, size_t *n*);
Far version: void far * far _fmemset (void far **s*, int *c*, size_t *n*)

	DOS	UNIX	Windows	ANSI C	C++ only
Near version	■	■	■	■	
Far version	■		■		

Remarks **memset** is available on UNIX System V systems

memset sets the first *n* bytes of the array *s* to the character *c*.

Return Value **memset** returns *s*.

See also **memccpy, memcpy, setmem**

Example

```
#include <string.h>
#include <stdio.h>
#include <mem.h>

int main(void)
{
   char buffer[] = "Hello world\n";
   printf("Buffer before memset: %s\n", buffer);
```

```
   memset(buffer, '*', strlen(buffer) - 1);
   printf("Buffer after memset:  %s\n", buffer);
   return 0;
}
```

min

Function Returns the smaller of two values.

Syntax #include <stdlib.h>
(type) min(*a*, *b*);

DOS	UNIX	Windows	ANSI C	C++ only
■		■		

Remarks **min** compares two values and returns the smaller of the two. Both arguments and the macro declaration must be of the same type.

Return Value **min** returns the smaller of two values.

See also **max**

Example

```
#include <stdlib.h>
#include <stdio.h>

int main()
{
   int x = 5, y = 6;
   printf("The smaller number is %d\n", min(x,y));
   return 0;
}
```

Program output

```
The smaller number is 5
```

mkdir

Function Creates a directory.

Syntax #include <dir.h>
int mkdir(const char **path*);

DOS	UNIX	Windows	ANSI C	C++ only
■	■	■		

K-M

Remarks **mkdir** is available on UNIX System V systems, though it then takes an additional parameter.

mkdir creates a new directory from the given path name *path*.

Return Value **mkdir** returns the value 0 if the new directory was created.

A return value of –1 indicates an error, and the global variable *errno* is set to one of the following values:

EACCES	Permission denied
ENOENT	No such file or directory

See also **chdir, getcurdir, getcwd, rmdir**

Example

```
#include <stdio.h>
#include <conio.h>
#include <process.h>
#include <dir.h>

int main(void)
{
  int status;

   clrscr();
   status = mkdir("asdfjklm");
   (!status) ? (printf("Directory created\n")) :
               (printf("Unable to create directory\n"));

   getch();
   system("dir");
   getch();
   status = rmdir("asdfjklm");
   if (status == 0)
     printf("Directory deleted\n");
   else
     perror("Unable to delete directory");
   return 0;
}
```

MK_FP

Function Makes a far pointer.

Syntax #include <dos.h>
void far * MK_FP(unsigned *seg*, unsigned *ofs*);

DOS	UNIX	Windows	ANSI C	C++ only
■		■		

Remarks **MK_FP** is a macro that makes a far pointer from its component segment (*seg*) and offset (*ofs*) parts.

Return Value **MK_FP** returns a far pointer.

See also **FP_OFF**, **FP_SEG**, **movedata**, **segread**

Example

```
#include <dos.h>
#include <graphics.h>

int main(void)
{
   int gd, gm, i;
   unsigned int far *screen;
   detectgraph(&gd, &gm);
   if (gd == HERCMONO)
       screen = MK_FP(0xB000, 0);
   else
       screen = MK_FP(0xB800, 0);
   for (i = 0; i < 26; i++)
      screen[i] = 0x0700 + ('a' + i);
   return 0;
}
```

mktemp

Function Makes a unique file name.

Syntax #include <dir.h>
char *mktemp(char **template*);

DOS	UNIX	Windows	ANSI C	C++ only
■	■	■		

Remarks **mktemp** replaces the string pointed to by *template* with a unique file name and returns *template*.

template should be a null-terminated string with six trailing Xs. These Xs are replaced with a unique collection of letters plus a period, so that there are two letters, a period, and three suffix letters in the new file name.

Starting with AA.AAA, the new file name is assigned by looking up the name on the disk and avoiding pre-existing names of the same format.

K-M

Return Value If *template* is well-formed, **mktemp** returns the address of the *template* string. Otherwise, it returns null.

Example

```
#include <dir.h>
#include <stdio.h>

int main(void)
{
   /* fname defines template for temporary file */
   char *fname = "TXXXXXX", *ptr;
   ptr = mktemp(fname);
   printf("%s\n",ptr);
   return 0;
}
```

mktime

Function Converts time to calendar format.

Syntax #include <time.h>
time_t mktime(struct tm **t*);

DOS	UNIX	Windows	ANSI C	C++ only
■		■	■	

Remarks Converts the time in the structure pointed to by *t* into a calendar time with the same format used by the **time** function. The original values of the fields *tm_sec*, *tm_min*, *tm_hour*, *tm_mday*, and *tm_mon* are not restricted to the ranges described in the *tm* structure. If the fields are not in their proper ranges, they are adjusted. Values for fields *tm_wday* and *tm_yday* are computed after the other fields have been adjusted. If the calender time cannot be represented, **mktime** returns –1.

The allowable range of calender times is Jan 1 1970 00:00:00 to Jan 19 2038 03:14:07.

Return Value See Remarks.

See also **localtime, strftime, time**

Example

```
#include <stdio.h>
#include <time.h>

char *wday[] = { "Sunday", "Monday", "Tuesday", "Wednesday", Thursday", "Friday",
                 "Saturday", "Unknown"};

int main(void)
```

```
{
   struct tm time_check;
   int year, month, day;

   /* input year, month, and day to find the weekday for */
   printf("Year:  ");
   scanf("%d", &year);
   printf("Month: ");
   scanf("%d", &month);
   printf("Day:   ");
   scanf("%d", &day);

   /* load the time_check structure with the data */
   time_check.tm_year = year - 1900;
   time_check.tm_mon  = month - 1;
   time_check.tm_mday = day;
   time_check.tm_hour = 0;
   time_check.tm_min  = 0;
   time_check.tm_sec  = 1;
   time_check.tm_isdst = -1;

   /* call mktime to fill in the structure's weekday field */
   if (mktime(&time_check) == -1)
      time_check.tm_wday = 7;

   /* print out the day of the week */
   printf("That day is a %s\n", wday[time_check.tm_wday]);
   return 0;
}
```


modf, modfl

Function Splits a **double** or **long double** into integer and fractional parts.

Syntax #include <math.h>
double modf(double *x*, double **ipart*);
long double modfl(long double *x*, long double **ipart*);

	DOS	UNIX	Windows	ANSI C	C++ only
modf	■	■	■	■	
modfl	■		■		

Remarks **modf** breaks the double *x* into two parts: the integer and the fraction. **modf** stores the integer in *ipart* and returns the fraction.
modfl is the long double version; it takes long double arguments and returns a long double result.

Return Value **modf** and **modfl** return the fractional part of *x*.

See also **fmod, ldexp**

Example

```
#include <math.h>
#include <stdio.h>

int main(void)
{
   double fraction, integer, number = 100000.567;
   fraction = modf(number, &integer);
   printf("The whole and fractional parts of %lf are %lf and %lf\n", number,
         integer, fraction);
   return 0;
}
```

movedata

Function Copies *n* bytes.

Syntax #include <mem.h>
void movedata(unsigned *srcseg*, unsigned *srcoff*, unsigned *dstseg*,
unsigned *dstoff*, size_t *n*);

DOS	UNIX	Windows	ANSI C	C++ only
■		■		

Remarks **movedata** copies *n* bytes from the source address (*srcseg:srcoff*) to the destination address (*dstseg:dstoff*).

movedata is a means of moving blocks of data that is independent of memory model.

Return Value None.

See also **FP_OFF, memcpy, MK_FP, movmem, segread**

Example

```
#include <mem.h>

#define MONO_BASE 0xB000

char buf[80*25*2];

/* Saves the contents of the monochrome screen in buffer. */
void save_mono_screen(char near *buffer)
{
   movedata(MONO_BASE, 0, _DS, (unsigned)buffer, 80*25*2);
}

int main(void)
{
```

```
   save_mono_screen(buf);
   return(0);
}
```

movmem

Function Moves a block of *length* bytes.

Syntax #include <mem.h>
void movmem(void **src*, void **dest*, unsigned *length*);

DOS	UNIX	Windows	ANSI C	C++ only
■		■		

Remarks **movmem** moves a block of *length* bytes from *src* to *dest*. Even if the source and destination blocks overlap, the move direction is chosen so that the data is always moved correctly.

K-M

Return Value None.

See also **memcpy, memmove, movedata**

Example

```
#include <mem.h>
#include <alloc.h>
#include <stdio.h>
#include <string.h>

int main(void)
{
   char *source = "Borland International";
   char *destination;
   int length;
   length = strlen(source);
   destination = malloc(length + 1);
   movmem(source,destination,length);
   printf("%s\n",destination);
   return 0;
}
```

moverel

Function Moves the current position (CP) a relative distance.

Syntax #include <graphics.h>
void far moverel(int *dx*, int *dy*);

DOS	UNIX	Windows	ANSI C	C++ only
■				

Remarks **moverel** moves the current position (CP) *dx* pixels in the *x* direction and *dy* pixels in the *y* direction.

Return Value None.

See also **moveto**

Example

```
#include <graphics.h>
#include <stdlib.h>
#include <stdio.h>
#include <conio.h>

int main(void)
{
   /* request autodetection */
   int gdriver = DETECT, gmode, errorcode;
   char msg[80];

   /* initialize graphics and local variables */
   initgraph(&gdriver, &gmode, "");

   /* read result of initialization */
   errorcode = graphresult();
   if (errorcode != grOk) {   /* an error occurred */
      printf("Graphics error: %s\n", grapherrormsg(errorcode));
      printf("Press any key to halt:");
      getch();
      exit(1);               /* terminate with an error code */
   }

   /* move the CP to location (20,30) */
   moveto(20,30);

   /* plot a pixel at the CP */
   putpixel(getx(), gety(), getmaxcolor());

   /* create and output a message at (20,30) */
   sprintf(msg, " (%d, %d)", getx(), gety());
   outtextxy(20,30, msg);

   /* move to a point a relative distance away from the current CP */
   moverel(100, 100);

   /* plot a pixel at the CP */
   putpixel(getx(), gety(), getmaxcolor());

   /* create and output a message at CP */
   sprintf(msg, " (%d, %d)", getx(), gety());
   outtext(msg);
```

```
    /* clean up */
    getch();
    closegraph();
    return 0;
}
```

movetext

Function Copies text onscreen from one rectangle to another.

Syntax #include <conio.h>
int movetext(int *left*, int *top*, int *right*, int *bottom*, int *destleft*, int *desttop*);

DOS	UNIX	Windows	ANSI C	C++ only
■				

Remarks **movetext** copies the contents of the onscreen rectangle defined by *left*, *top*, *right*, and *bottom* to a new rectangle of the same dimensions. The new rectangle's upper left corner is position (*destleft*, *desttop*).

All coordinates are absolute screen coordinates. Rectangles that overlap are moved correctly.

movetext is a text mode function performing direct video output.

Return Value **movetext** returns nonzero if the operation succeeded. If the operation failed (for example, if you gave coordinates outside the range of the current screen mode), **movetext** returns 0.

See also **gettext, puttext**

Example

```
#include <conio.h>
#include <string.h>

int main(void)
{
    char *str = "This is a test string";
    clrscr();
    cputs(str);
    getch();
    movetext(1, 1, strlen(str), 2, 10, 10);
    getch();
    return 0;
}
```

moveto

Function	Moves the current position (CP) to (*x*,*y*).
Syntax	#include <graphics.h> void far moveto(int *x*, int *y*);

DOS	UNIX	Windows	ANSI C	C++ only
■				

Remarks **moveto** moves the current position (CP) to viewport position (*x*,*y*).

Return Value None.

See also **moverel**

Example

```
#include <graphics.h>
#include <stdlib.h>
#include <stdio.h>
#include <conio.h>

int main(void)
{
   /* request autodetection */
   int gdriver = DETECT, gmode, errorcode;
   char msg[80];

   /* initialize graphics and local variables */
   initgraph(&gdriver, &gmode, "");

   /* read result of initialization */
   errorcode = graphresult();
   if (errorcode != grOk) {  /* an error occurred */
      printf("Graphics error: %s\n", grapherrormsg(errorcode));
      printf("Press any key to halt:");
      getch();
      exit(1);               /* terminate with an error code */
   }

   /* move the CP to location (20,30) */
   moveto(20,30);

   /* plot a pixel at the CP */
   putpixel(getx(), gety(), getmaxcolor());

   /* create and output a message at (20,30) */
   sprintf(msg, " (%d, %d)", getx(), gety());
   outtextxy(20,30, msg);

   /* move to (100,100) */
   moveto(100,100);
```

```
    /* plot a pixel at the CP */
    putpixel(getx(), gety(), getmaxcolor());

    /* create and output a message at CP */
    sprintf(msg, " (%d, %d)", getx(), gety());
    outtext(msg);

    /* clean up */
    getch();
    closegraph();
    return 0;
}
```

norm

Function Returns the square of the absolute value.

Syntax #include <complex.h>
double norm(complex *x*);

DOS	UNIX	Windows	ANSI C	C++ only
■		■		■

Remarks **norm** can overflow if either the real or imaginary part is sufficiently large.

Return Value `norm(x)` returns the magnitude `real(x) * real(x) + imag(x) * imag(x)`.

See also **arg, complex, polar**

Example

```
#include <complex.h>

int main(void)
{
   double x = 3.1, y = 4.2;
   complex z = complex(x,y);
   cout << "z = " << z << "\n";
   cout << "  has real part = " << real(z) << "\n";
   cout << "  and imaginary real part = " << imag(z) << "\n";
   cout << "z has complex conjugate = " << conj(z) << "\n";
   double mag = sqrt(norm(z));
   double ang = arg(z);
   cout << "The polar form of z is:\n";
   cout << "   magnitude = " << mag << "\n";
   cout << "   angle (in radians) = " << ang << "\n";
   cout << "Reconstructing z from its polar form gives:\n";
   cout << "   z = " << polar(mag,ang) << "\n";
   return 0;
}
```

K-M

normvideo

Function Selects normal-intensity characters.

Syntax #include <conio.h>
void normvideo(void);

DOS	UNIX	Windows	ANSI C	C++ only
■				

Remarks **normvideo** selects normal characters by returning the text attribute (foreground and background) to the value it had when the program started.

This function does not affect any characters currently on the screen, only those displayed by functions (such as **cprintf**) performing direct console output functions *after* **normvideo** is called.

Return Value None.

See also **highvideo, lowvideo, textattr, textcolor**

Example

```
#include <conio.h>

int main(void)
{
   clrscr();
   lowvideo();
   cprintf("LOW    Intensity Text\r\n");
   highvideo();
   cprintf("HIGH   Intensity Text\r\n");
   normvideo();
   cprintf("NORMAL Intensity Text\r\n");
   return 0;
}
```

nosound

Function Turns PC speaker off.

Syntax #include <dos.h>
void nosound(void);

DOS	UNIX	Windows	ANSI C	C++ only
■				

Remarks Turns the speaker off after it has been turned on by a call to **sound**.

Return Value None.

See also **delay, sound**

Example

```
/* Emits a 7-Hz tone for 10 seconds. Your PC may not be able to emit a 7-Hz
   tone. */

#include <dos.h>

int main(void)
{
   sound(7);
   delay(10000);
   nosound();
}
```

_open, _dos_open

Function Opens a file for reading or writing.

Syntax #include <fcntl.h>
int _open(const char **filename*, int *oflags*);

#include <fcntl.h>
#include <share.h>
#include <dos.h>
unsigned _dos_open(const char **filename*, unsigned *oflags*, int **handlep*);

DOS	UNIX	Windows	ANSI C	C++ only
■		■		

Remarks **_open** and **_dos_open** open the file specified by *filename*, then prepares it for reading or writing, as determined by the value of *oflags*. The file is always opened in binary mode. The file handle is stored at the location pointed to by *handlep*.

oflags must include one of the following values:

O_RDONLY	Open for reading.
O_WRONLY	Open for writing.
O_RDWR	Open for reading and writing.

On DOS 3.0 or later, the following additional values can be included in *oflags* (using an OR operation):

N-P

These symbolic constants are defined in fcntl.h and share.h.

O_NOINHERIT	The file is not passed to child programs.
SH_COMPAT	Allow other opens with SH_COMPAT. The call will fail if the file has already been opened in any other shared mode.
SH_DENYRW	Only the current handle may have access to the file.
SH_DENYWR	Allow only reads from any other open to the file.
SH_DENYRD	Allow only writes from any other open to the file.
SH_DENYNO	Allow other shared opens to the file, but not other SH_COMPAT opens.

Only one of the SH_DENY*xx* values can be included in a single **_dos_open** or **_open** under DOS 3.0 or later. These file-sharing attributes are in addition to any locking performed on the files.

The maximum number of simultaneously open files is defined by HANDLE_MAX.

Return Value On successful completion, **_open** returns a nonnegative integer (the file handle). On successful completion, **_dos_open** returns 0, and stores the file handle at the location pointed to by *handlep*. The file pointer, which marks the current position in the file, is set to the beginning of the file.

On error, **_open** returns –1 and **_dos_open** returns the DOS error code. For both functions, the global variable *errno* is set to one of the following:

ENOENT	Path or file not found
EMFILE	Too many open files
EACCES	Permission denied
EINVACC	Invalid access code

See also **open, _read, sopen**

Example

```
#include <string.h>
#include <stdio.h>
#include <fcntl.h>
#include <io.h>

int main(void) /* Example for _open. */
{
   int handle;
   char msg[] = "Hello world\n";
   if ((handle = _open("TEST.$$$", O_RDWR)) == -1) {
      perror("Error:");
      return 1;
```

```
    }
    _write(handle, msg, strlen(msg));
    _close(handle);
    return 0;
}

#include <string.h>
#include <stdio.h>
#include <fcntl.h>
#include <dos.h>

int main(void)  /* Example for _dos_open. */
{
    int handle;
    unsigned nbytes;
    char msg[] = "Hello world\n";
    if (_dos_open("TEST.$$$", O_RDWR, &handle) != 0) {
        perror("Unable to open TEST.$$$");
        return 1;
    }
    if (_dos_write(handle, msg, strlen(msg),&nbytes) != 0)
        perror("Unable to write to TEST.$$$");
    printf("%u bytes written to TEST.$$$\n",nbytes);
    _dos_close(handle);
    return 0;
}
```

N-P

open

Function Opens a file for reading or writing.

Syntax #include <fcntl.h>
#include<sys\stat.h>
int open(const char **path*, int *access* [, unsigned *mode*]);

DOS	UNIX	Windows	ANSI C	C++ only
■	■	■		

Remarks **open** opens the file specified by *path*, then prepares it for reading and/or writing as determined by the value of *access*.

To create a file in a particular mode, you can either assign to the global variable *_fmode* or call **open** with the O_CREAT and O_TRUNC options ORed with the translation mode desired. For example, the call

```
open("xmp",O_CREAT|O_TRUNC|O_BINARY,S_IREAD)
```

will create a binary-mode, read-only file named XMP, truncating its length to 0 bytes if it already existed.

For **open**, *access* is constructed by bitwise ORing flags from the following two lists. Only one flag from the first list can be used (and one *must* be used); the remaining flags can be used in any logical combination.

List 1: Read/write flags

These symbolic constants are defined in fcntl.h.

O_RDONLY	Open for reading only.
O_WRONLY	Open for writing only.
O_RDWR	Open for reading and writing.

List 2: Other access flags

O_NDELAY	Not used; for UNIX compatibility.
O_APPEND	If set, the file pointer will be set to the end of the file prior to each write.
O_CREAT	If the file exists, this flag has no effect. If the file does not exist, the file is created, and the bits of *mode* are used to set the file attribute bits as in **chmod**.
O_TRUNC	If the file exists, its length is truncated to 0. The file attributes remain unchanged.
O_EXCL	Used only with O_CREAT. If the file already exists, an error is returned.
O_BINARY	Can be given to explicitly open the file in binary mode.
O_TEXT	Can be given to explicitly open the file in text mode.

If neither O_BINARY nor O_TEXT is given, the file is opened in the translation mode set by the global variable *_fmode*.

If the O_CREAT flag is used in constructing *access*, you need to supply the *mode* argument to **open** from the following symbolic constants defined in sys\stat.h.

Value of *mode*	Access permission
S_IWRITE	Permission to write
S_IREAD	Permission to read
S_IREAD | S_IWRITE	Permission to read and write

Return Value

On successful completion, **open** returns a nonnegative integer (the file handle). The file pointer, which marks the current position in the file, is set to the beginning of the file. On error, **open** returns –1 and the global variable *errno* is set to one of the following:

ENOENT	No such file or directory
EMFILE	Too many open files

EACCES	Permission denied
EINVACC	Invalid access code

See also **chmod, chsize, close, _creat, creat, creatnew, creattemp, dup, dup2, fdopen, filelength, fopen, freopen, getftime, lseek, lock, _open, read, sopen, _write, write**

Example

```
#include <string.h>
#include <stdio.h>
#include <fcntl.h>
#include <io.h>

int main(void)
{
   int handle;
   char msg[] = "Hello world";
   if ((handle = open("TEST.$$$", O_CREAT | O_TEXT)) == -1) {
      perror("Error:");
      return 1;
   }
   write(handle, msg, strlen(msg));
   close(handle);
   return 0;
}
```


opendir

Function Opens a directory stream for reading.

Syntax #include <dirent.h>
DIR *opendir(char **dirname*);

DOS	UNIX	Windows	ANSI C	C++ only
■	■	■		

Remarks **opendir** is available on POSIX-compliant UNIX systems.

The **opendir** function opens a directory stream for reading. The name of the directory to read is *dirname*. The stream is set to read the first entry in the directory.

A directory stream is represented by the **DIR** structure, defined in dirent.h. This structure contains no user-accessible fields. More than one directory stream may be opened and read simultaneously. Directory entries can be created or deleted while a directory stream is being read.

Use the **readdir** function to read successive entries from a directory stream. Use the **closedir** function to remove a directory stream when it is no longer needed.

Return Value If successful, **opendir** returns a pointer to a directory stream that can be used in calls to **readdir**, **rewinddir**, and **closedir**. If the directory cannot be opened, **opendir** returns NULL and sets the global variable *errno* to

ENOENT	The directory does not exist.
ENOMEM	Not enough memory to allocate a DIR object.

See also **closedir, readdir, rewinddir**

Example

```
/* Using opendir, readdir, closedir */

#include <dirent.h>
#include <stdio.h>
#include <stdlib.h>

void scandir(char *dirname)
{
   DIR *dir;
   struct dirent *ent;

   printf("First pass on '%s':\n",dirname);
   if ((dir = opendir(dirname)) == NULL) {
     perror("Unable to open directory");
     exit(1);
   }
   while ((ent = readdir(dir)) != NULL)
     printf("%s\n",ent->d_name);

   printf("Second pass on '%s':\n",dirname);
   rewinddir(dir);
   while ((ent = readdir(dir)) != NULL)
     printf("%s\n",ent->d_name);
   if (closedir(dir) != 0)
     perror("Unable to close directory");
}

void main(int argc,char *argv[])
{
   if (argc != 2) {
     printf("usage: opendir dirname\n");
     exit(1);
   }
   scandir(argv[1]);
   exit(0);
}
```

outp

Function Outputs a byte to a hardware port.

Syntax #include <conio.h>
int outp(unsigned *portid*, int *value*);

DOS	UNIX	Windows	ANSI C	C++ only
■		■		

Remarks **outp** is a macro that writes the low byte of *value* to the output port specified by *portid*.

If **outp** is called when conio.h has been included, it will be treated as a macro that expands to inline code. If you don't include conio.h, or if you do include conio.h and **#undef** the macro **outp**, you'll get the **outp** function.

Return Value **outp** returns *value*.

See also **inp**, **inpw**, **outpw**

Example

```
#include <stdio.h>
#include <conio.h>

int main(void)
{
   unsigned port = 0;
   int value;
   value = outp(port, 'C');
   printf("Value %c sent to port number %d\n", value, port);
   return 0;
}
```

outport, outportb

Function Outputs a word or byte to a hardware port.

Syntax #include <dos.h>
void outport(int *portid*, int *value*);
void outportb(int *portid*, unsigned char *value*);

DOS	UNIX	Windows	ANSI C	C++ only
■		■		

N-P

Remarks **outport** works just like the 80x86 instruction **out**. It writes the low byte of the word given by *value* to the output port specified by *portid* and writes the high byte of the word to *portid* +1.

outportb is a macro that writes the byte given by *value* to the output port specified by *portid*.

If **outportb** is called when dos.h has been included, it will be treated as a macro that expands to inline code. If you don't include dos.h, or if you do include dos.h and #**undef** the macro **outportb**, you'll get the **outportb** function.

Return Value None.

See also **inport, inportb**

Example

```
#include <stdio.h>
#include <dos.h>

int main(void)
{
   int value = 64, port = 0;
   unsigned char c_value = 'C';

   outportb(port, value);
   printf("Value %d sent to port number %d\n", value, port);
   outportb(port, c_value);
   printf("Character %c sent to port number %d\n", c_value, port);
   return 0;
}
```

outpw

Function Outputs a word to a hardware port.

Syntax #include <conio.h>
unsigned outpw(unsigned *portid*, unsigned *value*);

DOS	UNIX	Windows	ANSI C	C++ only
■		■		

Remarks **outpw** is a macro that writes the 16-bit word given by *value* to the output port specified by *portid*. It writes the low byte of *value* to *portid*, and the high byte of the word to *portid* +1, using a single 16-bit OUT instruction.

If **outpw** is called when conio.h has been included, it will be treated as a macro that expands to inline code. If you don't include conio.h, or if you do include conio.h and **#undef** the macro **outpw**, you'll get the **outpw** function.

Return Value **outpw** returns *value*.

See also **inp, inpw, outp**

Example

```
#include <stdio.h>
#include <conio.h>

int main(void)
{
   unsigned value, port = 0;
   value = outpw(port, 64);
   printf("Value %d sent to port number %d\n", value, port);
   return 0;
}
```


outtext

Function Displays a string in the viewport.

Syntax #include <graphics.h>
void far outtext(char far **textstring*);

DOS	UNIX	Windows	ANSI C	C++ only
■				

Remarks **outtext** displays a text string in the viewport, using the current justification settings and the current font, direction, and size.

outtext outputs *textstring* at the current position (CP). If the horizontal text justification is LEFT_TEXT and the text direction is HORIZ_DIR, the CP's x-coordinate is advanced by **textwidth**(*textstring*). Otherwise, the CP remains unchanged.

To maintain code compatibility when using several fonts, use **textwidth** and **textheight** to determine the dimensions of the string.

➡ If a string is printed with the default font using **outtext**, any part of the string that extends outside the current viewport is truncated.

outtext is for use in graphics mode; it will not work in text mode.

Return Value None.

See also **gettextsettings, outtextxy, settextjustify, textheight, textwidth**

Example

```
#include <graphics.h>
#include <stdlib.h>
#include <stdio.h>
#include <conio.h>

int main(void)
{
   /* request autodetection */
   int gdriver = DETECT, gmode, errorcode;
   int midx, midy;

   /* initialize graphics and local variables */
   initgraph(&gdriver, &gmode, "");

   /* read result of initialization */
   errorcode = graphresult();
   if (errorcode != grOk) {  /* an error occurred */
      printf("Graphics error: %s\n", grapherrormsg(errorcode));
      printf("Press any key to halt:");
      getch();
      exit(1);               /* terminate with an error code */
   }

   midx = getmaxx() / 2;
   midy = getmaxy() / 2;

   /* move the CP to the center of the screen */
   moveto(midx, midy);

   /* output text starting at the CP */
   outtext("This ");
   outtext("is ");
   outtext("a ");
   outtext("test.");

   /* clean up */
   getch();
   closegraph();
   return 0;
}
```

outtextxy

Function Displays a string at a specified location.

Syntax #include <graphics.h>
void far outtextxy(int *x*, int *y*, char far **textstring*);

DOS	UNIX	Windows	ANSI C	C++ only
■				

Remarks **outtextxy** displays a text string in the viewport at the given position (*x*, *y*), using the current justification settings and the current font, direction, and size.

To maintain code compatibility when using several fonts, use **textwidth** and **textheight** to determine the dimensions of the string.

If a string is printed with the default font using **outtext** or **outtextxy**, any part of the string that extends outside the current viewport is truncated.

outtext is for use in graphics mode; it will not work in text mode.

Return Value None.

See also **gettextsettings**, **outtext**, **textheight**, **textwidth**

Example

```
#include <graphics.h>
#include <stdlib.h>
#include <stdio.h>
#include <conio.h>

int main(void)
{
   /* request autodetection */
   int gdriver = DETECT, gmode, errorcode;
   int midx, midy;

   /* initialize graphics and local variables */
   initgraph(&gdriver, &gmode, "");

   /* read result of initialization */
   errorcode = graphresult();
   if (errorcode != grOk) {  /* an error occurred */
      printf("Graphics error: %s\n", grapherrormsg(errorcode));
      printf("Press any key to halt:");
      getch();
      exit(1);              /* terminate with an error code */
   }

   midx = getmaxx() / 2;
   midy = getmaxy() / 2;

   /* output text at center of the screen; CP doesn't get changed */
   outtextxy(midx, midy, "This is a test.");
```

```
   /* clean up */
   getch();
   closegraph();
   return 0;
}
```

_OvrlnitEms

Function Initializes expanded memory swapping for the overlay manager.

Syntax #include <dos.h>
int cdecl far _OvrInitEms(unsigned *emsHandle*, unsigned *firstPage*, unsigned *pages*);

DOS	UNIX	Windows	ANSI C	C++ only
▪				

Remarks **_OvrlnitEms** checks for the presence of expanded memory by looking for an EMS driver and allocating memory from it. If *emsHandle* is zero, the overlay manager allocates EMS pages and uses them for swapping. If *emsHandle* is not zero, then it should be a valid EMS handle; the overlay manager will use it for swapping. In that case, you can specify *firstPage*, where the swapping can start inside that area.

In both cases, a nonzero *pages* parameter gives the limit of the usable pages by the overlay manager.

Return Value **_OvrlnitEms** returns 0 if the overlay manager is able to use expanded memory for swapping.

See also **_OvrlnitExt**, *_ovrbuffer* (global variable)

Example

```
#include <dos.h>

int main(void)
{
   /* ask overlay manager to check for expanded memory and allow it to use 16
      pages (256K) available only in medium, large, and huge memory models */
   _OvrInitEms (0, 0, 16);

   return 0;
}
```

_OvrlnitExt

Function Initializes extended memory swapping for the overlay manager.

Syntax #include <dos.h>
int cdecl far _OvrInitExt(unsigned long *startAddress*,
unsigned long *length*);

DOS	UNIX	Windows	ANSI C	C++ only
■				

Remarks **_OvrInitExt** checks for the presence of extended memory, using the known methods to detect the presence of other programs using extended memory, and allocates memory from it. If *startAddress* is zero, the overlay manager determines the start address and uses, at most, the size of the overlays. If *startAddress* is not zero, then the overlay manager uses the extended memory above that address.

In both cases, a nonzero *length* parameter gives the limit of the usable extended memory by the overlay manager.

Return Value **_OvrInitExt** returns 0 if the overlay manager is able to use extended memory for swapping.

See also **_OvrInitEms**, *_ovrbuffer* (global variable)

Example

```
#include <dos.h>

int main(void)
{
   /* use the extended memory from the linear address 0x200000L (2MB), as much as
      necessary */
   _OvrInitExt (0x200000L, 0);
   return 0;
}
```

N-P

parsfnm

Function Parses file name.

Syntax #include <dos.h>
char *parsfnm(const char **cmdline*, struct fcb **fcb*, int *opt*);

DOS	UNIX	Windows	ANSI C	C++ only
■		■		

Remarks **parsfnm** parses a string pointed to by *cmdline* for a file name. The string is normally a command line. The file name is placed in a file control block (FCB) as a drive, file name, and extension. The FCB is pointed to by *fcb*.

The *opt* parameter is the value documented for AL in the DOS parse system call. See your DOS reference manuals under system call 0x29 for a description of the parsing operations performed on the file name.

Return Value On success, **parsfnm** returns a pointer to the next byte after the end of the file name. If there is any error in parsing the file name, **parsfnm** returns null.

Example

```
#include <process.h>
#include <string.h>
#include <stdio.h>
#include <dos.h>

int main(void)
{
   char line[80];
   struct fcb blk;

   /* get file name */
   printf("Enter drive and file name (no path - ie. a:file.dat)\n");
   gets(line);

   /* put file name in fcb */
   if (parsfnm(line, &blk, 1) == NULL)
      printf("Error in parsfm call\n");
   else
      printf("Drive #%d  Name: %11s\n", blk.fcb_drive, blk.fcb_name);
   return 0;
}
```

peek

Function Returns the word at memory location specified by *segment:offset*.

Syntax #include <dos.h>
int peek(unsigned *segment*, unsigned *offset*);

DOS	UNIX	Windows	ANSI C	C++ only
■		■		

Remarks **peek** returns the word at the memory location *segment:offset*.

If **peek** is called when dos.h has been included, it is treated as a macro that expands to inline code. If you don't include dos.h, or if you do include it and **#undef peek**, you'll get the function rather than the macro.

Return Value **peek** returns the word of data stored at the memory location *segment:offset*.

See also **harderr, peekb, poke**

Example

```
#include <stdio.h>
#include <conio.h>
#include <dos.h>

int main(void)
{
   int value = 0;
   printf("The current status of your keyboard is:\n");
   value = peek(0x0040, 0x0017);
   if (value & 1)
      printf("Right shift on\n");
   else
      printf("Right shift off\n");
   if (value & 2)
      printf("Left shift on\n");
   else
      printf("Left shift off\n");
   if (value & 4)
      printf("Control key on\n");
   else
      printf("Control key off\n");
   if (value & 8)
      printf("Alt key on\n");
   else
      printf("Alt key off\n");
   if (value & 16)
      printf("Scroll lock on\n");
   else
      printf("Scroll lock off\n");
   if (value & 32)
      printf("Num lock on\n");
   else
      printf("Num lock off\n");
   if (value & 64)
      printf("Caps lock on\n");
   else
      printf("Caps lock off\n");
   return 0;
}
```


peekb

Function Returns the byte of memory specified by *segment:offset*.

Syntax #include <dos.h>

char peekb(unsigned *segment*, unsigned *offset*);

DOS	UNIX	Windows	ANSI C	C++ only
■		■		

Remarks **peekb** returns the byte at the memory location addressed by *segment:offset*.

If **peekb** is called when dos.h has been included, it is treated as a macro that expands to inline code. If you don't include dos.h, or if you do include it and #**undef peekb**, you'll get the function rather than the macro.

Return Value **peekb** returns the byte of information stored at the memory location *segment:offset*.

See also **peek, pokeb**

Example

```
#include <stdio.h>
#include <conio.h>
#include <dos.h>

int main(void)
{
   int value = 0;
   printf("The current status of your keyboard is:\n");
   value = peekb(0x0040, 0x0017);
   if (value & 1)
      printf("Right shift on\n");
   else
      printf("Right shift off\n");
   if (value & 2)
      printf("Left shift on\n");
   else
      printf("Left shift off\n");
   if (value & 4)
      printf("Control key on\n");
   else
      printf("Control key off\n");
   if (value & 8)
      printf("Alt key on\n");
   else
      printf("Alt key off\n");
   if (value & 16)
      printf("Scroll lock on\n");
   else
      printf("Scroll lock off\n");
   if (value & 32)
      printf("Num lock on\n");
   else
      printf("Num lock off\n");
```

```
   if (value & 64)
      printf("Caps lock on\n");
   else
      printf("Caps lock off\n");
   return 0;
}
```

perror

Function Prints a system error message.

Syntax #include <stdio.h>
void perror(const char *s);

DOS	UNIX	Windows	ANSI C	C++ only
■	■		■	

Remarks **perror** prints to the *stderr* stream (normally the console) the system error message for the last library routine that produced the error.

First the argument *s* is printed, then a colon, then the message corresponding to the current value of the global variable *errno*, and finally a newline. The convention is to pass the file name of the program as the argument string.

The array of error message strings is accessed through the global variable *sys_errlist*. The global variable *errno* can be used as an index into the array to find the string corresponding to the error number. None of the strings includes a newline character.

The global variable *sys_nerr* contains the number of entries in the array.

Refer to *errno*, *sys_errlist*, and *sys_nerr* in Chapter 3, "Global variables," for more information.

Return Value None.

See also **clearerr, eof, _strerror, strerror**

Example

```
#include <stdio.h>
int main(void)
{
   FILE *fp;
   fp = fopen("perror.dat", "r");
   if (!fp)
      perror("Unable to open file for reading");
```

N-P

```
   return 0;
}
```

pieslice

Function Draws and fills in pie slice.

Syntax #include <graphics.h>
void far pieslice(int *x*, int *y*, int *stangle*, int *endangle*, int *radius*);

DOS	UNIX	Windows	ANSI C	C++ only
■				

Remarks **pieslice** draws and fills a pie slice centered at (*x,y*) with a radius given by *radius*. The slice travels from *stangle* to *endangle*. The slice is outlined in the current drawing color and then filled using the current fill pattern and fill color.

The angles for **pieslice** are given in degrees. They are measured counter-clockwise, with 0 degrees at 3 o'clock, 90 degrees at 12 o'clock, and so on.

➡ If you are using a CGA or monochrome adapter, the examples in this book of how to use graphics functions may not produce the expected results. If your system runs on a CGA or monochrome adapter, use the value 1 (one) instead of the symbolic color constant, and consult the second example under **arc** on how to use the **pieslice** function.

Return Value None.

See also **fillellipse**, *fill_patterns* (enumerated type), **graphresult**, **sector**, **setfillstyle**

Example

```
#include <graphics.h>
#include <stdlib.h>
#include <stdio.h>
#include <conio.h>

int main(void)
{
   /* request autodetection */
   int gdriver = DETECT, gmode, errorcode;
   int midx, midy;
   int stangle = 45, endangle = 135, radius = 100;

   /* initialize graphics and local variables */
   initgraph(&gdriver, &gmode, "");

   /* read result of initialization */
   errorcode = graphresult();
```

```
   if (errorcode != grOk)    /* an error occurred */
   {
      printf("Graphics error: %s\n", grapherrormsg(errorcode));
      printf("Press any key to halt:");
      getch();
      exit(1);               /* terminate with an error code */
   }

   midx = getmaxx() / 2;
   midy = getmaxy() / 2;

   /* set fill style and draw a pie slice */
   setfillstyle(EMPTY_FILL, getmaxcolor());
   pieslice(midx, midy, stangle, endangle, radius);

   /* clean up */
   getch();
   closegraph();
   return 0;
}
```

poke

Function Stores an integer value at a memory location given by *segment*:*offset*.

Syntax #include <dos.h>
void poke(unsigned *segment*, unsigned *offset*, int *value*);

DOS	UNIX	Windows	ANSI C	C++ only
■		■		

Remarks **poke** stores the integer *value* at the memory location *segment*:*offset*.

If this routine is called when dos.h has been included, it will be treated as a macro that expands to inline code. If you don't include dos.h, or if you do include it and **#undef poke**, you'll get the function rather than the macro.

Return Value None.

See also **harderr, peek, pokeb**

Example

```
#include <dos.h>
#include <conio.h>

int main(void)
{
   clrscr();
   cprintf("Make sure the scroll lock key is off and press any key\r\n");
```

```
    getch();
    poke(0x0000,0x0417,16);
    cprintf("The scroll lock is now on\r\n");
    return 0;
}
```

pokeb

Function Stores a byte value at memory location *segment:offset*.

Syntax #include <dos.h>
void pokeb(unsigned *segment*, unsigned *offset*, char *value*);

DOS	UNIX	Windows	ANSI C	C++ only
■		■		

Remarks **pokeb** stores the byte *value* at the memory location *segment:offset*.

If this routine is called when dos.h has been included, it will be treated as a macro that expands to inline code. If you don't include dos.h, or if you do include it and **#undef pokeb**, you'll get the function rather than the macro.

Return Value None.

See also **peekb**, **poke**

Example

```
#include <dos.h>
#include <conio.h>

int main(void)
{
   clrscr();
   cprintf("Make sure the scroll lock key is off and press any key\r\n");
   getch();
   pokeb(0x0000,0x0417,16);
   cprintf("The scroll lock is now on\r\n");
   return 0;
}
```

polar

Function Returns a complex number with a given magnitude and angle.

Syntax #include <complex.h>
complex polar(double *mag*, double *angle*);

DOS	UNIX	Windows	ANSI C	C++ only
■		■		■

Remarks `polar(mag,angle)` is the same as `complex(mag*cos(angle), mag*sin(angle))`.

Return Value The complex number with the given magnitude (absolute value) and angle (argument).

See also **arg, complex, norm**

Example

```
#include <complex.h>

int main()
{
   double x = 3.1, y = 4.2;
   complex z = complex(x,y);
   cout << "z = " << z << "\n";
   cout << "  has real part = " << real(z) << "\n";
   cout << "  and imaginary real part = " << imag(z) << "\n";
   cout << "z has complex conjugate = " << conj(z) << "\n";

   double mag = sqrt(norm(z));
   double ang = arg(z);
   cout << "The polar form of z is:\n";
   cout << "   magnitude = " << mag << "\n";
   cout << "   angle (in radians) = " << ang << "\n";
   cout << "Reconstructing z from its polar form gives:\n";
   cout << "   z = " << polar(mag,ang) << "\n";
   return 0;
}
```


poly, polyl

Function Generates a polynomial from arguments.

Syntax #include <math.h>
double poly(double *x*, int *degree*, double *coeffs[]*);
long double polyl(long double *x*, int *degree*, long double *coeffs[]*);

	DOS	UNIX	Windows	ANSI C	C++ only
poly	■	■	■		
polyl	■		■		

Remarks **poly** generates a polynomial in *x*, of degree *degree*, with coefficients *coeffs[0]*, *coeffs[1]*, ..., *coeffs[degree]*. For example, if $n = 4$, the generated polynomial is

$$coeffs[4]x^4 + coeffs[3]x^3 + coeffs[2]x^2 + coeffs[1]x + coeffs[0]$$

polyl is the long double version; it takes long double arguments and returns a long double result.

Return Value **poly** and **polyl** return the value of the polynomial as evaluated for the given *x*.

Example

```
#include <stdio.h>
#include <math.h>

/* polynomial:  x**3 - 2x**2 + 5x - 1 */
int main(void)
{
   double result, array[] = { -1.0, 5.0, -2.0, 1.0 };
   result = poly(2.0, 3, array);
   printf("The polynomial: x**3 - 2.0x**2 + 5x - 1"
          " at 2.0 is %lf\n", result);
   return 0;
}
```

pow, powl

Function Calculates *x* to the power of *y*.

Syntax

Real versions:
#include <math.h>
double pow(double *x*, double *y*);
long double powl(long double *x*, long double *y*)

Complex version:
#include <complex.h>
complex pow(complex *x*, complex *y*);
complex pow(complex *x*, double *y*);
complex pow(double *x*, complex *y*);

	DOS	UNIX	Windows	ANSI C	C++ only
powl	■		■		
Real **pow**	■	■	■	■	
Complex **pow**	■		■		■

Remarks **pow** calculates x^y.

powl is the long double version; it takes long double arguments and returns a long double result.

The complex **pow** is defined by

pow(*base*, *expon*) = **exp**(*expon* **log**(*base*))

Return Value On success, **pow** and **powl** return the value calculated, x^y.

Sometimes the arguments passed to these functions produce results that overflow or are incalculable. When the correct value would overflow, the functions return the value HUGE_VAL (**pow**) or _LHUGE_VAL (**powl**). Results of excessively large magnitude can cause the global variable *errno* to be set to

ERANGE	Result out of range

If the argument *x* passed to **pow** or **powl** is real and less than 0, and *y* is not a whole number, the global variable *errno* is set to

EDOM	Domain error

If the arguments *x* and *y* passed to **pow** or **powl** are both 0, they return 1.

Error handling for these functions can be modified through the functions **matherr** and **_matherrl**.

See also **complex, exp, pow10, sqrt**

Example

```
#include <math.h>
#include <stdio.h>

int main(void)
{
   double x = 2.0, y = 3.0;
   printf("%lf raised to %lf is %lf\n", x, y, pow(x, y));
   return 0;
}
```

N-P

pow10, pow10l

Function Calculates 10 to the power of *p*.

Syntax #include <math.h>
double pow10(int *p*);
long double pow10l(int *p*);

	DOS	UNIX	Windows	ANSI C	C++ only
pow10	■	■	■		
pow10l	■		■		

Remarks **pow10** computes 10^p.

Return Value On success, **pow10** returns the value calculated, 10^p.

The result is actually calculated to long double accuracy. All arguments are valid, though some can cause an underflow or overflow.

powl is the long double version; it returns a long double result.

See also **exp, pow**

Example

```
#include <math.h>
#include <stdio.h>

int main(void)
{
   double p = 3.0;
   printf("Ten raised to %lf is %lf\n", p, pow10(p));
   return 0;
}
```

printf

Function Writes formatted output to stdout.

Syntax #include <stdio.h>
int printf(const char **format*[, *argument*, ...]);

DOS	UNIX	Windows	ANSI C	C++ only
■	■		■	

Remarks **printf** accepts a series of arguments, applies to each a format specifier contained in the format string given by *format*, and outputs the formatted data to *stdout*. There must be the same number of format specifiers as arguments.

The format string The format string, present in each of the **...printf** function calls, controls how each function will convert, format, and print its arguments. *There must be enough arguments for the format; if there are not, the results will be unpredictable and likely disastrous.* Excess arguments (more than required by the format) are merely ignored.

The format string is a character string that contains two types of objects—*plain characters* and *conversion specifications*:

- Plain characters are simply copied verbatim to the output stream.
- Conversion specifications fetch arguments from the argument list and apply formatting to them.

Format specifiers

...printf format specifiers have the following form:

```
% [flags] [width] [.prec] [F|N|h|l|L] type
```

Each conversion specification begins with the percent character (**%**). After the **%** come the following, in this order:

- an optional sequence of flag characters, `[flags]`
- an optional width specifier, `[width]`
- an optional precision specifier, `[.prec]`
- an optional input-size modifier, `[F|N|h|l|L]`
- the conversion-type character, `[type]`

Optional format string components

These are the general aspects of output formatting controlled by the optional characters, specifiers, and modifiers in the format string:

Character or specifier	What it controls or specifies
flags	Output justification, numeric signs, decimal points, trailing zeros, octal and hex prefixes
width	Minimum number of characters to print, padding with blanks or zeros
precision	Maximum number of characters to print; for integers, minimum number of digits to print
size	Override default size of argument: **N** = near pointer **F** = far pointer **h** = **short int** **l** = **long** **L** = **long double**

...printf conversion-type characters

The following table lists the **...printf** conversion-type characters, the type of input argument accepted by each, and in what format the output appears.

The information in this table of type characters is based on the assumption that no flag characters, width specifiers, precision specifiers, or input-size modifiers were included in the format specifier. To see how the addition of the optional characters and specifiers affects the **...printf** output, refer to the tables following this one.

N-P

Type character	Input argument	Format of output
Numerics		
d	integer	**signed** decimal **int**.
i	integer	**signed** decimal **int**.
o	integer	**unsigned** octal **int**.
u	integer	**unsigned** decimal **int.**
x	integer	**unsigned** hexadecimal **int** (with **a**, **b**, **c**, **d**, **e**, **f**).
X	integer	**unsigned** hexadecimal **int** (with **A**, **B**, **C**, **D**, **E**, **F**).
f	floating-point	**signed** value of the form [-]*dddd.dddd*.
e	floating-point	**signed** value of the form [-]*d.dddd* or **e** [+/-]*ddd*.
g	floating-point	**signed** value in either **e** or **f** form, based on given value and precision. Trailing zeros and the decimal point are printed only if necessary.
E	floating-point	Same as **e**, but with **E** for exponent.
G	floating-point	Same as **g**, but with **E** for exponent if **e** format used.
Characters		
c	character	Single character.
s	string pointer	Prints characters until a null-terminator is pressed or precision is reached.
%	none	The **%** character is printed.
Pointers		
n	pointer to **int**	Stores (in the location pointed to by the input argument) a count of the characters written so far.
p	pointer	Prints the input argument as a pointer; format depends on which memory model was used. It will be either XXXX:YYYY or YYYY (offset only).

Conventions Certain conventions accompany some of these specifications, as summarized in the following table:

Characters	Conventions
e or **E**	The argument is converted to match the style [-] *d.ddd*...**e**[+/-]*ddd*, where ■ one digit precedes the decimal point. ■ the number of digits after the decimal point is equal to the precision. ■ the exponent always contains at least two digits.
f	The argument is converted to decimal notation in the style [-] *ddd.ddd*..., where the number of digits after the decimal point is equal to the precision (if a nonzero precision was given).
g or **G**	The argument is printed in style **e**, **E** or **f**, with the precision specifying the number of significant digits. Trailing zeros are removed from the result, and a decimal point appears only if necessary. The argument is printed in style **e** or **f** (with some restraints) if **g** is the conversion character, and in style **E** if the character is **G**. Style **e** is used only if the exponent that results from the conversion is either greater than the precision or less than –4.
x or **X**	For **x** conversions, the letters **a**, **b**, **c**, **d**, **e**, and **f** appear in the output; for **X** conversions, the letters **A**, **B**, **C**, **D**, **E**, and **F** appear.

Infinite floating-point numbers are printed as +INF and –INF. An IEEE Not-a-Number is printed as +NAN or –NAN.

N-P

Flag characters

The flag characters are minus (-), plus (+), sharp (#), and blank (). They can appear in any order and combination.

Flag	What it specifies
–	Left-justifies the result, pads on the right with blanks. If not given, right-justifies result, pads on left with zeros or blanks.
+	Signed conversion results always begin with a plus (+) or minus (-) sign.
blank	If value is nonnegative, the output begins with a blank instead of a plus; negative values still begin with a minus.
#	Specifies that *arg* is to be converted using an "alternate form." See the following table.

Plus (+) takes precedence over blank () if both are given.

Alternate forms

If the # flag is used with a conversion character, it has the following effect on the argument (*arg*) being converted:

Conversion character	How # affects *arg*
c,s,d,i,u	No effect.
0	0 is prepended to a nonzero *arg*.
x or **X**	0x (or 0X) is prepended to *arg*.
e, **E**, or **f**	The result always contains a decimal point even if no digits follow the point. Normally, a decimal point appears in these results only if a digit follows it.
g or **G**	Same as **e** and **E**, with the addition that trailing zeros are not removed.

Width specifiers

The width specifier sets the minimum field width for an output value.

Width is specified in one of two ways: directly, through a decimal digit string, or indirectly, through an asterisk (*). If you use an asterisk for the width specifier, the next argument in the call (which must be an **int**) specifies the minimum output field width.

In no case does a nonexistent or small field width cause truncation of a field. If the result of a conversion is wider than the field width, the field is simply expanded to contain the conversion result.

Width specifier	How output width is affected
n	At least *n* characters are printed. If the output value has less than *n* characters, the output is padded with blanks (right-padded if – flag given, left-padded otherwise).
0*n*	At least *n* characters are printed. If the output value has less than *n* characters, it is filled on the left with zeros.
*	The argument list supplies the width specifier, which must precede the actual argument being formatted.

Precision specifiers

A precision specification always begins with a period (.) to separate it from any preceding width specifier. Then, like width, precision is specified either directly through a decimal digit string, or indirectly through an asterisk (*). If you use an asterisk for the precision specifier, the next argument in the call (treated as an **int**) specifies the precision.

If you use asterisks for the width or the precision, or for both, the width argument must immediately follow the specifiers, followed by the precision argument, then the argument for the data to be converted.

Precision specifier	How output precision is affected
(none given)	Precision set to default: default = 1 for *d*, *i*, *o*, *u*, *x*, *X* types default = 6 for *e*, *E*, *f* types default = all significant digits for *g*, *G* types default = print to first null character for *s* types; no effect on *c* types
.0	For *d*, *i*, *o*, *u*, *x* types, precision set to default; for *e*, *E*, *f* types, no decimal point is printed.
.*n*	*n* characters or *n* decimal places are printed. If the output value has more than *n* characters, the output might be truncated or rounded. (Whether this happens depends on the type character.)
*	The argument list supplies the precision specifier, which must precede the actual argument being formatted.

If an explicit precision of zero is specified, *and* the format specifier for the field is one of the integer formats (that is, *d*, *i*, *o*, *u*, *x*), *and* the value to be printed is 0, no numeric characters will be output for that field (that is, the field will be blank).

Conversion character	How precision specification (.n) affects conversion
d **i** **o** **u** **x** **X**	.*n* specifies that at least *n* digits are printed. If the input argument has less than *n* digits, the output value is left-padded with zeros. If the input argument has more than *n* digits, the output value is not truncated.
e **E** **f**	.*n* specifies that *n* characters are printed after the decimal point, and the last digit printed is rounded.
g **G**	.*n* specifies that at most *n* significant digits are printed.
c	.*n* has no effect on the output.
s	.*n* specifies that no more than *n* characters are printed.

Input-size modifier

The input-size modifier character (*F*, *N*, *h*, *l*, or *L*) gives the size of the subsequent input argument:

F = far pointer
N = near pointer

h = **short int**
l = **long**
L = **long double**

The input-size modifiers (*F*, *N*, *h*, *l*, and *L*) affect how the **...printf** functions interpret the data type of the corresponding input argument *arg*. *F* and *N* apply only to input *args* that are pointers (*%p*, *%s*, and *%n*). *h*, *L*, and *L* apply to input *args* that are numeric (integers and floating-point).

Both *F* and *N* reinterpret the input *arg*. Normally, the *arg* for a *%p*, *%s*, or *%n* conversion is a pointer of the default size for the memory model. *F* says "interpret *arg* as a far pointer." *N* says "interpret *arg* as a near pointer."

h, *l*, and *L* override the default size of the numeric data input arguments: *l* and *L* apply to integer (*d*, *i*, *o*, *u*, *x*, *X*) and floating-point (*e*, *E*, *f*, *g*, and *G*) types, while *h* applies to integer types only. Neither *h* nor *l* affect character (*c*, *s*) or pointer (*p*, *n*) types.

Input-size modifier	How *arg* is interpreted
F	*arg* is read as a **far** pointer.
N	*arg* is read as a **near** pointer. *N* cannot be used with any conversion in huge model.
h	*arg* is interpreted as a **short int** for *d*, *i*, *o*, *u*, *x*, or *X*.
l	*arg* is interpreted as a **long int** for *d*, *i*, *o*, *u*, *x*, or *X*; *arg* is interpreted as a **double** for *e*, *E*, *f*, *g*, or *G*.
L	*arg* is interpreted as a **long double** for *e*, *E*, *f*, *g*, or *G*.

Return Value **printf** returns the number of bytes output. In the event of error, **printf** returns EOF.

See also **cprintf, ecvt, fprintf, fread, fscanf, putc, puts, putw, scanf, sprintf, vprintf, vsprintf**

Example

```
#include <stdio.h>
#include <string.h>

#define I 555
#define R 5.5

int main(void)
{
   int i,j,k,l;
   char buf[7];
   char *prefix = buf;
   char tp[20];
```

```
printf("prefix  6d      6o      8x          10.2e         "
       "10.2f\n");
strcpy(prefix,"%");
for (i = 0; i < 2; i++) {
   for (j = 0; j < 2; j++)
      for (k = 0; k < 2; k++)
         for (l = 0; l < 2; l++) {
            if (i==0)  strcat(prefix,"-");
            if (j==0)  strcat(prefix,"+");
            if (k==0)  strcat(prefix,"#");
            if (l==0)  strcat(prefix,"0");
            printf("%5s |",prefix);
            strcpy(tp,prefix);
            strcat(tp,"6d |");
            printf(tp,I);
            strcpy(tp,"");
            strcpy(tp,prefix);
            strcat(tp,"6o |");
            printf(tp,I);
            strcpy(tp,"");
            strcpy(tp,prefix);
            strcat(tp,"8x |");
            printf(tp,I);
            strcpy(tp,"");
            strcpy(tp,prefix);
            strcat(tp,"10.2e |");
            printf(tp,R);
            strcpy(tp,prefix);
            strcat(tp,"10.2f |");
            printf(tp,R);
            printf("  \n");
            strcpy(prefix,"%");
         }
      }
   return 0;
}
```

N-P

Program output

```
prefix    6d      6o        8x          10.2e        10.2f
 %-+#0 |+555   |01053  |0x22b    |+5.50e+00  |+5.50       |
  %-+# |+555   |01053  |0x22b    |+5.50e+00  |+5.50       |
  %-+0 |+555   |1053   |22b      |+5.50e+00  |+5.50       |
   %-+ |+555   |1053   |22b      |+5.50e+00  |+5.50       |
  %-#0 |555    |01053  |0x22b    |5.50e+00   |5.50        |
   %-# |555    |01053  |0x22b    |5.50e+00   |5.50        |
   %-0 |555    |1053   |22b      |5.50e+00   |5.50        |
    %- |555    |1053   |22b      |5.50e+00   |5.50        |
  %+#0 |+00555 |001053 |0x00022b |+05.50e+00 |+000005.50 |
   %+# |  +555 | 01053 |    0x22b | +5.50e+00 |      +5.50 |
   %+0 |+00555 |001053 |0000022b |+05.50e+00 |+000005.50 |
    %+ |  +555 |  1053 |      22b | +5.50e+00 |      +5.50 |
   %#0 |000555 |001053 |0x00022b |005.50e+00 |0000005.50 |
    %# |   555 | 01053 |    0x22b |  5.50e+00 |       5.50 |
    %0 |000555 |001053 |0000022b |005.50e+00 |0000005.50 |
     % |   555 |  1053 |      22b |  5.50e+00 |       5.50 |
```

putc

Function Outputs a character to a stream.

Syntax #include <stdio.h>
int putc(int *c*, FILE **stream*);

DOS	UNIX	Windows	ANSI C	C++ only
■	■	■	■	

Remarks **putc** is a macro that outputs the character *c* to the stream given by *stream*.

Return Value On success, **putc** returns the character printed, *c*. On error, **putc** returns EOF.

See also **fprintf, fputc, fputch, fputchar, fputs, fwrite, getc, getchar, printf, putch, putchar, putw, vprintf**

Example

```
#include <stdio.h>

int main(void)
{
   char msg[] = "Hello world\n";
   int i = 0;
   while (msg[i])
      putc(msg[i++], stdout);
   return 0;
}
```

putch

Function Outputs character to screen.

Syntax #include <conio.h>
int putch(int *c*);

DOS	UNIX	Windows	ANSI C	C++ only
■				

Remarks **putch** outputs the character *c* to the current text window. It is a text mode function performing direct video output to the console. **putch** does not translate linefeed characters (\n) into carriage-return/linefeed pairs.

The string is written either directly to screen memory or by way of a BIOS call, depending on the value of the global variable *directvideo*.

Return Value On success, **putch** returns the character printed, *c*. On error, it returns EOF.

See also **cprintf, cputs, getch, getche, putc, putchar**

Example

```
#include <stdio.h>
#include <conio.h>

int main(void)
{
   char ch = 0;
   printf("Input a string:");
   while ((ch != '\r')) {
      ch = getch();
      putch(ch);
   }
   return 0;
}
```

N-P

putchar

Function Outputs character on stdout.

Syntax #include <stdio.h>
int putchar(int *c*);

DOS	UNIX	Windows	ANSI C	C++ only
■	■	■	■	

Remarks **putchar**(*c*) is a macro defined to be **putc**(*c*, *stdout*).

Return Value On success, **putchar** returns the character *c*. On error, **putchar** returns EOF.

See also **fputchar, getc, getchar, printf, putc, putch, puts, putw, vprintf**

Example

```
#include <stdio.h>

/* define some box drawing characters */
#define LEFT_TOP  0xDA
#define RIGHT_TOP 0xBF
#define HORIZ     0xC4
#define VERT      0xB3
#define LEFT_BOT  0xC0
#define RIGHT_BOT 0xD9

int main(void)
{
   char i, j;

   /* draw the top of the box */
   putchar(LEFT_TOP);
   for (i=0; i<10; i++)
      putchar(HORIZ);
   putchar(RIGHT_TOP);
   putchar('\n');

   /* draw the middle */
   for (i=0; i<4; i++) {
      putchar(VERT);
      for (j=0; j<10; j++)
         putchar(' ');
      putchar(VERT);
      putchar('\n');
   }

   /* draw the bottom */
   putchar(LEFT_BOT);
   for (i=0; i<10; i++)
      putchar(HORIZ);
   putchar(RIGHT_BOT);
   putchar('\n');
   return 0;
}
```

putenv

Function Adds string to current environment.

Syntax #include <stdlib.h>

int putenv(const char **name*);

DOS	UNIX	Windows	ANSI C	C++ only
■	■	■		

Remarks **putenv** accepts the string *name* and adds it to the environment of the *current* process. For example,

```
putenv("PATH=C:\\BC");
```

putenv can also be used to modify or delete an existing *name*. You can set a variable to an empty value by specifying an empty string.

putenv can be used only to modify the current program's environment. Once the program ends, the old environment is restored.

Note that the string given to **putenv** must be static or global. Unpredictable results will occur if a local or dynamic string given to **putenv** is used after the string memory is released.

Return Value On success, **putenv** returns 0; on failure, –1.

See also **getenv**

Example

```
#include <stdio.h>
#include <stdlib.h>
#include <alloc.h>
#include <string.h>
#include <dos.h>

int main(void)
{
   char *path, *ptr;
   int i = 0;

   /* Get the current path environment. */
   ptr = getenv("PATH");

   /* set up new path */
   path = (char *) malloc(strlen(ptr)+15);
   strcpy(path,"PATH=");
   strcat(path,ptr);
   strcat(path,";c:\\temp");

   /* replace the current path and display current environment */
   putenv(path);
   while (environ[i])
       printf("%s\n",environ[i++]);
   return 0;
}
```

N-P

putimage

Function Outputs a bit image to screen.

Syntax #include <graphics.h>
void far putimage(int *left*, int *top*, void far *bitmap*, int *op*);

DOS	UNIX	Windows	ANSI C	C++ only
■				

Remarks **putimage** puts the bit image previously saved with **getimage** back onto the screen, with the upper left corner of the image placed at (*left*,*top*). *bitmap* points to the area in memory where the source image is stored.

The *op* parameter to **putimage** specifies a combination operator that controls how the color for each destination pixel onscreen is computed, based on the pixel already onscreen and the corresponding source pixel in memory.

The enumeration *putimage_ops*, as defined in graphics.h, gives names to these operators.

Name	Value	Description
COPY_PUT	0	Copy
XOR_PUT	1	Exclusive or
OR_PUT	2	Inclusive or
AND_PUT	3	And
NOT_PUT	4	Copy the inverse of the source

In other words, COPY_PUT copies the source bitmap image onto the screen, XOR_PUT XORs the source image with that already onscreen, OR_PUT ORs the source image with that onscreen, and so on.

Return Value None.

See also **getimage**, **imagesize**, **putpixel**, **setvisualpage**

Example

```
#include <graphics.h>
#include <stdlib.h>
#include <stdio.h>
#include <conio.h>

#define ARROW_SIZE 10

void draw_arrow(int x, int y);

int main()
{
   /* request autodetection */
```

```
   int gdriver = DETECT, gmode, errorcode;
   void *arrow;
   int x, y, maxx;
   unsigned int size;

   /* initialize graphics and local variables */
   initgraph(&gdriver, &gmode, "");

   errorcode = graphresult();
   if (errorcode != grOk)    /* an error occurred */
   {
      printf("Graphics error: %s\n", grapherrormsg(errorcode));
      printf("Press any key to halt:");
      getch();
      exit(1);               /* terminate with an error code */
   }

   maxx = getmaxx();
   x = 0;
   y = getmaxy() / 2;
   draw_arrow(x, y);

   /* calculate the size of the image and allocate space for it */
   size = imagesize(x, y-ARROW_SIZE, x+(4*ARROW_SIZE), y+ARROW_SIZE);
   arrow = malloc(size);

   /* grab the image */
   getimage(x, y-ARROW_SIZE, x+(4*ARROW_SIZE), y+ARROW_SIZE, arrow);

   /* repeat until a key is pressed */
   while (!kbhit()) {
      /* erase old image */
      putimage(x, y-ARROW_SIZE, arrow, XOR_PUT);
      x += ARROW_SIZE;
      if (x >= maxx)
         x = 0;

      /* plot new image */
      putimage(x, y-ARROW_SIZE, arrow, XOR_PUT);
   }
   free(arrow);
   closegraph();
   return 0;
}
void draw_arrow(int x, int y) {
   moveto(x, y);
   linerel(4*ARROW_SIZE, 0);
   linerel(-2*ARROW_SIZE, -1*ARROW_SIZE);
   linerel(0, 2*ARROW_SIZE);
   linerel(2*ARROW_SIZE, -1*ARROW_SIZE);
}
```

putpixel

Function Plots a pixel at a specified point.

Syntax #include <graphics.h>
void far putpixel(int *x*, int *y*, int *color*);

DOS	UNIX	Windows	ANSI C	C++ only
■				

Remarks **putpixel** plots a point in the color defined by *color* at (*x*,*y*).

Return Value None.

See also **getpixel, putimage**

Example

```
#include <graphics.h>
#include <stdlib.h>
#include <stdio.h>
#include <conio.h>
#include <dos.h>

#define PIXEL_COUNT 1000
#define DELAY_TIME  100  /* in milliseconds */

int main()
{
   /* request autodetection */
   int gdriver = DETECT, gmode, errorcode;
   int i, x, y, color, maxx, maxy, maxcolor, seed;

   /* initialize graphics and local variables */
   initgraph(&gdriver, &gmode, "");

   /* read result of initialization */
   errorcode = graphresult();
   if (errorcode != grOk) {  /* an error occurred */
      printf("Graphics error: %s\n", grapherrormsg(errorcode));
      printf("Press any key to halt:");
      getch();
      exit(1);               /* terminate with an error code */
   }

   maxx = getmaxx() + 1;
   maxy = getmaxy() + 1;
   maxcolor = getmaxcolor() + 1;

   while (!kbhit())
```

```
   {
      /* seed the random number generator */
      seed = random(32767);
      srand(seed);
      for (i=0; i<PIXEL_COUNT; i++) {
         x = random(maxx);
         y = random(maxy);
         color = random(maxcolor);
         putpixel(x, y, color);
      }
      delay(DELAY_TIME);
      srand(seed);
      for (i=0; i<PIXEL_COUNT; i++) {
         x = random(maxx);
         y = random(maxy);
         color = random(maxcolor);
         if (color == getpixel(x, y))
            putpixel(x, y, 0);
      }
   }

   /* clean up */
   getch();
   closegraph();
   return 0;
}
```


puts

Function Outputs a string to stdout.

Syntax #include <stdio.h>
int puts(const char *s);

DOS	UNIX	Windows	ANSI C	C++ only
■	■		■	

Remarks **puts** copies the null-terminated string *s* to the standard output stream stdout and appends a newline character.

Return Value On successful completion, **puts** returns a nonnegative value. Otherwise, it returns a value of EOF.

See also **cputs, fputs, gets, printf, putchar**

puttext

Function Copies text from memory to the text mode screen.

Syntax #include <conio.h>
int puttext(int *left*, int *top*, int *right*, int *bottom*, void **source*);

DOS	UNIX	Windows	ANSI C	C++ only
■				

Remarks **puttext** writes the contents of the memory area pointed to by *source* out to the onscreen rectangle defined by *left*, *top*, *right*, and *bottom*.

All coordinates are absolute screen coordinates, not window-relative. The upper left corner is (1,1).

puttext places the contents of a memory area into the defined rectangle sequentially from left to right and top to bottom.

puttext is a text mode function performing direct video output.

Return Value **puttext** returns a nonzero value if the operation succeeds; it returns 0 if it fails (for example, if you gave coordinates outside the range of the current screen mode).

See also **gettext**, **movetext**, **window**

putw

Function Puts an integer on a stream.

Syntax #include <stdio.h>
int putw(int *w*, FILE **stream*);

DOS	UNIX	Windows	ANSI C	C++ only
■	■	■		

Remarks **putw** outputs the integer *w* to the given stream. **putw** neither expects nor causes special alignment in the file.

Return Value On success, **putw** returns the integer *w*. On error, **putw** returns EOF. Because EOF is a legitimate integer, use **ferror** to detect errors with **putw**.

See also **getw**, **printf**

Example

```
#include <stdio.h>
#include <stdlib.h>
```

```
#define FNAME "test.$$$"

int main(void)
{
   FILE *fp;
   int word;

   /* place the word in a file */
   fp = fopen(FNAME, "wb");
   if (fp == NULL) {
      printf("Error opening file %s\n", FNAME);
      exit(1);
   }
   word = 94;
   putw(word,fp);
   if (ferror(fp))
       printf("Error writing to file\n");
   else
       printf("Successful write\n");
   fclose(fp);

   /* reopen the file */
   fp = fopen(FNAME, "rb");
   if (fp == NULL) {
      printf("Error opening file %s\n", FNAME);
      exit(1);
   }

   /* extract the word */
   word = getw(fp);
   if (ferror(fp))
       printf("Error reading file\n");
   else
       printf("Successful read: word = %d\n", word);

   /* clean up */
   fclose(fp);
   unlink(FNAME);
   return 0;
}
```

N-P

qsort

Function Sorts using the quicksort algorithm.

Syntax #include <stdlib.h>
void qsort(void **base*, size_t *nelem*, size_t *width*,
int (**fcmp*)(const void *, const void *));

DOS	UNIX	Windows	ANSI C	C++ only
■	■	■	■	

Remarks **qsort** is an implementation of the "median of three" variant of the quicksort algorithm. **qsort** sorts the entries in a table by repeatedly calling the user-defined comparison function pointed to by *fcmp*.

- *base* points to the base (0th element) of the table to be sorted.
- *nelem* is the number of entries in the table.
- *width* is the size of each entry in the table, in bytes.

fcmp*, the comparison function, accepts two arguments, *elem1* and *elem2*, each a pointer to an entry in the table. The comparison function compares each of the pointed-to items (elem1* and **elem2*), and returns an integer based on the result of the comparison.

**elem1* < **elem2* *fcmp* returns an integer < 0
**elem1* == **elem2* *fcmp* returns 0
**elem1* > **elem2* *fcmp* returns an integer > 0

In the comparison, the less-than symbol (<) means the left element should appear before the right element in the final, sorted sequence. Similarly, the greater-than (>) symbol means the left element should appear after the right element in the final, sorted sequence.

Return Value None.

See also **bsearch, lsearch**

Example

```
#include <stdio.h>
#include <stdlib.h>
#include <string.h>

int sort_function( const void *a, const void *b);

char list[5][4] = { "cat", "car", "cab", "cap", "can" };

int main(void)
{
   int  x;
   qsort((void *)list, 5, sizeof(list[0]), sort_function);
   for (x = 0; x < 5; x++)
      printf("%s\n", list[x]);
   return 0;
}
int sort_function(const void *a, const void *b)
{
   return( strcmp((char *)a,(char *)b) );
}
```

raise

Function Sends a software signal to the executing program.

Syntax #include <signal.h>
int raise(int *sig*);

DOS	UNIX	Windows	ANSI C	C++ only
▪	▪	▪	▪	

Remarks **raise** sends a signal of type *sig* to the program. If the program has installed a signal handler for the signal type specified by *sig*, that handler will be executed. If no handler has been installed, the default action for that signal type will be taken.

The signal types currently defined in signal.h are noted here:

Signal	Meaning
SIGABRT	Abnormal termination (*)
SIGFPE	Bad floating-point operation
SIGILL	Illegal instruction (#)
SIGINT	Control break interrupt
SIGSEGV	Invalid access to storage (#)
SIGTERM	Request for program termination (*)

Signal types marked with a (*) aren't generated by DOS or Borland C++ during normal operation. However, they can be generated with **raise**. Signals marked by (#) *can't* be generated asynchronously on 8088 or 8086 processors but *can* be generated on some other processors (see **signal** for details).

Q-R

Return Value **raise** returns 0 if successful, nonzero otherwise.

See also **abort, signal**

Example

```
#include <signal.h>

int main()
{
   int a, b;
   a = 10;
   b = 0;
   if (b == 0)
      raise(SIGFPE);    /* preempt divide by zero error */
   a = a / b;
```

```
    return 0;
}
```

rand

Function Random number generator.

Syntax #include <stdlib.h>
int rand(void);

DOS	UNIX	Windows	ANSI C	C++ only
■	■	■	■	

Remarks **rand** uses a multiplicative congruential random number generator with period 2^{32} to return successive pseudorandom numbers in the range from 0 to RAND_MAX. The symbolic constant RAND_MAX is defined in stdlib.h; its value is $2^{15} - 1$.

Return Value **rand** returns the generated pseudorandom number.

See also **random, randomize, srand**

Example

```
#include <stdlib.h>
#include <stdio.h>

int main(void)
{
   int i;
   printf("Ten random numbers from 0 to 99\n\n");
   for(i=0; i<10; i++)
      printf("%d\n", rand() % 100);
   return 0;
}
```

randbrd

Function Reads random block.

Syntax #include <dos.h>
int randbrd(struct fcb *fcb*, int *rcnt*);

DOS	UNIX	Windows	ANSI C	C++ only
■				

Remarks **randbrd** reads *rcnt* number of records using the open file control block (FCB) pointed to by *fcb*. The records are read into memory at the current disk transfer address (DTA). They are read from the disk record indicated in the random record field of the FCB. This is accomplished by calling DOS system call 0x27.

The actual number of records read can be determined by examining the random record field of the FCB. The random record field is advanced by the number of records actually read.

Return Value The following values are returned, depending on the result of the **randbrd** operation:

0 All records are read.
1 End-of-file is reached and the last record read is complete.
2 Reading records would have wrapped around address 0xFFFF (as many records as possible are read).
3 End-of-file is reached with the last record incomplete.

See also **getdta, randbwr, setdta**

Example

```
#include <process.h>
#include <string.h>
#include <stdio.h>
#include <dos.h>

int main(void)
{
   char far *save_dta;
   char line[80], buffer[256];
   struct fcb blk;
   int i, result;

   /* get user input file name for dta */
   printf("Enter drive and file name (no path - i.e. a:file.dat)\n");
   gets(line);

   /* put file name in fcb */
   if (!parsfnm(line, &blk, 1)) {
      printf("Error in call to parsfnm\n");
      exit(1);
   }
   printf("Drive #%d  File: %s\n\n", blk.fcb_drive, blk.fcb_name);

   /* open file with DOS fcb open file */
   bdosptr(0x0F, &blk, 0);

   /* save old dta and set new one */
   save_dta = getdta();
   setdta(buffer);
```

```
    /* set up information for the new dta */
    blk.fcb_recsize = 128;
    blk.fcb_random = 0L;
    result = randbrd(&blk, 1);

    /* check results from randbrd */
    if (!result)
       printf("Read OK\n\n");
    else {
       perror("Error during read");
       exit(1);
    }

    /* read in data from the new dta */
    printf("The first 128 characters are:\n");
    for (i=0; i<128; i++)
       putchar(buffer[i]);

    /* restore previous dta */
    setdta(save_dta);
    return 0;
}
```

randbwr

Function Writes random block.

Syntax #include <dos.h>
int randbwr(struct fcb **fcb*, int *rcnt*);

DOS	UNIX	Windows	ANSI C	C++ only
■				

Remarks **randbwr** writes *rcnt* number of records to disk using the open file control block (FCB) pointed to by *fcb*. This is accomplished using DOS system call 0x28. If *rcnt* is 0, the file is truncated to the length indicated by the random record field.

The actual number of records written can be determined by examining the random record field of the FCB. The random record field is advanced by the number of records actually written.

Return Value The following values are returned, depending upon the result of the **randbwr** operation:

0 All records are written.
1 There is not enough disk space to write the records (no records are written).

2 Writing records would have wrapped around address 0xFFFF (as many records as possible are written).

See also **randbrd**

Example

```
#include <process.h>
#include <string.h>
#include <stdio.h>
#include <dos.h>

int main(void)
{
   char far *save_dta;
   char line[80];
   char buffer[256] = "RANDBWR test!";
   struct fcb blk;
   int result;

   /* get new file name from user */
   printf("Enter a file name to create (no path - ie. a:file.dat\n");
   gets(line);

   /* parse the new file name to the dta */
   parsfnm(line,&blk,1);
   printf("Drive #%d  File: %s\n", blk.fcb_drive, blk.fcb_name);

   /* request DOS services to create file */
   if (bdosptr(0x16, &blk, 0) == -1) {
      perror("Error creating file");
      exit(1);
   }

   /* save old dta and set new dta */
   save_dta = getdta();
   setdta(buffer);

   /* write new records */
   blk.fcb_recsize = 256;
   blk.fcb_random = 0L;
   result = randbwr(&blk, 1);

   if (!result)
      printf("Write OK\n");
   else {
      perror("Disk error");
      exit(1);
   }

   /* request DOS services to close the file */
   if (bdosptr(0x10, &blk, 0) == -1) {
      perror("Error closing file");
      exit(1);
```

Q-R

```
   }

   /* reset the old dta */
   setdta(save_dta);
   return 0;
}
```

random

Function Random number generator.

Syntax #include <stdlib.h>
int random(int *num*);

DOS	UNIX	Windows	ANSI C	C++ only
■		■		

Remarks **random** returns a random number between 0 and (*num*-1). **random**(*num*) is a macro defined in stdlib.h. Both *num* and the random number returned are integers.

Return Value **random** returns a number between 0 and (*num*-1).

See also **rand, randomize, srand**

Example

```
#include <stdlib.h>
#include <stdio.h>
#include <time.h>

int main()       /* prints a random number in the range 0 to 99 */
{
   randomize();
   printf("Random number in the 0-99 range: %d\n", random (100));
   return 0;
}
```

randomize

Function Initializes random number generator.

Syntax #include <stdlib.h>
#include <time.h>
void randomize(void);

DOS	UNIX	Windows	ANSI C	C++ only
■		■		

Remarks **randomize** initializes the random number generator with a random value. Because **randomize** is implemented as a macro that calls the **time** function prototyped in time.h, we recommend that you also include time.h when you use this routine.

Return Value None.

See also **rand, random, srand**

Example

```
#include <stdlib.h>
#include <stdio.h>
#include <time.h>

int main(void)
{
   int i;
   randomize();
   printf("Ten random numbers from 0 to 99\n\n");
   for(i=0; i<10; i++)
      printf("%d\n", rand() % 100);
   return 0;
}
```

_read, _dos_read

Function Reads from file.

Syntax #include <io.h>
int _read(int *handle*, void **buf*, unsigned *len*);

#include <dos.h>
unsigned _dos_read(int *handle*, void far **buf*, unsigned **nread*);

DOS	UNIX	Windows	ANSI C	C++ only
■		■		

Remarks **_read** attempts to read *len* bytes from the file associated with *handle* into the buffer pointed to by *buf*.

When a file is opened in text mode, **_read** does not remove carriage returns.

_dos_read uses DOS function 0x3F to read *len* bytes from the file associated with *handle* into the buffer pointed to by the far pointer *buf*. The

Q-R

actual number of bytes read is stored at the location pointed to by *nread*; when an error occurs, or the end-of-file is encountered, this number may be less than *len*.

_dos_read does not remove carriage returns because all its files are binary files.

handle is a file handle obtained from a **_dos_creat**, **_dos_creatnew**, or **_dos_open** call.

For **_read**, *handle* is a file handle obtained from a **creat**, **open**, **dup**, or **dup2** call.

On disk files, **_dos_read** and **_read** begin reading at the current file pointer. When the reading is complete, they increment the file pointer by the number of bytes read. On devices, the bytes are read directly from the device.

The maximum number of bytes that **_dos_read** or **_read** can read is 65,534, because 65,535 (0xFFFF) is the same as –1, the error return indicator.

Return Value

On successful completion, **_dos_read** returns 0. Otherwise, the function returns the DOS error code and sets the global variable *errno*.

On successful completion, **_read** returns a positive integer indicating the number of bytes placed in the buffer. On end-of-file, **_read** returns zero. On error, it returns –1, and the global variable *errno*.

The global variable *errno* is set to one of the following:

EACCES	Permission denied
EBADF	Bad file number

See also

_open, **read**, **_write**

Example

```
#include <stdio.h>
#include <io.h>
#include <alloc.h>
#include <fcntl.h>
#include <process.h>
#include <sys\stat.h>

int main(void)  /* Example for _read. */
{
   void *buf;
   int handle, bytes;
   buf = malloc(10);
```

```
   /* Looks for a file in the current directory named TEST.$$$ and attempts to
      read 10 bytes from it. To use this example you should create the file
      TEST.$$$ */
   if ((handle = open("TEST.$$$", O_RDONLY )) == -1) {
      printf("Error Opening File\n");
      exit(1);
   }
   if ((bytes = _read(handle, buf, 10)) == -1) {
      printf("Read Failed.\n");
      exit(1);
   }
   else printf("Read: %d bytes read.\n", bytes);
   return 0;
}

#include <stdio.h>
#include <fcntl.h>
#include <dos.h>

int main(void)  /* Example for _dos_read. */
{
   int handle;
   unsigned bytes;
   char buf[10];

   /* Looks for a file in the current directory named TEST.$$$ and
      attempts to read 10 bytes from it. To use this example you
      should create the file TEST.$$$ */
   if (_dos_open("TEST.$$$", O_RDONLY, &handle) != 0) {
      perror("Unable to open TEST.$$$");
      return 1;
   }
   if (_dos_read(handle, buf, 10, &bytes) != 0) {
      perror("Unable to read from TEST.$$$");
      return 1;
   }
   else printf("_dos_read: %d bytes read.\n", bytes);
   return 0;
}
```

Q-R

read

Function Reads from file.

Syntax #include <io.h>
int read(int *handle*, void **buf*, unsigned *len*);

DOS	UNIX	Windows	ANSI C	C++ only
■	■	■		

Remarks **read** attempts to read *len* bytes from the file associated with *handle* into the buffer pointed to by *buf*.

For a file opened in text mode, **read** removes carriage returns and reports end-of-file when it reaches a *Ctrl-Z*.

For **_dos_read**, *handle* is a file handle obtained from a **creat**, **open**, **dup**, or **dup2** call.

On disk files, **read** begins reading at the current file pointer. When the reading is complete, it increments the file pointer by the number of bytes read. On devices, the bytes are read directly from the device.

The maximum number of bytes that **read** can read is 65,534, because 65,535 (0xFFFF) is the same as –1, the error return indicator.

Return Value On successful completion, **read** returns an integer indicating the number of bytes placed in the buffer. If the file was opened in text mode, **read** does not count carriage returns or *Ctrl-Z* characters in the number of bytes read.

On end-of-file, **read** returns 0. On error, **read** returns –1 and sets the global variable *errno* to one of the following:

EACCES	Permission denied
EBADF	Bad file number

See also **open, _read, write**

Example

```
#include <stdio.h>
#include <io.h>
#include <alloc.h>
#include <fcntl.h>
#include <process.h>
#include <sys\stat.h>

int main(void)
{
   void *buf;
   int handle, bytes;
   buf = malloc(10);

   /* Looks for a file in the current directory named TEST.$$$ and attempts to
      read 10 bytes from it. To use this example you should create the file
      TEST.$$$ */
   if ((handle = open("TEST.$$$", O_RDONLY | O_BINARY,
                      S_IWRITE | S_IREAD)) == -1) {
      printf("Error Opening File\n");
```

```
      exit(1);
   }
   if ((bytes = read(handle, buf, 10)) == -1) {
      printf("Read Failed.\n");
      exit(1);
   }
   else {
      printf("Read: %d bytes read.\n", bytes);
   }
   return 0;
}
```

readdir

Function Reads the current entry from a directory stream.

Syntax #include <dirent.h>
struct dirent readdir(DIR **dirp*);

DOS	UNIX	Windows	ANSI C	C++ only
■	■	■		

Remarks **readdir** is available on POSIX-compliant UNIX systems.

The **readdir** function reads the current directory entry in the directory stream pointed to by *dirp*. The directory stream is advanced to the next entry.

The **readdir** function returns a pointer to a **dirent** structure that is overwritten by each call to the function on the same directory stream. The structure is not overwritten by a **readdir** call on a different directory stream.

The **dirent** structure corresponds to a single directory entry. It is defined in dirent.h, and contains (in addition to other non-accessible members) the following member:

```
char  d_name[];
```

where *d_name* is an array of characters containing the null terminated file name for the current directory entry. The size of the array is indeterminate; use **strlen** to determine the length of the filename.

All valid directory entries are returned, including subdirectories, "." and ".." entries, system files, hidden files, and volume labels. Unused or deleted directory entries are skipped.

Q-R

A directory entry can be created or deleted while a directory stream is being read, but **readdir** may or may not return the affected directory entry. Rewinding the directory with **rewinddir** or reopening it with **opendir** will ensure that **readdir** will reflect the current state of the directory.

Return Value If successful, **readdir** returns a pointer to the current directory entry for the directory stream. If the end of the directory has been reached, or *dirp* does not refer to an open directory stream, **readdir** returns NULL.

See also **closedir**, **opendir**, **rewinddir**

Example See the example for **opendir**.

real

Function Returns the real part of a complex number or converts a BCD number back to **float**, **double** or **long double**.

Syntax

As defined in ***complex***:
#include <complex.h>
double real(complex *x*);

As defined in ***bcd***:
#include <bcd.h>
double real(bcd *x*);

DOS	UNIX	Windows	ANSI C	C++ only
■		■		■

Remarks The data associated to a complex number consists of two floating-point numbers. **real** returns the one considered to be the real part.

You can also use **real** to convert a binary coded decimal number back to a **float**, **double**, or **long double**.

Return Value The real part of part of the complex number.

See also **bcd**, **complex**, **imag**

Example 1

```
#include <complex.h>

int main(void)
{
   double x = 3.1, y = 4.2;
   complex z = complex(x,y);
   cout << "z = " << z << "\n";
   cout << "  has real part = " << real(z) << "\n";
   cout << "  and imaginary real part = " << imag(z) << "\n";
   cout << "z has complex conjugate = " << conj(z) << "\n";
   return 0;
}
```

Example 2

```
#include <bcd.h>
#include <iostream.h>

int main(void)
{
   bcd x = 3.1;
   cout << "The bcd number x = " << x << "\n";
   cout << "Its binary equivalent is " << real(x) << "\n";
   return 0;
}
```

realloc

Function Reallocates main memory.

Syntax #include <stdlib.h>
void *realloc(void **block*, size_t *size*);

DOS	UNIX	Windows	ANSI C	C++ only
■	■	■	■	

Remarks **realloc** attempts to shrink or expand the previously allocated block to *size* bytes. The *block* argument points to a memory block previously obtained by calling **malloc**, **calloc**, or **realloc**. If *block* is a null pointer, **realloc** works just like **malloc**.

realloc adjusts the size of the allocated block to *size*, copying the contents to a new location if necessary.

Return Value **realloc** returns the address of the reallocated block, which can be different than the address of the original block. If the block cannot be reallocated or *size* == 0, **realloc** returns null.

See also **calloc, farrealloc, free, malloc**

Example

```
#include <stdio.h>
#include <alloc.h>
#include <string.h>

int main(void)
{
   char *str;

   /* allocate memory for string */
   str = (char *) malloc(10);

   /* copy "Hello" into string */
   strcpy(str, "Hello");
```

Q-R

```
   printf("String is %s\n  Address is %p\n", str, str);
   str = (char *) realloc(str, 20);
   printf("String is %s\n  New address is %p\n", str, str);

   /* free memory */
   free(str);
   return 0;
}
```

rectangle

Function Draws a rectangle.

Syntax #include <graphics.h>
void far rectangle(int *left*, int *top*, int *right*, int *bottom*);

DOS	UNIX	Windows	ANSI C	C++ only
■				

Remarks **rectangle** draws a rectangle in the current line style, thickness, and drawing color.

(*left*,*top*) is the upper left corner of the rectangle, and (*right*,*bottom*) is its lower right corner.

Return Value None.

See also **bar, bar3d, setcolor, setlinestyle**

Example

```
#include <graphics.h>
#include <stdlib.h>
#include <stdio.h>
#include <conio.h>

int main(void)
{
   /* request autodetection */
   int gdriver = DETECT, gmode, errorcode;
   int left, top, right, bottom;

   /* initialize graphics and local variables */
   initgraph(&gdriver, &gmode, "");

   /* read result of initialization */
   errorcode = graphresult();
   if (errorcode != grOk) {  /* an error occurred */
      printf("Graphics error: %s\n", grapherrormsg(errorcode));
      printf("Press any key to halt:");
      getch();
```

```
      exit(1);               /* terminate with an error code */
   }

   left = getmaxx() / 2 - 50;
   top = getmaxy() / 2 - 50;
   right = getmaxx() / 2 + 50;
   bottom = getmaxy() / 2 + 50;

   /* draw a rectangle */
   rectangle(left,top,right,bottom);

   /* clean up */
   getch();
   closegraph();
   return 0;
}
```

registerbgidriver

Function Registers a user-loaded or linked-in graphics driver code with the graphics system.

Syntax #include <graphics.h>
int registerbgidriver(void (**driver*)(void));

DOS	UNIX	Windows	ANSI C	C++ only
■				

Remarks **registerbgidriver** enables a user to load a driver file and "register" the driver. Once its memory location has been passed to **registerbgidriver**, **initgraph** uses the registered driver. A user-registered driver can be loaded from disk onto the heap, or converted to an .OBJ file (using BINOBJ.EXE) and linked into the .EXE.

Calling **registerbgidriver** informs the graphics system that the driver pointed to by *driver* was included at link time. This routine checks the linked-in code for the specified driver; if the code is valid, it registers the code in internal tables. Linked-in drivers are discussed in detail in UTIL.DOC, included with your distribution disks.

By using the name of a linked-in driver in a call to **registerbgidriver**, you also tell the compiler (and linker) to link in the object file with that public name.

Return Value **registerbgidriver** returns a negative graphics error code if the specified driver or font is invalid. Otherwise, **registerbgidriver** returns the driver number.

If you register a user-supplied driver, you *must* pass the result of **registerbgidriver** to **initgraph** as the drive number to be used.

See also **graphresult, initgraph, installuserdriver, registerbgifont**

Example

```
#include <graphics.h>
#include <stdlib.h>
#include <stdio.h>
#include <conio.h>

int main(void)
{
   /* request autodetection */
   int gdriver = DETECT, gmode, errorcode;

   /* register a driver that was added into GRAPHICS.LIB */
   errorcode = registerbgidriver(EGAVGA_driver);

   /* report any registration errors */
   if (errorcode < 0) {
      printf("Graphics error: %s\n", grapherrormsg(errorcode));
      printf("Press any key to halt:");
      getch();
      exit(1);                /* terminate with an error code */
   }

   /* initialize graphics and local variables */
   initgraph(&gdriver, &gmode, "");

   /* read result of initialization */
   errorcode = graphresult();
   if (errorcode != grOk) {  /* an error occurred */
      printf("Graphics error: %s\n", grapherrormsg(errorcode));
      printf("Press any key to halt:");
      getch();
      exit(1);                /* terminate with an error code */
   }

   /* draw a line */
   line(0, 0, getmaxx(), getmaxy());

   /* clean up */
   getch();
   closegraph();
   return 0;
}
```

registerbgifont

Function Registers linked-in stroked font code.

Syntax #include <graphics.h>
int registerbgifont(void (**font*)(void));

DOS	UNIX	Windows	ANSI C	C++ only
■				

Remarks Calling **registerbgifont** informs the graphics system that the font pointed to by *font* was included at link time. This routine checks the linked-in code for the specified font; if the code is valid, it registers the code in internal tables. Linked-in fonts are discussed in detail under BGIOBJ in UTIL.DOC included with your distribution disks.

By using the name of a linked-in font in a call to **registerbgifont**, you also tell the compiler (and linker) to link in the object file with that public name.

If you register a user-supplied font, you *must* pass the result of **registerbgifont** to **settextstyle** as the font number to be used.

Return Value **registerbgifont** returns a negative graphics error code if the specified font is invalid. Otherwise, **registerbgifont** returns the font number of the registered font.

See also **graphresult, initgraph, installuserdriver, registerbgidriver, settextstyle**

Example

```
#include <graphics.h>
#include <stdlib.h>
#include <stdio.h>
#include <conio.h>

int main(void)
{
   /* request autodetection */
   int gdriver = DETECT, gmode, errorcode;
   int midx, midy;

   /* register a font file that was added into GRAPHICS.LIB */
   errorcode = registerbgifont(triplex_font);

   /* report any registration errors */
   if (errorcode < 0) {
      printf("Graphics error: %s\n", grapherrormsg(errorcode));
      printf("Press any key to halt:");
      getch();
      exit(1);              /* terminate with an error code */
   }

   /* initialize graphics and local variables */
   initgraph(&gdriver, &gmode, "");
```

Q-R

```
   /* read result of initialization */
   errorcode = graphresult();
   if (errorcode != grOk) {  /* an error occurred */
      printf("Graphics error: %s\n", grapherrormsg(errorcode));
      printf("Press any key to halt:");
      getch();
      exit(1);               /* terminate with an error code */
   }

   midx = getmaxx() / 2;
   midy = getmaxy() / 2;

   /* select the registered font */
   settextstyle(TRIPLEX_FONT, HORIZ_DIR, 4);

   /* output some text */
   settextjustify(CENTER_TEXT, CENTER_TEXT);
   outtextxy(midx, midy, "The TRIPLEX FONT");

   /* clean up */
   getch();
   closegraph();
   return 0;
}
```

remove

Function Removes a file.

Syntax #include <stdio.h>
int remove(const char **filename*);

DOS	UNIX	Windows	ANSI C	C++ only
■	■	■	■	

Remarks **remove** deletes the file specified by *filename*. It is a macro that simply translates its call to a call to **unlink**. If your file is open, be sure to close it before removing it.

➡ The string pointed to by **filename* may include a full DOS path.

Return Value On successful completion, **remove** returns 0. On error, it returns –1, and the global variable *errno* is set to one of the following:

ENOENT	No such file or directory
EACCES	Permission denied

See also **unlink**

Example

```
#include <stdio.h>

int main(void)
{
   char file[80];

   /* prompt for file name to delete */
   printf("File to delete: ");
   gets(file);

   /* delete the file */
   if (remove(file) == 0)
      printf("Removed %s.\n",file);
   else
      perror("remove");
   return 0;
}
```

rename

Function Renames a file.

Syntax #include <stdio.h>
int rename(const char **oldname*, const char **newname*);

DOS	UNIX	Windows	ANSI C	C++ only
■		■	■	

Remarks **rename** changes the name of a file from *oldname* to *newname*. If a drive specifier is given in *newname*, the specifier must be the same as that given in *oldname*.

Directories in *oldname* and *newname* need not be the same, so **rename** can be used to move a file from one directory to another. Wildcards are not allowed.

Return Value On successfully renaming the file, **rename** returns 0. In the event of error, –1 is returned, and the global variable *errno* is set to one of the following:

ENOENT	No such file or directory
EACCES	Permission denied
ENOTSAM	Not same device

Example

```
#include <stdio.h>

int main(void)
{
   char oldname[80], newname[80];
```

Q-R

```
   /* prompt for file to rename and new name */
   printf("File to rename: ");
   gets(oldname);
   printf("New name: ");
   gets(newname);

   /* rename the file */
   if (rename(oldname, newname) == 0)
      printf("Renamed %s to %s.\n", oldname, newname);
   else
      perror("rename");
   return 0;
}
```

restorecrtmode

Function Restores the screen mode to its pre-**initgraph** setting.

Syntax #include <graphics.h>
void far restorecrtmode(void);

DOS	UNIX	Windows	ANSI C	C++ only
■				

Remarks **restorecrtmode** restores the original video mode detected by **initgraph**.

This function can be used in conjunction with **setgraphmode** to switch back and forth between text and graphics modes. **textmode** should not be used for this purpose; use it only when the screen is in text mode, to change to a different text mode.

Return Value None.

See also **getgraphmode, initgraph, setgraphmode**

Example

```
#include <graphics.h>
#include <stdlib.h>
#include <stdio.h>
#include <conio.h>

int main(void)
{
   /* request autodetection */
   int gdriver = DETECT, gmode, errorcode;
   int x, y;

   /* initialize graphics and local variables */
   initgraph(&gdriver, &gmode, "");
```

```
    /* read result of initialization */
    errorcode = graphresult();
    if (errorcode != grOk) {  /* an error occurred */
       printf("Graphics error: %s\n", grapherrormsg(errorcode));
       printf("Press any key to halt:");
       getch();
       exit(1);               /* terminate with an error code */
    }

    x = getmaxx() / 2;
    y = getmaxy() / 2;

    /* output a message */
    settextjustify(CENTER_TEXT, CENTER_TEXT);
    outtextxy(x, y, "Press any key to exit graphics:");
    getch();

    /* restore system to text mode */
    restorecrtmode();
    printf("We're now in text mode.\n");
    printf("Press any key to return to graphics mode:");
    getch();

    /* return to graphics mode */
    setgraphmode(getgraphmode());

    /* output a message */
    settextjustify(CENTER_TEXT, CENTER_TEXT);
    outtextxy(x, y, "We're back in graphics mode.");
    outtextxy(x, y+textheight("W"), "Press any key to halt:");

    /* clean up */
    getch();
    closegraph();
    return 0;
}
```

Q-R

rewind

Function Repositions a file pointer to the beginning of a stream.

Syntax #include <stdio.h>
void rewind(FILE **stream*);

DOS	UNIX	Windows	ANSI C	C++ only
■	■	■	■	

Remarks **rewind**(*stream*) is equivalent to **fseek**(*stream*, 0L, SEEK_SET), except that **rewind** clears the end-of-file and error indicators, while **fseek** only clears the end-of-file indicator.

After **rewind**, the next operation on an update file can be either input or output.

Return Value None.

See also **fopen, fseek, ftell**

Example See **fseek**

Example

```
#include <stdio.h>
#include <dir.h>

int main(void)
{
   FILE *fp;
   char *fname = "TXXXXXX", *newname, first;
   newname = mktemp(fname);
   fp = fopen(newname,"w+");
   fprintf(fp,"abcdefghijklmnopqrstuvwxyz");
   rewind(fp);
   fscanf(fp,"%c",&first);
   printf("The first character is: %c\n",first);
   fclose(fp);
   remove(newname);
   return 0;
}
```

rewinddir

Function Resets a directory stream to the first entry.

Syntax #include <dirent.h>
void rewinddir(DIR **dirp*);

DOS	UNIX	Windows	ANSI C	C++ only
■	■	■		

Remarks **rewinddir** is available on POSIX-compliant UNIX systems.

The **rewinddir** function repositions the directory stream *dirp* at the first entry in the directory. It also ensures that the directory stream accurately reflects any directory entries that may have been created or deleted since the last **opendir** or **rewinddir** on that directory stream.

Return Value None.

See also **closedir, opendir, readdir**

Example See the example for **opendir**.

rmdir

Function Removes a DOS file directory.

Syntax #include <dir.h>
int rmdir(const char **path*);

DOS	UNIX	Windows	ANSI C	C++ only
■	■	■		

Remarks **rmdir** deletes the directory whose path is given by *path*. The directory named by *path*

- must be empty.
- must not be the current working directory.
- must not be the root directory.

Return Value **rmdir** returns 0 if the directory is successfully deleted. A return value of –1 indicates an error, and the global variable *errno* is set to one of the following:

EACCES	Permission denied
ENOENT	Path or file function not found

See also **chdir, getcurdir, getcwd, mkdir**

Example

```
#include <stdio.h>
#include <conio.h>
#include <process.h>
#include <dir.h>

#define DIRNAME "testdir.$$$"

int main(void)
{
   int stat;
   stat = mkdir(DIRNAME);
   if (!stat)
      printf("Directory created\n");
   else {
      printf("Unable to create directory\n");
```

Q-R

```
      exit(1);
   }
   getch();
   system("dir/p");
   getch();
   stat = rmdir(DIRNAME);
   if (!stat)
      printf("\nDirectory deleted\n");
   else {
      perror("\nUnable to delete directory\n");
      exit(1);
   }
   return 0;
}
```

rmtmp

Function Removes temporary files.

Syntax #include <stdio.h>
int rmtmp(void);

DOS	UNIX	Windows	ANSI C	C++ only
■		■		

Remarks The **rmtmp** function closes and deletes all open temporary file streams, which were previously created with **tmpfile**. The current directory must the same as when the files were created, or the files will not be deleted.

Return Value **rmtmp** returns the total number of temporary files it closed and deleted.

See also **tmpfil**

Example

```
#include <stdio.h>
#include <process.h>

void main()
{
   FILE *stream;
   int i;

   /* Create temporary files */
   for (i = 1; i <= 10; i++) {
     if ((stream = tmpfile()) == NULL)
       perror("Could not open temporary file\n");
     else
       printf("Temporary file %d created\n", i);
   }
```

```
   /* Remove temporary files */
   if (stream != NULL)
     printf("%d temporary files deleted\n", rmtmp());
}
```

_rotl

Function Bit-rotates an **unsigned** integer value to the left.

Syntax #include <stdlib.h>
unsigned _rotl(unsigned *value*, int *count*);

DOS	UNIX	Windows	ANSI C	C++ only
■		■		

Remarks **_rotl** rotates the given *value* to the left *count* bits. The value rotated is an **unsigned** integer.

Return Value **_rotl** returns the value of *value* left-rotated *count* bits.

See also **_lrotl, _lrotr, _rotr**

Example

```
#include <stdlib.h>
#include <stdio.h>

/* rotl example */
int rotl_example(void)
{
   unsigned value, result;

   value = 32767;
   result = _rotl(value, 1);
   printf("The value %u rotated left"
          " one bit is: %u\n", value, result);
   return 0;
}

/* rotr example */
int rotr_example(void)
{
   unsigned value, result;

   value = 32767;
   result = _rotr(value, 1);
   printf("The value %u rotated right"
          " one bit is: %u\n", value, result);
   return 0;
}
```

Q-R

```
int main(void)
{
   rotl_example();
   rotr_example();
   return 0;
}
```

_rotr

Function Bit-rotates an **unsigned** integer value to the right.

Syntax #include <stdlib.h>
unsigned _rotr(unsigned *value*, int *count*);

DOS	UNIX	Windows	ANSI C	C++ only
■		■		

Remarks **_rotr** rotates the given *value* to the right *count* bits. The value rotated is an **unsigned** integer.

Return Value **_rotr** returns the value of *value* right-rotated *count* bits.

See also **_lrotl**, **_lrotr**, **_rotl**

Example

```
#include <stdlib.h>
#include <stdio.h>

int main(void)
{
   unsigned value, result;
   value = 32767;
   result = _rotr(value, 1);
   printf("The value %u rotated right one bit is: %u\n", value, result);
   return 0;
}
```

sbrk

Function Changes data segment space allocation.

Syntax #include <alloc.h>
void *sbrk(int *incr*);

DOS	UNIX	Windows	ANSI C	C++ only
■	■			

Remarks **sbrk** adds *incr* bytes to the break value and changes the allocated space accordingly. *incr* can be negative, in which case the amount of allocated space is decreased.

sbrk will fail without making any change in the allocated space if such a change would result in more space being allocated than is allowable.

Return value Upon successful completion, **sbrk** returns the old break value. On failure, **sbrk** returns a value of –1, and the global variable *errno* is set to

ENOMEM   Not enough core

See also **brk**

Example

```
#include <stdio.h>
#include <alloc.h>

int main(void)
{
   printf("Changing allocation with sbrk()\n");
   printf("Before sbrk() call: %lu bytes free\n", (unsigned long) coreleft());
   sbrk(1000);
   printf("After sbrk() call: %lu bytes free\n", (unsigned long) coreleft());

   return 0;
}
```

scanf

Function Scans and formats input from the stdin stream.

Syntax #include <stdio.h>
int scanf(const char **format*[, address, ...]);

DOS	UNIX	Windows	ANSI C	C++ only
■	■		■	

Remarks **scanf** scans a series of input fields, one character at a time, reading from the stdin stream. Then each field is formatted according to a format specifier passed to **scanf** in the format string pointed to by *format*. Finally, **scanf** stores the formatted input at an address passed to it as an argument following *format*. There must be the same number of format specifiers and addresses as there are input fields.

The format string The format string present in **scanf** and the related functions **cscanf**, **fscanf**, **sscanf**, **vscanf**, **vfscanf**, and **vsscanf** controls how each function scans, converts, and stores its input fields. There must be enough address

S

arguments for the given format specifiers; if not, the results are unpredictable and likely disastrous. Excess address arguments (more than required by the format) are merely ignored.

scanf often leads to unexpected results if you diverge from an expected pattern. You need to remember to teach **scanf** how to synchronize at the end of a line. The combination of **gets** or **fgets** followed by **sscanf** is safe and easy, and therefore preferred.

The format string is a character string that contains three types of objects: whitespace characters, non-whitespace characters, and format specifiers.

- The whitespace characters are blank, tab (\t) or newline (\n). If a **...scanf** function encounters a whitespace character in the format string, it will read, but not store, all consecutive whitespace characters up to the next non-whitespace character in the input.
- The non-whitespace characters are all other ASCII characters except the percent sign (%). If a **...scanf** function encounters a non-whitespace character in the format string, it will read, but not store, a matching non-whitespace character.
- The format specifiers direct the **...scanf** functions to read and convert characters from the input field into specific types of values, then store them in the locations given by the address arguments.

Trailing whitespace is left unread (including a newline), unless explicitly matched in the format string.

Format specifiers

...scanf format specifiers have the following form:

```
% [*] [width] [F|N] [h|l|L] type_character
```

Each format specifier begins with the percent character (%). After the % come the following, in this order:

- an optional assignment-suppression character, `[*]`
- an optional width specifier, `[width]`
- an optional pointer size modifier, `[F|N]`
- an optional argument-type modifier, `[h|l|L]`
- the type character

Optional format string components

These are the general aspects of input formatting controlled by the optional characters and specifiers in the **...scanf** format string:

Character or specifier	What it controls or specifies
*	Suppresses assignment of the next input field.
width	Maximum number of characters to read; fewer characters might be read if the **...scanf** function encounters a whitespace or unconvertible character.
size	Overrides default size of address argument: *N* = near pointer *F* = far pointer
argument type	Overrides default type of address argument: *h* = **short int** *l* = **long int** (if the type character specifies an integer conversion) *l* = **double** (if the type character specifies a floating-point conversion) *L* = **long double** (valid only with floating-point conversions)

***...scanf* type characters**

The following table lists the **...scanf** type characters, the type of input expected by each, and in what format the input will be stored.

The information in this table is based on the assumption that no optional characters, specifiers, or modifiers (*, width, or size) were included in the format specifier. To see how the addition of the optional elements affects the **...scanf** input, refer to the tables following this one.

S

Type character	Expected input	Type of argument
Numerics		
d	Decimal integer	Pointer to **int** (int **arg*)
D	Decimal integer	Pointer to **long** (long **arg*)
o	Octal integer	Pointer to **int** (int **arg*)
O	Octal integer	Pointer to **long** (long **arg*)
i	Decimal, octal, or hexadecimal integer	Pointer to **int** (int **arg*)
I	Decimal, octal, or hexadecimal integer	Pointer to **long** (long **arg*)
u	Unsigned decimal integer	Pointer to **unsigned int** (unsigned int **arg*)
U	Unsigned decimal integer	Pointer to **unsigned long** (unsigned long **arg*)
x	Hexadecimal integer	Pointer to **int** (int **arg*)
X	Hexadecimal integer	Pointer to **int** (int **arg*)
e, E	Floating point	Pointer to **float** (float **arg*)
f	Floating point	Pointer to **float** (float **arg*)
g, G	Floating point	Pointer to **float** (float **arg*)
Characters		
s	Character string	Pointer to array of characters (char *arg[]*)
c	Character	Pointer to character (char **arg*) if a field width *W* is given along with the *c*-type character (such as %5*c*).
		Pointer to array of *W* characters (char *arg*[W])
%	% character	No conversion done; % is stored.
Pointers		
n		Pointer to **int** (int **arg*). The number of characters read successfully up to %*n* is stored in this **int**.
p	Hexadecimal form YYYY:ZZZZ or ZZZZ	Pointer to an object (*far** or *near**) %*p* conversions default to the pointer size native to the memory model.

Input fields Any one of the following is an input field:

- all characters up to (but not including) the next whitespace character
- all characters up to the first one that cannot be converted under the current format specifier (such as an 8 or 9 under octal format)

■ up to *n* characters, where *n* is the specified field width

Conventions Certain conventions accompany some of these format specifiers, as summarized here.

%c conversion

This specification reads the next character, including a whitespace character. To skip one whitespace character and read the next non-whitespace character, use %1s.

%Wc conversion (W = width specification)

The address argument is a pointer to an array of characters; the array consists of *W* elements (char *arg*[*W*]).

%s conversion

The address argument is a pointer to an array of characters (**char** *arg*[]).

The array size must be *at least* (*n*+1) bytes, where *n* equals the length of string *s* (in characters). A space or new line terminates the input field. A null-terminator is automatically appended to the string and stored as the last element in the array.

%[search_set] conversion

The set of characters surrounded by square brackets can be substituted for the *s*-type character. The address argument is a pointer to an array of characters (char *arg*[]).

These square brackets surround a set of characters that define a *search set* of possible characters making up the string (the input field).

If the first character in the brackets is a caret (^), the search set is inverted to include all ASCII characters except those between the square brackets. (Normally, a caret will be included in the inverted search set unless explicitly listed somewhere after the first caret.)

The input field is a string not delimited by whitespace. **...scanf** reads the corresponding input field up to the first character it reaches that does not appear in the search set (or in the inverted search set). Two examples of this type of conversion are

`%[abcd]`	Searches for any of the characters *a*, *b*, *c*, and *d* in the input field.
`%[^abcd]`	Searches for any characters *except a*, *b*, *c*, and *d* in the input field.

You can also use a range facility shortcut to define a range of characters (numerals or letters) in the search set. For example, to catch all decimal digits, you could define the search set by using `%[0123456789]`, or you could use the shortcut to define the same search set by using `%[0-9]`.

S

To catch alphanumeric characters, use the following shortcuts:

`%[A-Z]`	Catches all uppercase letters.
`%[0-9A-Za-z]`	Catches all decimal digits and all letters (uppercase and lowercase).
`%[A-FT-Z]`	Catches all uppercase letters from *A* through *F* and from *T* through *Z*.

The rules covering these search set ranges are straightforward:

- The character prior to the hyphen (-) must be lexically less than the one after it.
- The hyphen must not be the first nor the last character in the set. (If it is first or last, it is considered to just be the hyphen character, not a range definer.)
- The characters on either side of the hyphen must be the ends of the range and not part of some other range.

Here are some examples where the hyphen just means the hyphen character, not a range between two ends:

`%[-+*/]`	The four arithmetic operations
`%[z-a]`	The characters *z*, –, and *a*
`%[+0-9-A-Z]`	The characters + and – and the ranges 0-9 and *A-Z*
`%[+0-9A-Z-]`	Also the characters + and – and the ranges 0-9 and *A-Z*
`%[^-0-9+A-Z]`	All characters except + and – and those in the ranges 0-9 and *A-Z*

%e, %E. %f, %g, and %G (floating-point) conversions

Floating-point numbers in the input field must conform to the following generic format:

```
[+/-] ddddddddd [.] dddd [E | e] [+/-] ddd
```

where [*item*] indicates that *item* is optional, and *ddd* represents decimal, octal, or hexadecimal digits.

INF = infinity; NAN = not a number

In addition, +INF, –INF, +NAN, and –NAN are recognized as floating-point numbers. Note that the sign and capitalization are required.

%d, %i, %o, %x, %D, %I, %O, %X, %c, %n conversions

A pointer to **unsigned** character, **unsigned** integer, or **unsigned long** can be used in any conversion where a pointer to a character, integer, or **long** is allowed.

The assignment-suppression character is an asterisk (*); it is not to be confused with the C indirection (pointer) operator (also an asterisk).

Assignment-suppression character

If the asterisk follows the percent sign (%) in a format specifier, the next input field will be scanned but will not be assigned to the next address argument. The suppressed input data is assumed to be of the type specified by the type character that follows the asterisk character.

The success of literal matches and suppressed assignments is not directly determinable.

Width specifiers

The width specifier (*n*), a decimal integer, controls the maximum number of characters that will be read from the current input field.

If the input field contains fewer than *n* characters, **...scanf** reads all the characters in the field, then proceeds with the next field and format specifier.

If a whitespace or nonconvertible character occurs before width characters are read, the characters up to that character are read, converted, and stored, then the function attends to the next format specifier.

A nonconvertible character is one that cannot be converted according to the given format (such as an 8 or 9 when the format is octal, or a *J* or *K* when the format is hexadecimal or decimal).

Width specifier	How width of stored input is affected
n	Up to *n* characters are read, converted, and stored in the current address argument.

Input-size and argument-type modifiers

The input-size modifiers (*N* and *F*) and argument-type modifiers (*h*, *l*, and *L*) affect how the **...scanf** functions interpret the corresponding address argument *arg[f*.

F and *N* override the default or declared size of *arg*.

h, *l*, and *L* indicate which type (version) of the following input data is to be used (*h* = **short**, *l* = **long**, *L* = **long double**). The input data will be converted to the specified version, and the *arg* for that input data should point to an object of the corresponding size (**short** object for **%h**, **long** or **double** object for **%l**, and **long double** object for **%L**).

S

Modifier	How conversion is affected
F	Overrides default or declared size; *arg* interpreted as far pointer.
N	Overrides default or declared size; *arg* interpreted as near pointer. Cannot be used with any conversion in huge model.
h	For *d, i, o, u, x* types, convert input to **short int**, store in **short** object.
	For *D, I, O, U, X* types, no effect.
	For *e, f, c, s, n, p* types, no effect.
l	For *d, i, o, u, x* types, convert input to **long int**, store in **long** object.
	For *e, f, g* types, convert input to **double**, store in **double** object.
	For *D, I, O, U, X* types, no effect.
	For *c, s, n, p* types, no effect.
L	For *e, f, g* types, convert input to a **long double**, store in **long double** object. **L** has no effect on other formats.

When scanf stops scanning

scanf might stop scanning a particular field before reaching the normal field-end character (whitespace), or might terminate entirely, for a variety of reasons.

scanf stops scanning and storing the current field and proceed to the next input field if any of the following occurs:

- An assignment-suppression character (*) appears after the percent character in the format specifier; the current input field is scanned but not stored.
- *width* characters have been read (*width* = width specification, a positive decimal integer in the format specifier).
- The next character read cannot be converted under the current format (for example, an *A* when the format is decimal).
- The next character in the input field does not appear in the search set (or does appear in an inverted search set).

When **scanf** stops scanning the current input field for one of these reasons, the next character is assumed to be unread and to be the first character of the following input field, or the first character in a subsequent read operation on the input.

scanf will terminate under the following circumstances:

- The next character in the input field conflicts with a corresponding non-whitespace character in the format string.
- The next character in the input field is EOF.

■ The format string has been exhausted.

If a character sequence that is not part of a format specifier occurs in the format string, it must match the current sequence of characters in the input field; **scanf** will scan but not store the matched characters. When a conflicting character occurs, it remains in the input field as if it were never read.

Return value **scanf** returns the number of input fields successfully scanned, converted, and stored; the return value does not include scanned fields that were not stored.

If **scanf** attempts to read at end-of-file, the return value is EOF.

If no fields were stored, the return value is 0.

See also **atof, cscanf, fscanf, getc, printf, sscanf, vfscanf, vscanf, vsscanf**

Example

```
#include <stdio.h>
#include <conio.h>

int main(void)
{
   char label[20];
   char name[20];
   int entries = 0;
   int loop, age;
   double salary;
   struct Entry_struct {
      char  name[20];
      int   age;
      float salary;
   } entry[20];

   /* input a label as character string restricted to 20 characters */
   printf("\n\nPlease enter a label for the chart: ");
   scanf("%20s", label);
   fflush(stdin);     /* flush input stream in case of bad input */

   /* input number of entries as integer */
   printf("How many entries will there be? (less than 20) ");
   scanf("%d", &entries);

   /* flush the input stream in case of bad input */
   fflush(stdin);

   /* input a name, restricting input to only upper- or lowercase letters */
   for (loop=0;loop<entries;++loop) {
      printf("Entry %d\n", loop);
      printf("  Name   : ");
      scanf("%[A-Za-z]", entry[loop].name);
      fflush(stdin);  /* flush input stream in case of bad input */
```

S

```
         /* input an age as integer */
         printf("  Age    : ");
         scanf("%d", &entry[loop].age);
         fflush(stdin);  /* flush input stream in case of bad input */

         /* input a salary as a float */
         printf("  Salary : ");
         scanf("%f", &entry[loop].salary);
         fflush(stdin);  /* flush input stream in case of bad input */
      }

      /* input name, age, and salary as string, integer, and double */
      printf("\nPlease enter your name, age and salary\n");
      scanf("%20s %d %lf", name, &age, &salary);

      /* print out the data that was input */
      printf("\n\nTable %s\n",label);
      printf("Compiled by %s  age %d  $%15.2lf\n", name, age, salary);
      printf("-----------------------------------------------------\n");
      for (loop=0;loop<entries;++loop)
         printf("%4d | %-20s | %5d | %15.2lf\n", loop + 1, entry[loop].name,
                entry[loop].age, entry[loop].salary);
      printf("-----------------------------------------------------\n");
      return 0;
   }
```

_searchenv

Function Searches an environment path for a file.

Syntax #include <stdlib.h>
char *_searchenv(const char **file*, const char **varname*, char **buf*);

DOS	UNIX	Windows	ANSI C	C++ only
■		■		

Remarks **_searchenv** attempts to locate *file*, searching along the path specified by the DOS environment variable *varname*. Typical environment variables that contain paths are PATH, LIB, and INCLUDE.

_searchenv searches for the file in the current directory of the current drive first. If the file is not found there, the environment variable *varname* is fetched, and each directory in the path it specifies is searched in turn until the file is found, or the path is exhausted.

When the file is located, the full path name is stored in the buffer pointed to by *buf*. This string can be used in a call to access the file (for example, with **fopen** or **exec...**). The buffer is assumed to be large enough to store any possible filename. If the file cannot be successfully located, an empty string (consisting of only a null character) will be stored at *buf*.

Return value None.

See also **exec..., _dos_findfirst, _dos_findnext, spawn..., system**

Example

```
#include <stdio.h>
#include <stdlib.h>

char buf[_MAX_PATH];

int main(void)
{
   /* looks for TLINK */
   _searchenv("TLINK.EXE","PATH",buf);
   if (buf[0] == '\0')
      printf("TLINK.EXE not found\n");
   else
      printf("TLINK.EXE found in %s\n", buf);

   /* looks for non-existent file */
   _searchenv("NOTEXIST.FIL","PATH",buf);
   if (buf[0] == '\0')
      printf("NOTEXIST.FIL not found\n");
   else
      printf("NOTEXIST.FIL found in %s\n", buf);
   return 0;
}
```

Program output

```
TLINK.EXE found in C:\BIN\TLINK.EXE
NOTEXIST.FIL not found
```

S

searchpath

Function Searches the DOS path for a file.

Syntax #include <dir.h>
char *searchpath(const char **file*);

DOS	UNIX	Windows	ANSI C	C++ only
■		■		

Remarks **searchpath** attempts to locate *file*, searching along the DOS path, which is the PATH=... string in the environment. A pointer to the complete path-name string is returned as the function value.

searchpath searches for the file in the current directory of the current drive first. If the file is not found there, the PATH environment variable is fetched, and each directory in the path is searched in turn until the file is found, or the path is exhausted.

When the file is located, a string is returned containing the full path name. This string can be used in a call to access the file (for example, with **fopen** or **exec...**).

The string returned is located in a static buffer and is overwritten on each subsequent call to **searchpath**.

Return value **searchpath** returns a pointer to a file name string if the file is successfully located; otherwise, **searchpath** returns null.

See also **exec..., findfirst, findnext, spawn..., system**

Example

```
#include <stdio.h>
#include <dir.h>

int main(void)
{
   char *p;

   /* looks for TLINK and returns a pointer to the path */
   p = searchpath("TLINK.EXE");
   printf("Search for TLINK.EXE : %s\n", p);

   /* looks for non-existent file */
   p = searchpath("NOTEXIST.FIL");
   printf("Search for NOTEXIST.FIL : %s\n", p);
   return 0;
}
```

Program output

```
Search for TLINK.EXE : C:\BIN\TLINK.EXE
Search for NOTEXIST.FIL : (NULL)
```

sector

Function Draws and fills an elliptical pie slice.

Syntax #include <graphics.h>

void far sector(int *x*, int *y*, int *stangle*, int *endangle*, int *xradius*, int *yradius*);

DOS	UNIX	Windows	ANSI C	C++ only
■				

Remarks Draws and fills an elliptical pie slice using (*x*,*y*) as the center point, *xradius* and *yradius* as the horizontal and vertical radii, respectively, and drawing from *stangle* to *endangle*. The pie slice is outlined using the current color, and filled using the pattern and color defined by **setfillstyle** or **setfillpattern**.

The angles for **sector** are given in degrees. They are measured counter-clockwise with 0 degrees at 3 o'clock, 90 degrees at 12 o'clock, and so on.

If an error occurs while the pie slice is filling, **graphresult** returns a value of –6 (grNoScanMem).

Return value None.

See also **arc, circle, ellipse, getarccoords, getaspectratio, graphresult, pieslice, setfillpattern, setfillstyle, setgraphbufsize**

Example

```
#include <graphics.h>
#include <stdlib.h>
#include <stdio.h>
#include <conio.h>

int main(void)
{
   /* request autodetection */
   int gdriver = DETECT, gmode, errorcode;
   int midx, midy, i;
   int stangle = 45, endangle = 135;
   int xrad = 100, yrad = 50;

   /* initialize graphics and local variables */
   initgraph(&gdriver, &gmode, "");

   /* read result of initialization */
   errorcode = graphresult();
   if (errorcode != grOk) {  /* an error occurred */
      printf("Graphics error: %s\n", grapherrormsg(errorcode));
      printf("Press any key to halt:");
      getch();
      exit(1);              /* terminate with an error code */
   }

   midx = getmaxx() / 2;
   midy = getmaxy() / 2;

   /* loop through the fill patterns */
```

S

```
    for (i=EMPTY_FILL; i<USER_FILL; i++) {

       /* set the fill style */
       setfillstyle(i, getmaxcolor());

       /* draw the sector slice */
       sector(midx, midy, stangle, endangle, xrad, yrad);
       getch();
    }

    /* clean up */
    closegraph();
    return 0;
}
```

segread

Function Reads segment registers.

Syntax #include <dos.h>
void segread(struct SREGS **segp*);

DOS	UNIX	Windows	ANSI C	C++ only
■		■		

Remarks **segread** places the current values of the segment registers into the structure pointed to by *segp*.

This call is intended for use with **intdosx** and **int86x**.

Return value None.

See also **FP_OFF, int86, int86x, intdos, intdosx, MK_FP, movedata**

Example

```
#include <stdio.h>
#include <dos.h>

int main(void)
{
   struct SREGS segs;
   segread(&segs);
   printf("Current segment register settings\n\n");
   printf("CS: %X   DS: %X\n", segs.cs, segs.ds);
   printf("ES: %X   SS: %X\n", segs.es, segs.ss);
   return 0;
}
```

setactivepage

Function Sets active page for graphics output.

Syntax #include <graphics.h>
void far setactivepage(int *page*);

DOS	UNIX	Windows	ANSI C	C++ only
■				

Remarks **setactivepage** makes *page* the active graphics page. All subsequent graphics output will be directed to that graphics page.

The active graphics page might not be the one you see onscreen, depending on how many graphics pages are available on your system. Only the EGA, VGA, and Hercules graphics cards support multiple pages.

Return value None.

See also **setvisualpage**

Example

```
#include <graphics.h>
#include <stdlib.h>
#include <stdio.h>
#include <conio.h>

int main(void)
{
   /* select driver and mode that supports multiple pages */
   int gdriver = EGA, gmode = EGAHI, errorcode;
   int x, y, ht;

   /* initialize graphics and local variables */
   initgraph(&gdriver, &gmode, "");

   /* read result of initialization */
   errorcode = graphresult();
   if (errorcode != grOk)    /* an error occurred */
   {
      printf("Graphics error: %s\n", grapherrormsg(errorcode));
      printf("Press any key to halt:");
      getch();
      exit(1);               /* terminate with an error code */
   }

   x = getmaxx() / 2;
   y = getmaxy() / 2;
   ht = textheight("W");
```

S

```
   /*  select the off screen page for drawing */
   setactivepage(1);

   /* draw a line on page #1 */
   line(0, 0, getmaxx(), getmaxy());

   /* output a message on page #1 */
   settextjustify(CENTER_TEXT, CENTER_TEXT);
   outtextxy(x, y, "This is page #1:");
   outtextxy(x, y+ht, "Press any key to halt:");

   /* select drawing to page #0 */
   setactivepage(0);

   /* output a message  on page #0 */
   outtextxy(x, y, "This is page #0.");
   outtextxy(x, y+ht, "Press any key to view page #1:");
   getch();

   /* select page #1 as the visible page */
   setvisualpage(1);

   /* clean up */
   getch();
   closegraph();
   return 0;
}
```

setallpalette

Function Changes all palette colors as specified.

Syntax #include <graphics.h>
void far setallpalette(struct palettetype far **palette*);

DOS	UNIX	Windows	ANSI C	C++ only
■				

Remarks **setallpalette** sets the current palette to the values given in the **palettetype** structure pointed to by *palette*.

You can partially (or completely) change the colors in the EGA/VGA palette with **setallpalette**.

The MAXCOLORS constant and the **palettetype** structure used by **setallpalette** are defined in graphics.h as follows:

```
#define MAXCOLORS  15

struct palettetype {
```

```
    unsigned char size;
    signed char colors[MAXCOLORS + 1];
};
```

size gives the number of colors in the palette for the current graphics driver in the current mode.

colors is an array of *size* bytes containing the actual raw color numbers for each entry in the palette. If an element of *colors* is –1, the palette color for that entry is not changed.

The elements in the *colors* array used by **setallpalette** can be represented by symbolic constants defined in graphics.h.

Table 2.6
Actual color table

CGA Name	Value	EGA/VGA Name	Value
BLACK	0	EGA_BLACK	0
BLUE	1	EGA_BLUE	1
GREEN	2	EGA_GREEN	2
CYAN	3	EGA_CYAN	3
RED	4	EGA_RED	4
MAGENTA	5	EGA_MAGENTA	5
BROWN	6	EGA_LIGHTGRAY	7
LIGHTGRAY	7	EGA_BROWN	20
DARKGRAY	8	EGA_DARKGRAY	56
LIGHTBLUE	9	EGA_LIGHTBLUE	57
LIGHTGREEN	10	EGA_LIGHTGREEN	58
LIGHTCYAN	11	EGA_LIGHTCYAN	59
LIGHTRED	12	EGA_LIGHTRED	60
LIGHTMAGENTA	13	EGA_LIGHTMAGENTA	61
YELLOW	14	EGA_YELLOW	62
WHITE	15	EGA_WHITE	63

Note that valid colors depend on the current graphics driver and current graphics mode.

Changes made to the palette are seen immediately onscreen. Each time a palette color is changed, all occurrences of that color onscreen will change to the new color value.

setallpalette cannot be used with the IBM-8514 driver.

Return value If invalid input is passed to **setallpalette**, **graphresult** returns –11 (grError), and the current palette remains unchanged.

See also **getpalette, getpalettesize, graphresult, setbkcolor, setcolor, setpalette**

Example

```
#include <graphics.h>
#include <stdlib.h>
#include <stdio.h>
```

S

```
#include <conio.h>

int main(void)
{
   /* request autodetection */
   int gdriver = DETECT, gmode, errorcode;
   struct palettetype pal;
   int color, maxcolor, ht;
   int y = 10;
   char msg[80];

   /* initialize graphics and local variables */
   initgraph(&gdriver, &gmode, "");

   /* read result of initialization */
   errorcode = graphresult();
   if (errorcode != grOk)    /* an error occurred */
   {
      printf("Graphics error: %s\n", grapherrormsg(errorcode));
      printf("Press any key to halt:");
      getch();
      exit(1);               /* terminate with an error code */
   }

   maxcolor = getmaxcolor();
   ht = 2 * textheight("W");

   /* grab a copy of the palette */
   getpalette(&pal);

   /* display the default palette colors */
   for (color=1; color<=maxcolor; color++) {
      setcolor(color);
      sprintf(msg, "Color: %d", color);
      outtextxy(1, y, msg);
      y += ht;
   }

   /* wait for a key */
   getch();

   /* black out the colors one by one */
   for (color=1; color<=maxcolor; color++) {
      setpalette(color, BLACK);
      getch();
   }

   /* restore the palette colors */
   setallpalette(&pal);

   /* clean up */
   getch();
   closegraph();
```

```
   return 0;
}
```

setaspectratio

Function Changes the default aspect ratio correction factor.

Syntax #include <graphics.h>
void far setaspectratio(int *xasp*, int *yasp*);

DOS	UNIX	Windows	ANSI C	C++ only
■				

Remarks **setaspectratio** changes the default aspect ratio of the graphics system. The graphics system uses the aspect ratio to make sure that circles are round onscreen. If circles appear elliptical, the monitor is not aligned properly. You could correct this in the hardware by realigning the monitor, but it's easier to change in the software by using **setaspectratio** to set the aspect ratio. To obtain the current aspect ratio from the system, call **getaspectratio**.

Return value None.

See also **circle, getaspectratio**

Example

```
#include <graphics.h>
#include <stdlib.h>
#include <stdio.h>
#include <conio.h>

int main(void)
{
   /* request autodetection */
   int gdriver = DETECT, gmode, errorcode;
   int xasp, yasp, midx, midy;

   /* initialize graphics and local variables */
   initgraph(&gdriver, &gmode, "");

   /* read result of initialization */
   errorcode = graphresult();
   if (errorcode != grOk)    /* an error occurred */
   {
      printf("Graphics error: %s\n", grapherrormsg(errorcode));
      printf("Press any key to halt:");
      getch();
      exit(1);               /* terminate with an error code */
```

S

```
   }

   midx = getmaxx() / 2;
   midy = getmaxy() / 2;
   setcolor(getmaxcolor());

   /* get current aspect ratio settings */
   getaspectratio(&xasp, &yasp);

   /* draw normal circle */
   circle(midx, midy, 100);
   getch();

   /* clear the screen */
   cleardevice();

   /* adjust the aspect for a wide circle */
   setaspectratio(xasp/2, yasp);
   circle(midx, midy, 100);
   getch();

   /* adjust the aspect for a narrow circle */
   cleardevice();
   setaspectratio(xasp, yasp/2);
   circle(midx, midy, 100);

   /* clean up */
   getch();
   closegraph();
   return 0;
}
```

setbkcolor

Function Sets the current background color using the palette.

Syntax #include <graphics.h>
void far setbkcolor(int *color*);

DOS	UNIX	Windows	ANSI C	C++ only
■				

Remarks **setbkcolor** sets the background to the color specified by *color*. The argument *color* can be a name or a number, as listed in the following table:

These symbolic names are defined in graphics.h.

Number	Name	Number	Name
0	BLACK	8	DARKGRAY
1	BLUE	9	LIGHTBLUE
2	GREEN	10	LIGHTGREEN
3	CYAN	11	LIGHTCYAN
4	RED	12	LIGHTRED
5	MAGENTA	13	LIGHTMAGENTA
6	BROWN	14	YELLOW
7	LIGHTGRAY	15	WHITE

For example, if you want to set the background color to blue, you can call

```
setbkcolor(BLUE) /* or */ setbkcolor(1)
```

On CGA and EGA systems, **setbkcolor** changes the background color by changing the first entry in the palette.

If you use an EGA or a VGA, and you change the palette colors with **setpalette** or **setallpalette**, the defined symbolic constants might not give you the correct color. This is because the parameter to **setbkcolor** indicates the entry number in the current palette rather than a specific color (unless the parameter passed is 0, which always sets the background color to black).

Return value None.

See also **getbkcolor**, **setallpalette**, **setcolor**, **setpalette**

Example

```
#include <graphics.h>
#include <stdlib.h>
#include <stdio.h>
#include <conio.h>

int main(void)
{
   /* select driver and mode that supports multiple background colors */
   int gdriver = EGA, gmode = EGAHI, errorcode;
   int bkcol, maxcolor, x, y;
   char msg[80];

   /* initialize graphics and local variables */
   initgraph(&gdriver, &gmode, "");

   /* read result of initialization */
   errorcode = graphresult();
   if (errorcode != grOk) {    /* an error occurred */
      printf("Graphics error: %s\n", grapherrormsg(errorcode));
      printf("Press any key to halt:");
      getch();
      exit(1);               /* terminate with an error code */
```

S

```
   }

   /* maximum color index supported */
   maxcolor = getmaxcolor();

   /* for centering text messages */
   settextjustify(CENTER_TEXT, CENTER_TEXT);
   x = getmaxx() / 2;
   y = getmaxy() / 2;

   /* loop through the available colors */
   for (bkcol=0; bkcol<=maxcolor; bkcol++) {

      /* clear the screen */
      cleardevice();

      /* select a new background color */
      setbkcolor(bkcol);

      /* output a messsage */
      if (bkcol == WHITE)
         setcolor(EGA_BLUE);
      sprintf(msg, "Background color: %d", bkcol);
      outtextxy(x, y, msg);
      getch();
   }

   /* clean up */
   closegraph();
   return 0;
}
```

setblock, _dos_setblock

Function Modifies the size of a previously allocated block.

Syntax #include <dos.h>
int setblock(unsigned *segx*, unsigned *newsize*);
unsigned _dos_setblock(unsigned *newsize*, unsigned *segx*,
unsigned **maxp*);

DOS	UNIX	Windows	ANSI C	C++ only
■				

Remarks **setblock** and **_dos_setblock** modify the size of a memory segment. *segx* is the segment address returned by a previous call to **allocmem** or **_dos_allocmem**. *newsize* is the new, requested size in paragraphs. If the sement cannot be changed to the new size, **_dos_setblock** stores the sizeof the largest possible segment at the location pointed to by *maxp*.

Return value **setblock** returns –1 on success. In the event of error, it returns the size of the largest possible block (in paragraphs), and the global variable *_doserrno* is set.

_dos_setblock returns 0 on success. In the event of error, it returns the DOS error code, and the global variable *errno* is set to the following:

ENOMEM Not enough memory, or bad segment address

See also **allocmem, freemem**

Example

```
#include <dos.h>
#include <alloc.h>
#include <stdio.h>
#include <stdlib.h>

int main(void)  /* Example for setblock. */
{
   unsigned int size, segp;
   int stat;
   size = 64;               /* (64 x 16) = 1024 bytes */
   stat = allocmem(size, &segp);
   if (stat == -1)
      printf("Allocated memory at segment: %X\n", segp);
   else {
      printf("Failed: maximum number of paragraphs available is %d\n", stat);
      exit(1);
   }

   stat = setblock(segp, size * 2);
   if (stat == -1)
      printf("Expanded memory block at segment: %X\n", segp);
   else
      printf("Failed: maximum number of paragraphs available is %d\n", stat);
   freemem(segp);
   return 0;
}

#include <dos.h>
#include <stdio.h>

int main(void)  /* Example for _dos_setblock. */
{
   unsigned int size, segp, err, maxb;
   size = 64; /* (64 x 16) = 1024 bytes */
   err = _dos_allocmem(size, &segp);
   if (err == 0)
      printf("Allocated memory at segment: %x\n", segp);
   else {
      perror("Unable to allocate block");
```

S

```
      printf("Maximum no. of paragraphs available is %u\n", segp);
      return 1;
   }
   if (_dos_setblock(size * 2, segp, &maxb) == 0)
      printf("Expanded memory block at segment: %X\n", segp);
   else {
      perror("Unable to expand block");
      printf("Maximum no. of paragraphs available is %u\n", maxb);
   }
   _dos_freemem(segp);
   return 0;
}
```

setbuf

Function Assigns buffering to a stream.

Syntax #include <stdio.h>
void setbuf(FILE **stream*, char **buf*);

DOS	UNIX	Windows	ANSI C	C++ only
■	■	■	■	

Remarks **setbuf** causes the buffer *buf* to be used for I/O buffering instead of an automatically allocated buffer. It is used after *stream* has been opened.

If *buf* is null, I/O will be unbuffered; otherwise, it will be fully buffered. The buffer must be BUFSIZ bytes long (specified in stdio.h).

stdin and *stdout* are unbuffered if they are not redirected; otherwise, they are fully buffered. **setbuf** can be used to change the buffering style being used.

Unbuffered means that characters written to a stream are immediately output to the file or device, while *buffered* means that the characters are accumulated and written as a block.

setbuf produces unpredictable results unless it is called immediately after opening *stream* or after a call to **fseek**. Calling **setbuf** after *stream* has been unbuffered is legal and will not cause problems.

A common cause for error is to allocate the buffer as an automatic (local) variable and then fail to close the file before returning from the function where the buffer was declared.

Return value None.

See also **fflush, fopen, fseek, setvbuf**

Example

```
#include <stdio.h>

/* bufsiz is defined in stdio.h */
char outbuf[BUFSIZ];

int main(void)
{
   /* attach buffer to standard output stream */
   setbuf(stdout, outbuf);

   /* put some characters into the buffer */
   puts("This is a test of buffered output.\n\n");
   puts("This output will go into outbuf\n");
   puts("and won't appear until the buffer\n");
   puts("fills up or we flush the stream.\n");

   /* flush the output buffer */
   fflush(stdout);
   return 0;
}
```

setcbrk

Function Sets control-break setting.

Syntax #include <dos.h>
int setcbrk(int *cbrkvalue*);

DOS	UNIX	Windows	ANSI C	C++ only
■		■		

Remarks **setcbrk** uses the DOS system call 0x33 to turn control-break checking on or off.

value = 0 Turns checking off (check only during I/O to console, printer, or communications devices).

value = 1 Turns checking on (check at every system call).

Return value **setcbrk** returns *cbrkvalue*, the value passed.

See also **getcbrk**

Example

```
#include <dos.h>
#include <conio.h>
#include <stdio.h>
```

```
int main(void)
{
   int break_flag;
   printf("Enter 0 to turn control break off\n");
   printf("Enter 1 to turn control break on\n");
   break_flag = getch() - 0;
   setcbrk(break_flag);
   if (getcbrk())
      printf("Cntrl-brk flag is on\n");
   else
      printf("Cntrl-brk flag is off\n");
   return 0;
}
```

setcolor

Function Sets the current drawing color using the palette.

Syntax #include <graphics.h>
void far setcolor(int *color*);

DOS	UNIX	Windows	ANSI C	C++ only
■				

Remarks **setcolor** sets the current drawing color to *color*, which can range from 0 to **getmaxcolor**.

The current drawing color is the value to which pixels are set when lines, and so on are drawn. The following tables show the drawing colors available for the CGA and EGA, respectively.

Palette number	Constant assigned to color number (pixel value) 1	2	3
0	CGA_LIGHTGREEN	CGA_LIGHTRED	CGA_YELLOW
1	CGA_LIGHTCYAN	CGA_LIGHTMAGENTA	CGA_WHITE
2	CGA_GREEN	CGA_RED	CGA_BROWN
3	CGA_CYAN	CGA_MAGENTA	CGA_LIGHTGRAY

Numeric value	Symbolic name		
0	BLACK	8	DARKGRAY
1	BLUE	9	LIGHTBLUE
2	GREEN	10	LIGHTGREEN
3	CYAN	11	LIGHTCYAN
4	RED	12	LIGHTRED
5	MAGENTA	13	LIGHTMAGENTA

6	BROWN	14	YELLOW
7	LIGHTGRAY	15	WHITE

You select a drawing color by passing either the color number itself or the equivalent symbolic name to **setcolor**. For example, in CGAC0 mode, the palette contains four colors: the background color, light green, light red, and yellow. In this mode, either **setcolor**(3) or **setcolor**(CGA_YELLOW) selects a drawing color of yellow.

Return value None.

See also **getcolor**, **getmaxcolor**, **graphresult**, **setallpalette**, **setbkcolor**, **setpalette**

Example

```
#include <graphics.h>
#include <stdlib.h>
#include <stdio.h>
#include <conio.h>

int main(void)
{
   /* select driver and mode that supports multiple drawing colors */
   int gdriver = EGA, gmode = EGAHI, errorcode;
   int color, maxcolor, x, y;
   char msg[80];

   /* initialize graphics and local variables */
   initgraph(&gdriver, &gmode, "");

   /* read result of initialization */
   errorcode = graphresult();
   if (errorcode != grOk)     /* an error occurred */
   {
      printf("Graphics error: %s\n", grapherrormsg(errorcode));
      printf("Press any key to halt:");
      getch();
      exit(1);                /* terminate with an error code */
   }

   /* maximum color index supported */
   maxcolor = getmaxcolor();

   /* for centering text messages */
   settextjustify(CENTER_TEXT, CENTER_TEXT);
   x = getmaxx() / 2;
   y = getmaxy() / 2;

   /* loop through the available colors */
   for (color=1; color<=maxcolor; color++) {
      cleardevice();          /* clear the screen */
      setcolor(color);        /* select new background color */

      /* output a messsage */
```

S

```
      sprintf(msg, "Color: %d", color);
      outtextxy(x, y, msg);
      getch();
   }

   /* clean up */
   closegraph();
   return 0;
}
```

_setcursortype

Function Selects cursor appearance.

Syntax #include <conio.h>
void _setcursortype(int *cur_t*);

DOS	UNIX	Windows	ANSI C	C++ only
■				

Remarks Sets the cursor type to

_NOCURSOR	Turns off the cursor
_SOLIDCURSOR	Solid block cursor
_NORMALCURSOR	Normal underscore cursor

Return value None.

Example

```
#include <conio.h>

int main(void)
{
   /* display the normal cursor */
   cprintf("\n\rNormal Cursor: ");
   getch();

   /* turn off the cursor */
   _setcursortype(_NOCURSOR);
   cprintf("\n\rNo Cursor    : ");
   getch();

   /* switch to a solid cursor */
   _setcursortype(_SOLIDCURSOR);
   cprintf("\n\rSolid Cursor : ");
   getch();

   /* switch back to the normal cursor */
   _setcursortype(_NORMALCURSOR);
   cprintf("\n\rNormal Cursor: ");
```

```
   getch();
   return 0;
}
```

setdta

Function Sets disk-transfer address.

Syntax #include <dos.h>
void setdta(char far **dta*);

DOS	UNIX	Windows	ANSI C	C++ only
■		■		

Remarks **setdta** changes the current setting of the DOS disk-transfer address (DTA) to the value given by *dta*.

Return value None.

See also **getdta**

Example

```
#include <process.h>
#include <string.h>
#include <stdio.h>
#include <dos.h>

int main(void)
{
   char line[80], far *save_dta;
   char buffer[256] = "SETDTA test!";
   struct fcb blk;
   int result;

   /* get new file name from user */
   printf("Enter a file name to create:");
   gets(line);

   /* parse the new file name to the dta */
   parsfnm(line, &blk, 1);
   printf("%d %s\n", blk.fcb_drive, blk.fcb_name);

   /* request DOS services to create file */
   if (bdosptr(0x16, &blk, 0) == -1) {
      perror("Error creating file");
      exit(1);
   }

   /* save old dta and set new dta */
   save_dta = getdta();
```

S

```
   setdta(buffer);

   /* write new records */
   blk.fcb_recsize = 256;
   blk.fcb_random = 0L;
   result = randbwr(&blk, 1);
   printf("result = %d\n", result);

   if (!result)
      printf("Write OK\n");
   else {
      perror("Disk error");
      exit(1);
   }

   /* request DOS services to close the file */
   if (bdosptr(0x10, &blk, 0) == -1) {
      perror("Error closing file");
      exit(1);
   }

   /* reset the old dta */
   setdta(save_dta);

   return 0;
}
```

setfillpattern

Function Selects a user-defined fill pattern.

Syntax #include <graphics.h>
void far setfillpattern(char far **upattern*, int *color*);

DOS	UNIX	Windows	ANSI C	C++ only
■				

Remarks **setfillpattern** is like **setfillstyle**, except that you use it to set a user-defined 8×8 pattern rather than a predefined pattern.

upattern is a pointer to a sequence of 8 bytes, with each byte corresponding to 8 pixels in the pattern. Whenever a bit in a pattern byte is set to 1, the corresponding pixel is plotted.

Return value None.

See also **getfillpattern, getfillsettings, graphresult, sector, setfillstyle**

Example

```
#include <graphics.h>
#include <stdlib.h>
```

```
#include <stdio.h>
#include <conio.h>

int main(void)
{
   /* request autodetection */
   int gdriver = DETECT, gmode, errorcode;
   int maxx, maxy;

   /* a user-defined fill pattern */
   char pattern[8] = {0x00, 0x70, 0x20, 0x27, 0x24, 0x24, 0x07, 0x00};

   /* initialize graphics and local variables */
   initgraph(&gdriver, &gmode, "");

   /* read result of initialization */
   errorcode = graphresult();
   if (errorcode != grOk)     /* an error occurred */
   {
      printf("Graphics error: %s\n", grapherrormsg(errorcode));
      printf("Press any key to halt:");
      getch();
      exit(1);                /* terminate with an error code */
   }

   maxx = getmaxx();
   maxy = getmaxy();
   setcolor(getmaxcolor());

   /* select a user-defined fill pattern */
   setfillpattern(pattern, getmaxcolor());

   /* fill the screen with the pattern */
   bar(0, 0, maxx, maxy);

   /* clean up */
   getch();
   closegraph();
   return 0;
}
```

S

setfillstyle

Function Sets the fill pattern and color.

Syntax #include <graphics.h>
void far setfillstyle(int *pattern*, int *color*);

DOS	UNIX	Windows	ANSI C	C++ only
▪				

Remarks **setfillstyle** sets the current fill pattern and fill color. To set a user-defined fill pattern, do *not* give a *pattern* of 12 (USER_FILL) to **setfillstyle**; instead, call **setfillpattern**.

The enumeration *fill_patterns*, defined in graphics.h, gives names for the predefined fill patterns, plus an indicator for a user-defined pattern.

Name	Value	Description
EMPTY_FILL	0	Fill with background color
SOLID_FILL	1	Solid fill
LINE_FILL	2	Fill with ——
LTSLASH_FILL	3	Fill with ///
SLASH_FILL	4	Fill with ///, thick lines
BKSLASH_FILL	5	Fill with \\\, thick lines
LTBKSLASH_FILL	6	Fill with \\\
HATCH_FILL	7	Light hatch fill
XHATCH_FILL	8	Heavy crosshatch fill
INTERLEAVE_FILL	9	Interleaving line fill
WIDE_DOT_FILL	10	Widely spaced dot fill
CLOSE_DOT_FILL	11	Closely spaced dot fill
USER_FILL	12	User-defined fill pattern

All but EMPTY_FILL fill with the current fill color; EMPTY_FILL uses the current background color.

If invalid input is passed to **setfillstyle**, **graphresult** returns –11 (grError), and the current fill pattern and fill color remain unchanged.

Return value None.

See also **bar, bar3d, fillpoly, floodfill, getfillsettings, graphresult, pieslice, sector, setfillpattern**

Example

```
#include <graphics.h>
#include <stdlib.h>
#include <string.h>
#include <stdio.h>
#include <conio.h>

/* the names of the fill styles supported */
char *fname[] = { "EMPTY_FILL", "SOLID_FILL", "LINE_FILL", "LTSLASH_FILL",
                  "SLASH_FILL", "BKSLASH_FILL", "LTBKSLASH_FILL", "HATCH_FILL",
                  "XHATCH_FILL", "INTERLEAVE_FILL", "WIDE_DOT_FILL",
                  "CLOSE_DOT_FILL", "USER_FILL" };

int main(void)
{
   /* request autodetection */
   int gdriver = DETECT, gmode, errorcode;
```

```
   int style, midx, midy;
   char stylestr[40];

   /* initialize graphics and local variables */
   initgraph(&gdriver, &gmode, "");

   /* read result of initialization */
   errorcode = graphresult();
   if (errorcode != grOk) {  /* an error occurred */
      printf("Graphics error: %s\n", grapherrormsg(errorcode));
      printf("Press any key to halt:");
      getch();
      exit(1);               /* terminate with an error code */
   }

   midx = getmaxx() / 2;
   midy = getmaxy() / 2;
   for (style = EMPTY_FILL; style < USER_FILL; style++) {
      /* select the fill style */
      setfillstyle(style, getmaxcolor());

      /* convert style into a string */
      strcpy(stylestr, fname[style]);

      /* fill a bar */
      bar3d(0, 0, midx-10, midy, 0, 0);

      /* output a message */
      outtextxy(midx, midy, stylestr);

      /* wait for a key */
      getch();
      cleardevice();
   }

   /* clean up */
   getch();
   closegraph();
   return 0;
}
```

S

setgraphbufsize

Function Changes the size of the internal graphics buffer.

Syntax #include <graphics.h>
unsigned far setgraphbufsize(unsigned *bufsize*);

DOS	UNIX	Windows	ANSI C	C++ only
■				

Remarks Some of the graphics routines (such as **floodfill**) use a memory buffer that is allocated when **initgraph** is called, and released when **closegraph** is called. The default size of this buffer, allocated by **_graphgetmem**, is 4,096 bytes.

You might want to make this buffer smaller (to save memory space) or bigger (if, for example, a call to **floodfill** produces error –7: Out of flood memory).

setgraphbufsize tells **initgraph** how much memory to allocate for this internal graphics buffer when it calls **_graphgetmem**.

You *must* call **setgraphbufsize** before calling **initgraph**. Once **initgraph** has been called, all calls to **setgraphbufsize** are ignored until after the next call to **closegraph**.

Return value **setgraphbufsize** returns the previous size of the internal buffer.

See also **closegraph, _graphfreemem, _graphgetmem, initgraph, sector**

Example

```
#include <graphics.h>
#include <stdlib.h>
#include <stdio.h>
#include <conio.h>

#define BUFSIZE 1000 /* internal graphics buffer size */

int main(void)
{
   /* request autodetection */
   int gdriver = DETECT, gmode, errorcode;
   int x, y, oldsize;
   char msg[80];

   /* set size of internal graphics buffer before calling initgraph */
   oldsize = setgraphbufsize(BUFSIZE);


   /* initialize graphics and local variables */
   initgraph(&gdriver, &gmode, "");

   /* read result of initialization */
   errorcode = graphresult();
   if (errorcode != grOk) {  /* an error occurred */
      printf("Graphics error: %s\n", grapherrormsg(errorcode));
      printf("Press any key to halt:");
      getch();
      exit(1);               /* terminate with an error code */
```

```
   }

   x = getmaxx() / 2;
   y = getmaxy() / 2;

   /* output some messages */
   sprintf(msg, "Graphics buffer size: %d", BUFSIZE);
   settextjustify(CENTER_TEXT, CENTER_TEXT);
   outtextxy(x, y, msg);
   sprintf(msg, "Old graphics buffer size: %d", oldsize);
   outtextxy(x, y+textheight("W"), msg);

   /* clean up */
   getch();
   closegraph();
   return 0;
}
```

setgraphmode

Function Sets the system to graphics mode and clears the screen.

Syntax #include <graphics.h>
void far setgraphmode(int *mode*);

DOS	UNIX	Windows	ANSI C	C++ only
■				

Remarks **setgraphmode** selects a graphics mode different than the default one set by **initgraph**. *mode* must be a valid mode for the current device driver. **setgraphmode** clears the screen and resets all graphics settings to their defaults (current position, palette, color, viewport, and so on).

You can use **setgraphmode** in conjunction with **restorecrtmode** to switch back and forth between text and graphics modes.

Return value If you give **setgraphmode** an invalid mode for the current device driver, **graphresult** returns a value of –10 (grInvalidMode).

See also **getgraphmode**, **getmoderange**, **graphresult**, **initgraph**, **restorecrtmode**

Example

```
#include <graphics.h>
#include <stdlib.h>
#include <stdio.h>
#include <conio.h>

int main(void)
{
   /* request autodetection */
```

```
    int gdriver = DETECT, gmode, errorcode;
    int x, y;

    /* initialize graphics and local variables */
    initgraph(&gdriver, &gmode, "");

    /* read result of initialization */
    errorcode = graphresult();
    if (errorcode != grOk) {  /* an error occurred */
       printf("Graphics error: %s\n", grapherrormsg(errorcode));
       printf("Press any key to halt:");
       getch();
       exit(1);               /* terminate with an error code */
    }

    x = getmaxx() / 2;
    y = getmaxy() / 2;

    /* output a message */
    settextjustify(CENTER_TEXT, CENTER_TEXT);
    outtextxy(x, y, "Press any key to exit graphics:");
    getch();

    /* restore system to text mode */
    restorecrtmode();
    printf("We're now in text mode.\n");
    printf("Press any key to return to graphics mode:");
    getch();

    /* return to graphics mode */
    setgraphmode(getgraphmode());

    /* output a message */
    settextjustify(CENTER_TEXT, CENTER_TEXT);
    outtextxy(x, y, "We're back in graphics mode.");
    outtextxy(x, y+textheight("W"), "Press any key to halt:");


    /* clean up */
    getch();
    closegraph();
    return 0;
}
```

setjmp

Function Sets up for nonlocal goto.

Syntax #include <setjmp.h>
int setjmp(jmp_buf *jmpb*);

DOS	UNIX	Windows	ANSI C	C++ only
■	■	■	■	

Remarks **setjmp** captures the complete *task state* in *jmpb* and returns 0.

A later call to **longjmp** with *jmpb* restores the captured task state and returns in such a way that **setjmp** appears to have returned with the value *val*.

A task state is

- all segment registers (CS, DS, ES, SS)
- register variables (SI, DI)
- stack pointer (SP)
- frame base pointer (BP)
- flags

A task state is complete enough that **setjmp** can be used to implement coroutines.

setjmp must be called before **longjmp**. The routine that calls **setjmp** and sets up *jmpb* must still be active and cannot have returned before the **longjmp** is called. If it has returned, the results are unpredictable.

setjmp is useful for dealing with errors and exceptions encountered in a low-level subroutine of a program.

➡ You can't use **setjmp** and **longjmp** for implementing co-routines if your program is overlaid. Normally, **setjmp** and **longjmp** save and restore all the registers needed for co-routines, but the overlay manager needs to keep track of stack contents and assumes there is only one stack. When you implement co-routines there are usually either two stacks or two partitions of one stack, and the overlay manager will not track them properly.

You can have background tasks which run with their own stacks or sections of stack, but you must ensure that the background tasks do not invoke any overlaid code, and you must not use the overlay versions of **setjmp** or **longjmp** to switch to and from background. When you avoid using overlay code or support routines, the existence of the background stacks does not disturb the overlay manager.

Return value **setjmp** returns 0 when it is initially called. If the return is from a call to **longjmp**, **setjmp** returns a nonzero value (as in the example).

See also **longjmp**, **signal**

S

Example

```
#include <stdio.h>
#include <process.h>
#include <setjmp.h>

void subroutine(void);

jmp_buf jumper;

int main()
{
   int value;
   value = setjmp(jumper);
   if (value != 0) {
      printf("Longjmp with value %d\n", value);
      exit(value);
   }
   printf("About to call subroutine ... \n");
   subroutine();
   return 0;
}

void subroutine(void) {
   longjmp(jumper,1);
}
```

setlinestyle

Function Sets the current line width and style.

Syntax #include <graphics.h>
void far setlinestyle(int *linestyle*, unsigned *upattern*, int *thickness*);

DOS	UNIX	Windows	ANSI C	C++ only
■				

Remarks **setlinestyle** sets the style for all lines drawn by **line, lineto, rectangle, drawpoly**, and so on.

The *linesettingstype* structure is defined in graphics.h as follows:

```
struct linesettingstype {
   int linestyle;
   unsigned upattern;
   int thickness;
};
```

linestyle specifies in which of several styles subsequent lines will be drawn (such as solid, dotted, centered, dashed). The enumeration *line_styles*, defined in graphics.h, gives names to these operators:

Name	Value	Description
SOLID_LINE	0	Solid line
DOTTED_LINE	1	Dotted line
CENTER_LINE	2	Centered line
DASHED_LINE	3	Dashed line
USERBIT_LINE	4	User-defined line style

thickness specifies whether the width of subsequent lines drawn will be normal or thick.

Name	Value	Description
NORM_WIDTH	1	1 pixel wide
THICK_WIDTH	3	3 pixels wide

upattern is a 16-bit pattern that applies only if *linestyle* is USERBIT_LINE (4). In that case, whenever a bit in the pattern word is 1, the corresponding pixel in the line is drawn in the current drawing color. For example, a solid line corresponds to a *upattern* of 0xFFFF (all pixels drawn), while a dashed line can correspond to a *upattern* of 0x3333 or 0x0F0F. If the *linestyle* parameter to **setlinestyle** is not USERBIT_LINE (in other words, if it is not equal to 4), you must still provide the *upattern* parameter, but it will be ignored.

The *linestyle* parameter does not affect arcs, circles, ellipses, or pie slices. Only the *thickness* parameter is used.

Return value If invalid input is passed to **setlinestyle**, **graphresult** returns –11, and the current line style remains unchanged.

See also **arc, bar3d, circle, drawpoly, ellipse, getlinesettings, graphresult, line, linerel, lineto, pieslice, rectangle**

Example

```
#include <graphics.h>
#include <stdlib.h>
#include <string.h>
#include <stdio.h>
#include <conio.h>

/* the names of the line styles supported */
char *lname[] = { "SOLID_LINE", "DOTTED_LINE", "CENTER_LINE", "DASHED_LINE",
                  "USERBIT_LINE" };

int main(void)
{
```

```
   /* request autodetection */
   int gdriver = DETECT, gmode, errorcode;
   int style, midx, midy, userpat;
   char stylestr[40];

   /* initialize graphics and local variables */
   initgraph(&gdriver, &gmode, "");

   /* read result of initialization */
   errorcode = graphresult();
   if (errorcode != grOk) {  /* an error occurred */
      printf("Graphics error: %s\n", grapherrormsg(errorcode));
      printf("Press any key to halt:");
      getch();
      exit(1);               /* terminate with an error code */
   }

   midx = getmaxx() / 2;
   midy = getmaxy() / 2;

   /* a user-defined line pattern */
   /* binary: "0000000000000001" */
   userpat = 1;
   for (style=SOLID_LINE; style<=USERBIT_LINE; style++)
   {
      /* select the line style */
      setlinestyle(style, userpat, 1);

      /* convert style into a string */
      strcpy(stylestr, lname[style]);

      /* draw a line */
      line(0, 0, midx-10, midy);

      /* draw a rectangle */
      rectangle(0, 0, getmaxx(), getmaxy());

      /* output a message */
      outtextxy(midx, midy, stylestr);

      /* wait for a key */
      getch();
      cleardevice();
   }

   /* clean up */
   closegraph();
   return 0;
}
```

setlocale

Function Selects a locale.

Syntax #include <locale.h>
char *setlocale(int *category*, char **locale*);

DOS	UNIX	Windows	ANSI C	C++ only
■		■	■	

Remarks Borland C++ supports only the "C" locale at present, so invoking this function has no effect.

Possible values for the argument category:

LC_ALL
LC_COLLATE
LC_CTYPE
LC_MONETARY
LC_NUMERIC
LC_TIME

Return value If selection is successful, a string is returned to indicate the locale that was in effect prior to invoking the function. If it is not successful, a NULL pointer is returned.

See also **localeconv**

Example

```
#include <locale.h>
#include <stdio.h>

int main( void )
{
   char *old_locale;

   /* only locale supported in Borland C++ is "C" */
   old_locale = setlocale(LC_ALL,"C");
   printf("Old locale was %s\n",old_locale);
   return 0;
}
```

setmem

Function Assigns a value to a range of memory.

S

Syntax #include <mem.h>
void setmem(void **dest*, unsigned *length*, char *value*);

DOS	UNIX	Windows	ANSI C	C++ only
■		■		

Remarks **setmem** sets a block of *length* bytes, pointed to by *dest*, to the byte *value*.

Return value None.

See also **memset, strset**

Example

```
#include <stdio.h>
#include <alloc.h>
#include <mem.h>

int main(void)
{
   char *dest;

   dest = (char *) calloc(21, sizeof(char));
   setmem(dest, 20, 'c');
   printf("%s\n", dest);
   return 0;
}
```

setmode

Function Sets mode of an open file.

Syntax #include <fcntl.h>
int setmode(int *handle*, int *amode*);

DOS	UNIX	Windows	ANSI C	C++ only
■		■		

Remarks **setmode** sets the mode of the open file associated with *handle* to either binary or text. The argument *amode* must have a value of either O_BINARY or O_TEXT, never both. (These symbolic constants are defined in fcntl.h.)

Return value **setmode** returns the previous translation mode if successful. On error it returns –1 and sets the global variable *errno* to

EINVAL Invalid argument

See also **_creat, creat, _open, open**

Example

```
#include <stdio.h>
#include <fcntl.h>
#include <io.h>

int main(void)
{
   int result;
   result = setmode(fileno(stdprn), O_TEXT);
   if (result == -1)
      perror("Mode not available\n");
   else
      printf("Mode successfully switched\n");
   return 0;
}
```

set_new_handler

Function Sets the function to be called when a request for memory allocation cannot be satisfied.

Syntax #include <new.h>
void (* set_new_handler(void (* *my_handler*)()))();

DOS	UNIX	Windows	ANSI C	C++ only
▪	▪	▪		▪

Remarks **set_new_handler** sets the function to be called when **operator new** cannot allocate the requested memory. By default **operator new** will return zero if it cannot allocate memory. You can affect this default behavior by setting a new handler and calling **set_new_handler**.

If **new** cannot allocate the requested memory it calls the handler that was set by a previous call to **set_new_handler**. *my_handler* should specify the actions to be taken when **new** cannot satisfy a request for memory allocation. If *my_handler* returns, then **new** will again attempt to satisfy the request.

Ideally, *my_handler* would free up memory and return. **new** would then be able to satisfy the request and the program would continue. However, if *my_handler* cannot provide memory for **new**, *my_handler* must terminate the program. Otherwise, an infinite loop will be created.

The default handler is reset by **set_new_handler(0)**.

Preferably, you should overload the **operator new()** to take appropriate actions for your applications.

Return value **set_new_handler** returns the old handler, if it has been defined. By default, no handler is installed.

The user-defined argument function, *my_handler*, should not return a value.

See Also *_new_handler* (global variable)

Example

```
#include <iostream.h>
#include <new.h>
#include <stdlib.h>

void mem_warn() {
   cerr << "\nCannot allocate!";
   exit(1);
   }

void main(void) {
   set_new_handler(mem_warn);

   char *ptr = new char[100];
   cout << "\nFirst allocation: ptr = " << hex << long(ptr);
   ptr = new char[64000U];
   cout << "\nFinal allocation: ptr = " << hex << long(ptr);
   set_new_handler(0);  // Reset to default.
   }
```

Program output

```
First allocation: ptr = 283e0f30
Cannot allocate!
```

setpalette

Function Changes one palette color.

Syntax #include <graphics.h>
void far setpalette(int *colornum*, int *color*);

DOS	UNIX	Windows	ANSI C	C++ only
■				

Remarks **setpalette** changes the *colornum* entry in the palette to *color*. For example, **setpalette**(0,5) changes the first color in the current palette (the background color) to actual color number 5. If *size* is the number of entries in the current palette, *colornum* can range between 0 and (*size* – 1).

You can partially (or completely) change the colors in the EGA/VGA palette with **setpalette**. On a CGA, you can only change the first entry in the palette (*colornum* equals 0, the background color) with a call to **setpalette**.

The *color* parameter passed to **setpalette** can be represented by symbolic constants defined in graphics.h.

CGA		EGA/VGA	
Name	**Value**	**Name**	**Value**
BLACK	0	EGA_BLACK	0
BLUE	1	EGA_BLUE	1
GREEN	2	EGA_GREEN	2
CYAN	3	EGA_CYAN	3
RED	4	EGA_RED	4
MAGENTA	5	EGA_MAGENTA	5
BROWN	6	EGA_LIGHTGRAY	7
LIGHTGRAY	7	EGA_BROWN	20
DARKGRAY	8	EGA_DARKGRAY	56
LIGHTBLUE	9	EGA_LIGHTBLUE	57
LIGHTGREEN	10	EGA_LIGHTGREEN	58
LIGHTCYAN	11	EGA_LIGHTCYAN	59
LIGHTRED	12	EGA_LIGHTRED	60
LIGHTMAGENTA	13	EGA_LIGHTMAGENTA	61
YELLOW	14	EGA_YELLOW	62
WHITE	15	EGA_WHITE	63

Note that valid colors depend on the current graphics driver and current graphics mode.

Changes made to the palette are seen immediately onscreen. Each time a palette color is changed, all occurrences of that color onscreen change to the new color value.

setpalette cannot be used with the IBM-8514 driver; use **setrgbpalette** instead.

Return value If invalid input is passed to **setpalette**, **graphresult** returns –11, and the current palette remains unchanged.

See also **getpalette, graphresult, setallpalette, setbkcolor, setcolor, setrgbpalette**

Example

```
#include <graphics.h>
#include <stdlib.h>
#include <stdio.h>
#include <conio.h>

int main(void)
{
   /* request autodetection */
   int gdriver = DETECT, gmode, errorcode;
   int color, maxcolor, ht;
```

S

```
   int y = 10;
   char msg[80];

   /* initialize graphics and local variables */
   initgraph(&gdriver, &gmode, "");

   /* read result of initialization */
   errorcode = graphresult();
   if (errorcode != grOk) {  /* an error occurred */
      printf("Graphics error: %s\n", grapherrormsg(errorcode));
      printf("Press any key to halt:");
      getch();
      exit(1);               /* terminate with an error code */
   }

   maxcolor = getmaxcolor();
   ht = 2 * textheight("W");

   /* display the default colors */
   for (color=1; color<=maxcolor; color++) {
      setcolor(color);
      sprintf(msg, "Color: %d", color);
      outtextxy(1, y, msg);
      y += ht;
   }

   /* wait for a key */
   getch();

   /* black out the colors one by one */
   for (color=1; color<=maxcolor; color++) {
      setpalette(color, BLACK);
      getch();
   }

   /* clean up */
   closegraph();
   return 0;
}
```

setrgbpalette

Function Allows user to define colors for the IBM 8514.

Syntax #include <graphics.h>
void far setrgbpalette(int *colornum*, int *red*, int *green*, int *blue*);

DOS	UNIX	Windows	ANSI C	C++ only
■				

Remarks **setrgbpalette** can be used with the IBM 8514 and VGA drivers.

colornum defines the palette entry to be loaded, while *red*, *green*, and *blue* define the component colors of the palette entry.

For the IBM 8514 display (and the VGA in 256K color mode), *colornum* is in the range 0 to 255. For the remaining modes of the VGA, *colornum* is in the range 0 to 15. Only the lower byte of *red*, *green*, or *blue* is used, and out of each byte, only the 6 most significant bits are loaded in the palette.

➡ For compatibility with other IBM graphics adapters, the BGI driver defines the first 16 palette entries of the IBM 8514 to the default colors of the EGA/VGA. These values can be used as is, or they can be changed using **setrgbpalette**.

Return value None.

See also **setpalette**

Example

```
#include <graphics.h>
#include <stdlib.h>
#include <stdio.h>
#include <conio.h>

int main(void)
{
   /* select driver and mode that supports use of setrgbpalette */
   int gdriver = VGA, gmode = VGAHI, errorcode;
   struct palettetype pal;
   int i, ht, y, xmax;

   /* initialize graphics and local variables */
   initgraph(&gdriver, &gmode, "");

   /* read result of initialization */
   errorcode = graphresult();
   if (errorcode != grOk) {  /* an error occurred */
      printf("Graphics error: %s\n", grapherrormsg(errorcode));
      printf("Press any key to halt:");
      getch();
      exit(1);               /* terminate with an error code */
   }

   /* grab a copy of the palette */
   getpalette(&pal);


   /* create gray scale */
   for (i=0; i<pal.size; i++)
      setrgbpalette(pal.colors[i], i*4, i*4, i*4);
```

```
   /* display the gray scale */
   ht = getmaxy() / 16;
   xmax = getmaxx();
   y = 0;
   for (i=0; i<pal.size; i++) {
      setfillstyle(SOLID_FILL, i);
      bar(0, y, xmax, y+ht);
      y += ht;
   }

   /* clean up */
   getch();
   closegraph();
   return 0;
}
```

settextjustify

Function Sets text justification for graphics functions.

Syntax #include <graphics.h>
void far settextjustify(int *horiz*, int *vert*);

DOS	UNIX	Windows	ANSI C	C++ only
■				

Remarks Text output after a call to **settextjustify** is justified around the current position (CP) horizontally and vertically, as specified. The default justification settings are LEFT_TEXT (for horizontal) and TOP_TEXT (for vertical). The enumeration *text_just* in graphics.h provides names for the *horiz* and *vert* settings passed to **settextjustify**.

Description	Name	Value	Action
horiz	LEFT_TEXT	0	left-justify text
	CENTER_TEXT	1	center text
	RIGHT_TEXT	2	right-justify text
vert	BOTTOM_TEXT	0	justify from bottom
	CENTER_TEXT	1	center text
	TOP_TEXT	2	justify from top

If *horiz* is equal to LEFT_TEXT and *direction* equals HORIZ_DIR, the CP's *x* component is advanced after a call to **outtext**(*string*) by **textwidth**(*string*).

settextjustify affects text written with **outtext** and cannot be used with text mode and stream functions.

Return value If invalid input is passed to **settextjustify**, **graphresult** returns –11, and the current text justification remains unchanged.

See also **gettextsettings, graphresult, outtext, settextstyle**

Example

```
#include <graphics.h>
#include <stdlib.h>
#include <stdio.h>
#include <conio.h>

/* function prototype */
void xat(int x, int y);

/* horizontal text justification settings */
char *hjust[] = { "LEFT_TEXT", "CENTER_TEXT", "RIGHT_TEXT" };

/* vertical text justification settings */
char *vjust[] = { "LEFT_TEXT", "CENTER_TEXT", "RIGHT_TEXT" };

int main(void)
{
   /* request autodetection */
   int gdriver = DETECT, gmode, errorcode;
   int midx, midy, hj, vj;
   char msg[80];

   /* initialize graphics and local variables */
   initgraph(&gdriver, &gmode, "");

   /* read result of initialization */
   errorcode = graphresult();
   if (errorcode != grOk) {  /* an error occurred */
      printf("Graphics error: %s\n", grapherrormsg(errorcode));
      printf("Press any key to halt:");
      getch();
      exit(1);               /* terminate with an error code */
   }

   midx = getmaxx() / 2;
   midy = getmaxy() / 2;

   /* loop through text justifications */
   for (hj=LEFT_TEXT; hj<=RIGHT_TEXT; hj++)
      for (vj=LEFT_TEXT; vj<=RIGHT_TEXT; vj++) {
         cleardevice();

         /* set the text justification */
         settextjustify(hj, vj);

         /* create a message string */
         sprintf(msg, "%s  %s", hjust[hj], vjust[vj]);

         /* create crosshairs on the screen */
```

```
         xat(midx, midy);

         /* output the message */
         outtextxy(midx, midy, msg);
         getch();
      }

   /* clean up */
   closegraph();
   return 0;
}

void xat(int x, int y)          /* draw an x at (x,y) */
{
  line(x-4, y, x+4, y);
  line(x, y-4, x, y+4);
}
```

settextstyle

Function Sets the current text characteristics for graphics output.

Syntax #include <graphics.h>
void far settextstyle(int *font*, int *direction*, int *charsize*);

DOS	UNIX	Windows	ANSI C	C++ only
■				

Remarks **settextstyle** sets the text font, the direction in which text is displayed, and the size of the characters. A call to **settextstyle** affects all text output by **outtext** and **outtextxy**.

The parameters *font, direction,* and *charsize* passed to **settextstyle** are described in the following:

font: One 8×8 bit-mapped font and several "stroked" fonts are available. The 8×8 bit-mapped font is the default. The enumeration *font_names,* defined in graphics.h, provides names for these different font settings:

Name	Value	Description
DEFAULT_FONT	0	8×8 bit-mapped font
TRIPLEX_FONT	1	Stroked triplex font
SMALL_FONT	2	Stroked small font
SANS_SERIF_FONT	3	Stroked sans-serif font
GOTHIC_FONT	4	Stroked gothic font
SCRIPT_FONT	5	Stroked script font
SIMPLEX_FONT	6	Stroked triplex script font

TRIPLEX_SCR_FONT	7	Stroked triplex script font
COMPLEX_FONT	8	Stroked complex font
EUROPEAN_FONT	9	Stroked European font
BOLD_FONT	10	Stroked bold font

The default bit-mapped font is built into the graphics system. Stroked fonts are stored in *.CHR disk files, and only one at a time is kept in memory. Therefore, when you select a stroked font (different from the last selected stroked font), the corresponding *.CHR file must be loaded from disk.

To avoid this loading when several stroked fonts are used, you can link font files into your program. Do this by converting them into object files with the BGIOBJ utility, then registering them through **registerbgifont**, as described in UTIL.DOC, included with your distributions disks.

direction: Font directions supported are horizontal text (left to right) and vertical text (rotated 90 degrees counterclockwise). The default direction is HORIZ_DIR.

Name	Value	Description
HORIZ_DIR	0	Left to right
VERT_DIR	1	Bottom to top

charsize: The size of each character can be magnified using the *charsize* factor. If *charsize* is nonzero, it can affect bit-mapped or stroked characters. A *charsize* value of 0 can be used only with stroked fonts.

- If *charsize* equals 1, **outtext** and **outtextxy** displays characters from the 8×8 bit-mapped font in an 8×8 pixel rectangle onscreen.
- If *charsize* equals 2, these output functions display characters from the 8×8 bit-mapped font in a 16×16 pixel rectangle, and so on (up to a limit of ten times the normal size).
- When *charsize* equals 0, the output functions **outtext** and **outtextxy** magnify the stroked font text using either the default character magnification factor (4) or the user-defined character size given by **setusercharsize**.

Always use **textheight** and **textwidth** to determine the actual dimensions of the text.

Return value None.

See also **gettextsettings**, **graphresult**, **installuserfont**, **settextjustify**, **setusercharsize**, **textheight**, **textwidth**

S

Example

```
#include <graphics.h>
#include <stdlib.h>
#include <stdio.h>
#include <conio.h>

/* the names of the text styles supported */
char *fname[] = { "DEFAULT font",  "TRIPLEX font",
                  "SMALL font",    "SANS SERIF font",
                  "GOTHIC font",   "SCRIPT font",
                  "SIMPLEX font",  "TRIPLEX SCRIPT font",
                  "COMPLEX font",  "EUROPEAN font",
                  "BOLD font"};

int main(void)
{
   /* request autodetection */
   int gdriver = DETECT, gmode, errorcode;
   int style, midx, midy;
   int size = 1;

   /* initialize graphics and local variables */
   initgraph(&gdriver, &gmode, "");

   /* read result of initialization */
   errorcode = graphresult();
   if (errorcode != grOk) {  /* an error occurred */
      printf("Graphics error: %s\n", grapherrormsg(errorcode));
      printf("Press any key to halt:");
      getch();
      exit(1);               /* terminate with an error code */
   }

   midx = getmaxx() / 2;
   midy = getmaxy() / 2;
   settextjustify(CENTER_TEXT, CENTER_TEXT);

   /* loop through the available text styles */
   for (style=DEFAULT_FONT; style<=BOLD_FONT; style++) {
      cleardevice();
      if (style == TRIPLEX_FONT)
         size = 4;
      /* select the text style */
      settextstyle(style, HORIZ_DIR, size);

      /* output a message */
      outtextxy(midx, midy, fname[style]);
      getch();
   }
   /* clean up */
   closegraph();
```

```
   return 0;
}
```

setusercharsize

Function Varies character width and height for stroked fonts.

Syntax #include <graphics.h>
void far setusercharsize(int *multx*, int *divx*, int *multy*, int *divy*);

DOS	UNIX	Windows	ANSI C	C++ only
■				

Remarks **setusercharsize** gives you finer control over the size of text from stroked fonts used with graphics functions. The values set by **setusercharsize** are active *only* if *charsize* equals 0, as set by a previous call to **settextstyle**.

With **setusercharsize**, you specify factors by which the width and height are scaled. The default width is scaled by *multx* : *divx*, and the default height is scaled by *multy* : *divy*. For example, to make text twice as wide and 50% taller than the default, set

```
multx = 2;  divx = 1;
multy = 3;  divy = 2;
```

Return value None.

See also **gettextsettings**, **graphresult**, **settextstyle**

Example

```
#include <graphics.h>
#include <stdlib.h>
#include <stdio.h>
#include <conio.h>

int main(void)
{
   /* request autodetection */
   int gdriver = DETECT, gmode, errorcode;

   /* initialize graphics and local variables */
   initgraph(&gdriver, &gmode, "");

   /* read result of initialization */
   errorcode = graphresult();
   if (errorcode != grOk) {  /* an error occurred */
      printf("Graphics error: %s\n", grapherrormsg(errorcode));
      printf("Press any key to halt:");
      getch();
      exit(1);               /* terminate with an error code */
```

```
   }

   /* select a text style */
   settextstyle(TRIPLEX_FONT, HORIZ_DIR, 4);

   /* move to the text starting position */
   moveto(0, getmaxy() / 2);

   /* output some normal text */
   outtext("Norm ");

   /* make the text 1/3 the normal width */
   setusercharsize(1, 3, 1, 1);
   outtext("Short ");

   /* make the text 3 times normal width */
   setusercharsize(3, 1, 1, 1);
   outtext("Wide");

   /* clean up */
   getch();
   closegraph();
   return 0;
}
```

setvbuf

Function Assigns buffering to a stream.

Syntax #include <stdio.h>
int setvbuf(FILE **stream*, char **buf*, int *type*, size_t *size*);

DOS	UNIX	Windows	ANSI C	C++ only
■	■	■	■	

Remarks **setvbuf** causes the buffer *buf* to be used for I/O buffering instead of an automatically allocated buffer. It is used after the given stream is opened.

If *buf* is null, a buffer will be allocated using **malloc**; the buffer will use *size* as the amount allocated. The buffer will be automatically freed on close. The *size* parameter specifies the buffer size and must be greater than zero.

➥ The parameter *size* is limited to a maximum of 32,767.

stdin and *stdout* are unbuffered if they are not redirected; otherwise, they are fully buffered. *Unbuffered* means that characters written to a stream are immediately output to the file or device, while *buffered* means that the characters are accumulated and written as a block.

The *type* parameter is one of the following:

_IOFBF The file is *fully buffered*. When a buffer is empty, the next input operation will attempt to fill the entire buffer. On output, the buffer will be completely filled before any data is written to the file.

_IOLBF The file is *line buffered*. When a buffer is empty, the next input operation will still attempt to fill the entire buffer. On output, however, the buffer will be flushed whenever a newline character is written to the file.

_IONBF The file is *unbuffered*. The *buf* and *size* parameters are ignored. Each input operation will read directly from the file, and each output operation will immediately write the data to the file.

A common cause for error is to allocate the buffer as an automatic (local) variable and then fail to close the file before returning from the function where the buffer was declared.

Return value **setvbuf** returns 0 on success. It returns nonzero if an invalid value is given for *type* or *size*, or if there is not enough space to allocate a buffer.

See also **fflush, fopen, setbuf**

Example

```
#include <stdio.h>

int main(void)
{
   FILE *input, *output;
   char bufr[512];
   input = fopen("file.in", "r+b");
   output = fopen("file.out", "w");

   /* set up input stream for minimal disk access, using our own character buffer
      */
   if (setvbuf(input, bufr, _IOFBF, 512) != 0)
      printf("failed to set up buffer for input file\n");
   else
      printf("buffer set up for input file\n");

   /* set up output stream for line buffering using space that is obtained
      through an indirect call to malloc */
   if (setvbuf(output, NULL, _IOLBF, 132) != 0)
      printf("failed to set up buffer for output file\n");
   else
      printf("buffer set up for output file\n");

   /* perform file I/O here */

   /* close files */
   fclose(input);
   fclose(output);
```

S

```
    return 0;
}
```

setverify

Function Sets the state of the verify flag in DOS.

Syntax #include <dos.h>
void setverify(int *value*);

DOS	UNIX	Windows	ANSI C	C++ only
■		■		

Remarks **setverify** sets the current state of the verify flag to *value*.

- A *value* of 0 = verify flag off.
- A *value* of 1 = verify flag on.

The verify flag controls output to the disk. When verify is off, writes are not verified; when verify is on, all disk writes are verified to ensure proper writing of the data.

Return value None.

See also **getverify**

Example

```
#include <stdio.h>
#include <conio.h>
#include <dos.h>

int main(void)
{
   int verify_flag;
   printf("Enter 0 to set verify flag off\n");
   printf("Enter 1 to set verify flag on\n");
   verify_flag = getch() - 0;
   setverify(verify_flag);
   if (getverify())
      printf("DOS verify flag is on\n");
   else
      printf("DOS verify flag is off\n");
   return 0;
}
```

setviewport

Function Sets the current viewport for graphics output.

Syntax #include <graphics.h>
void far setviewport(int *left*, int *top*, int *right*, int *bottom*, int *clip*);

DOS	UNIX	Windows	ANSI C	C++ only
■				

Remarks **setviewport** establishes a new viewport for graphics output.

The viewport's corners are given in absolute screen coordinates by (*left*,*top*) and (*right*,*bottom*). The current position (CP) is moved to (0,0) in the new window.

The parameter *clip* determines whether drawings are clipped (truncated) at the current viewport boundaries. If *clip* is nonzero, all drawings will be clipped to the current viewport.

Return value If invalid input is passed to **setviewport**, **graphresult** returns –11, and the current view settings remain unchanged.

See also **clearviewport**, **getviewsettings**, **graphresult**

Example

```
#include <graphics.h>
#include <stdlib.h>
#include <stdio.h>
#include <conio.h>

#define CLIP_ON 1            /* activates clipping in viewport */

int main(void)
{
   /* request autodetection */
   int gdriver = DETECT, gmode, errorcode;


   /* initialize graphics and local variables */
   initgraph(&gdriver, &gmode, "");

   /* read result of initialization */
   errorcode = graphresult();
   if (errorcode != grOk)    /* an error occurred */
   {
      printf("Graphics error: %s\n", grapherrormsg(errorcode));
      printf("Press any key to halt:");
      getch();
```

S

```
      exit(1);                /* terminate with an error code */
   }

   setcolor(getmaxcolor());

   /* message in default full-screen viewport */
   outtextxy(0, 0, "* <-- (0, 0) in default viewport");

   /* create a smaller viewport */
   setviewport(50, 50, getmaxx()-50, getmaxy()-50, CLIP_ON);

   /* display some text */
   outtextxy(0, 0, "* <-- (0, 0) in smaller viewport");

   /* clean up */
   getch();
   closegraph();
   return 0;
}
```

setvisualpage

Function Sets the visual graphics page number.

Syntax #include <graphics.h>
void far setvisualpage(int *page*);

DOS	UNIX	Windows	ANSI C	C++ only
■				

Remarks **setvisualpage** makes *page* the visual graphics page.

Return value None.

See also **graphresult, setactivepage**

Example

```
#include <graphics.h>
#include <stdlib.h>
#include <stdio.h>
#include <conio.h>

int main(void)
{
   /* select driver and mode that supports multiple pages */
   int gdriver = EGA, gmode = EGAHI, errorcode;
   int x, y, ht;

   /* initialize graphics and local variables */
   initgraph(&gdriver, &gmode, "");

   /* read result of initialization */
```

```
   errorcode = graphresult();
   if (errorcode != grOk)     /* an error occurred */
   {
      printf("Graphics error: %s\n", grapherrormsg(errorcode));
      printf("Press any key to halt:");
      getch();
      exit(1);                /* terminate with an error code */
   }

   x = getmaxx() / 2;
   y = getmaxy() / 2;
   ht = textheight("W");

   /*  select the off screen page for drawing */
   setactivepage(1);

   /* draw a line on page #1 */
   line(0, 0, getmaxx(), getmaxy());

   /* output a message on page #1 */
   settextjustify(CENTER_TEXT, CENTER_TEXT);
   outtextxy(x, y, "This is page #1:");
   outtextxy(x, y+ht, "Press any key to halt:");

   /* select drawing to page #0 */
   setactivepage(0);

   /* output a message  on page #0 */
   outtextxy(x, y, "This is page #0.");
   outtextxy(x, y+ht, "Press any key to view page #1:");
   getch();

   /* select page #1 as the visible page */
   setvisualpage(1);

   /* clean up */
   getch();
   closegraph();
   return 0;
}
```

S

setwritemode

Function Sets the writing mode for line drawing in graphics mode.

Syntax #include <graphics.h>
void far setwritemode(int *mode*);

DOS	UNIX	Windows	ANSI C	C++ only
■				

Remarks The following constants are defined:

```
COPY_PUT = 0      /* MOV */
XOR_PUT  = 1      /* XOR */
```

Each constant corresponds to a binary operation between each byte in the line and the corresponding bytes onscreen. COPY_PUT uses the assembly language **MOV** instruction, overwriting with the line whatever is on the screen. XOR_PUT uses the **XOR** command to combine the line with the screen. Two successive **XOR** commands will erase the line and restore the screen to its original appearance.

➡ **setwritemode** currently works only with **line, linerel, lineto, rectangle,** and **drawpoly**.

Return value None.

See also **drawpoly, line, linerel, lineto, putimage**

Example

```
#include <graphics.h>
#include <stdlib.h>
#include <stdio.h>
#include <conio.h>

int main()
{
   /* request autodetection */
   int gdriver = DETECT, gmode, errorcode;
   int xmax, ymax;

   /* initialize graphics and local variables */
   initgraph(&gdriver, &gmode, "");

   /* read result of initialization */
   errorcode = graphresult();
   if (errorcode != grOk)    /* an error occurred */
   {
      printf("Graphics error: %s\n", grapherrormsg(errorcode));
      printf("Press any key to halt:");
      getch();
      exit(1);               /* terminate with an error code */
   }

   xmax = getmaxx();
   ymax = getmaxy();

   /* select XOR drawing mode */
   setwritemode(XOR_PUT);

   /* draw a line */
   line(0, 0, xmax, ymax);
```

```
   getch();

   /* erase the line by drawing over it */
   line(0, 0, xmax, ymax);
   getch();

   /* select overwrite drawing mode */
   setwritemode(COPY_PUT);

   /* draw a line */
   line(0, 0, xmax, ymax);

   /* clean up */
   getch();
   closegraph();
   return 0;
}
```

signal

Function Specifies signal-handling actions.

Syntax #include <signal.h>
void (*signal(int *sig*, void (**func*) (int *sig*[, int *subcode*])))(int);

DOS	UNIX	Windows	ANSI C	C++ only
■		■	■	

Remarks **signal** determines how receipt of signal number *sig* will subsequently be treated. You can install a user-specified handler routine or use one of the two predefined handlers, SIG_DFL and SIG_IGN, in signal.h.

Function pointer	Meaning
SIG_DFL	Terminates the program
SIG_IGN	Ignore this type signal
SIG_ERR	Indicates an error return from **signal**

The signal types and their defaults are as follows:

Signal type	Meaning
SIGABRT	Abnormal termination. Default action is equivalent to calling **_exit**(3).
SIGFPE	Arithmetic error caused by division by 0, invalid operation, and the like. Default action is equivalent to calling **_exit**(1).
SIGILL	Illegal operation. Default action is equivalent to calling **_exit**(1).
SIGINT	*CTRL-C* interrupt. Default action is to do an INT 23h.
SIGSEGV	Illegal storage access. Default action is equivalent to calling **_exit**(1).
SIGTERM	Request for program termination. Default action is equivalent to calling **_exit**(1).

signal.h defines a type called *sig_atomic_t*, the largest integer type the processor can load or store atomically in the presence of asynchronous interrupts (for the 8086 family, this is a 16-bit word; that is, a Borland C++ integer).

When a signal is generated by the **raise** function or by an external event, the following happens:

1. If a user-specified handler has been installed for the signal, the action for that signal type is set to SIG_DFL.
2. The user-specified function is called with the signal type as the parameter.

User-specified handler functions can terminate by a return or by a call to **abort**, **_exit**, **exit**, or **longjmp**.

Borland C++ implements an extension to ANSI C when the signal type is SIGFPE, SIGSEGV, or SIGILL. The user-specified handler function is called with one or two extra parameters. If SIGFPE, SIGSEGV, or SIGILL has been raised as the result of an explicit call to the **raise** function, the user-specified handler is called with one extra parameter, an integer specifying that the handler is being explicitly invoked. The explicit activation values for SIGFPE, SIGSEGV and SIGILL are as follows (see declarations in float.h):

SIGSEGV signal	Meaning
SIGFPE	FPE_EXPLICITGEN
SIGSEGV	SEGV_EXPLICITGEN
SIGILL	ILL_EXPLICITGEN

If SIGFPE is raised because of a floating-point exception, the user handler is called with one extra parameter that specifies the FPE_xxx type of the signal. If SIGSEGV, SIGILL, or the integer-related variants of SIGFPE signals (FPE_INTOVFLOW or FPE_INTDIV0) are raised as the result of a processor exception, the user handler is called with two extra parameters:

1. The SIGFPE, SIGSEGV, or SIGILL exception type (see float.h for all these types). This first parameter is the usual ANSI signal type.
2. An integer pointer into the stack of the interrupt handler that called the user-specified handler. This pointer points to a list of the processor registers saved when the exception occurred. The registers are in the same order as the parameters to an interrupt function; that is, BP, DI, SI, DS, ES, DX, CX, BX, AX, IP, CS, FLAGS. To have a register value changed when the handler returns, change one of the locations in this list. For example, to have a new SI value on return, do something like this:

   ```
   *((int*)list_pointer + 2) = new_SI_value;
   ```

   In this way, the handler can examine and make any adjustments to the registers that you want. (See Example 2 for a demonstration.)

The following SIGFPE-type signals can occur (or be generated). They correspond to the exceptions that the 8087 family is capable of detecting, as well as the "INTEGER DIVIDE BY ZERO" and the "INTERRUPT ON OVERFLOW" on the main CPU. (The declarations for these are in float.h.)

SIGFPE signal	Meaning
FPE_INTOVFLOW	INTO executed with OF flag set
FPE_INTDIV0	Integer divide by zero
FPE_INVALID	Invalid operation
FPE_ZERODIVIDE	Division by zero
FPE_OVERFLOW	Numeric overflow
FPE_UNDERFLOW	Numeric underflow
FPE_INEXACT	Precision
FPE_EXPLICITGEN	User program executed **raise**(SIGFPE)

The FPE_INTOVFLOW and FPE_INTDIV0 signals are generated by integer operations, and the others are generated by floating-point operations. Whether the floating-point exceptions are generated depends on the coprocessor control word, which can be modified with **_control87**. Denormal exceptions are handled by Borland C++ and not passed to a signal handler.

The following SIGSEGV-type signals can occur:

SEGV_BOUND	Bound constraint exception
SEGV_EXPLICITGEN	**raise**(SIGSEGV) was executed

The 8088 and 8086 processors *don't* have a bound instruction. The 186, 286, 386, and NEC V series processors *do* have this instruction. So, on the 8088 and 8086 processors, the SEGV_BOUND type of SIGSEGV signal won't occur. Borland C++ doesn't generate bound instructions, but they can be used in inline code and separately compiled assembler routines that are linked in.

The following SIGILL-type signals can occur:

ILL_EXECUTION	Illegal operation attempted.
ILL_EXPLICITGEN	**raise**(SIGILL) was executed.

The 8088, 8086, NEC V20, and NEC V30 processors *don't* have an illegal operation exception. The 186, 286, 386, NEC V40, and NEC V50 processors *do* have this exception type. So, on 8088, 8086, NEC V20, and NEC V30 processors, the ILL_EXECUTION type of SIGILL won't occur.

When the signal type is SIGFPE, SIGSEGV, or SIGILL, a return from a signal handler is generally not advisable because the state of the 8087 is corrupt, the results of an integer division are wrong, an operation that shouldn't have overflowed did, a bound instruction failed, or an illegal operation was attempted. The only time a return is reasonable is when the handler alters the registers so that a reasonable return context exists *or* the signal type indicates that the signal was generated explicitly (for example, FPE_EXPLICITGEN, SEGV_EXPLICITGEN, or ILL_EXPLICITGEN). Generally in this case you would print an error message and terminate the program using **_exit**, **exit**, or **abort**. If a return is executed under any other conditions, the program's action will probably be unpredictable upon resuming.

Return value If the call succeeds, **signal** returns a pointer to the previous handler routine for the specified signal type. If the call fails, **signal** returns SIG_ERR, and the external variable *errno* is set to EINVAL.

See also **abort, _control87, ctrlbrk, exit, longjmp, raise, setjmp**

Example 1

```
/* This example installs a signal handler routine to be run when Ctrl-Break is
   pressed. */
#include <stdio.h>
#include <signal.h>
#include <stdlib.h>

void catcher(void)
{
   printf("\nNow in break routine\n");
```

```
   exit(1);
}

int main(void) {
   signal(SIGINT,catcher);
   for (;;)
      printf("\nIn main() program\n");
}
```

Example 2

```
/* This example installs a signal handler routine for SIGFPE, catches an integer
   overflow condition, makes an adjustment to AX register, and returns. This
   example program MAY cause your computer to crash, and will produce runtime
   errors depending on which memory model is used. */
#pragma inline
#include <stdio.h>
#include <signal.h>

void Catcher(int *reglist)
{
   printf("Caught it!\n");
   *(reglist + 8) = 3;              /* make return AX = 3 */
}

int main(void)
{
   signal(SIGFPE, Catcher);
   asm    mov    ax,07FFFH          /* AX = 32767 */
   asm    inc    ax                 /* cause overflow */
   asm    into                      /* activate handler */

   /* The handler set AX to 3 on return. If that hadn't happened, there would
      have been another exception when the next 'into' was executed after the
      'dec' instruction. */
   asm    dec    ax                 /* no overflow now */
   asm    into                      /* doesn't activate */
   return 0;
}
```

S

sin, sinl

Function Calculates sine.

Syntax *Real versions*:
#include <math.h>
double sin(double *x*);
long double sinl(long double *x*);

Complex version:
#include <complex.h>
complex sin(complex *x*);

	DOS	UNIX	Windows	ANSI C	C++ only
sinl	■		■		
Real ***sin***	■	■	■	■	
Complex ***sin***	■		■		■

Remarks **sin** computes the sine of the input value. Angles are specified in radians.

sinl is the long double version; it takes a long double argument and returns a long double result.

Error handling for these functions can be modified through the functions **matherr** and **_matherrl**.

Return value **sin** and **sinl** return the sine of the input value.

The complex sine is defined by

$$\sin(z) = (\exp(i * z) - \exp(-i * z))/(2i)$$

See also **acos, asin, atan, atan2, complex, cos, tan**

Example

```
#include <stdio.h>
#include <math.h>

int main(void)
{
   double result, x = 0.5;
   result = sin(x);
   printf("The sin() of %lf is %lf\n", x, result);
   return 0;
}
```

sinh, sinhl

Function Calculates hyperbolic sine.

Syntax

Real versions:
#include <math.h>
double sinh(double *x*);
long double sinhl(long double *x*);

Complex version:
#include <complex.h>
complex sinh(complex *x*);

	DOS	UNIX	Windows	ANSI C	C++ only
sinhl	■		■		
Real ***sinh***	■	■	■	■	
Complex ***sinh***	■	■	■		■

Remarks **sinh** computes the hyperbolic sine, $(e^x - e^{-x})/2$.
sinl is the long double version; it takes a long double argument and returns a long double result.

Error handling for **sinh** and **sinhl** can be modified through the functions **matherr** and **_matherrl**.

The complex hyperbolic sine is defined by

sinh(z) = (exp(z) – exp(-z))/2

Return value **sinh** and **sinhl** return the hyperbolic sine of *x*.

When the correct value overflows, these functions return the value HUGE_VAL (**sinh**) or _LHUGE_VAL (**sinhl**) of appropriate sign. Also, the global variable *errno* is set to ERANGE.
See **cosh**.

See also **acos**, **asin**, **atan**, **atan2**, **complex**, **cos**, **cosh**, **sin**, **tan**, **tanh**

Example

```
#include <stdio.h>
#include <math.h>

int main(void)
{
   double result, x = 0.5;
   result = sinh(x);
   printf("The hyperbolic sin() of %lf is %lf\n", x, result);
   return 0;
}
```

sleep

Function Suspends execution for an interval (seconds).

Syntax #include <dos.h>
void sleep(unsigned *seconds*);

DOS	UNIX	Windows	ANSI C	C++ only
■	■			

Remarks With a call to **sleep**, the current program is suspended from execution for the number of seconds specified by the argument *seconds*. The interval is only accurate to the nearest hundredth of a second or the accuracy of the DOS clock, whichever is less accurate.

Return value None.

See also **delay**

Example

```
#include <dos.h>
#include <stdio.h>

int main(void)
{
   int i;
   for (i=1; i<5; i++) {
      printf("Sleeping for %d seconds\n", i);
      sleep(i);
   }
   return 0;
}
```

sopen

Function Opens a shared file.

Syntax #include <fcntl.h>
#include <sys\stat.h>
#include <share.h>
#include <io.h>
int sopen(char **path*, int *access*, int *shflag*[, int *mode*]);

DOS	UNIX	Windows	ANSI C	C++ only
■	■	■		

Remarks **sopen** opens the file given by *path* and prepares it for shared reading or writing, as determined by *access*, *shflag*, and *mode*.

For **sopen**, *access* is constructed by ORing flags bitwise from the following two lists. Only one flag from the first list can be used; the remaining flags can be used in any logical combination.

List 1: Read/write flags

O_RDONLY	Open for reading only.
O_WRONLY	Open for writing only.
O_RDWR	Open for reading and writing.

List 2: Other access flags

O_NDELAY	Not used; for UNIX compatibility.
O_APPEND	If set, the file pointer is set to the end of the file prior to each write.

O_CREAT	If the file exists, this flag has no effect. If the file does not exist, the file is created, and the bits of *mode* are used to set the file attribute bits as in **chmod**.
O_TRUNC	If the file exists, its length is truncated to 0. The file attributes remain unchanged.
O_EXCL	Used only with O_CREAT. If the file already exists, an error is returned.
O_BINARY	This flag can be given to explicitly open the file in binary mode.
O_TEXT	This flag can be given to explicitly open the file in text mode.

These O_... symbolic constants are defined in fcntl.h.

If neither O_BINARY nor O_TEXT is given, the file is opened in the translation mode set by the global variable *_fmode*.

If the O_CREAT flag is used in constructing *access*, you need to supply the *mode* argument to **sopen** from the following symbolic constants defined in sys\stat.h.

Value of *mode*	Access permission
S_IWRITE	Permission to write
S_IREAD	Permission to read
S_IREAD | S_IWRITE	Permission to read/write

shflag specifies the type of file-sharing allowed on the file *path*. Symbolic constants for *shflag* are defined in share.h.

Value of *shflag*	What it does
SH_COMPAT	Sets compatibility mode
SH_DENYRW	Denies read/write access
SH_DENYWR	Denies write access
SH_DENYRD	Denies read access
SH_DENYNONE	Permits read/write access
SH_DENYNO	Permits read/write access

Return value On successful completion, **sopen** returns a nonnegative integer (the file handle), and the file pointer (that marks the current position in the file) is set to the beginning of the file. On error, it returns –1, and the global variable *errno* is set to

ENOENT	Path or file function not found
EMFILE	Too many open files
EACCES	Permission denied
EINVACC	Invalid access code

S

See also **chmod, close, creat, lock, lseek, _open, open, unlock, unmask**

Example

```
#include <io.h>
#include <fcntl.h>
#include <sys\stat.h>
#include <process.h>
#include <share.h>
#include <stdio.h>

int main(void)
{
   int handle, status;
   handle = sopen("c:\\autoexec.bat", O_RDONLY, SH_DENYNO, S_IREAD);
   if (handle < 0) {
      printf("sopen failed\n");
      exit(1);
   }
   status = access("c:\\autoexec.bat", 6);
   if (status == 0)
      printf("read/write access allowed\n");
   else
      printf("read/write access not allowed\n");
   close(handle);
   return 0;
}
```

sound

Function Turns PC speaker on at specified frequency.

Syntax #include <dos.h>
void sound(unsigned *frequency*);

DOS	UNIX	Windows	ANSI C	C++ only
■				

Remarks **sound** turns on the PC's speaker at a given frequency. *frequency* specifies the frequency of the sound in hertz (cycles per second). To turn the speaker off after a call to **sound**, call the function **nosound.**

See also **delay, nosound**

Example

```
/* Emits a 440-Hz tone for 1 seconds. */
#include <dos.h>

int main(void)
{
```

```
    sound(440);
    delay(1000);
    nosound();
    return 0;
}
```

spawnl, spawnle, spawnlp, spawnlpe, spawnv, spawnve, spawnvp, and spawnvpe

Function Creates and runs child processes.

Syntax #include <process.h>
#include <stdio.h>
int spawnl(int *mode*, char **path*, char **arg0*, *arg1*, ..., *argn*, NULL);
int spawnle(int *mode*, char **path*, char **arg0*, *arg1*, ..., *argn*, NULL,
char **envp[]*);

int spawnlp(int *mode*, char **path*, char **arg0*, *arg1*, ..., *argn*, NULL);
int spawnlpe(int *mode*, char **path*, char **arg0*, *arg1*, ..., *argn*, NULL, char
**envp[]*);

int spawnv(int *mode*, char **path*, char **argv[]*);
int spawnve(int *mode*, char **path*, char **argv[]*, char **envp[]*);

int spawnvp(int *mode*, char **path*, char **argv[]*);
int spawnvpe(int *mode*, char **path*, char **argv[]*, char **envp[]*);

DOS	UNIX	Windows	ANSI C	C++ only
■				

Remarks The functions in the **spawn...** family create and run (execute) other files, known as *child processes*. There must be sufficient memory available for loading and executing a child process.

The value of *mode* determines what action the calling function (the *parent process*) takes after the **spawn...** call. The possible values of *mode* are

P_WAIT — Puts parent process "on hold" until child process completes execution.

P_NOWAIT — Continues to run parent process while child process runs.

P_OVERLAY — Overlays child process in memory location formerly occupied by parent. Same as an **exec...** call.

➡ P_NOWAIT is currently not available; using it generates an error value.

S

path is the file name of the called child process. The **spawn...** function calls search for *path* using the standard DOS search algorithm:

- No extension or no period: Search for exact file name; if not successful, DOS adds .COM and searches again. If still not successful, it adds .EXE and searches again.
- Extension given: Search only for exact file name.
- Period given: Search only for file name with no extension.
- If *path* does not contain an explicit directory, **spawn...** functions that have the ***p*** suffix will search the current directory, then the directories set with the DOS PATH environment variable.

The suffixes *l*, *v*, *p*, and *e* added to the **spawn...** "family name" specify that the named function operates with certain capabilities.

p The function will search for the file in those directories specified by the PATH environment variable. Without the *p* suffix, the function will search only the current working directory.

l The argument pointers *arg0*, *arg1*, ..., *argn* are passed as separate arguments. Typically, the *l* suffix is used when you know in advance the number of arguments to be passed.

v The argument pointers *argv[0]*, ..., *arg[n]* are passed as an array of pointers. Typically, the *v* suffix is used when a variable number of arguments is to be passed.

e The argument *envp* can be passed to the child process, allowing you to alter the environment for the child process. Without the *e* suffix, child processes inherit the environment of the parent process.

Each function in the **spawn...** family *must* have one of the two argument-specifying suffixes (either *l* or *v*). The path search and environment inheritance suffixes (*p* and *e*) are optional.

For example,

- **spawnl** takes separate arguments, searches only the current directory for the child, and passes on the parent's environment to the child.
- **spawnvpe** takes an array of argument pointers, incorporates PATH in its search for the child process, and accepts the *envp* argument for altering the child's environment.

The **spawn...** functions must pass at least one argument to the child process (*arg0* or *argv[0]*): This argument is, by convention, a copy of *path*. (Using a different value for this 0th argument won't produce an error.) If you want to pass an empty argument list to the child process, then *arg0* or *argv[0]* must be NULL.

Under DOS 3.x, *path* is available for the child process; under earlier versions, the child process cannot use the passed value of the 0th argument (*arg0* or *argv[0]*).

When the *l* suffix is used, *arg0* usually points to *path*, and *arg1*, ..., *argn* point to character strings that form the new list of arguments. A mandatory null following *argn* marks the end of the list.

When the *e* suffix is used, you pass a list of new environment settings through the argument *envp*. This environment argument is an array of character pointers. Each element points to a null-terminated character string of the form

envvar = value

where *envvar* is the name of an environment variable, and *value* is the string value to which *envvar* is set. The last element in *envp[]* is null. When *envp* is null, the child inherits the parents' environment settings.

The combined length of *arg0* + *arg1* + ... + *argn* (or of *argv[0]* + *argv[1]* + ... + *argv[n]*), including space characters that separate the arguments, must be < 128 bytes. Null-terminators are not counted.

When a **spawn...** function call is made, any open files remain open in the child process.

Return value On a successful execution, the **spawn...** functions return the child process's exit status (0 for a normal termination). If the child specifically calls **exit** with a nonzero argument, its exit status can be set to a nonzero value.

On error, the **spawn...** functions return –1, and the global variable *errno* is set to

E2BIG	Arg list too long
EINVAL	Invalid argument
ENOENT	Path or file name not found
ENOEXEC	Exec format error
ENOMEM	Not enough core

See also **abort, atexit, _exit, exit, exec..., _fpreset, searchpath, system**

Example 1

```
#include <process.h>
#include <stdio.h>
#include <conio.h>

void spawnl_example(void)
```

S

```
{
   int result;

   clrscr();
   result = spawnl(P_WAIT, "bcc.exe", NULL);
   if (result == -1) {
      perror("Error from spawnl");
      exit(1);
   }
}

void spawnle_example(void)
{
   int result;

   clrscr();
   result = spawnle(P_WAIT, "bcc.exe", NULL, NULL);
   if (result == -1) {
      perror("Error from spawnle");
      exit(1);
   }
}

int main(void)
{
   spawnl_example();
   spawnle_example();
}
```

_splitpath

Function Splits a full path name into its components.

Syntax #include <stdlib.h>
void _splitpath(const char **path*, char **drive*, char **dir*, char **name*, char **ext*);

DOS	UNIX	Windows	ANSI C	C++ only
■		■		

Remarks **_splitpath** takes a file's full path name (*path*) as a string in the form

X:\DIR\SUBDIR\NAME.EXT

and splits *path* into its four components. It then stores those components in the strings pointed to by *drive*, *dir*, *name*, and *ext*. (All five components must be passed, but any of them can be a null, which means the corresponding component will be parsed but not stored.)

The maximum sizes for these strings are given by the constants _MAX_DRIVE, _MAX_DIR, _MAX_PATH, _MAX_FNAME, and _MAX_EXT (defined in stdlib.h), and each size includes space for the null-terminator. These constants are defined in stdlib.h.

Constant	Max	String
_MAX_PATH	(80)	*path*
_MAX_DRIVE	(3)	*drive*; includes colon (:)
_MAX_DIR	(66)	*dir*; includes leading and trailing backslashes (\)
_MAX_FNAME	(9)	*name*
_MAX_EXT	(5)	*ext*; includes leading dot (.)

_splitpath assumes that there is enough space to store each non-null component.

When **_splitpath** splits *path*, it treats the punctuation as follows:

- *drive* includes the colon (C:, A:, and so on).
- *dir* includes the leading and trailing backslashes (\BC\include\, \source\, and so on).
- *name* includes the file name.
- *ext* includes the dot preceding the extension (.C, .EXE, and so on).

_makepath and **_splitpath** are invertible; if you split a given *path* with **_splitpath**, then merge the resultant components with **_makepath**, you end up with *path*.

Return value None.

See also **_fullpath**, **_makepath**

Example

```
#include <dir.h>
#include <string.h>
#include <stdio.h>
#include <stdlib.h>

int main(void)
{
   char s[_MAX_PATH];
   char drive[_MAX_DRIVE];
   char dir[_MAX_DIR];
   char file[_MAX_FNAME];
   char ext[_MAX_EXT];

   getcwd(s,_MAX_PATH);             /* get current working directory */
   if (s[strlen(s)-1] != '\\')
      strcat(s,"\\");               /* append a trailing \ character */
   _splitpath(s,drive,dir,file,ext); /* split the string to separate elems */
```

S

```
   strcpy(file,"DATA");
   strcpy(ext,".TXT");
   _makepath(s,drive,dir,file,ext); /* merge everything into one string */
   puts(s);                         /* display resulting string */
   return 0;
}
```

sprintf

Function Writes formatted output to a string.

Syntax #include <stdio.h>
int sprintf(char **buffer*, const char **format*[, *argument*, ...]);

DOS	UNIX	Windows	ANSI C	C++ only
■	■	■	■	

Remarks **sprintf** accepts a series of arguments, applies to each a format specifier contained in the format string pointed to by *format*, and outputs the formatted data to a string.

*See **printf** for details on format specifiers.*

sprintf applies the first format specifier to the first argument, the second to the second, and so on. There must be the same number of format specifiers as arguments.

Return value **sprintf** returns the number of bytes output. **sprintf** does not include the terminating null byte in the count. In the event of error, **sprintf** returns EOF.

See also **fprintf, printf**

Example

```
#include <stdio.h>
#include <math.h>

int main(void)
{
   char buffer[80];
   sprintf(buffer, "An approximation of pi is %f\n", M_PI);
   puts(buffer);
   return 0;
}
```

sqrt, sqrtl

Function Calculates the positive square root.

Syntax

Real versions:
#include <math.h>
double sqrt(double *x*);
long double sqrtl(long double *x*);

Complex version:
#include <complex.h>
complex sqrt(complex *x*);

	DOS	UNIX	Windows	ANSI C	C++ only
sqrtl	■		■		
*Real **sqrt***	■	■	■	■	
*Complex **sqrt***	■		■		■

Remarks **sqrt** calculates the positive square root of the argument *x*. **sqrtl** is the long double version; it takes a long double argument and returns a long double result.

Error handling for these functions can be modified through the functions **matherr** and **_matherrl**.

For complex numbers *x*, `sqrt(x)` gives the complex root whose *arg* is *arg* (*x*)/2.

The complex square root is defined by

sqrt(*z*) = **sqrt**(**abs**(*z*)) (**cos**(**arg**(*z*)/2) + *i* **sin**(**arg**(*z*)/2))

Return value On success, **sqrt** and **sqrtl** return the value calculated, the square root of *x*. If *x* is real and positive, the result is positive. If *x* is real and negative, the global variable *errno* is set to

EDOM Domain error

See also **complex**, **exp**, **log**, **pow**

Example

```
#include <math.h>
#include <stdio.h>

int main(void)
{
   double x = 4.0, result;
   result = sqrt(x);
   printf("The square root of %lf is %lf\n", x, result);
   return 0;
}
```

srand

Function Initializes random number generator.

S

Syntax #include <stdlib.h>
void srand(unsigned *seed*);

DOS	UNIX	Windows	ANSI C	C++ only
■	■	■	■	

Remarks The random number generator is reinitialized by calling **srand** with an argument value of 1. It can be set to a new starting point by calling **srand** with a given *seed* number.

Return value None.

See also **rand, random, randomize**

Example

```
#include <stdlib.h>
#include <stdio.h>
#include <time.h>

int main(void)
{
   int i;
   time_t t;
   srand((unsigned) time(&t));
   printf("Ten random numbers from 0 to 99\n\n");
   for(i=0; i<10; i++)
      printf("%d\n", rand() % 100);
   return 0;
}
```

sscanf

Function Scans and formats input from a string.

Syntax #include <stdio.h>
int sscanf(const char **buffer*, const char **format*[, *address*, ...]);

DOS	UNIX	Windows	ANSI C	C++ only
■	■	■	■	

Remarks **sscanf** scans a series of input fields, one character at a time, reading from a string. Then each field is formatted according to a format specifier passed to **sscanf** in the format string pointed to by *format*. Finally, **sscanf** stores the formatted input at an address passed to it as an argument following *format*. There must be the same number of format specifiers and addresses as there are input fields.

*See **scanf** for details on format specifiers.*

sscanf might stop scanning a particular field before it reaches the normal end-of-field (whitespace) character, or it might terminate entirely, for a number of reasons. See **scanf** for a discussion of possible causes.

Return value **sscanf** returns the number of input fields successfully scanned, converted, and stored; the return value does not include scanned fields that were not stored. If no fields were stored, the return value is 0.

If **sscanf** attempts to read at end-of-string, the return value is EOF.

See also **fscanf**, **scanf**

Example

```
#include <stdio.h>
#include <conio.h>
#include <stdlib.h>

char *names[4] = {"Peter", "Mike", "Shea", "Jerry"};

#define NUMITEMS 4

int main(void)
{
   int   loop, age;
   char  temp[4][80], name[20];
   long  salary;

   /* clear the screen */
   clrscr();

   /* create name, age and salary data */
   for (loop=0; loop < NUMITEMS; ++loop)
      sprintf(temp[loop], "%s %d %ld", names[loop],
              random(10) + 20,
              random(5000) + 27500L
              );

   /* print title bar */
   printf("%4s | %-20s | %5s | %15s\n",
          "#", "Name", "Age", "Salary");
   printf("   --------------------------"
          "---------------------------\n");

   /* input a name, age and salary data */
   for (loop=0; loop < NUMITEMS; ++loop) {
      sscanf(temp[loop],"%s %d %ld", &name, &age, &salary);
      printf("%4d | %-20s | %5d | %15ld\n",
             loop + 1, name, age, salary);
      }
   return 0;
}
```

_status87

Function Gets floating-point status.

Syntax #include <float.h>
unsigned int _status87(void);

DOS	UNIX	Windows	ANSI C	C++ only
■		■		

Remarks **_status87** gets the floating-point status word, which is a combination of the 80x87 status word and other conditions detected by the 80x87 exception handler.

Return value The bits in the return value give the floating-point status. See float.h for a complete definition of the bits returned by **_status87**.

Example

```
#include <stdio.h>
#include <float.h>

int main(void)
{
   float x;
   double y = 1.5e-100;
   printf("Status 87 before error: %x\n", _status87());
   x = y;                /* force an error to occur */
   y = x;
   printf("Status 87 after error : %x\n", _status87());
   return 0;
}
```

stime

Function Sets system date and time.

Syntax #include <time.h>
int stime(time_t **tp*);

DOS	UNIX	Windows	ANSI C	C++ only
■	■	■		

Remarks **stime** sets the system time and date. *tp* points to the value of the time as measured in seconds from 00:00:00 GMT, January 1, 1970.

Return value **stime** returns a value of 0.

See also **asctime, ftime, gettime, gmtime, localtime, time, tzset**

Example

```
#include <stdio.h>
#include <time.h>

int main(void)
{
   time_t t;
   t = time(NULL);

   printf("Current date is %s", ctiem(&t));
   t -= 24L*60L*60L;  /* Back up to same time previous day. */
   stime(&t);
   printf("\nNew date is %s", ctime(&t));
   return 0;
}
```

stpcpy

Function Copies one string into another.

Syntax #include <string.h>
char *stpcpy(char **dest*, const char **src*);

DOS	UNIX	Windows	ANSI C	C++ only
■	■	■		

Remarks **stpcpy** copies the string *src* to *dest*, stopping after the terminating null character of *src* has been reached.

Return value **stpcpy** returns *dest* + **strlen**(*src*).

See also **strcpy**

Example

```
#include <stdio.h>
#include <string.h>

int main(void)
{
   char string[10];
   char *str1 = "abcdefghi";
   stpcpy(string, str1);
   printf("%s\n", string);
   return 0;
}
```

strcat, _fstrcat

Function Appends one string to another.

Syntax #include <string.h>
Near version: char *strcat(char **dest*, const char **src*);
Far version: char far * far _fstrcat(char far **dest*, const char far **src*)

	DOS	UNIX	Windows	ANSI C	C++ only
Near version	■	■	■	■	
Far version	■		■		

Remarks **strcat** appends a copy of *src* to the end of *dest*. The length of the resulting string is **strlen**(*dest*) + **strlen**(*src*).

Return value **strcat** returns a pointer to the concatenated strings.

Example

```
#include <string.h>
#include <stdio.h>

int main(void)
{
   char destination[25];
   char *blank = " ", *c = "C++", *turbo = "Turbo";
   strcpy(destination, turbo);
   strcat(destination, blank);
   strcat(destination, c);
   printf("%s\n", destination);
   return 0;
}
```

strchr, _fstrchr

Function Scans a string for the first occurrence of a given character.

Syntax #include <string.h>
Near version: char *strchr(const char **s*, int *c*);
Far version: char far * far _fstrchr(const char far **s*, int *c*)

	DOS	UNIX	Windows	ANSI C	C++ only
Near version	■	■	■	■	
Far version	■		■		

Remarks **strchr** scans a string in the forward direction, looking for a specific character. **strchr** finds the *first* occurrence of the character *c* in the string *s*. The null-terminator is considered to be part of the string, so that, for example,

```
strchr(strs,0)
```

returns a pointer to the terminating null character of the string *strs*.

Return value **strchr** returns a pointer to the first occurrence of the character *c* in *s*; if *c* does not occur in *s*, **strchr** returns null.

See also **strcspn, strrchr**

Example

```
#include <string.h>
#include <stdio.h>

int main(void)
{
   char string[15];
   char *ptr, c = 'r';
   strcpy(string, "This is a string");
   ptr = strchr(string, c);
   if (ptr)
      printf("The character %c is at position: %d\n", c, ptr-string);
   else
      printf("The character was not found\n");
   return 0;
}
```

strcmp

Function Compares one string to another.

Syntax #include <string.h>
int strcmp(const char **s1*, const char **s2*);

DOS	UNIX	Windows	ANSI C	C++ only
■	■	■	■	

Remarks **strcmp** performs an unsigned comparison of *s1* to *s2*, starting with the first character in each string and continuing with subsequent characters until the corresponding characters differ or until the end of the strings is reached.

Return value **strcmp** returns a value that is

S

< 0 if *s1* is less than *s2*
== 0 if *s1* is the same as *s2*
> 0 if *s1* is greater than *s2*

See also **strcmpi, strcoll, stricmp, strncmp, strncmpi, strnicmp**

Example

```
#include <string.h>
#include <stdio.h>

int main(void)
{
   char *buf1 = "aaa", *buf2 = "bbb", *buf3 = "ccc";
   int ptr;
   ptr = strcmp(buf2, buf1);
   if (ptr > 0)
      printf("buffer 2 is greater than buffer 1\n");
   else
      printf("buffer 2 is less than buffer 1\n");
   ptr = strcmp(buf2, buf3);
   if (ptr > 0)
      printf("buffer 2 is greater than buffer 3\n");
   else
      printf("buffer 2 is less than buffer 3\n");
   return 0;
}
```

strcmpi

Function Compares one string to another, without case sensitivity.

Syntax #include <string.h>
int strcmpi(const char **s1*, const char **s2*);

DOS	UNIX	Windows	ANSI C	C++ only
■		■		

Remarks **strcmpi** performs an unsigned comparison of *s1* to *s2*, without case sensitivity (same as **stricmp**—implemented as a macro).

It returns a value (< 0, 0, or > 0) based on the result of comparing *s1* (or part of it) to *s2* (or part of it).

The routine **strcmpi** is the same, respectively, as **stricmp**. **strcmpi** is implemented through a macro in string.h and translates calls from **strcmpi** to **stricmp**. Therefore, in order to use **strcmpi**, you must include the header file string.h for the macro to be available. This macro is provided for compatibility with other C compilers.

Return value **strcmpi** returns an **int** value that is

< 0 if *s1* is less than *s2*
== 0 if *s1* is the same as *s2*
> 0 if *s1* is greater than *s2*

See also **strcmp**, **strcoll**, **stricmp**, **strncmp**, **strncmpi**, **strnicmp**

Example

```
#include <string.h>
#include <stdio.h>

int main(void)
{
   char *buf1 = "BBB", *buf2 = "bbb";
   int ptr;
   ptr = strcmpi(buf2, buf1);
   if (ptr > 0)
      printf("buffer 2 is greater than buffer 1\n");
   if (ptr < 0)
      printf("buffer 2 is less than buffer 1\n");
   if (ptr == 0)
      printf("buffer 2 equals buffer 1\n");
   return 0;
}
```

strcoll

Function Compares two strings.

Syntax #include <string.h>
int strcoll(char **s1*, char **s2*);

DOS	UNIX	Windows	ANSI C	C++ only
■		■	■	

Remarks **strcoll** compares the string pointed to by *s1* to the string pointed to by *s2*, according to the collating sequence set by **setlocale**.

Return value **strcoll** returns a value that is

< 0 if *s1* is less than *s2*
== 0 if *s1* is the same as *s2*
> 0 if *s1* is greater than *s2*

See also **strcmp**, **strcmpi**, **stricmp**, **strncmp**, **strncmpi**, **strnicmp**, **strxfrm**

Example

```
#include <stdio.h>
```

S

```
#include <string.h>

int main(void)
{
   char *two = "International";
   char *one = "Borland";
   int check;
   check = strcoll(one, two);
   if (check == 0)
      printf("The strings are equal\n");
   if (check <  0)
      printf("%s comes before %s\n", one, two);
   if (check >  0)
      printf("%s comes before %s\n", two, one);
   return 0;
}
```

strcpy

Function Copies one string into another.

Syntax #include <string.h>
char *strcpy(char **dest*, const char **src*);

DOS	UNIX	Windows	ANSI C	C++ only
■	■	■	■	

Remarks Copies string *src* to *dest*, stopping after the terminating null character has been moved.

Return value **strcpy** returns *dest*.

See also **stpcpy**

Example

```
#include <stdio.h>
#include <string.h>

int main(void)
{
   char string[10];
   char *str1 = "abcdefghi";
   strcpy(string, str1);
   printf("%s\n", string);
   return 0;
}
```

strcspn, _fstrcspn

Function Scans a string for the initial segment not containing any subset of a given set of characters.

Syntax #include <string.h>
Near version: size_t strcspn(const char **s1*, const char **s2*);
Far version: size_t far far _fstrcspn(const char far **s1*, const char far **s2*)

	DOS	UNIX	Windows	ANSI C	C++ only
Near version	■	■	■	■	
Far version	■		■		

Return value **strcspn** returns the length of the initial segment of string *s1* that consists entirely of characters *not* from string *s2*.

See also **strchr, strrchr**

Example

```
#include <stdio.h>
#include <string.h>
#include <alloc.h>

int main(void)
{
   char *string1 = "1234567890", *string2 = "747DC8";
   int length;
   length = strcspn(string1, string2);
   printf("Character where strings intersect is at position %d\n", length);
   return 0;
}
```

_strdate

Function Converts current date to string.

Syntax #include <time.h>
char *_strdate(char **buf*);

DOS	UNIX	Windows	ANSI C	C++ only
■		■		

Remarks **_strdate** converts the current date to a string, storing the string in the buffer *buf*. The buffer must be at least 9 characters long.

S

The string has the following form:

```
MM/DD/YY
```

where MM, DD, and YY are all two-digit numbers representing the month, day, and year. The string is terminated by a null character.

Return value **_strdate** returns *buf*, the address of the date string.

See also **asctime, ctime, localtime, strftime, _strtime, time**

Example

```
#include <time.h>
#include <stdio.h>
void main(void)
{
    char datebuf[9], timebuf[9];

    _strdate(datebuf);
    _strtime(timebuf);
    printf("Date: %s  Time: %s\n",datebuf,timebuf);
}
```

strdup, _fstrdup

Function Copies a string into a newly created location.

Syntax #include <string.h>
Near version: char *strdup(const char *s);
Far version: char far * far _fstrdup(const char far *s)

	DOS	UNIX	Windows	ANSI C	C++ only
Near version	■	■	■		
Far version	■		■		

Remarks **strdup** makes a duplicate of string *s*, obtaining space with a call to **malloc**. The allocated space is (**strlen**(*s*) + 1) bytes long. The user is responsible for freeing the space allocated by **strdup** when it is no longer needed.

Return value **strdup** returns a pointer to the storage location containing the duplicated string, or returns null if space could not be allocated.

See also **free**

Example

```
#include <stdio.h>
#include <string.h>
#include <alloc.h>

int main(void)
{
   char *dup_str, *string = "abcde";
```

```
   dup_str = strdup(string);
   printf("%s\n", dup_str);
   free(dup_str);

   return 0;
}
```

_strerror

Function Builds a customized error message.

Syntax #include <string.h>
char *_strerror(const char *s);

DOS	UNIX	Windows	ANSI C	C++ only
■		■		

Remarks **_strerror** allows you to generate customized error messages; it returns a pointer to a null-terminated string containing an error message.

- If *s* is null, the return value points to the most recent error message.
- If *s* is not null, the return value contains *s* (your customized error message), a colon, a space, the most-recently generated system error message, and a new line. *s* should be 94 characters or less.

_strerror is the same as **strerror** in version 1.0 of Turbo C.

Return value **_strerror** returns a pointer to a constructed error string. The error message string is constructed in a static buffer that is overwritten with each call to **_strerror**.

See also **perror, strerror**

Example

```
#include <stdio.h>

int main(void)
{
   FILE *fp;

   /* open a file for writing */
   fp = fopen("TEST.$$$", "w");

   /* force an error condition by attempting to read */
   if (!fp) fgetc(fp);
   if (ferror(fp))
      /* display a custom error message */
      printf("%s", _strerror("Custom"));
   fclose(fp);
```

S

```
    return 0;
}
```

strerror

Function Returns a pointer to an error message string.

Syntax #include <string.h>
char *strerror(int *errnum*);

DOS	UNIX	Windows	ANSI C	C++ only
■		■	■	

Remarks **strerror** takes an **int** parameter *errnum*, an error number, and returns a pointer to an error message string associated with *errnum*.

Return value **strerror** returns a pointer to a constructed error string. The error message string is constructed in a static buffer that is overwritten with each call to **strerror**.

See also **perror**, **_strerror**

Example

```
#include <stdio.h>
#include <errno.h>

int main(void)
{
   char *buffer;
   buffer = strerror(errno);
   printf("Error: %s\n", buffer);
   return 0;
}
```

strftime

Function Formats time for output.

Syntax #include <time.h>
size_t strftime(char **s*, size_t *maxsize*, const char **fmt*, const struct tm **t*);

DOS	UNIX	Windows	ANSI C	C++ only
■		■	■	

Remarks **strftime** formats the time in the argument *t* into the array pointed to by the argument *s* according to the *fmt* specifications. The format string consists of zero or more directives and ordinary characters. Like **printf**, a directive consists of the % character followed by a character that determines the substitution that is to take place. All ordinary characters are copied unchanged. No more than *maxsize* characters are placed in *s*.

Return value **strftime** returns the number of characters placed into *s*. If the number of characters required is greater than *maxsize*, **strftime** returns 0.

Format specifier	Substitutes
%%	Character %
%a	Abbreviated weekday name
%A	Full weekday name
%b	Abbreviated month name
%B	Full month name
%c	Date and time
%d	Two-digit day of the month (01 to 31)
%H	Two-digit hour (00 to 23)
%I	Two-digit hour (01 to 12)
%j	Three-digit day of the year (001 to 366)
%m	Two-digit month as a decimal number (1 – 12)
%M	Two-digit minute (00 to 59)
%p	AM or PM
%S	Two-digit second (00 to 59)
%U	Two-digit week number where Sunday is the first day of the week (00 to 53)
%w	Weekday where 0 is Sunday (0 to 6)
%W	Two-digit week number where Monday is the first day of the week (00 to 53)
%x	Date
%X	Time
%y	Two-digit year without century (00 to 99)
%Y	Year with century
%Z	Time zone name, or no characters if no time zone

See also **localtime, mktime, time**

Example

```
#include <stdio.h>
#include <time.h>
#include <dos.h>

int main(void)
{
   struct tm *time_now;
   time_t secs_now;
   char str[80];
   tzset();
   time(&secs_now);
   time_now = localtime(&secs_now);
   strftime(str, 80, "It is %M minutes after %I o'clock (%Z)  %A, %B %d 19%y",
         time_now);
```

S

```
   printf("%s\n",str);

   return 0;
}
```

stricmp, _fstricmp

Function Compares one string to another, without case sensitivity.

Syntax #include <string.h>
Near version: int stricmp(const char **s1*, const char **s2*);
Far version: int far _fstricmp(const char far **s1*, const char far **s2*)

DOS	UNIX	Windows	ANSI C	C++ only
■		■		

Remarks **stricmp** performs an unsigned comparison of *s1* to *s2*, starting with the first character in each string and continuing with subsequent characters until the corresponding characters differ or until the end of the strings is reached. The comparison is not case sensitive.

It returns a value (< 0, 0, or > 0) based on the result of comparing *s1* (or part of it) to *s2* (or part of it).

The routines **stricmp** and **strcmpi** are the same; **strcmpi** is implemented through a macro in string.h that translates calls from **strcmpi** to **stricmp**. Therefore, in order to use **strcmpi**, you must include the header file string.h for the macro to be available.

Return value **stricmp** returns an **int** value that is

< 0 if *s1* is less than *s2*
== 0 if *s1* is the same as *s2*
> 0 if *s1* is greater than *s2*

See also **strcmp**, **strcmpi**, **strcoll**, **strncmp**, **strncmpi**, **strnicmp**

Example

```
#include <string.h>
#include <stdio.h>

int main(void)
{
   char *buf1 = "BBB", *buf2 = "bbb";
   int ptr;
   ptr = strcmpi(buf2, buf1);
   if (ptr > 0)
      printf("buffer 2 is greater than buffer 1\n");
   if (ptr < 0)
```

```
      printf("buffer 2 is less than buffer 1\n");
   if (ptr == 0)
      printf("buffer 2 equals buffer 1\n");
   return 0;
}
```

strlen, _fstrlen

Function Calculates the length of a string.

Syntax #include <string.h>
Near version: size_t strlen(const char *s);
Far version: size_t _fstrlen(const char far *s)

	DOS	UNIX	Windows	ANSI C	C++ only
Near version	■	■	■	■	
Far version	■		■		

Remarks **strlen** calculates the length of *s*.

Return value **strlen** returns the number of characters in *s*, not counting the null-terminating character.

Example

```
#include <stdio.h>
#include <string.h>

int main(void)
{
   char *string = "Borland International";
   printf("%d\n", strlen(string));
   return 0;
}
```

S

strlwr, _fstrlwr

Function Converts uppercase letters in a string to lowercase.

Syntax #include <string.h>
Near version: char *strlwr(char *s);
Far version: char far * far _fstrlwr(char char far *s)

DOS	UNIX	Windows	ANSI C	C++ only
■		■		

Remarks **strlwr** converts uppercase letters (*A* to *Z*) in string *s* to lowercase (*a* to *z*). No other characters are changed.

Return value **strlwr** returns a pointer to the string *s*.

See also **strupr**

Example

```
#include <stdio.h>
#include <string.h>

int main(void)
{
   char *string = "Borland International";
   printf("string prior to strlwr: %s\n", string);
   strlwr(string);
   printf("string after strlwr:    %s\n", string);
   return 0;
}
```

strncat, _fstrncat

Function Appends a portion of one string to another.

Syntax #include <string.h>
Near version: char *strncat(char **dest*, const char **src*, size_t *maxlen*);
Far version: char far * far _fstrncat(char far **dest*, const char far **src*, size_t *maxlen*)

	DOS	UNIX	Windows	ANSI C	C++ only
Near version	■	■	■	■	
Far version	■		■		

Remarks **strncat** copies at most *maxlen* characters of *src* to the end of *dest* and then appends a null character. The maximum length of the resulting string is **strlen**(*dest*) + *maxlen*.

Return value **strncat** returns *dest*.

Example

```
#include <string.h>
#include <stdio.h>

int main(void)
{
   char destination[25];
   char *source = " States";
   strcpy(destination, "United");
   strncat(destination, source, 7);
```

```
   printf("%s\n", destination);
   return 0;
}
```

strncmp, _fstrncmp

Function Compares a portion of one string to a portion of another.

Syntax #include <string.h>
Near version: int strncmp(const char **s1*, const char **s2*, size_t *maxlen*);
Far version: int far _fstrncmp(const char far **s1*, const char far **s2*, size_t *maxlen*)

	DOS	UNIX	Windows	ANSI C	C++ only
Near version	■	■	■	■	
Far version	■		■		

Remarks **strncmp** makes the same unsigned comparison as **strcmp**, but looks at no more than *maxlen* characters. It starts with the first character in each string and continues with subsequent characters until the corresponding characters differ or until it has examined *maxlen* characters.

Return value **strncmp** returns an **int** value based on the result of comparing *s1* (or part of it) to *s2* (or part of it).

< 0 if *s1* is less than *s2*
== 0 if *s1* is the same as *s2*
> 0 if *s1* is greater than *s2*

See also **strcmp, strcoll, stricmp, strncmpi, strnicmp**

Example

```
#include <string.h>
#include <stdio.h>

int main(void)
{
   char *buf1 = "aaabbb", *buf2 = "bbbccc", *buf3 = "ccc";
   int ptr;
   ptr = strncmp(buf2,buf1,3);
   if (ptr > 0)
      printf("buffer 2 is greater than buffer 1\n");
   else
      printf("buffer 2 is less than buffer 1\n");
   ptr = strncmp(buf2,buf3,3);
   if (ptr > 0)
      printf("buffer 2 is greater than buffer 3\n");
   else
```

S

```
      printf("buffer 2 is less than buffer 3\n");
   return(0);
}
```

strncmpi

Function Compares a portion of one string to a portion of another, without case sensitivity.

Syntax #include <string.h>
int strncmpi(const char **s1*, const char **s2*, size_t *n*);

DOS	UNIX	Windows	ANSI C	C++ only
■		■		

Remarks **strncmpi** performs a signed comparison of *s1* to *s2*, for a maximum length of *n* bytes, starting with the first character in each string and continuing with subsequent characters until the corresponding characters differ or until *n* characters have been examined. The comparison is not case sensitive. (**strncmpi** is the same as **strnicmp**—implemented as a macro). It returns a value (< 0, 0, or > 0) based on the result of comparing *s1* (or part of it) to *s2* (or part of it).

The routines **strnicmp** and **strncmpi** are the same; **strncmpi** is implemented through a macro in string.h that translates calls from **strncmpi** to **strnicmp**. Therefore, in order to use **strncmpi**, you must include the header file string.h for the macro to be available. This macro is provided for compatibility with other C compilers.

Return value **strncmpi** returns an **int** value that is

< 0 if *s1* is less than *s2*
== 0 if *s1* is the same as *s2*
> 0 if *s1* is greater than *s2*

Example

```
#include <string.h>
#include <stdio.h>

int main(void)
{
   char *buf1 = "BBBccc", *buf2 = "bbbccc";
   int ptr;
   ptr = strncmpi(buf2,buf1,3);
   if (ptr > 0)
      printf("buffer 2 is greater than buffer 1\n");
   if (ptr < 0)
```

```
    printf("buffer 2 is less than buffer 1\n");
  if (ptr == 0)
    printf("buffer 2 equals buffer 1\n");
  return 0;
}
```

strncpy, _fstrncpy

Function Copies a given number of bytes from one string into another, truncating or padding as necessary.

Syntax #include <stdio.h>
Near version: char *strncpy(char **dest*, const char **src*, size_t *maxlen*);
Far version: char far * far _fstrncpy(char far **dest*, const char far **src*, size_t *maxlen*)

	DOS	UNIX	Windows	ANSI C	C++ only
Near version	■	■	■	■	
Far version	■		■		

Remarks **strncpy** copies up to *maxlen* characters from *src* into *dest*, truncating or null-padding *dest*. The target string, *dest*, might not be null-terminated if the length of *src* is *maxlen* or more.

Return value **strncpy** returns *dest*.

Example

```
#include <stdio.h>
#include <string.h>

int main(void)
{
  char string[10];
  char *str1 = "abcdefghi";
  strncpy(string, str1, 3);
  string[3] = '\0';
  printf("%s\n", string);
  return 0;
}
```

strnicmp, _fstrnicmp

Function Compares a portion of one string to a portion of another, without case sensitivity.

Syntax #include <string.h>

Near version: int strnicmp(const char **s1*, const char **s2*, size_t *maxlen*);
Far version: int far _fstrnicmp(const char far **s1*, const char far **s2*,
size_t *maxlen*)

DOS	UNIX	Windows	ANSI C	C++ only
■		■		

Remarks **strnicmp** performs a signed comparison of *s1* to *s2*, for a maximum length of *maxlen* bytes, starting with the first character in each string and continuing with subsequent characters until the corresponding characters differ or until the end of the strings is reached. The comparison is not case sensitive.

It returns a value (< 0, 0, or > 0) based on the result of comparing *s1* (or part of it) to *s2* (or part of it).

Return value **strnicmp** returns an **int** value that is

< 0 if *s1* is less than *s2*
== 0 if *s1* is the same as *s2*
> 0 if *s1* is greater than *s2*

Example

```
#include <string.h>
#include <stdio.h>

int main(void)
{
   char *buf1 = "BBBccc", *buf2 = "bbbccc";
   int ptr;
   ptr = strnicmp(buf2, buf1, 3);
   if (ptr > 0)
      printf("buffer 2 is greater than buffer 1\n");
   if (ptr < 0)
      printf("buffer 2 is less than buffer 1\n");
   if (ptr == 0)
      printf("buffer 2 equals buffer 1\n");
   return 0;
}
```

strnset, _fstrnset

Function Sets a specified number of characters in a string to a given character.

Syntax #include <string.h>
Near version: char *strnset(char **s*, int *ch*, size_t *n*);
Far version: char far * far _fstrnset(char far **s*, int *ch*, size_t *n*)

DOS	UNIX	Windows	ANSI C	C++ only
■		■		

Remarks **strnset** copies the character *ch* into the first *n* bytes of the string *s* . If *n* > **strlen**(*s*), then **strlen**(*s*) replaces *n*. It stops when *n* characters have been set, or when a null character is found.

Return value **strnset** returns *s*.

Example

```
#include <stdio.h>
#include <string.h>

int main(void)
{
   char *string = "abcdefghijklmnopqrstuvwxyz";
   char letter = 'x';
   printf("string before strnset: %s\n", string);
   strnset(string, letter, 13);
   printf("string after  strnset: %s\n", string);
   return 0;
}
```

strpbrk, _fstrpbrk

Function Scans a string for the first occurrence of any character from a given set.

Syntax #include <string.h>
Near version: char *strpbrk(const char *s1, const char *s2);
Far version: char far * far _fstrpbrk(const char far *s1, const char far *s2)

	DOS	UNIX	Windows	ANSI C	C++ only
Near version	■	■	■	■	
Far version	■		■		

Remarks **strpbrk** scans a string, *s1*, for the first occurrence of any character appearing in *s2*.

Return value **strpbrk** returns a pointer to the first occurrence of any of the characters in *s2*. If none of the *s2* characters occurs in *s1*, it returns null.

Example

```
#include <stdio.h>
#include <string.h>

int main(void)
{
   char *string1 = "abcdefghijklmnopqrstuvwxyz";
```

```
   char *string2 = "onm";
   char *ptr;
   ptr = strpbrk(string1, string2);
   if (ptr)
      printf("strpbrk found first character: %c\n", *ptr);
   else
      printf("strpbrk didn't find character in set\n");
   return 0;
}
```

strrchr, _fstrrchr

Function Scans a string for the last occurrence of a given character.

Syntax #include <string.h>
Near version: char *strrchr(const char **s*, int *c*);
Far version: char far * far _fstrrchr(const char far **s*, int *c*)

	DOS	UNIX	Windows	ANSI C	C++ only
Near version	■	■	■	■	
Far version	■		■		

Remarks **strrchr** scans a string in the reverse direction, looking for a specific character. **strrchr** finds the *last* occurrence of the character *c* in the string *s*. The null-terminator is considered to be part of the string.

Return value **strrchr** returns a pointer to the last occurrence of the character *c*. If *c* does not occur in *s*, **strrchr** returns null.

See also **strcspn**, **strchr**

Example

```
#include <string.h>
#include <stdio.h>

int main(void)
{
   char string[15], *ptr, c = 'r';
   strcpy(string, "This is a string");
   ptr = strrchr(string, c);
   if (ptr)
      printf("The character %c is at position: %d\n", c, ptr-string);
   else
      printf("The character was not found\n");
   return 0;
}
```

strrev, _fstrrev

Function Reverses a string.

Syntax #include <string.h>
Near version: char *strrev(char **s*);
Far version: char far * far _fstrrev(char far **s*)

DOS	UNIX	Windows	ANSI C	C++ only
■		■		

Remarks **strrev** changes all characters in a string to reverse order, except the terminating null character. (For example, it would change *string\0* to *gnirts\0*.)

Return value **strrev** returns a pointer to the reversed string.

Example

```
#include <string.h>
#include <stdio.h>

int main(void)
{
   char *forward = "string";
   printf("Before strrev(): %s\n", forward);
   strrev(forward);
   printf("After strrev():  %s\n", forward);
   return 0;
}
```

strset, _fstrset

Function Sets all characters in a string to a given character.

Syntax #include <string.h>
Near version: char *strset(char **s*, int *ch*);
Far version: char far * far _fstrset(char far **s*, int *ch*)

DOS	UNIX	Windows	ANSI C	C++ only
■		■		

Remarks **strset** sets all characters in the string *s* to the character *ch*. It quits when the terminating null character is found.

Return value **strset** returns *s*.

S

See also **setmem**

Example

```
#include <stdio.h>
#include <string.h>

int main(void)
{
   char string[10] = "123456789";
   char symbol = 'c';
   printf("Before strset(): %s\n", string);
   strset(string, symbol);
   printf("After strset():  %s\n", string);
   return 0;
}
```

strspn, _fstrspn

Function Scans a string for the first segment that is a subset of a given set of characters.

Syntax #include <string.h>
Near version: size_t strspn(const char **s1*, const char **s2*);
Far version: size_t far _fstrspn(const char far **s1*, const char far **s2*)

	DOS	UNIX	Windows	ANSI C	C++ only
Near version	■	■	■	■	
Far version	■		■		

Remarks **strspn** finds the initial segment of string *s1* that consists entirely of characters from string *s2*.

Return value **strspn** returns the length of the initial segment of *s1* that consists entirely of characters from *s2*.

Example

```
#include <stdio.h>
#include <string.h>
#include <alloc.h>

int main(void)
{
   char *string1 = "1234567890", *string2 = "123DC8";
   int length;
   length = strspn(string1, string2);
   printf("Character where strings differ is at position %d\n", length);
   return 0;
}
```

strstr, _fstrstr

Function Scans a string for the occurrence of a given substring.

Syntax #include <string.h>
Near version: char *strstr(const char *s1*, const char *s2*);
Far version: char far * far _fstrstr(const char far *s1*, const char far *s2*)

	DOS	UNIX	Windows	ANSI C	C++ only
Near version	■	■	■	■	
Far version	■		■		

Remarks **strstr** scans *s1* for the first occurrence of the substring *s2*.

Return value **strstr** returns a pointer to the element in *s1*, where *s2* begins (points to *s2* in *s1*). If *s2* does not occur in *s1*, **strstr** returns null.

Example

```
#include <stdio.h>
#include <string.h>

int main(void)
{
   char *str1 = "Borland International", *str2 = "nation", *ptr;
   ptr = strstr(str1, str2);
   printf("The substring is: %s\n", ptr);
   return 0;
}
```

_strtime

Function Converts current time to string.

Syntax #include <time.h>
char *_strtime(char *buf*);

DOS	UNIX	Windows	ANSI C	C++ only
■		■		

Remarks **_strtime** converts the current time to a string, storing the string in the buffer *buf*. The buffer must be at least 9 characters long.

The string has the following form:

```
HH:MM:SS
```

S

where HH, MM, and SS are all two-digit numbers representing the hour, minute, and second, respectively. The string is terminated by a null character.

Return value **_strtime** returns *buf*, the address of the time string.

See also **asctime, ctime, localtime, strftime, _strdate, time**

Example

```
#include <time.h>
#include <stdio.h>
void main(void)
{
    char datebuf[9], timebuf[9];

    _strdate(datebuf);
    _strtime(timebuf);
    printf("Date: %s  Time: %s\n",datebuf,timebuf);
}
```

strtod, _strtold

Function Convert a string to a double or long double value.

Syntax #include <stdlib.h>
double strtod(const char *s, char **endptr);
long double _strtold(const char *s, char **endptr);

	DOS	UNIX	Windows	ANSI C	C++ only
strtod	■	■	■	■	
_strtold	■		■		

Remarks **strtod** converts a character string, *s*, to a double value. *s* is a sequence of characters that can be interpreted as a double value; the characters must match this generic format:

```
[ws] [sn] [ddd] [.] [ddd] [fmt[sn]ddd]
```

where

[ws] = optional whitespace
[sn] = optional sign (+ or –)
[ddd] = optional digits
[fmt] = optional *e* or *E*
[.] = optional decimal point

strtod also recognizes +INF and –INF for plus and minus infinity, and +NAN and –NAN for Not-a-Number.

For example, here are some character strings that **strtod** can convert to double:

+ 1231.1981 *e*-1
502.85E2
+ 2010.952

strtod stops reading the string at the first character that cannot be interpreted as an appropriate part of a **double** value.

If *endptr* is not null, **strtod** sets **endptr* to point to the character that stopped the scan (**endptr* = &*stopper*). *endptr* is useful for error detection.

_strtold is the long double version; it converts a string to a long double value.

Return value These functions return the value of *s* as a double (**strtod**) or a long double (**_strtold**). In case of overflow, they return plus or minus HUGE_VAL (**strtod**) or _LHUGE_VAL (**_strtold**).

See also **atof**

Example

```
#include <stdio.h>
#include <stdlib.h>

int main(void)
{
   char input[80], *endptr;
   double value;
   printf("Enter a floating point number:");
   gets(input);
   value = strtod(input, &endptr);
   printf("The string is %s the number is %lf\n", input, value);
   return 0;
}
```

S

strtok, _fstrtok

Function Searches one string for tokens, which are separated by delimiters defined in a second string.

Syntax #include <string.h>
Near version: char *strtok(char *s1*, const char *s2*);
Far version: char far * far _fstrtok(char far *s1*, const char far *s2*)

	DOS	UNIX	Windows	ANSI C	C++ only
Near version	■	■	■	■	
Far version	■		■		

Remarks **strtok** considers the string *s1* to consist of a sequence of zero or more text tokens, separated by spans of one or more characters from the separator string *s2*.

The first call to **strtok** returns a pointer to the first character of the first token in *s1* and writes a null character into *s1* immediately following the returned token. Subsequent calls with null for the first argument will work through the string *s1* in this way, until no tokens remain.

The separator string, *s2*, can be different from call to call.

Return value **strtok** returns a pointer to the token found in *s1*. A null pointer is returned when there are no more tokens.

Example

```
#include <string.h>
#include <stdio.h>

int main(void)
{
   char input[16] = "abc,d";
   char *p;

   /* strtok places a NULL terminator
   in front of the token, if found */
   p = strtok(input, ",");
   if (p)   printf("%s\n", p);

   /* a second call to strtok using a NULL as the first parameter returns a
      pointer to the character following the token */
   p = strtok(NULL, ",");
   if (p)   printf("%s\n", p);
   return 0;
}
```

strtol

Function Converts a string to a **long** value.

Syntax #include <stdlib.h>
long strtol(const char *s, char **endptr*, int *radix*);

DOS	UNIX	Windows	ANSI C	C++ only
■		■	■	

Remarks **strtol** converts a character string, *s*, to a **long** integer value. *s* is a sequence of characters that can be interpreted as a **long** value; the characters must match this generic format:

```
[ws] [sn] [0] [x] [ddd]
```

where

[ws] = optional whitespace
[sn] = optional sign (+ or –)
[0] = optional zero (0)
[x] = optional x or X
[ddd] = optional digits

strtol stops reading the string at the first character it doesn't recognize.

If *radix* is between 2 and 36, the long integer is expressed in base *radix*. If *radix* is 0, the first few characters of *s* determine the base of the value being converted.

First character	Second character	String interpreted as
0	1 – 7	Octal
0	*x* or X	Hexadecimal
1 – 9		Decimal

If *radix* is 1, it is considered to be an invalid value. If *radix* is less than 0 or greater than 36, it is considered to be an invalid value.

Any invalid value for *radix* causes the result to be 0 and sets the next character pointer **endptr* to the starting string pointer.

If the value in *s* is meant to be interpreted as octal, any character other than 0 to 7 will be unrecognized.

If the value in *s* is meant to be interpreted as decimal, any character other than 0 to 9 will be unrecognized.

If the value in *s* is meant to be interpreted as a number in any other base, then only the numerals and letters used to represent numbers in that base will be recognized. (For example, if *radix* equals 5, only 0 to 4 will be recognized; if *radix* equals 20, only 0 to 9 and *A* to *J* will be recognized.)

If *endptr* is not null, **strtol** sets **endptr* to point to the character that stopped the scan (**endptr* = &*stopper*).

Return value **strtol** returns the value of the converted string, or 0 on error.

See also **atoi, atol, strtoul**

Example

```
#include <stdlib.h>
#include <stdio.h>

int main(void)
{
   char *string = "87654321", *endptr;
   long lnumber;

   /* strtol converts string to long integer */
   lnumber = strtol(string, &endptr, 10);
   printf("string = %s  long = %ld\n", string, lnumber);
   return 0;
}
```

strtoul

Function Converts a string to an **unsigned long** in the given radix.

Syntax #include <stdlib.h>
unsigned long strtoul(const char **s*, char ***endptr*, int *radix*);

DOS	UNIX	Windows	ANSI C	C++ only
■		■	■	

Remarks **strtoul** operates the same as **strtol**, except that it converts a string *str* to an **unsigned long** value (where **strtol** converts to a **long**). Refer to the entry for **strtol** for more information.

Return value **strtoul** returns the converted value, an **unsigned long**, or 0 on error.

See also **atol, strtol**

Example

```
#include <stdlib.h>
#include <stdio.h>

int main(void)
{
   char *string = "87654321", *endptr;
   unsigned long lnumber;
   lnumber = strtoul(string, &endptr, 10);
   printf("string = %s  long = %lu\n", string, lnumber);
   return 0;
}
```

strupr, _fstrupr

Function Converts lowercase letters in a string to uppercase.

Syntax #include <string.h>
Near version: char *strupr(char *s);
Far version: char far * far _fstrupr(char far *s)

DOS	UNIX	Windows	ANSI C	C++ only
■		■		

Remarks **strupr** converts lowercase letters (*a-z*) in string *s* to uppercase (*A-Z*). No other characters are changed.

Return value **strupr** returns *s*.

See also **strlwr**

Example

```
#include <stdio.h>
#include <string.h>

int main(void)
{
   char *string = "abcdefghijklmnopqrstuvwxyz", *ptr;

   /* converts string to uppercase characters */
   ptr = strupr(string);
   printf("%s\n", ptr);
   return 0;
}
```

strxfrm

Function Transforms a portion of a string.

Syntax #include<string.h>
size_t strxfrm(char *s1, char *s2, size_t n);

DOS	UNIX	Windows	ANSI C	C++ only
■		■	■	

Remarks **strxfrm** transforms the string pointed to by *s2* into the string *s1* for no more than *n* characters.

Return value Number of characters copied.

S

See also **strcoll, strncpy**

Example

```
#include <stdio.h>
#include <string.h>
#include <alloc.h>

int main(void)
{
   char *target, *source = "Frank Borland";
   int length;

   /* allocate space for the target string */
   target = (char *) calloc(80, sizeof(char));

   /* copy the source over to the target and get the length */
   length = strxfrm(target, source, 80);

   /* print out the results */
   printf("%s has the length %d\n", target, length);
   return 0;
}
```

swab

Function Swaps bytes.

Syntax #include <stdlib.h>
void swab(char **from*, char **to*, int *nbytes*);

DOS	UNIX	Windows	ANSI C	C++ only
■	■	■		

Remarks **swab** copies *nbytes* bytes from the *from* string to the *to* string. Adjacent even- and odd-byte positions are swapped. This is useful for moving data from one machine to another machine with a different byte order. *nbytes* should be even.

Return value None.

Example

```
#include <stdlib.h>
#include <stdio.h>
#include <string.h>

char source[15] = "rFna koBlrna d";
char target[15];

int main(void)
{
   swab(source, target, strlen(source));
```

```
    printf("This is target: %s\n", target);
    return 0;
}
```

system

Function Issues a DOS command.

Syntax #include <stdlib.h>
int system(const char **command*);

DOS	UNIX	Windows	ANSI C	C++ only
■	■		■	

Remarks **system** invokes the DOS COMMAND.COM file to execute a DOS command, batch file, or other program named by the string *command*, from inside an executing C program.

To be located and executed, the program must be in the current directory or in one of the directories listed in the PATH string in the environment.

The COMSPEC environment variable is used to find the COMMAND.COM file, so that file need not be in the current directory.

Return value If *command* is a NULL pointer, then **system** returns nonzero if a command processor is available. If **command** is not a NULL pointer, **system** returns zero if the command processor was successfully started. If an error occurred, a –1 is returned and *errno* is set to ENOENT, ENOMEM, E2BIG, or ENOEXEC.

See also **exec..., _fpreset, searchpath, spawn...**

Example

```
#include <stdlib.h>
#include <stdio.h>

int main(void)
{
    printf("About to spawn command.com and run a DOS command\n");
    system("dir");
    return 0;
}
```

S

tan, tanl

Function Calculates the tangent.

Syntax

Real version:
#include <math.h>
double tan(double *x*);
long double tanl(long double *x*);

Complex version:
#include <complex.h>
complex tan(complex *x*);

	DOS	UNIX	Windows	ANSI C	C++ only
tanl	■		■		
Real **tan**	■	■	■	■	
Complex **tan**	■		■		■

Remarks **tan** calculates the tangent. Angles are specified in radians.

tanl is the long double version; it takes a long double argument and returns a long double result.

Error handling for these routines can be modified through the functions **matherr** and **_matherrl.**

The complex tangent is defined by

tan(*z*) = **sin**(*z*) / **cos**(*z*)

Return value **tan** and **tanl** return the tangent of *x*, sin(*x*)/cos(*x*).

See also **acos, asin, atan, atan2, complex, cos, sin**

Example

```
#include <stdio.h>
#include <math.h>

int main(void)
{
   double result, x = 0.5;
   result = tan(x);
   printf("The tangent of %lf is %lf\n", x, result);
   return 0;
}
```

tanh, tanhl

Function Calculates the hyperbolic tangent.

Syntax

Real versions:
#include <math.h>
double tanh(double *x*);
long double tanhl(long double *x*);

Complex version:
#include <complex.h>
complex tanh(complex *x*);

	DOS	UNIX	Windows	ANSI C	C++ only
tanhl	■		■		
Real ***tanh***	■	■	■	■	
Complex ***tanh***	■		■		■

Remarks **tanh** computes the hyperbolic tangent, sinh(*x*)/cosh(*x*).

tanhl is the long double version; it takes a long double argument and returns a long double result.

Error handling for these functions can be modified through the functions **matherr** and **_matherrl**.

The complex hyperbolic tangent is defined by

tanh(*z*) = **sinh**(*z*) / **cosh**(*z*)

Return value **tanh** and **tanhl** return the hyperbolic tangent of *x*.

See also **complex, cos, cosh, sin, sinh, tan**

Example

```
#include <stdio.h>
#include <math.h>

int main(void)
{
   double result, x = 0.5;
   result = tanh(x);
   printf("The hyperbolic tangent of %lf is %lf\n", x, result);
   return 0;
}
```

T-Z

tell

Function Gets the current position of a file pointer.

Syntax #include <io.h>
long tell(int *handle*);

DOS	UNIX	Windows	ANSI C	C++ only
■	■	■		

Remarks **tell** gets the current position of the file pointer associated with *handle* and expresses it as the number of bytes from the beginning of the file.

Return value **tell** returns the current file pointer position. A return of –1 (long) indicates an error, and the global variable *errno* is set to

EBADF Bad file number

See also **fgetpos, fseek, ftell, lseek**

Example

```
#include <string.h>
#include <stdio.h>
#include <fcntl.h>
#include <io.h>

int main(void)
{
   int handle;
   char msg[] = "Hello world";
   if ((handle = open("TEST.$$$", O_CREAT | O_TEXT | O_APPEND)) == -1) {
      perror("Error:");
      return 1;
   }
   write(handle, msg, strlen(msg));
   printf("The file pointer is at byte %ld\n", tell(handle));
   close(handle);
   return 0;
}
```

tempnam

Function Creates a unique file name in specified directory.

Syntax #include <stdio.h>
char *tempnam(char **dir*, char **prefix*)

DOS	UNIX	Windows	ANSI C	C++ only
■	■	■		

Remarks The **tempnam** function creates a unique filename in arbitrary directories. It attempts to use the following directories, in the order shown, when creating the file name:

- The directory specified by the TMP environment variable.
- The *dir* argument to **tempnam**.
- The **P_tmpdir** definition in stdio.h. If you edit stdio.h and change this definition, **tempnam** will NOT use the new definition.

- The current working directory.

If any of these directories is NULL, or undefined, or does not exist, it is skipped.

The *prefix* argument specifies the first part of the filename; it cannot be longer than 5 characters, and may not contain a period (.). A unique filename is created by concatenating the directory name, the *prefix*, and 6 unique characters. Space for the resulting filename is allocated with **malloc**; the caller should free this filename when no longer needed by calling **free**. The unique file is not actually created; **tempnam** only verifies that it does not currently exist.

➡ If you do create a temporary file using the name constructed by **tempnam**, it is your responsibility to delete the file name (for example, with a call to **remove**). It is not deleted automatically. (**tmpfile** *does* delete the file name.)

Return value If **tempnam** is successful, it returns a pointer to the unique temporary file name, which the caller may pass to **free** when it is no longer needed. Otherwise, if **tempnam** cannot create a unique filename, it returns NULL.

See also **mktemp, tmpfile, tmpnam**

Example

```
#include <stdio.h>
#include <stdlib.h>

void main(void)
{
   FILE *stream;
   int i;
   char *name;

   for (i = 1; i <= 10; i++) {
      if ((name = tempnam("\\tmp","wow")) == NULL)
         perror("tempnam couldn't create name");
      else {
         printf("Creating %s\n",name);
         if ((stream = fopen(name,"wb")) == NULL)
            perror("Could not open temporary file\n");
         else
            fclose(stream);
      }
      free(name);
   }
   printf("Warning: temp files not deleted.\n");
}
```

T-Z

textattr

Function Sets text attributes.

Syntax #include <conio.h>
void textattr(int *newattr*);

DOS	UNIX	Windows	ANSI C	C++ only
■				

Remarks **textattr** lets you set both the foreground and background colors in a single call. (Normally, you set the attributes with **textcolor** and **textbackground**.)

This function does not affect any characters currently on the screen; it only affects those displayed by functions (such as **cprintf**) performing text mode, direct video output *after* this function is called.

The color information is encoded in the *newattr* parameter as follows:

7	6	5	4	3	2	1	0
B	b	b	b	f	f	f	f

In this 8-bit *newattr* parameter,

ffff is the 4-bit foreground color (0 to 15).
bbb is the 3-bit background color (0 to 7).
B is the blink-enable bit.

If the blink-enable bit is on, the character blinks. This can be accomplished by adding the constant BLINK to the attribute.

If you use the symbolic color constants defined in conio.h for creating text attributes with **textattr**, note the following limitations on the color you select for the background:

- You can only select one of the first eight colors for the background.
- You must shift the selected background color left by 4 bits to move it into the correct bit positions.

These symbolic constants are listed in the following table:

Symbolic constant	Numeric value	Foreground or background?
BLACK	0	Both
BLUE	1	Both
GREEN	2	Both
CYAN	3	Both
RED	4	Both
MAGENTA	5	Both
BROWN	6	Both
LIGHTGRAY	7	Both
DARKGRAY	8	Foreground only
LIGHTBLUE	9	Foreground only
LIGHTGREEN	10	Foreground only
LIGHTCYAN	11	Foreground only
LIGHTRED	12	Foreground only
LIGHTMAGENTA	13	Foreground only
YELLOW	14	Foreground only
WHITE	15	Foreground only
BLINK	128	Foreground only

Return value None.

See also **gettextinfo, highvideo, lowvideo, normvideo, textbackground, textcolor**

Example

```
#include <conio.h>

int main(void)
{
   int i;
   clrscr();
   for (i = 0; i < 9; i++) {
       textattr(i + ((i+1) << 4));
       cprintf("This is a test\r\n");
   }
   return 0;
}
```

T-Z

textbackground

Function Selects new text background color.

Syntax #include <conio.h>
void textbackground(int *newcolor*);

DOS	UNIX	Windows	ANSI C	C++ only
■				

Remarks **textbackground** selects the background color. This function works for functions that produce output in text mode directly to the screen. *newcolor* selects the new background color. You can set *newcolor* to an integer from 0 to 7, or to one of the symbolic constants defined in conio.h. If you use symbolic constants, you must include conio.h.

Once you have called **textbackground**, all subsequent functions using direct video output (such as **cprintf**) will use *newcolor*. **textbackground** does not affect any characters currently onscreen.

The following table lists the symbolic constants and the numeric values of the allowable colors:

Symbolic constant	Numeric value
BLACK	0
BLUE	1
GREEN	2
CYAN	3
RED	4
MAGENTA	5
BROWN	6
LIGHTGRAY	7

Return value None.

See also **gettextinfo, textattr, textcolor**

Example

```
#include <conio.h>

int main(void)
{
   int i, j;
   clrscr();
   for (i=0; i<9; i++) {
      for (j=0; j<80; j++)
        cprintf("C");
      cprintf("\r\n");
      textcolor(i+1);
      textbackground(i);
   }
   return 0;
}
```

textcolor

Function Selects new character color in text mode.

Syntax #include <conio.h>
void textcolor(int *newcolor*);

DOS	UNIX	Windows	ANSI C	C++ only
■				

Remarks **textcolor** selects the foreground character color. This function works for the console output functions. *newcolor* selects the new foreground color. You can set *newcolor* to an integer as given in the table below, or to one of the symbolic constants defined in conio.h. If you use symbolic constants, you must include conio.h.

Once you have called **textcolor**, all subsequent functions using direct video output (such as **cprintf**) will use *newcolor*. **textcolor** does not affect any characters currently onscreen.

The following table lists the allowable colors (as symbolic constants) and their numeric values:

Symbolic constant	Numeric value
BLACK	0
BLUE	1
GREEN	2
CYAN	3
RED	4
MAGENTA	5
BROWN	6
LIGHTGRAY	7
DARKGRAY	8
LIGHTBLUE	9
LIGHTGREEN	10
LIGHTCYAN	11
LIGHTRED	12
LIGHTMAGENTA	13
YELLOW	14
WHITE	15
BLINK	128

You can make the characters blink by adding 128 to the foreground color. The predefined constant BLINK exists for this purpose; for example,

```
textcolor(CYAN + BLINK);
```

Some monitors do not recognize the intensity signal used to create the eight "light" colors (8-15). On such monitors, the light colors will be displayed as their "dark" equivalents (0-7). Also, systems that do not display in color can treat these numbers as shades of one color, special

T-Z

patterns, or special attributes (such as underlined, bold, italics, and so on). Exactly what you'll see on such systems depends on your hardware.

Return value None.

See also **gettextinfo, highvideo, lowvideo, normvideo, textattr, textbackground**

Example

```
#include <conio.h>

int main(void)
{
   int i;
   for (i=0; i<15; i++) {
      textcolor(i);
      cprintf("Foreground Color\r\n");
   }
   return 0;
}
```

textheight

Function Returns the height of a string in pixels.

Syntax #include <graphics.h>
int far textheight(char far **textstring*);

DOS	UNIX	Windows	ANSI C	C++ only
■				

Remarks The graphics function **textheight** takes the current font size and multiplication factor, and determines the height of *textstring* in pixels. This function is useful for adjusting the spacing between lines, computing viewport heights, sizing a title to make it fit on a graph or in a box, and so on.

For example, with the 8×8 bit-mapped font and a multiplication factor of 1 (set by **settextstyle**), the string *TurboC*++ is 8 pixels high.

➡ Use **textheight** to compute the height of strings, instead of doing the computations manually. By using this function, no source code modifications have to be made when different fonts are selected.

Return value **textheight** returns the text height in pixels.

See also **gettextsettings, outtext, outtextxy, settextstyle, textwidth**

Example

```
#include <graphics.h>
#include <stdlib.h>
```

```
#include <stdio.h>
#include <conio.h>

int main(void)
{
   /* request autodetection */
   int gdriver = DETECT, gmode, errorcode;
   int y = 0;
   int i;
   char msg[80];

   /* initialize graphics and local variables */
   initgraph(&gdriver, &gmode, "");

   /* read result of initialization */
   errorcode = graphresult();
   if (errorcode != grOk) {  /* an error occurred */
      printf("Graphics error: %s\n", grapherrormsg(errorcode));
      printf("Press any key to halt:");
      getch();
      exit(1);               /* terminate with an error code */
   }

   /* draw some text on the screen */
   for (i=1; i<11; i++) {
      /* select the text style, direction, and size */
      settextstyle(TRIPLEX_FONT, HORIZ_DIR, i);

      /* create a message string */
      sprintf(msg, "Size: %d", i);

      /* output the message */
      outtextxy(1, y, msg);

      /* advance to the next text line */
      y += textheight(msg);
   }

   /* clean up */
   getch();
   closegraph();
   return 0;
}
```

textmode

Function Puts screen in text mode.

Syntax #include <conio.h>
void textmode(int *newmode*);

DOS	UNIX	Windows	ANSI C	C++ only
■				

Remarks **textmode** selects a specific text mode.

You can give the text mode (the argument *newmode*) by using a symbolic constant from the enumeration type *text_modes* (defined in conio.h). If you use these constants, you must include conio.h.

The *text_modes* type constants, their numeric values, and the modes they specify are given in the following table:

Symbolic constant	Numeric value	Text mode
LASTMODE	–1	Previous text mode
BW40	0	Black and white, 40 columns
C40	1	Color, 40 columns
BW80	2	Black and white, 80 columns
C80	3	Color, 80 columns
MONO	7	Monochrome, 80 columns
C4350	64	EGA 43-line and VGA 50-line modes

When **textmode** is called, the current window is reset to the entire screen, and the current text attributes are reset to normal, corresponding to a call to **normvideo**.

Specifying LASTMODE to **textmode** causes the most recently selected text mode to be reselected.

textmode should be used only when the screen is in text mode (presumably to change to a different text mode). This is the only context in which **textmode** should be used. When the screen is in graphics mode, use **restorecrtmode** instead to escape temporarily to text mode.

Return value None.

See also **gettextinfo, window**

Example

```
#include <conio.h>

int main(void)
{
   textmode(BW40);
   cprintf("ABC");
   getch();
   textmode(C40);
   cprintf("ABC");
   getch();
   textmode(BW80);
```

```
   cprintf("ABC");
   getch();
   textmode(C80);
   cprintf("ABC");
   getch();
   textmode(MONO);
   cprintf("ABC");
   getch();

   return 0;
}
```

textwidth

Function Returns the width of a string in pixels.

Syntax #include <graphics.h>
int far textwidth(char far **textstring*);

DOS	UNIX	Windows	ANSI C	C++ only
■				

Remarks The graphics function **textwidth** takes the string length, current font size, and multiplication factor, and determines the width of *textstring* in pixels.

This function is useful for computing viewport widths, sizing a title to make it fit on a graph or in a box, and so on.

➡ Use **textwidth** to compute the width of strings, instead of doing the computations manually. When you use this function, no source code modifications have to be made when different fonts are selected.

Return value **textwidth** returns the text width in pixels.

See also **gettextsettings, outtext, outtextxy, settextstyle, textheight**

Example

```
#include <graphics.h>
#include <stdlib.h>
#include <stdio.h>
#include <conio.h>

int main(void)
{
   /* request autodetection */
   int gdriver = DETECT, gmode, errorcode;
   int x = 0, y = 0;
   int i;
   char msg[80];
```

T-Z

```
      /* initialize graphics and local variables */
      initgraph(&gdriver, &gmode, "");

      /* read result of initialization */
      errorcode = graphresult();
      if (errorcode != grOk) {  /* an error occurred */
         printf("Graphics error: %s\n", grapherrormsg(errorcode));
         printf("Press any key to halt:");
         getch();
         exit(1);               /* terminate with an error code */
      }

      y = getmaxy() / 2;
      settextjustify(LEFT_TEXT, CENTER_TEXT);
      for (i = 1; i < 11; i++) {
         /* select the text style, direction, and size */
         settextstyle(TRIPLEX_FONT, HORIZ_DIR, i);

         /* create a message string */
         sprintf(msg, "Size: %d", i);

         /* output the message */
         outtextxy(x, y, msg);

         /* advance to the end of the text */
         x += textwidth(msg);
      }

      /* clean up */
      getch();
      closegraph();
      return 0;
   }
```

time

Function Gets time of day.

Syntax #include <time.h>
time_t time(time_t **timer*);

DOS	UNIX	Windows	ANSI C	C++ only
■	■	■	■	

Remarks **time** gives the current time, in seconds, elapsed since 00:00:00 GMT, January 1, 1970, and stores that value in the location pointed to by *timer*, provided that *timer* is not a null pointer.

Return value **time** returns the elapsed time in seconds, as described.

See also **asctime**, **ctime**, **difftime**, **ftime**, **gettime**, **gmtime**, **localtime**, **settime**, **stime**, **tzset**

Example

```
#include <time.h>
#include <stdio.h>
#include <dos.h>

int main(void)
{
   time_t t;
   t = time(NULL);
   printf("The number of seconds since January 1, 1970 is %ld",t);
   return 0;
}
```

tmpfile

Function Opens a "scratch" file in binary mode.

Syntax #include <stdio.h>
FILE *tmpfile(void);

DOS	UNIX	Windows	ANSI C	C++ only
■	■	■	■	

Remarks **tmpfile** creates a temporary binary file and opens it for update (*w* + *b*). The file is automatically removed when it's closed or when your program terminates.

tmpfile creates the temporary file in the directory defined by the TMP environment variable. If TMP is not defined, the TEMP environment variable is used. If neither TMP or TEMP is defined, **tmpfile** creates the files in the current directory.

Return value **tmpfile** returns a pointer to the stream of the temporary file created. If the file can't be created, **tmpfile** returns null.

See also **fopen**, **tmpnam**

Example

```
#include <stdio.h>
#include <process.h>

int main(void)
{
   FILE *tempfp;
   tempfp = tmpfile();
   if (tempfp)
```

T-Z

```
      printf("Temporary file created\n");
   else {
      printf("Unable to create temporary file\n");
      exit(1);
   }
   return 0;
}
```

tmpnam

Function Creates a unique file name.

Syntax #include <stdio.h>
char *tmpnam(char *s);

DOS	UNIX	Windows	ANSI C	C++ only
■	■	■	■	

Remarks **tmpnam** creates a unique file name, which can safely be used as the name of a temporary file. **tmpnam** generates a different string each time you call it, up to TMP_MAX times. TMP_MAX is defined in stdio.h as 65,535.

The parameter to **tmpnam**, *s*, is either null or a pointer to an array of at least *L_tmpnam* characters. *L_tmpnam* is defined in stdio.h. If *s* is null, **tmpnam** leaves the generated temporary file name in an internal static object and returns a pointer to that object. If *s* is not null, **tmpnam** places its result in the pointed-to array, which must be at least *L_tmpnam* characters long, and returns *s*.

tmpnam creates the temporary file in the directory defined by the TMP environment variable. If TMP is not defined, the TEMP environment variable is used. If neither TMP or TEMP is defined, **tmpnam** creates the files in the current directory.

➡ If you do create such a temporary file with **tmpnam**, it is your responsibility to delete the file name (for example, with a call to **remove**). It is not deleted automatically. (**tmpfile** *does* delete the file name.)

Return value If *s* is null, **tmpnam** returns a pointer to an internal static object. Otherwise, **tmpnam** returns *s*.

See also **tmpfile**

Example

```
#include <stdio.h>

int main(void)
{
```

```
    char name[13];
    tmpnam(name);
    printf("Temporary name: %s\n", name);
    return 0;
}
```

toascii

Function Translates characters to ASCII format.

Syntax #include <ctype.h>
int toascii(int *c*);

DOS	UNIX	Windows	ANSI C	C++ only
■	■	■		

Remarks **toascii** is a macro that converts the integer *c* to ASCII by clearing all but the lower 7 bits; this gives a value in the range 0 to 127.

Return value **toascii** returns the converted value of *c*.

Example

```
#include <stdio.h>
#include <ctype.h>

int main(void)
{
   int number, result;
   number = 511;
   result = toascii(number);
   printf("%d %d\n", number, result);
   return 0;
}
```

_tolower

Function Translates characters to lowercase.

Syntax #include <ctype.h>
int _tolower(int *ch*);

DOS	UNIX	Windows	ANSI C	C++ only
■	■	■		

Remarks **_tolower** is a macro that does the same conversion as **tolower**, except that it should be used only when *ch* is known to be uppercase (*A-Z*).

To use **_tolower**, you must include ctype.h.

Return value **_tolower** returns the converted value of *ch* if it is uppercase; otherwise, the result is undefined.

Example

```
#include <string.h>
#include <stdio.h>
#include <ctype.h>

int main(void)
{
   int length, i;
   char *string = "THIS IS A STRING.";

   /* We should be checking each character to make sure it is an uppercase before
      passing it to _tolower! The result of passing it a non-uppercase is
      undefined. */
   length = strlen(string);
   for (i = 0; i < length; i++)
      string[i] = _tolower(string[i]);
   printf("%s\n",string);
   return 0;
}
```

tolower

Function Translates characters to lowercase.

Syntax #include <ctype.h>
int tolower(int *ch*);

DOS	UNIX	Windows	ANSI C	C++ only
■	■	■	■	

Remarks **tolower** is a function that converts an integer *ch* (in the range EOF to 255) to its lowercase value (*a* to *z*; if it was uppercase, *A* to *Z*). All others are left unchanged.

Return value **tolower** returns the converted value of *ch* if it is uppercase; it returns all others unchanged.

Example

```
#include <string.h>
#include <stdio.h>
#include <ctype.h>

int main(void)
{
   int length, i;
```

```
    char *string = "THIS IS A STRING";
    length = strlen(string);
    for (i = 0; i < length; i++)
       string[i] = tolower(string[i]);
    printf("%s\n",string);
    return 0;
}
```

_toupper

Function Translates characters to uppercase.

Syntax #include <ctype.h>
int _toupper(int *ch*);

DOS	UNIX	Windows	ANSI C	C++ only
■	■	■		

Remarks **_toupper** is a macro that does the same conversion as **toupper**, except that it should be used only when *ch* is known to be lowercase (*a* to *z*).

To use **_toupper**, you must include ctype.h.

Return value **_toupper** returns the converted value of *ch* if it is lowercase; otherwise, the result is undefined.

Example

```
#include <string.h>
#include <stdio.h>
#include <ctype.h>

int main(void)
{
   int length, i;
   char *string = "this is a string";

   /* We should be checking each character to make sure it is lowercase before
      passing it to _toupper. The result passing a non-lowercase is undefined. */
   length = strlen(string);
   for (i = 0; i < length; i++)
      string[i] = _toupper(string[i]);
   printf("%s\n",string);
   return 0;
}
```

T-Z

toupper

Function Translates characters to uppercase.

Syntax #include <ctype.h>
int toupper(int *ch*);

DOS	UNIX	Windows	ANSI C	C++ only
■	■	■	■	

Remarks **toupper** is a function that converts an integer *ch* (in the range EOF to 255) to its uppercase value (*A* to *Z*; if it was lowercase, *a* to *z*). All others are left unchanged.

Return value **toupper** returns the converted value of *ch* if it is lowercase; it returns all others unchanged.

Example

```
#include <string.h>
#include <stdio.h>
#include <ctype.h>

int main(void)
{
   int length, i;
   char *string = "this is a string";
   length = strlen(string);
   for (i = 0; i < length; i++)
      string[i] = toupper(string[i]);
   printf("%s\n",string);
   return 0;
}
```

tzset

Function Sets value of global variables *daylight*, *timezone*, and *tzname*.

Syntax #include <time.h>
void tzset(void)

DOS	UNIX	Windows	ANSI C	C++ only
■	■	■		

Remarks **tzset** is available on XENIX systems.

tzset sets the *daylight*, *timezone*, and *tzname* global variables based on the environment variable *TZ*. The library functions **ftime** and **localtime** use these global variables to correct Greenwich mean time (GMT) to whatever the local time zone is. The format of the *TZ* environment string follows:

```
TZ = zzz[+/-]d[d][lll]
```

zzz is a three-character string representing the name of the current time zone. All three characters are required. For example, the string "PST" could be used to represent Pacific Standard Time.

[+/-]*d*[*d*] is a required field containing an optionally signed number with 1 or more digits. This number is the local time zone's difference from GMT in hours. Positive numbers adjust westward from GMT. Negative numbers adjust eastward from GMT. For example, the number 5 = EST, +8 = PST, and –1 = continental Europe. This number is used in the calculation of the global variable *timezone*. *timezone* is the difference in seconds between GMT and the local time zone.

lll is an optional three-character field that represents the local time zone daylight saving time. For example, the string "PDT" could be used to represent Pacific daylight saving time. If this field is present, it will cause the global variable *daylight* to be set nonzero. If this field is absent, *daylight* will be set to zero.

If the *TZ* environment string isn't present or isn't in the preceding form, a default *TZ* = "EST5EDT" is presumed for the purposes of assigning values to the global variables *daylight*, *timezone*, and *tzname*.

The global variable *tzname*[0] points to a three-character string with the value of the time-zone name from the *TZ* environment string. *tzname*[1] points to a three-character string with the value of the daylight saving time-zone name from the *TZ* environment string. If no daylight saving name is present, *tzname*[1] points to a null string.

Return value None.

See also **asctime, ctime, ftime, gmtime, localtime, stime, time**

Example

```
#include   <time.h>
#include   <stdlib.h>
#include   <stdio.h>

int main(void)
{
   time_t td;
   putenv("TZ=PST8PDT");
   tzset();
   time(&td);
   printf("Current time = %s\n", asctime(localtime(&td)));
```

T-Z

```
    return 0;
}
```

ultoa

Function Converts an **unsigned long** to a string.

Syntax #include <stdlib.h>
char *ultoa(unsigned long *value*, char **string*, int *radix*);

DOS	UNIX	Windows	ANSI C	C++ only
■		■		

Remarks **ultoa** converts *value* to a null-terminated string and stores the result in *string*. *value* is an **unsigned long**.

radix specifies the base to be used in converting *value*; it must be between 2 and 36, inclusive. **ultoa** performs no overflow checking, and if *value* is negative and *radix* equals 10, it does not set the minus sign.

➡ The space allocated for *string* must be large enough to hold the returned string, including the terminating null character (\0). **ultoa** can return up to 33 bytes.

Return value **ultoa** returns *string*.

See also **itoa**, **ltoa**

Example

```
#include <stdlib.h>
#include <stdio.h>

int main(void)
{
   unsigned long lnumber = 3123456789L;
   char string[25];
   ultoa(lnumber,string,10);
   printf("string = %s  unsigned long = %lu\n",string,lnumber);
   return 0;
}
```

umask

Function Sets file read/write permission mask.

Syntax #include <io.h>
unsigned umask(unsigned *mode*);

DOS	UNIX	Windows	ANSI C	C++ only
■		■		

Remarks The **umask** function sets the access permission mask used by **open** and **creat**. Bits that are set in *mode* will be cleared in the access permission of files subsequently created by **open** and **creat**.

The *mode* can have one of the following values, defined in sys\stat.h:

Value of *mode*	Access permission
S_IWRITE	Permission to write
S_IREAD	Permission to read
S_IREAD|S_IWRITE	Permission to read and write

Return value The previous value of the mask. There is no error return.

See also **creat, open**

Example

```
#include <io.h>
#include <stdio.h>
#include <sys\stat.h>

#define FILENAME "TEST.$$$"

int main(void)
{
    unsigned oldmask;
    FILE *f;
    struct stat statbuf;

    /* Cause subsequent files to be created as read-only */
    oldmask = umask(S_IWRITE);
    printf("Old mask = 0x%x\n",oldmask);

    /* Create a zero-length file */
    if ((f = fopen(FILENAME,"w")) == NULL) {
        perror("Unable to create output file");
        return (1);
    }
```

T-Z

```
    fclose(f);

    /* Verify that the file is read-only */
    if (stat(FILENAME,&statbuf) != 0) {
        perror("Unable to get information about output file");
        return (1);
    }
    if (statbuf.st_mode & S_IWRITE)
        printf("Error! %s is writable!\n",FILENAME);
    else
        printf("Success! %s is not writable.\n",FILENAME);
    return(0);
}
```

ungetc

Function Pushes a character back into input stream.

Syntax #include <stdio.h>
int ungetc(int *c*, FILE **stream*);

DOS	UNIX	Windows	ANSI C	C++ only
■	■	■	■	

Remarks **ungetc** pushes the character *c* back onto the named input *stream*, which must be open for reading. This character will be returned on the next call to **getc** or **fread** for that *stream*. One character can be pushed back in all situations. A second call to **ungetc** without a call to **getc** will force the previous character to be forgotten. A call to **fflush**, **fseek**, **fsetpos**, or **rewind** erases all memory of any pushed-back characters.

Return value On success, **ungetc** returns the character pushed back; it returns EOF if the operation fails.

See also **fgetc**, **getc**, **getchar**

Example

```
#include <stdio.h>
#include <ctype.h>

int main(void)
{
   int i=0;
   char ch;
   puts("Input an integer followed by a char:");

   /* read chars until nondigit or EOF */
   while((ch = getchar()) != EOF && isdigit(ch))
```

```
      i = 10 * i + ch - 48;      /* convert ASCII into int value */

   /* if nondigit char was read, push it back into input buffer */
   if (ch != EOF)
      ungetc(ch, stdin);
   printf("i = %d, next char in buffer = %c\n", i, getchar());
   return 0;
}
```

ungetch

Function Pushes a character back to the keyboard buffer.

Syntax #include <conio.h>
int ungetch(int *ch*);

DOS	UNIX	Windows	ANSI C	C++ only
■	■			

Remarks **ungetch** pushes the character *ch* back to the console, causing *ch* to be the next character read. The **ungetch** function fails if it is called more than once before the next read.

Return value **ungetch** returns the character *ch* if it is successful. A return value of EOF indicates an error.

See also **getch, getche**

Example

```
#include <stdio.h>
#include <ctype.h>
#include <conio.h>

int main(void)
{
   int i=0;
   char ch;
   puts("Input an integer followed by a char:");

   /* read chars until nondigit or EOF */
   while((ch = getche()) != EOF && isdigit(ch))
      i = 10 * i + ch - 48;      /* convert ASCII into int value */

   /* if nondigit char was read, push it back into input buffer */
   if (ch != EOF)
      ungetch(ch);
   printf("\n\ni = %d, next char in buffer = %c\n", i, getch());
   return 0;
}
```

T-Z

unixtodos

Function Converts date and time from UNIX to DOS format.

Syntax #include <dos.h>
void unixtodos(long *time*, struct date **d*, struct time **t*);

DOS	UNIX	Windows	ANSI C	C++ only
■		■		

Remarks **unixtodos** converts the UNIX-format time given in *time* to DOS format and fills in the **date** and **time** structures pointed to by *d* and *t*.

time must not represent a calender time earlier than Jan 1 1980 00:00:00.

Return value None.

See also **dostounix**

Example

```
#include <stdio.h>
#include <dos.h>

char *month[] = { "---", "Jan", "Feb", "Mar", "Apr", "May", "Jun",
                  "Jul", "Aug", "Sep", "Oct", "Nov", "Dec"};

#define SECONDS_PER_DAY 86400L      /* number of secs in one day /

struct date dt;
struct time tm;

int main(void)
{
   unsigned long val;

   /* get today's date and time */
   getdate(&dt);
   gettime(&tm);
   printf("Today is %d %s %d\n", dt.da_day, month[dt.da_mon],
          dt.da_year);

   /* convert date and time to unix format (number of secs since Jan 1,
      1970 */
   val = dostounix(&dt, &tm);

   /* subtract 42 days worth of seconds */
   val -= (SECONDS_PER_DAY * 42);

   /* convert back to dos time and date */
   unixtodos(val, &dt, &tm);
```

```
   printf("42 days ago it was %d %s %d\n", dt.da_day, month[dt.da_mon],
          dt.da_year);
   return 0;
}
```

unlink

Function Deletes a file.

Syntax #include <io.h>
int unlink(const char **filename*);

DOS	UNIX	Windows	ANSI C	C++ only
■	■	■		

Remarks **unlink** deletes a file specified by *filename*. Any DOS drive, path, and file name can be used as a *filename*. Wildcards are not allowed.

Read-only files cannot be deleted by this call. To remove read-only files, first use **chmod** or **_chmod** to change the read-only attribute.

➥ If your file is open, be sure to close it before unlinking it.

Return value On successful completion, **unlink** returns 0. On error, it returns –1 and the global variable *errno* is set to one of the following values:

ENOENT	Path or file name not found
EACCES	Permission denied

See also **chmod, remove**

Example

```
#include <stdio.h>
#include <io.h>

int main(void)
{
   FILE *fp = fopen("junk.jnk","w");
   int status;
   fprintf(fp,"junk");
   status = access("junk.jnk",0);
   if (status == 0)
      printf("File exists\n");
   else
      printf("File doesn't exist\n");
   fclose(fp);
   unlink("junk.jnk");
```

T-Z

```
    status = access("junk.jnk",0);
    if (status == 0)
       printf("File exists\n");
    else
       printf("File doesn't exist\n");

    return 0;
}
```

unlock

Function Releases file-sharing locks.

Syntax #include <io.h>
int unlock(int *handle*, long *offset*, long *length*);

DOS	UNIX	Windows	ANSI C	C++ only
■		■		

Remarks **unlock** provides an interface to the DOS 3.x file-sharing mechanism.

unlock removes a lock previously placed with a call to **lock**. To avoid error, all locks must be removed before a file is closed. A program must release all locks before completing.

Return value **unlock** returns 0 on success, –1 on error.

See also **lock, sopen**

Example

```
#include <io.h>
#include <fcntl.h>
#include <sys\stat.h>
#include <process.h>
#include <share.h>
#include <stdio.h>

int main(void)
{
   int handle, status;
   long length;
   handle = sopen("c:\\autoexec.bat",O_RDONLY,SH_DENYNO,S_IREAD);
   if (handle < 0) {
       printf("sopen failed\n");
       exit(1);
   }

   length = filelength(handle);
   status = lock(handle,0L,length/2);
```

```
    if (status == 0)
       printf("lock succeeded\n");
    else
       printf("lock failed\n");
    status = unlock(handle,0L,length/2);
    if (status == 0)
       printf("unlock succeeded\n");
    else
       printf("unlock failed\n");
    close(handle);
    return 0;
}
```

utime

Function Sets file time and date.

Syntax #include <utime.h>
int utime(char **path*, struct utimbuf **times*);

DOS	UNIX	Windows	ANSI C	C++ only
■	■	■		

Remarks **utime** sets the modification time for the file *path*. The modification time is contained in the **utimbuf** structure pointed to by *times*. This structure is defined in utime.h, and has the following format:

```
struct utimbuf {
   time_t   actime;    /* access time */
   time_t   modtime;   /* modification time */
};
```

The DOS file system supports only a modification time; therefore, on DOS **utime** ignores *actime* and uses only *modtime* to set the file's modification time.

If *times* is NULL, the file's modification time is set to the current time.

Return value **utime** returns 0 if it is successful. Otherwise, it returns –1, and the global variable *errno* is set to one of the following:

EACCES	Permission denied
EMFILE	Too many open files
ENOENT	Path or file name not found

See also **setftime, stat, time**

T-Z

Example

```
/* Copy timestamp from one file to another */
#include <sys\stat.h>
#include <utime.h>
#include <stdio.h>

int main( int argc, char *argv[] )
{
   struct stat src_stat;
   struct utimbuf times;
   if(argc != 3) {
      printf( "Usage: copytime <source file> <dest file>\n" );
      return 1;
   }

   if (stat(argv[1],&src_stat) != 0) {
      perror("Unable to get status of source file");
      return 1;
   }

   times.modtime = times.actime = src_stat.st_mtime;
   if (utime(argv[2],&times) != 0) {
      perror("Unable to set time of destination file");
      return 1;
   }
   return 0;
}
```

va_arg, va_end, va_start

Function Implement a variable argument list.

Syntax #include <stdarg.h>
void va_start(va_list *ap*, *lastfix*);
type va_arg(va_list *ap*, *type*);
void va_end(va_list *ap*);

DOS	UNIX	Windows	ANSI C	C++ only
▪	▪	▪	▪	

Remarks Some C functions, such as **vfprintf** and **vprintf**, take variable argument lists in addition to taking a number of fixed (known) parameters. The **va_arg**, **va_end**, and **va_start** macros provide a portable way to access these argument lists. They are used for stepping through a list of arguments when the called function does not know the number and types of the arguments being passed.

The header file stdarg.h declares one type (*va_list*) and three macros (**va_start**, **va_arg**, and **va_end**).

va_list: This array holds information needed by **va_arg** and **va_end**. When a called function takes a variable argument list, it declares a variable *ap* of type *va_list*.

va_start: This routine (implemented as a macro) sets *ap* to point to the first of the variable arguments being passed to the function. **va_start** must be used before the first call to **va_arg** or **va_end**.

va_start takes two parameters: *ap* and *lastfix*. (*ap* is explained under *va_list* in the preceding paragraph; *lastfix* is the name of the last fixed parameter being passed to the called function.)

va_arg: This routine (also implemented as a macro) expands to an expression that has the same type and value as the next argument being passed (one of the variable arguments). The variable *ap* to **va_arg** should be the same *ap* that **va_start** initialized.

➥ Because of default promotions, you can't use **char**, **unsigned char**, or **float** types with **va_arg**.

The first time **va_arg** is used, it returns the first argument in the list. Each successive time **va_arg** is used, it returns the next argument in the list. It does this by first dereferencing *ap*, and then incrementing *ap* to point to the following item. **va_arg** uses the *type* to both perform the dereference and to locate the following item. Each successive time **va_arg** is invoked, it modifies *ap* to point to the next argument in the list.

va_end: This macro helps the called function perform a normal return. **va_end** might modify *ap* in such a way that it cannot be used unless **va_start** is recalled. **va_end** should be called after **va_arg** has read all the arguments; failure to do so might cause strange, undefined behavior in your program.

Return value **va_start** and **va_end** return no values; **va_arg** returns the current argument in the list (the one that *ap* is pointing to).

See also **v...printf**, **v...scanf**

Example 1

```
#include <stdio.h>
#include <stdarg.h>

/* calculate sum of a 0 terminated list */
void sum(char *msg, ...)
{
   int total = 0;
```

```
      va_list ap;
      int arg;
      va_start(ap, msg);
      while ((arg = va_arg(ap,int)) != 0)
         total += arg;
      printf(msg, total);
      va_end(ap);
   }

   int main(void) {
      sum("The total of 1+2+3+4 is %d\n", 1,2,3,4,0);
      return 0;
   }
```

Program output

```
The total of 1+2+3+4 is 10
```

Example 2

```
#include <stdio.h>
#include <stdarg.h>

void error(char *format,...)
{
   va_list argptr;
   printf("Error: ");
   va_start(argptr, format);
   vprintf(format, argptr);
   va_end(argptr);
}

int main(void) {
   int value = -1;
   error("This is just an error message\n");
   error("Invalid value %d encountered\n", value);
   return 0;
}
```

Program output

```
Error: This is just an error message
Error: Invalid value -1 encountered
```

vfprintf

Function Writes formatted output to a stream.

Syntax #include <stdio.h>
int vfprintf(FILE **stream*, const char **format*, *va_list arglist*);

DOS	UNIX	Windows	ANSI C	C++ only
■	■	■	■	

Remarks Available on UNIX System V.

The **v...printf** functions are known as *alternate entry points* for the **...printf** functions. They behave exactly like their **...printf** counterparts, but they accept a pointer to a list of arguments instead of an argument list.

*See **printf** for details on format specifiers.*

vfprintf accepts a pointer to a series of arguments, applies to each argument a format specifier contained in the format string pointed to by *format*, and outputs the formatted data to a stream. There must be the same number of format specifiers as arguments.

Return value **vfprintf** returns the number of bytes output. In the event of error, **vfprintf** returns EOF.

See also **printf, va_arg, va_end, va_start**

Example

```
#include <stdio.h>
#include <stdlib.h>

FILE *fp;
int vfpf(char *fmt, ...)
{
   va_list argptr;
   int cnt;
   va_start(argptr, fmt);
   cnt = vfprintf(fp, fmt, argptr);
   va_end(argptr);
   return(cnt);
}

int main(void)
{
   int inumber = 30;
   float fnumber = 90.0;
   char string[4] = "abc";
   fp = tmpfile();
   if (fp == NULL) {
      perror("tmpfile() call");
      exit(1);
   }
   vfpf("%d %f %s", inumber, fnumber, string);
   rewind(fp);
   fscanf(fp,"%d %f %s", &inumber, &fnumber, string);
   printf("%d %f %s\n", inumber, fnumber, string);
```

T-Z

```
   fclose(fp);
   return 0;
}
```

vfscanf

Function Scans and formats input from a stream.

Syntax #include <stdio.h>
int vfscanf(FILE **stream*, const char **format*, *va_list arglist*);

DOS	UNIX	Windows	ANSI C	C++ only
▪	▪	▪		

Remarks Available on UNIX System V.

The **v...scanf** functions are known as *alternate entry points* for the **...scanf** functions. They behave exactly like their **...scanf** counterparts, but they accept a pointer to a list of arguments instead of an argument list.

*See **scanf** for details on format specifiers.*

vfscanf scans a series of input fields, one character at a time, reading from a stream. Then each field is formatted according to a format specifier passed to **vfscanf** in the format string pointed to by *format*. Finally, **vfscanf** stores the formatted input at an address passed to it as an argument following *format*. There must be the same number of format specifiers and addresses as there are input fields.

vfscanf might stop scanning a particular field before it reaches the normal end-of-field (whitespace) character, or it might terminate entirely, for a number of reasons. See **scanf** for a discussion of possible causes.

Return value **vfscanf** returns the number of input fields successfully scanned, converted, and stored; the return value does not include scanned fields that were not stored. If no fields were stored, the return value is 0.

If **vfscanf** attempts to read at end-of-file, the return value is EOF.

See also **fscanf, scanf, va_arg, va_end, va_start**

Example

```
#include <stdio.h>
#include <stdlib.h>

FILE *fp;
```

```
int vfsf(char *fmt, ...)
{
   va_list  argptr;
   int cnt;
   va_start(argptr, fmt);
   cnt = vfscanf(fp, fmt, argptr);
   va_end(argptr);
   return(cnt);
}

int main(void)
{
   int inumber = 30;
   float fnumber = 90.0;
   char string[4] = "abc";
   fp = tmpfile();
   if (fp == NULL) {
      perror("tmpfile() call");
      exit(1);
   }
   fprintf(fp,"%d %f %s\n",inumber,fnumber,string);
   rewind(fp);
   vfsf("%d %f %s",&inumber,&fnumber,string);
   printf("%d %f %s\n",inumber,fnumber,string);
   fclose(fp);
   return 0;
}
```

vprintf

Function Writes formatted output to stdout.

Syntax #include <stdarg.h>
int vprintf(const char **format, va_list arglist*);

DOS	UNIX	Windows	ANSI C	C++ only
■	■		■	

T-Z

Remarks Available on UNIX System V.

The **v...printf** functions are known as *alternate entry points* for the **...printf** functions. They behave exactly like their **...printf** counterparts, but they accept a pointer to a list of arguments instead of an argument list.

*See **printf** for details on format specifiers.*

vprintf accepts a pointer to a series of arguments, applies to each a format specifier contained in the format string pointed to by *format*, and outputs the formatted data to stdout. There must be the same number of format specifiers as arguments.

When you use the SS!=DS flag, **vprintf** assumes that the address being passed is in the SS segment.

Return value **vprint** returns the number of bytes output. In the event of error, **vprint** returns EOF.

See also **printf, va_arg, va_end, va_start**

Example

```
#include <stdio.h>

int vpf(char *fmt, ...)
{
   va_list argptr;
   int cnt;
   va_start(argptr, format);
   cnt = vprintf(fmt, argptr);
   va_end(argptr);
   return(cnt);
}

int main(void)
{
   int inumber = 30;
   float fnumber = 90.0;
   char *string = "abc";
   vpf("%d %f %s\n",inumber,fnumber,string);
   return 0;
}
```

vscanf

Function Scans and formats input from stdin.

Syntax #include <stdarg.h>
int vscanf(const char **format*, *va_list arglist*);

DOS	UNIX	Windows	ANSI C	C++ only
■	■			

Remarks Available on UNIX system V.

The **v...scanf** functions are known as *alternate entry points* for the **...scanf** functions. They behave exactly like their **...scanf** counterparts, but they accept a pointer to a list of arguments instead of an argument list.

*See **scanf** for details on format specifiers.*

vscanf scans a series of input fields, one character at a time, reading from stdin. Then each field is formatted according to a format specifier passed to **vscanf** in the format string pointed to by *format*. Finally, **vscanf** stores the formatted input at an address passed to it as an argument following *format*. There must be the same number of format specifiers and addresses as there are input fields.

vscanf might stop scanning a particular field before it reaches the normal end-of-field (whitespace) character, or it might terminate entirely, for a number of reasons. See **scanf** for a discussion of possible causes.

Return value **vscanf** returns the number of input fields successfully scanned, converted, and stored; the return value does not include scanned fields that were not stored. If no fields were stored, the return value is 0.

If **vscanf** attempts to read at end-of-file, the return value is EOF.

See also **fscanf, scanf, va_arg, va_end, va_start**

Example

```
#include <stdio.h>
#include <conio.h>

int vscnf(char *fmt, ...)
{
   va_list argptr;
   int cnt;
   printf("Enter an integer, a float, and a string (e.g., i,f,s,)\n");
   va_start(argptr, fmt);
   cnt = vscanf(fmt, argptr);
   va_end(argptr);
   return(cnt);
}

int main(void)
{
   int inumber;
   float fnumber;
   char string[80];
   vscnf("%d, %f, %s", &inumber, &fnumber, string);
   printf("%d %f %s\n", inumber, fnumber, string);
   return 0;
}
```

T-Z

vsprintf

Function Writes formatted output to a string.

Syntax #include <stdarg.h>
int vsprintf(char **buffer*, const char **format*, *va_list arglist*);

DOS	UNIX	Windows	ANSI C	C++ only
■	■		■	

Remarks Available on UNIX system V. The **v...printf** functions are known as *alternate entry points* for the **...printf** functions. They behave exactly like their **...printf** counterparts, but they accept a pointer to a list of arguments instead of an argument list.

*See **printf** for details on format specifiers.*

vsprintf accepts a pointer to a series of arguments, applies to each a format specifier contained in the format string pointed to by *format*, and outputs the formatted data to a string. There must be the same number of format specifiers as arguments.

Return value **vsprintf** returns the number of bytes output. In the event of error, **vsprintf** returns EOF.

See also **printf, va_arg, va_end, va_start**

Example

```
#include <stdio.h>
#include <conio.h>

char buffer[80];
int vspf(char *fmt, ...)
{
   va_list argptr;
   int cnt;
   va_start(argptr, fmt);
   cnt = vsprintf(buffer, fmt, argptr);
   va_end(argptr);
   return(cnt);
}

int main(void)
{
   int inumber = 30;
   float fnumber = 90.0;
   char string[4] = "abc";
   vspf("%d %f %s", inumber, fnumber, string);
   printf("%s\n", buffer);
   return 0;
}
```

vsscanf

Function Scans and formats input from a stream.

Syntax #include <stdarg.h>
int vsscanf(const char *buffer, const char **format*, *va_list arglist*);

DOS	UNIX	Windows	ANSI C	C++ only
■	■	■		

Remarks Available on UNIX system V.

The **v...scanf** functions are known as *alternate entry points* for the **...scanf** functions. They behave exactly like their **...scanf** counterparts, but they accept a pointer to a list of arguments instead of an argument list.

*See **scanf** for details on format specifiers.*

vsscanf scans a series of input fields, one character at a time, reading from a stream. Then each field is formatted according to a format specifier passed to **vsscanf** in the format string pointed to by *format*. Finally, **vsscanf** stores the formatted input at an address passed to it as an argument following *format*. There must be the same number of format specifiers and addresses as there are input fields.

vsscanf might stop scanning a particular field before it reaches the normal end-of-field (whitespace) character, or it might terminate entirely, for a number of reasons. See **scanf** for a discussion of possible causes.

Return value **vsscanf** returns the number of input fields successfully scanned, converted, and stored; the return value does not include scanned fields that were not stored. If no fields were stored, the return value is 0.

If **vsscanf** attempts to read at end-of-string, the return value is EOF.

See also **fscanf**, **scanf**, **sscanf**, **va_arg**, **va_end**, **va_start**, **vfscanf**

Example

```
#include <stdio.h>
#include <conio.h>

char buffer[80] = "30 90.0 abc";
int vssf(char *fmt, ...)
```

```
{
   va_list  argptr;
   int cnt;
   fflush(stdin);
   va_start(argptr, fmt);
   cnt = vsscanf(buffer, fmt, argptr);
   va_end(argptr);
   return(cnt);
}

int main(void)
{
   int inumber;
   float fnumber;
   char string[80];
   vssf("%d %f %s", &inumber, &fnumber, string);
   printf("%d %f %s\n", inumber, fnumber, string);
   return 0;
}
```

wcstombs

Function Converts a wchar_t array into a multibyte string.

Syntax #include <stdlib.h>
size_t wcstombs(char *s, const wchar_t *pwcs, size_t n);

DOS	UNIX	Windows	ANSI C	C++ only
■	■	■	■	

Remarks **wcstombs** converts the type wchar_t elements contained in *pwcs* into a multibyte character string *s*. The process terminates if either a null character or an invalid multibyte character is encountered.

No more than *n* bytes are modified. If *n* number of bytes are processed before a null character is reached, the array *s* will not be null terminated.

The behavior of **wcstombs** is affected by the setting of LC_CTYPE category of the current locale.

Return value If an invalid multibyte character is encountered, **wcstombs** returns (size_t) –1. Otherwise, the function returns the number of bytes modified, not including the terminating code, if any.

wctomb

Function Converts wchar_t code to a multibyte character.

Syntax #include <stdlib.h>
int wctomb(char *s, wchar_t *wc*);

DOS	UNIX	Windows	ANSI C	C++ only
■	■	■	■	

Remarks If *s* is not null, **wctomb** determines the number of bytes needed to represent the multibyte character corresponding to *wc* (including any change in shift state). The multibyte character is stored in *s*. At most **MB_CUR_MAX** characters are stored. If the value of *wc* is zero, **wctomb** is left in the initial state.

The behavior of **wctomb** is affected by the setting of LC_CTYPE category of the current locale.

Return value If *s* is a null pointer, **wctomb** returns a nonzero or zero value, if multibyte characters encodings, respectively, do or do not have state-dependent encodings.

If *s* is not a null pointer, **wctomb** returns –1 if the *wc* value does not represent a valid multibyte character. Otherwise, **wctomb** returns the number of bytes that are contained in the multibyte character corresponding to *wc*. In no case will the return value be greater than the value of **MB_CUR_MAX** macro.

wherex

Function Gives horizontal cursor position within window.

Syntax #include <conio.h>
int wherex(void);

DOS	UNIX	Windows	ANSI C	C++ only
■				

Remarks **wherex** returns the x-coordinate of the current cursor position (within the current text window).

Return value **wherex** returns an integer in the range 1 to 80.

T-Z

See also **gettextinfo, gotoxy, wherey**

Example

```
#include <conio.h>

int main(void)
{
   clrscr();
   gotoxy(10,10);
   cprintf("Current location is X: %d  Y: %d\r\n", wherex(), wherey());
   getch();
   return 0;
}
```

wherey

Function Gives vertical cursor position within window.

Syntax #include <conio.h>
int wherey(void);

DOS	UNIX	Windows	ANSI C	C++ only
■				

Remarks **wherey** returns the y-coordinate of the current cursor position (within the current text window).

Return value **wherey** returns an integer in the range 1 to 25, 43, or 50.

See also **gettextinfo, gotoxy, wherex**

Example

```
#include <conio.h>

int main(void)
{
   clrscr();
   gotoxy(10,10);
   cprintf("Current location is X: %d  Y: %d\r\n", wherex(), wherey());
   getch();
   return 0;
}
```

window

Function Defines active text mode window.

Syntax #include <conio.h>

void window(int *left*, int *top*, int *right*, int *bottom*);

DOS	UNIX	Windows	ANSI C	C++ only
■				

Remarks **window** defines a text window onscreen. If the coordinates are in any way invalid, the call to **window** is ignored.

left and *top* are the screen coordinates of the upper left corner of the window. *right* and *bottom* are the screen coordinates of the lower right corner.

The minimum size of the text window is one column by one line. The default window is full screen, with these coordinates:

80-column mode:	1,1,80,25
40-column mode:	1,1,40,25

Return value None.

See also **clreol, clrscr, delline, gettextinfo, gotoxy, insline, puttext, textmode**

Example

```
#include <conio.h>

int main(void)
{
   window(10,10,40,11);
   textcolor(BLACK);
   textbackground(WHITE);
   cprintf("This is a test\r\n");
   return 0;
}
```

_write

Function Writes to a file.

Syntax #include <io.h>
int _write(int *handle*, void **buf*, unsigned *len*);

DOS	UNIX	Windows	ANSI C	C++ only
■		■		

Remarks **_write** attempts to write *len* bytes from the buffer pointed to by *buf* to the file associated with *handle*. The maximum number of bytes

T-Z

that **_write** can write is 65,534, because 65,535 (0xFFFF) is the same as –1, which is the error return indicator for **_write**.

_write does not translate a linefeed character (LF) to a CR/LF pair because all its files are binary files.

If the number of bytes actually written is less than that requested, the condition should be considered an error and probably indicates a full disk.

For disk files, writing, always proceeds from the current file pointer. On devices, bytes are directly sent to the device.

For files opened with the O_APPEND option, the file pointer is not positioned to EOF by **_write** before writing the data.

Return value **_write** returns the number of bytes written. In case of error, **_write** returns –1 and sets the global variable *errno* to one of the following:

EACCES	Permission denied
EBADF	Bad file number

See also **lseek, _read, write**

Example

```
#include <stdio.h>
#include <io.h>
#include <alloc.h>
#include <fcntl.h>
#include <process.h>
#include <sys\stat.h>

int main(void)
{
   void *buf;
   int handle, bytes;
   buf = malloc(200);

   /* Create a file TEST.$$$ in the current directory and write 200
      bytes to it. If TEST.$$$ already exists, overwrite. */
   if ((handle = open("TEST.$$$", O_CREAT | O_WRONLY | O_BINARY,
                     S_IWRITE | S_IREAD)) == -1)
   {
      printf("Error Opening File\n");
      exit(1);
   }
   if ((bytes = _write(handle, buf, 200)) == -1) {
      printf("Write Failed.\n");
      exit(1);
   }
```

```
    printf("_write: %d bytes written.\n",bytes);
    return 0;
}
```

write

Function Writes to a file.

Syntax #include <io.h>
int write(int *handle*, void **buf*, unsigned *len*);

DOS	UNIX	Windows	ANSI C	C++ only
■	■	■		

Remarks **write** writes a buffer of data to the file or device named by the given *handle*. *handle* is a file handle obtained from a **creat**, **open**, **dup**, or **dup2** call.

This function attempts to write *len* bytes from the buffer pointed to by *buf* to the file associated with *handle*. Except when **write** is used to write to a text file, the number of bytes written to the file will be no more than the number requested.

The maximum number of bytes that **write** can write is 65,534, because 65,535 (0xFFFF) is the same as –1, which is the error return indicator for **write**. On text files, when **write** sees a linefeed (LF) character, it outputs a CR/LF pair.

If the number of bytes actually written is less than that requested, the condition should be considered an error and probably indicates a full disk. For disks or disk files, writing, always proceeds from the current file pointer. For devices, bytes are sent directly to the device. For files opened with the O_APPEND option, the file pointer is positioned to EOF by **write** before writing the data.

T-Z

Return value **write** returns the number of bytes written. A **write** to a text file does not count generated carriage returns. In case of error, **write** returns –1 and sets the global variable *errno* to one of the following:

EACCES	Permission denied
EBADF	Bad file number

See also **creat**, **lseek**, **open**, **read**, **_write**

C H A P T E R

3

Global variables

Borland C++ provides you with predefined global variables for many common needs, such as dates, times, command-line arguments, and so on. This chapter defines and describes them.

_8087

Function Coprocessor chip flag.

Syntax extern int *_8087;*

Declared in dos.h

Remarks The *_8087* variable is set to a nonzero value (1, 2, or 3) if the startup code autodetection logic detects a floating-point coprocessor (an 8087, 80287, or 80387, respectively). The *_8087* variable is set to 0 otherwise.

The autodetection logic can be overridden by setting the 87 environment variable to `YES` or `NO`. (The commands are `SET 87=YES` and `SET 87=NO`; it is essential that there be no spaces before or after the equal sign.) In this case, the *_8087* variable will reflect the override.

Refer to Chapter 9, "Memory management," in the *Programmer's Guide* for more information about the 87 environment variable.

_argc

Function Keeps a count of command-line arguments.

Syntax extern int *_argc;*

Declared in dos.h

Remarks *_argc* has the value of *argc* passed to **main** when the program starts.

_argv

Function An array of pointers to command-line arguments.

Syntax extern char **_argv*[];

Declared in dos.h

Remarks *_argv* points to an array containing the original command-line arguments (the elements of *argv[]*) passed to **main** when the program starts.

_ctype

Function An array of character attribute information.

Syntax extern char *_ctype*[]

Declared in ctype.h

Remarks *_ctype* is an array of character attribute information indexed by ASCII value + 1. Each entry is a set of bits describing the character.

This array is used by **isdigit**, **isprint**, and so on.

daylight

Function Indicates whether daylight saving time adjustments will be made.

Syntax extern int *daylight;*

Declared in time.h

Remarks *daylight* is used by the time and date functions. It is set by the **tzset**, **ftime**, and **localtime** functions to 1 for daylight saving time, 0 for standard time.

directvideo

Function Flag that controls video output.

Syntax extern int *directvideo;*

Declared in conio.h

Remarks *directvideo* controls whether your program's console output (from **cputs**, for example) goes directly to the video RAM (*directvideo* = 1) or goes via ROM BIOS calls (*directvideo* = 0).

The default value is *directvideo* = 1 (console output goes directly to video RAM). In order to use *directvideo* = 1, your system's video hardware must be identical to IBM display adapters. Setting *directvideo* = 0 allows your console output to work on any system that is IBM BIOS-compatible.

environ

Function Accesses DOS environment variables.

Syntax extern char * *environ*[ ];

Declared in dos.h

Remarks *environ* is an array of pointers to strings; it is used to access and alter the DOS environment variables. Each string is of the form

envvar = *varvalue*

where *envvar* is the name of an environment variable (such as `PATH`), and *varvalue* is the string value to which *envvar* is set (such as `C:\BIN;C:\DOS`). The string *varvalue* may be empty.

When a program begins execution, the DOS environment settings are passed directly to the program. Note that *env*, the third argument to **main**, is equal to the initial setting of *environ*.

The *environ* array can be accessed by **getenv**; however, the **putenv** function is the only routine that should be used to add, change or delete the *environ* array entries. This is because modification can resize and relocate the process environment array, but *environ* is automatically adjusted so that it always points to the array.

See also **getenv**, **putenv**

errno, _doserrno, sys_errlist, sys_nerr

Function Enable **perror** to print error messages.

Syntax

extern int *errno;*
extern int *_doserrno;*
extern char * *sys_errlist*[ ];
extern int *sys_nerr;*

Declared in errno.h, stdlib.h (*errno, _doserrno, sys_errlist, sys_nerr*)
dos.h (*_doserrno*)

Remarks *errno, sys_errlist,* and *sys_nerr* are used by **perror** to print error messages when certain library routines fail to accomplish their appointed tasks. *_doserrno* is a variable that maps many DOS error codes to *errno*; however, **perror** does not use *_doserrno* directly.

_doserrno: When a DOS system call results in an error, *_doserrno* is set to the actual DOS error code. *errno* is a parallel error variable inherited from UNIX.

errno: When an error in a math or system call occurs, *errno* is set to indicate the type of error. Sometimes *errno* and *_doserrno* are equivalent. At other times, *errno* does not contain the actual DOS error code, which is contained in *_doserrno*. Still other errors might occur that set only *errno*, not *_doserrno*.

sys_errlist: To provide more control over message formatting, the array of message strings is provided in *sys_errlist*. You can use *errno* as an index into the array to find the string corresponding to the error number. The string does not include any newline character.

sys_nerr: This variable is defined as the number of error message strings in *sys_errlist*.

The following table gives mnemonics and their meanings for the values stored in *sys_errlist*.

Mnemonic	Meaning
E2BIG	Arg list too long
EACCES	Permission denied
EBADF	Bad file number
ECONTR	Memory blocks destroyed
ECURDIR	Attempt to remove CurDir
EDOM	Domain error
EEXIST	File already exists
EFAULT	Unknown error
EINVACC	Invalid access code
EINVAL	Invalid argument
EINVDAT	Invalid data
EINVDRV	Invalid drive specified
EINVENV	Invalid environment
EINVFMT	Invalid format
EINVFNC	Invalid function number
EINVMEM	Invalid memory block address
EMFILE	Too many open files
ENMFILE	No more files
ENODEV	No such device
ENOENT	No such file or directory
ENOEXEC	Exec format error
ENOFILE	No such file or directory
ENOMEM	Not enough memory
ENOPATH	Path not found
ENOTSAM	Not same device
ERANGE	Result out of range
EXDEV	Cross-device link
EZERO	Error 0

The following list gives mnemonics for the actual DOS error codes to which *_doserrno* can be set. (This value of *_doserrno* may or may not be mapped (through *errno*) to an equivalent error message string in *sys_errlist*.

Mnemonic	DOS error code
E2BIG	Bad environ
EACCES	Access denied
EACCES	Bad access
EACCES	Is current dir
EBADF	Bad handle
EFAULT	Reserved
EINVAL	Bad data
EINVAL	Bad function
EMFILE	Too many open
ENOENT	No such file or directory
ENOEXEC	Bad format

ENOMEM	Mcb destroyed
ENOMEM	Out of memory
ENOMEM	Bad block
EXDEV	Bad drive
EXDEV	Not same device

Refer to your DOS reference manual for more information about DOS error return codes.

Example

```
#include <errno.h>
#include <stdio.h>

extern char *sys_errlist[];

main()
{
   int i = 0;

   while(sys_errlist[i++]) printf("%s\n", sys_errlist[i]);
   return 0;
}
```

_fmode

Function Determines default file-translation mode.

Syntax extern int *_fmode;*

Declared in fcntl.h

Remarks *_fmode* determines in which mode (text or binary) files will be opened and translated. The value of *_fmode* is O_TEXT by default, which specifies that files will be read in text mode. If *_fmode* is set to O_BINARY, the files are opened and read in binary mode. (O_TEXT and O_BINARY are defined in fcntl.h.)

In text mode, on input carriage-return/linefeed (CR/LF) combinations are translated to a single linefeed character (LF). On output, the reverse is true: LF characters are translated to CR/LF combinations.

In binary mode, no such translation occurs.

You can override the default mode as set by *_fmode* by specifying a *t* (for text mode) or *b* (for binary mode) in the argument *type* in the library routines **fopen**, **fdopen**, and **freopen**. Also, in the routine **open**, the argument *access* can include either O_BINARY or O_TEXT, which will explicitly define the file being opened (given by the **open** *pathname* argument) to be in either binary or text mode.

_heaplen

Function Holds the length of the near heap.

Syntax extern unsigned *_heaplen;*

Declared in dos.h

Remarks *_heaplen* specifies the size (in bytes) of the near heap in the small data models (tiny, small, and medium). *_heaplen* does not exist in the large data models (compact, large, and huge), as they do not have a near heap.

In the small and medium models, the data segment size is computed as follows:

```
data segment [small,medium] = global data + heap + stack
```

where the size of the stack can be adjusted with *_stklen*.

If *_heaplen* is set to 0, the program allocates 64K bytes for the data segment, and the effective heap size is

```
64K - (global data + stack) bytes
```

By default, *_heaplen* equals 0, so you'll get a 64K data segment unless you specify a particular *_heaplen* value.

In the tiny model, everything (including code) is in the same segment, so the data segment computations are adjusted to include the code plus 256 bytes for the program segment prefix (PSP).

```
data segment[tiny] = 256 + code + global data + heap + stack
```

If *_heaplen* equals 0 in the tiny model, the effective heap size is obtained by subtracting the PSP, code, global data, and stack from 64K.

In the compact and large models, there is no near heap, and the stack is in its own segment, so the data segment is simply

```
data segment [compact,large] = global data
```

In the huge model, the stack is a separate segment, and each module has its own data segment.

See also *_stklen*

_new_handler

Function Traps new allocation miscues.

Syntax typedef void (*pvf)();
pvf _new_handler;

Or, as an alternative, you can set using the function **set_new_handler**, *like this:*

pvf set_new_handler(pvf p);

Remarks *_new_handler* contains a pointer to a function that takes no arguments and returns **void**. If **operator new()** is unable to allocate the space required, it will call the function pointed to by *_new_handler*; if that function returns it will try the allocation again. By default, the function pointed to by *_new_handler* simply terminates the application. The application can replace this handler, however, with a function that can try to free up some space. This is done by assigning directly to *_new_handler* or by calling the function **set_new_handler**, which returns a pointer to the former handler.

_new_handler is provided primarily for compatibility with C++ version 1.2. In most cases this functionality can be better provided by overloading **operator new**().

_osmajor, _osminor

Function Contain the major and minor DOS version numbers.

Syntax extern unsigned char *_osmajor*;
extern unsigned char *_osminor*;

Declared in dos.h

Remarks The major and minor version numbers are available individually through *_osmajor* and *_osminor*. *_osmajor* is the major version number, and *_osminor* is the minor version number. For example, if you are running DOS version 3.2, *_osmajor* will be 3, and *_osminor* will be 20.

These variables can be useful when you want to write modules that will run on DOS versions 2.x and 3.x. Some library routines behave differently depending on the DOS version number, while others only work under DOS 3.x. (For example, refer to **_open**, **creatnew**, and **ioctl** in the lookup section of this *Reference Guide*.)

_ovrbuffer

Function Change the size of the overlay buffer.

Syntax unsigned _ovrbuffer = *size;*

Declared in dos.h

Remarks The default overlay buffer size is twice the size of the largest overlay. This is adequate for some applications. But imagine that a particular function of a program is implemented through many modules, each of which is overlaid. If the total size of those modules is larger than the overlay buffer, a substantial amount of swapping will occur if the modules make frequent calls to each other.

The solution is to increase the size of the overlay buffer so that enough memory is available at any given time to contain all overlays that make frequent calls to each other. You can do this by setting the *_ovrbuffer* global variable to the required size in paragraphs. For example, to set the overlay buffer to 128K, include the following statement in your code:

```
unsigned _ovrbuffer = 0x2000;
```

There is no general formula for determining the ideal overlay buffer size. Borland's Turbo Profiler can help provide a suitable value.

See also **_OvrInitEms, _OvrInitExt**

_psp

Function Contains the segment address of the program segment prefix (PSP) for the current program.

Syntax extern unsigned int *_psp;*

Declared in dos.h

Remarks The PSP is a DOS process descriptor; it contains initial DOS information about the program.

Refer to the *DOS Programmer's Reference Manual* for more information on the PSP.

_stklen

Function Holds size of the stack.

Syntax extern unsigned *_stklen*;

Declared in dos.h

Remarks *_stklen* specifies the size of the stack for all six memory models. The minimum stack size allowed is 128 words; if you give a smaller value, *_stklen* is automatically adjusted to the minimum. The default stack size is 4K.

In the small and medium models, the data segment size is computed as follows:

```
data segment [small,medium] = global data + heap + stack
```

where the size of the heap can be adjusted with *_heaplen*.

In the tiny model, everything (including code) is in the same segment, so the data segment computations are adjusted to include the code plus 256 bytes for the program segment prefix (PSP).

```
data segment[tiny] = 256 + code + global data + heap + stack
```

In the compact and large models, there is no near heap, and the stack is in its own segment, so the data segment is simply

```
data segment [compact,large] = global data
```

In the huge model, the stack is a separate segment, and each module has its own data segment.

See also *_heaplen*

Example

```
#include <stdio.h>

/* Set the stack size to be greater than the default. */
/* This declaration must go in the global data area.  */

extern unsigned _stklen = 54321U;

main()
{
   /* show the current stack length */
   printf("The stack length is: %u\n", _stklen);
   return 0;
}
```

timezone

Function Contains difference in seconds between local time and GMT.

Syntax extern long *timezone;*

Declared in time.h

Remarks *timezone* is used by the time-and-date functions.

This variable is calculated by the **tzset** function; it is assigned a long value that is the difference, in seconds, between the current local time and Greenwich mean time.

tzname

Function Array of pointers to time zone names.

Syntax extern char * *tzname*[2]

Declared in time.h

Remarks The global variable *tzname* is an array of pointers to strings containing abbreviations for time zone names. *tzname*[0] points to a three-character string with the value of the time zone name from the *TZ* environment string. The global variable *tzname*[1] points to a three-character string with the value of the daylight saving time zone name from the *TZ* environment string. If no daylight saving name is present, *tzname*[1] points to a null string.

_version

Function Contains the DOS version number.

Syntax extern unsigned int *_version;*

Declared in dos.h

Remarks *_version* contains the DOS version number, with the major version number in the low byte and the minor version number in the high byte. (For DOS version *x.y*, the *x* is the major version number, and *y* is the minor.)

_wscroll

Function Enables or disables scrolling in console I/O functions.

Syntax extern int *_wscroll*

Declared in conio.h

Remarks *_wscroll* is a console I/O flag. Its default value is 1. If you set *_wscroll* to 0, scrolling is disabled. This can be useful for drawing along the edges of a window without having your screen scroll.

A P P E N D I X

A

Run-time library cross-reference

This appendix is an overview of the Borland C++ library routines and include files.

In this chapter, we

- explain why you might want to obtain the source code for the Borland C++ run-time library
- list and describe the header files
- summarize the different categories of tasks performed by the library routines

Borland C++ comes equipped with over 600 functions and macros that you call from within your C and C++ programs to perform a wide variety of tasks, including low- and high-level I/O, string and file manipulation, memory allocation, process control, data conversion, mathematical calculations, and much more. These functions and macros, called library routines, are documented in Chapter 2 of this book.

Borland C++'s routines are contained in the library files C*x*.LIB, MATH*x*.LIB, and GRAPHICS.LIB. Support for Windows development is provided by CW*x*.LIB, MATHW*x*.LIB, and OVERLAY.LIB. The letter *x* represents one of the six distinct memory models supported by Borland. Each model except the tiny model has its own library file and math file, containing versions of the routines written for that particular model. (The tiny model shares the small model's library and math files.) See the *Programmer's Guide*, Chapter 9, "Memory management" for complete details.

*In C++, you **must** always use prototypes.*

Borland C++ implements the ANSI C standard which, among other things, allows (and strongly recommends) function prototypes to be given for the routines in your C programs. All of Borland C++'s library routines are declared with prototypes in one or more header files.

Reasons to access the run-time library source code

There are several good reasons why you may wish to obtain the source code for the run-time library routines:

- You may find that a particular function you want to write is similar to, but not the same as, a Borland C++ function. With access to the run-time library source code, you could tailor the library function to your own needs, and avoid having to write a separate function of your own.
- Sometimes, when you are debugging code, you may wish to know more about the internals of a library function. Having the source code to the run-time library would be of great help in this situation.
- You may want to eliminate leading underscores on C symbols. Access to the run-time library source code will let you eliminate them.
- You can learn a lot from studying tight, professionally written library source code.

For all these reasons, and more, you will want to have access to the Borland C++ run-time library source code. Because Borland believes strongly in the concept of "open architecture," we have made the Borland C++ run-time library source code available for licensing. All you have to do is fill out the order form distributed with your Borland C++ package, include your payment, and we'll ship you the Borland C++ run-time library source code.

The Borland C++ header files

C++ header files, and header files defined by ANSI C, are marked in the margin.

Header files, also called include files, provide function prototype declarations for library functions. Data types and symbolic constants used with the library functions are also defined in them, along with global variables defined by Borland C++ and by the library functions. The Borland C++ library follows the ANSI C standard on names of header files and their contents.

	alloc.h	Declares memory management functions (allocation, deallocation, etc.).
ANSI C	assert.h	Defines the **assert** debugging macro.
	bcd.h	Declares the C++ class **bcd** and the overloaded operators for **bcd** and **bcd** math functions.
	bios.h	Declares various functions used in calling IBM-PC ROM BIOS routines.
	complex.h	Declares the C++ complex math functions.
	conio.h	Declares various functions used in calling the DOS console I/O routines.
	constrea.h	Declares C++ classes and methods to support console output.
ANSI C	ctype.h	Contains information used by the character classification and character conversion macros (such as **isalpha** and **toascii**).
	dir.h	Contains structures, macros, and functions for working with directories and path names.
	direct.h	Defines structures, macros, and functions for dealing with directories and path names.
	dirent.h	Declares functions and structures for POSIX directory operations.
	dos.h	Defines various constants and gives declarations needed for DOS and 8086-specific calls.
ANSI C	errno.h	Defines constant mnemonics for the error codes.
	fcntl.h	Defines symbolic constants used in connection with the library routine **open**.
ANSI C	float.h	Contains parameters for floating-point routines.
	fstream.h	Declares the C++ stream classes that support file input and output.
	generic.h	Contains macros for generic class declarations.
	graphics.h	Declares prototypes for the graphics functions.

	io.h	Contains structures and declarations for low-level input/output routines.
C++	iomanip.h	Declares the C++ streams I/O manipulators and contains macros for creating parameterized manipulators.
C++	iostream.h	Declares the basic C++ (version 2.0) streams (I/O) routines.
ANSI C	limits.h	Contains environmental parameters, information about compile-time limitations, and ranges of integral quantities.
ANSI C	locale.h	Declares functions that provide country- and language-specific information.
	sys\locking.h	Definitions for *mode* parameter of **locking** function.
	malloc.h	Memory management functions and variables.
ANSI C	math.h	Declares prototypes for the math functions and math error handlers.
	mem.h	Declares the memory-manipulation functions. (Many of these are also defined in string.h.)
	memory.h	Memory manipulation functions.
C++	new.h	Access to operator **new** and **newhandler**.
	process.h	Contains structures and declarations for the **spawn...** and **exec...** functions.
	search.h	Declares functions for searching and sorting.
ANSI C	setjmp.h	Defines a type *jmp_buf* used by the **longjmp** and **setjmp** functions and declares the functions **longjmp** and **setjmp**.
	share.h	Defines parameters used in functions that make use of file-sharing.
ANSI C	signal.h	Defines constants and declarations for use by the **signal** and **raise** functions.
ANSI C	stdarg.h	Defines macros used for reading the argument list in functions declared to accept a variable number of arguments (such as **vprintf**, **vscanf**, etc.).
ANSI C	stddef.h	Defines several common data types and macros.

ANSI C	stdio.h	Defines types and macros needed for the Standard I/O Package defined in Kernighan and Ritchie and extended under UNIX System V. Defines the standard I/O predefined streams *stdin, stdout, stdprn,* and *stderr,* and declares stream-level I/O routines.
C++	stdiostr.h	Declares the C++ (version 2.0) stream classes for use with stdio FILE structures.
ANSI C	stdlib.h	Declares several commonly used routines: conversion routines, search/sort routines, and other miscellany.
ANSI C	string.h	Declares several string-manipulation and memory-manipulation routines.
C++	strstrea.h	Declares the C++ stream classes for use with byte arrays in memory.
	sys\stat.h	Defines symbolic constants used for opening and creating files.
ANSI C	time.h	Defines a structure filled in by the time-conversion routines **asctime**, **localtime**, and **gmtime**, and a type used by the routines **ctime**, **difftime**, **gmtime**, **localtime**, and **stime**; also provides prototypes for these routines.
	sys\timeb.h	Declares the function **ftime** and the structure **timeb** that **ftime** returns.
	sys\types.h	Declares the type *time_t* used with time functions.
	utime.h	Declares the **utime** function and the **utimbuf** struct that it returns.
	values.h	Defines important constants, including machine dependencies; provided for UNIX System V compatibility.
	varargs.h	Definitions for accessing parameters in functions that accept a variable number of arguments. Provided for UNIX compatibility; you should use stdarg.h for new code.

Library routines by category

The Borland C++ library routines perform a variety of tasks. In this section, we list the routines, along with the include files in which they are declared, under several general categories of task performed. Chapter 2 contains complete information about the functions listed below.

Classification routines

These routines classify ASCII characters as letters, control characters, punctuation, uppercase, etc.

isalnum	(ctype.h)	**isdigit**	(ctype.h)	**ispunct**	(ctype.h)
isalpha	(ctype.h)	**isgraph**	(ctype.h)	**isspace**	(ctype.h)
isascii	(ctype.h)	**islower**	(ctype.h)	**isupper**	(ctype.h)
iscntrl	(ctype.h)	**isprint**	(ctype.h)	**isxdigit**	(ctype.h)

Conversion routines

These routines convert characters and strings from alpha to different numeric representations (floating-point, integers, longs) and vice versa, and from uppercase to lowercase and vice versa.

atof	(stdlib.h)	**ltoa**	(stdlib.h)	**toascii**	(ctype.h)
atoi	(stdlib.h)	**_strdate**	(time.h)	**_tolower**	(ctype.h)
atol	(stdlib.h)	**_strtime**	(time.h)	**tolower**	(ctype.h)
ecvt	(stdlib.h)	**strtod**	(stdlib.h)	**_toupper**	(ctype.h)
fcvt	(stdlib.h)	**strtol**	(stdlib.h)	**toupper**	(ctype.h)
gcvt	(stdlib.h)	**_strtold**	(stdlib.h)	**ultoa**	(stdlib.h)
itoa	(stdlib.h)	**strtoul**	(stdlib.h)		

Directory control routines

These routines manipulate directories and path names.

chdir	(dir.h)	**_fullpath**	(stdlib.h)
_chdrive	(direct.h)	**getcurdir**	(dir.h)
closedir	(dirent.h)	**getcwd**	(dir.h)
_dos_findfirst	(dos.h)	**_getdcwd**	(direct.h)
_dos_findnext	(dos.h)	**getdisk**	(dir.h)
_dos_getdiskfree	(dos.h)	**_getdrive**	(direct.h)
_dos_getdrive	(dos.h)	**_makepath**	(stdlib.h)
_dos_setdrive	(dos.h)	**mkdir**	(dir.h)
findfirst	(dir.h)	**mktemp**	(dir.h)
findnext	(dir.h)	**opendir**	(dirent.h)
fnmerge	(dir.h)	**readdir**	(dirent.h)
fnsplit	(dir.h)	**rewinddir**	(dirent.h)

rmdir	(dir.h)	**setdisk**	(dir.h)
_searchenv	(stdlib.h)	**_splitpath**	(stdlib.h)
searchpath	(dir.h)		

Diagnostic routines

These routines provide built-in troubleshooting capability.

assert	(assert.h)
matherr	(math.h)
_matherrl	(math.h)
perror	(errno.h)

Graphics routines

These routines let you create onscreen graphics with text.

arc	(graphics.h)	**getpalettesize**	(graphics.h)
bar	(graphics.h)	**getpixel**	(graphics.h)
bar3d	(graphics.h)	**gettextsettings**	(graphics.h)
circle	(graphics.h)	**getviewsettings**	(graphics.h)
cleardevice	(graphics.h)	**getx**	(graphics.h)
clearviewport	(graphics.h)	**gety**	(graphics.h)
closegraph	(graphics.h)	**graphdefaults**	(graphics.h)
detectgraph	(graphics.h)	**grapherrormsg**	(graphics.h)
drawpoly	(graphics.h)	**_graphfreemem**	(graphics.h)
ellipse	(graphics.h)	**_graphgetmem**	(graphics.h)
fillellipse	(graphics.h)	**graphresult**	(graphics.h)
fillpoly	(graphics.h)	**imagesize**	(graphics.h)
floodfill	(graphics.h)	**initgraph**	(graphics.h)
getarccoords	(graphics.h)	**installuserdriver**	(graphics.h)
getaspectratio	(graphics.h)	**installuserfont**	(graphics.h)
getbkcolor	(graphics.h)	**line**	(graphics.h)
getcolor	(graphics.h)	**linerel**	(graphics.h)
getdefaultpalette	(graphics.h)	**lineto**	(graphics.h)
getdrivername	(graphics.h)	**moverel**	(graphics.h)
getfillpattern	(graphics.h)	**moveto**	(graphics.h)
getfillsettings	(graphics.h)	**outtext**	(graphics.h)
getgraphmode	(graphics.h)	**outtextxy**	(graphics.h)
getimage	(graphics.h)	**pieslice**	(graphics.h)
getlinesettings	(graphics.h)	**putimage**	(graphics.h)
getmaxcolor	(graphics.h)	**putpixel**	(graphics.h)
getmaxmode	(graphics.h)	**rectangle**	(graphics.h)
getmaxx	(graphics.h)	**registerbgidriver**	(graphics.h)
getmaxy	(graphics.h)	**registerbgifont**	(graphics.h)
getmodename	(graphics.h)	**restorecrtmode**	(graphics.h)
getmoderange	(graphics.h)	**sector**	(graphics.h)
getpalette	(graphics.h)	**setactivepage**	(graphics.h)

setallpalette	(graphics.h)	**setpalette**	(graphics.h)
setaspectratio	(graphics.h)	**setrgbpalette**	(graphics.h)
setbkcolor	(graphics.h)	**settextjustify**	(graphics.h)
setcolor	(graphics.h)	**settextstyle**	(graphics.h)
setcursortype	(conio.h)	**setusercharsize**	(graphics.h)
setfillpattern	(graphics.h)	**setviewport**	(graphics.h)
setfillstyle	(graphics.h)	**setvisualpage**	(graphics.h)
setgraphbufsize	(graphics.h)	**setwritemode**	(graphics.h)
setgraphmode	(graphics.h)	**textheight**	(graphics.h)
setlinestyle	(graphics.h)	**textwidth**	(graphics.h)

Inline routines

These routines have inline versions. The compiler will generate code for the inline versions when you use #**pragma intrinsic** or if you specify program optimization. See the *User's Guide,* Appendix A, "The Optimizer" for more details.

fabs	(math.h)	**strcmp**	(string.h)
memchr	(mem.h)	**strcpy**	(string.h)
memcmp	(mem.h)	**strlen**	(string.h)
memcpy	(mem.h)	**strncat**	(string.h)
_rotl	(stdlib.h)	**strncmp**	(string.h)
_rotr	(stdlib.h)	**strncpy**	(string.h)
stpcpy	(string.h)	**strnset**	(string.h)
strcat	(string.h)	**strset**	(string.h)

Input/output routines

These routines provide stream-level and DOS-level I/O capability.

access	(io.h)	**_dos_creat**	(dos.h)
cgets	(conio.h)	**_dos_creatnew**	(dos.h)
_chmod	(io.h)	**_dos_getfileattr**	(dos.h)
chmod	(io.h)	**_dos_getftime**	(dos.h)
chsize	(io.h)	**_dos_open**	(dos.h)
clearerr	(stdio.h)	**_dos_read**	(dos.h)
_close	(io.h)	**_dos_setfileattr**	(dos.h)
close	(io.h)	**_dos_setftime**	(dos.h)
cprintf	(conio.h)	**_dos_write**	(dos.h)
cputs	(conio.h)	**dup**	(io.h)
_creat	(io.h)	**dup2**	(io.h)
creat	(io.h)	**eof**	(io.h)
creatnew	(io.h)	**fclose**	(stdio.h)
creattemp	(io.h)	**fcloseall**	(stdio.h)
cscanf	(conio.h)	**fdopen**	(stdio.h)
_dos_close	(dos.h)	**feof**	(stdio.h)

ferror	(stdio.h)	**printf**	(stdio.h)
fflush	(stdio.h)	**putc**	(stdio.h)
fgetc	(stdio.h)	**putch**	(conio.h)
fgetchar	(stdio.h)	**putchar**	(stdio.h)
fgetpos	(stdio.h)	**puts**	(stdio.h)
fgets	(stdio.h)	**putw**	(stdio.h)
filelength	(io.h)	**_read**	(io.h)
fileno	(stdio.h)	**read**	(io.h)
flushall	(stdio.h)	**remove**	(stdio.h)
fopen	(stdio.h)	**rename**	(stdio.h)
fprintf	(stdio.h)	**rewind**	(stdio.h)
fputc	(stdio.h)	**rmtmp**	(stdio.h)
fputchar	(stdio.h)	**scanf**	(stdio.h)
fputs	(stdio.h)	**setbuf**	(stdio.h)
fread	(stdio.h)	**setcursortype**	(conio.h)
freopen	(stdio.h)	**setftime**	(io.h)
fscanf	(stdio.h)	**setmode**	(io.h)
fseek	(stdio.h)	**setvbuf**	(stdio.h)
fsetpos	(stdio.h)	**sopen**	(io.h)
_fsopen	(stdio.h)	**sprintf**	(stdio.h)
fstat	(sys\stat.h)	**sscanf**	(stdio.h)
ftell	(stdio.h)	**stat**	(sys\stat.h)
fwrite	(stdio.h)	**_strerror**	(string.h, stdio.h)
getc	(stdio.h)	**strerror**	(stdio.h)
getch	(conio.h)	**tell**	(io.h)
getchar	(stdio.h)	**tempnam**	(stdio.h)
getche	(conio.h)	**tmpfile**	(stdio.h)
getftime	(io.h)	**tmpnam**	(stdio.h)
getpass	(conio.h)	**umask**	(io.h)
gets	(stdio.h)	**ungetc**	(stdio.h)
getw	(stdio.h)	**ungetch**	(conio.h)
ioctl	(io.h)	**unlock**	(io.h)
isatty	(io.h)	**utime**	(utime.h)
kbhit	(conio.h)	**vfprintf**	(stdio.h)
lock	(io.h)	**vfscanf**	(stdio.h)
locking	(io.h)	**vprintf**	(stdio.h)
lseek	(io.h)	**vscanf**	(stdio.h)
_open	(io.h)	**vsprintf**	(stdio.h)
open	(io.h)	**vsscanf**	(io.h)
perror	(stdio.h)	**_write**	(io.h)

Interface routines (DOS, 8086, BIOS)

These routines provide DOS, BIOS and machine-specific capabilities.

absread	(dos.h)	**bdosptr**	(dos.h)
abswrite	(dos.h)	**bioscom**	(bios.h)
bdos	(dos.h)	**_bios_disk**	(bios.h)

biosdisk	(bios.h)
_bios_equiplist	(bios.h)
biosequip	(bios.h)
_bios_keybrd	(bios.h)
bioskey	(bios.h)
biosmemory	(bios.h)
biosprint	(bios.h)
_bios_printer	(bios.h)
_bios_serialcom	(bios.h)
biostime	(bios.h)
_chain_intr	(dos.h)
country	(dos.h)
ctrlbrk	(dos.h)
_disable	(dos.h)
disable	(dos.h)
dosexterr	(dos.h)
_dos_getvect	(dos.h)
_dos_keep	(dos.h)
_dos_setvect	(dos.h)
_enable	(dos.h)
enable	(dos.h)
FP_OFF	(dos.h)
FP_SEG	(dos.h)
freemem	(dos.h)
geninterrupt	(dos.h)
getcbrk	(dos.h)
getdfree	(dos.h)
getdta	(dos.h)
getfat	(dos.h)
getfatd	(dos.h)
getpsp	(dos.h)
getvect	(dos.h)
getverify	(dos.h)
_harderr	(dos.h)
harderr	(dos.h)
_hardresume	(dos.h)
hardresume	(dos.h)
_hardretn	(dos.h)
hardretn	(dos.h)
inp	(conio.h
inpw	(conio.h
inport	(dos.h)
inportb	(dos.h)
int86	(dos.h)
int86x	(dos.h)
intdos	(dos.h)
intdosx	(dos.h)
intr	(dos.h)
keep	(dos.h)
MK_FP	(dos.h)
outp	(conio.h)
outpw	(conio.h)
outport	(dos.h)
outportb	(dos.h)
parsfnm	(dos.h)
peek	(dos.h)
peekb	(dos.h)
poke	(dos.h)
pokeb	(dos.h)
randbrd	(dos.h)
randbwr	(dos.h)
segread	(dos.h)
setcbrk	(dos.h)
setdta	(dos.h)
setvect	(dos.h)
setverify	(dos.h)
sleep	(dos.h)
unlink	(dos.h)

Manipulation routines

These routines handle strings and blocks of memory: copying, comparing, converting, and searching.

mblen	(stdlib.h)
mbstowcs	(stdlib.h)
mbtowc	(stdlib.h)
memccpy	(mem.h, string.h)
memchr	(mem.h, string.h)
memcmp	(mem.h, string.h)
memcpy	(mem.h, string.h)
memicmp	(mem.h, string.h)
memmove	(mem.h, string.h)
memset	(mem.h, string.h)
movedata	(mem.h, string.h)
movmem	(mem.h, string.h)
setmem	(mem.h)
stpcpy	(string.h)
strcat	(string.h)
strchr	(string.h)
strcmp	(string.h)
strcoll	(string.h)

strcpy	(string.h)
strcspn	(string.h)
strdup	(string.h)
strerror	(string.h)
stricmp	(string.h)
strcmpi	(string.h)
strlen	(string.h)
strlwr	(string.h)
strncat	(string.h)
strncmp	(string.h)
strncmpi	(string.h)
strncpy	(string.h)
strnicmp	(string.h)
strnset	(string.h)
strpbrk	(string.h)
strrchr	(string.h)
strrev	(string.h)
strset	(string.h)
strspn	(string.h)
strstr	(string.h)
strtok	(string.h)
strupr	(string.h)
strxfrm	(string.h)
wcstombs	(stdlib.h)
wctomb	(stdlib.h)

Math routines

These routines perform mathematical calculations and conversions.

abs	(complex.h, stdlib.h)
acos	(complex.h, math.h)
acosl	(math.h)
arg	(complex.h)
asin	(complex.h, math.h)
asinl	(math.h)
atan	(complex.h, math.h)
atanl	(math.h)
atan2	(complex.h, math.h)
atan2l	(math.h)
atof	(stdlib.h, math.h)
atoi	(stdlib.h)
atol	(stdlib.h)
_atold	(math.h)
bcd	(bcd.h)
cabs	(math.h)
cabsl	(math.h)
ceil	(math.h)
ceill	(math.h)
_clear87	(float.h)
complex	(complex.h)
conj	(complex.h)
_control87	(float.h)
cos	(complex.h, math.h)
cosl	(math.h)
cosh	(complex.h, math.h)
coshl	(math.h)
div	(math.h)
ecvt	(stdlib.h)
exp	(complex.h, math.h)
expl	(math.h)
fabs	(math.h)
fabsl	(math.h)
fcvt	(stdlib.h)
floor	(math.h)
floorl	(math.h)
fmod	(math.h)
fmodl	(math.h)
_fpreset	(float.h)
frexp	(math.h)
frexpl	(math.h)
gcvt	(stdlib.h)
hypot	(math.h)
hypotl	(math.h)
imag	(complex.h)
itoa	(stdlib.h)
labs	(stdlib.h)
ldexp	(math.h)
ldexpl	(math.h)
ldiv	(math.h)
log	(complex.h, math.h)
logl	(math.h)
log10	(complex.h, math.h)
log10l	(math.h)
_lrotl	(stdlib.h)
_lrotr	(stdlib.h)
ltoa	(stdlib.h)
matherr	(math.h)
_matherrl	(math.h)
modf	(math.h)

modfl	(math.h)	**sinl**	(math.h)
norm	(complex.h)	**sinh**	(complex.h, math.h)
polar	(complex.h)	**sinhl**	(math.h)
poly	(math.h)	**sqrt**	(complex.h, math.h)
polyl	(math.h)	**sqrtl**	(math.h)
pow	(complex.h, math.h)	**srand**	(stdlib.h)
powl	(math.h)	**_status87**	(float.h)
pow10	(math.h)	**strtod**	(stdlib.h)
pow10l	(math.h)	**strtol**	(stdlib.h)
rand	(stdlib.h)	**_strtold**	(stdlib.h)
random	(stdlib.h)	**strtoul**	(stdlib.h)
randomize	(stdlib.h)	**tan**	(complex.h, math.h)
real	(complex.h)	**tanl**	(math.h)
_rotl	(stdlib.h)	**tanh**	(complex.h, math.h)
_rotr	(stdlib.h)	**tanhl**	(complex.h, math.h)
sin	(complex.h, math.h)	**ultoa**	(stdlib.h)

Memory routines

These routines provide dynamic memory allocation in the small-data and large-data models.

alloca	(malloc.h)	**farheapfillfree**	(alloc.h)
allocmem	(dos.h)	**farheapwalk**	(alloc.h)
_bios_memsize	(bios.h)	**farmalloc**	(alloc.h)
brk	(alloc.h)	**farrealloc**	(alloc.h)
calloc	(alloc.h, stdlib.h)	**free**	(alloc.h, stdlib.h)
coreleft	(alloc.h, stdlib.h)	**heapcheck**	(alloc.h)
_dos_allocmem	(dos.h)	**heapcheckfree**	(alloc.h)
_dos_freemem	(dos.h)	**heapchecknode**	(alloc.h)
_dos_setblock	(dos.h)	**heapwalk**	(alloc.h)
farcalloc	(alloc.h)	**malloc**	(alloc.h, stdlib.h)
farcoreleft	(alloc.h)	**realloc**	(alloc.h, stdlib.h)
farfree	(alloc.h)		
farheapcheck	(alloc.h)	**sbrk**	(alloc.h)
farheapcheckfree	(alloc.h)	**setblock**	(dos.h)
farheapchecknode	(alloc.h)	**set_new_handler**	(new.h)

Miscellaneous routines

These routines provide nonlocal goto capabilities, sound effects, and locale.

delay	(dos.h)	**setjmp**	(setjmp.h)
localeconv	(locale.h)	**setlocale**	(locale.h)
longjmp	(setjmp.h)	**sound**	(dos.h)
nosound	(dos.h)		

Process control routines

These routines invoke and terminate new processes from within another.

abort	(process.h)	**execve**	(process.h)	**spawnl**	(process.h)
_c_exit	(process.h)	**execvp**	(process.h)	**spawnle**	(process.h)
_cexit	(process.h)	**execvpe**	(process.h)	**spawnlp**	(process.h)
execl	(process.h)	**_exit**	(process.h)	**spawnlpe**	(process.h)
execle	(process.h)	**exit**	(process.h)	**spawnv**	(process.h)
execlp	(process.h)	**getpid**	(process.h)	**spawnve**	(process.h)
execlpe	(process.h)	**raise**	(signal.h)	**spawnvp**	(process.h)
execv	(process.h)	**signal**	(signal.h)	**spawnvpe**	(process.h)

Text window display routines

These routines output text to the screen.

clreol	(conio.h)	**normvideo**	(conio.h)
clrscr	(conio.h)	**puttext**	(conio.h)
delline	(conio.h)	**setcursortype**	(conio.h)
gettext	(conio.h)	**textattr**	(conio.h)
gettextinfo	(conio.h)	**textbackground**	(conio.h)
gotoxy	(conio.h)	**textcolor**	(conio.h)
highvideo	(conio.h)	**textmode**	(conio.h)
insline	(conio.h)	**wherex**	(conio.h)
lowvideo	(conio.h)	**wherey**	(conio.h)
movetext	(conio.h)	**window**	(conio.h)

Time and date routines

These are time conversion and time manipulation routines.

asctime	(time.h)	**gettime**	(dos.h)
_bios_timeofday	(bios.h)	**gmtime**	(time.h)
ctime	(time.h)	**localtime**	(time.h)
difftime	(time.h)	**mktime**	(time.h)
_dos_getdate	(dos.h)	**setdate**	(dos.h)
_dos_gettime	(dos.h)	**settime**	(dos.h)
_dos_setdate	(dos.h)	**stime**	(time.h)
_dos_settime	(dos.h)	**strftime**	(time.h)
dostounix	(dos.h)	**time**	(time.h)
ftime	(sys\timeb.h)	**tzset**	(time.h)
getdate	(dos.h)	**unixtodos**	(dos.h)

Variable argument list routines

These routines are for use when accessing variable argument lists (such as with **vprintf**, etc).

va_arg (stdarg.h)
va_end (stdarg.h)
va_start (stdarg.h)

I N D E X

D

F

G

H

I

M

Q

R

S

T

U

V

W

X

Y